James Mozley

Essays, historical and theological

James Mozley

Essays, historical and theological

ISBN/EAN: 9783337204273

Printed in Europe, USA, Canada, Australia, Japan

Cover: Foto ©Lupo / pixelio.de

More available books at **www.hansebooks.com**

ESSAYS

HISTORICAL AND THEOLOGICAL

BY

J. B. MOZLEY, D.D.

LATE CANON OF CHRIST CHURCH, AND REGIUS PROFESSOR OF DIVINITY
IN THE UNIVERSITY OF OXFORD

IN TWO VOLUMES

VOL. II.

RIVINGTONS
WATERLOO PLACE, LONDON
Oxford and Cambridge
MDCCCLXXVIII

CONTENTS OF VOL. II.

DR. ARNOLD.

Details of Arnold's childhood—His early tastes—His Oxford character by Judge Coleridge—His married life at Laleham—State of public schools—Appointed to Rugby—His hatred of evil—Rule of sending away unsatisfactory boys—The Sixth Form—Fagging and flogging—Described with his class—His exuberances of feeling—His delight in scenery—His happiness—His nature German and Lutheran—State of political feeling towards the Church—Speculative Liberalism in Oxford—Copleston—Whately—Bunsen—Arnold's pamphlet on Church Reform—His system ecclesiastical and doctrinal—Remonstrances of his friends—His surprise at the opposition raised—Arnold and Froude—The Tracts for the Times—The Hampden controversy—Arnold's article in the *Edinburgh*—His combativeness—Confidence a leading characteristic—Want of intellectual sympathy—Greater with boys than with his equals—He has founded no school of opinion, ... 1

BLANCO WHITE.

Blanco White—His character literary rather than theological—Aspect of his mind—Value of his Autobiography—Their contents—Birth and parentage of B. White—His temper

—His childhood and youth—His literary taste—State of the Spanish Church—Its effect on B. White's mind—The Inquisition, etc.—His theological course in Spain—Review of his life up to this point—His political career—He quits Spain for England—The *Español*—His political friendships in England—His morbid and irritable temperament—His religious biography—He signs the Thirty-nine Articles—His secret and growing doubts—His residence with Archbishop Whately terminates—B. White becomes an Unitarian—Worship and devotion contrasted—Idea of God, through the human medium—The Incarnation—B. White's hatred of the human aspect of faith—His religion only abstract—His view of the Bible—Results of his religious course—His dejection and isolation—Effects of moral inferiority—Immortality of the soul—B. White of the French infidel school—His philosophy—His state of suffering—Probation of the intellect—The intellectual passion for truth, ... 68

DR. PUSEY'S SERMON.

The occasion of the Sermon—Dr. Pusey's manner—Average state of a Church—Dr. Pusey's course of mind—Comparison of his earlier and later works—His estimate of sin—Baptism : Extracts—Pardon—The Holy Eucharist: Extracts—Dr. Pusey a teacher needed in our times, . 149

THE BOOK OF JOB.

Preliminary difficulty in the Book of Job—Main argument of the book—Jewish estimate of the future state—Arguments of Job's friends—Is this visible state conducted upon principles of justice?—Illustrations from *Hamlet*—from the *Prometheus Vinctus*—Ingratitude—Morality and expediency—Job's language about himself—His lan-

guage towards God—Scripture sympathises with this—
Position and place of the Book of Job in the Bible—
Character of Job typical—Job's retractations—Balance
of moral truth restored—Contrast with the sentimental
philosophy and communism—Remedies for this scene of
injustice and crime—The especial Christian type of
character, ... 164

MAURICE'S THEOLOGICAL ESSAYS.

General philosophical character of the writer's speculations:
On Conscience—On Bishop Butler's views—On the Atonement—On the Eternity of Punishment—Postscript, . 255

INDIAN CONVERSION.

Prediction may be founded on two grounds—Can Brahmanism stand ?—The normal idea of the human race the worship of one God—Intellectual Paganism and Brahmanism—Their philosophy as to the relation of man with God—Hume—Seneca—Brahmanical belief in a future state—Doctrine of the metempsychosis—Confusion of personal identity—Development of revealed religion on a future life, different from that of Brahmanism—Hindoo moral system—Lying—Murder—Hindoo metaphysics—Hindoo inspiration undertakes all subjects—Succession of truths contradicted by Hindooism—Indian education—The vernacular and the English learning—The Hindoo catches quickly European ideas—The Government schools secular—Effect of secular education to demolish Hindooism—The Missionary schools—Deism not possible as a national religion—Sir C. Trevelyan's anticipations for the future of Christianity in India—Lord Stanley's policy—Caste—Civilisation does not adopt philosophical ideas of the Deity—The Gospel has conquered philosophy—Prophecy requires time, ... 310

ARGUMENT OF DESIGN.

Basis of the argument—The end of the physical apparatus is the evidence of design—Necessity of admission of the spiritual principle in Nature—Man the great discloser of design in Nature—Abnormal appendages in Nature—Rudimental organs in animals—Charge of want of fixed intention in Nature—Mr. Lewes's charge of tentatives and corrections in Nature—Enigmatical facts of Nature—Objections to design drawn from the infinity of the Deity—Startling opposites in the idea of infinity—Failure in one stage of the analogy of human contriv ncetoa divine—Formulas of the Encyclopædists—Geoffrey St. Hilaire—Collocation the evidence of design—Mr. Darwin's theory of natural selection—Developments from infinite chance variability—The eye—His admission that the first life-germ was a creation—Paley's demonstration, . 363

THE PRINCIPLE OF CAUSATION.

The idea of Cause, the key to the eternal past—Sir W. Hamilton—Leibnitz—Kant—Dean Mansel—Locke—Clarke—Maxim that every event has a cause—The idea of cause demands finality, and becomes a proof of an eternal self-existent Being—The atheist's idea—Clarke's argument—Wordsworth's sonnet—The attributes of God—Clarke—Cudworth's argument of an adequate cause—Materialists of the last century—The received view of Matter—The attitude of scientific men on the question—Mind in Nature—If in Nature, how can it be excluded from Design in Nature?—The argument demands a personal God—Man's ignorance—Extract from Kant—Existence of an ideal in Man, ... 415

IN MEMORIAM, ... 445

LIST OF THE AUTHOR'S ARTICLES AND WORKS, . . 451

DR. ARNOLD.*

(October 1844.)

This is a most genuine, hearty, real, and vivid book—most striking, most glowing, and most pictorial. It gives Dr. Arnold to the life, and portrays the man completely. We may say this without professing to have had more than an exoteric knowledge of Dr. Arnold's character, before we read it, to test the likeness by. There is a kind of intuitive power, however, by which we recognise a good portrait even when we did not know the original. Truth and nature tell their own tale: we see when the features are harmonious, when the face is a characteristic one, when the composition is a whole. This book is a clear, full, and rich representation of a particular species of religious mind; what species we mean we shall have occasion to explain farther on. We will take Dr. Arnold, for the present, simply as Mr. Stanley lays him before us, without any comments of our own. And we cannot forbear thus early thanking Mr. Stanley most sincerely for the taste and feeling with which he has managed his own editorial part of the business, and for the tact which has enabled him to carry out the representation of Dr. Arnold's character, opinions, and system, in their very strongest light and most ticklish collision with existing parties, and yet to distinguish throughout between loving the warrior and identifying himself with the combat; which has made him combine the most intense feeling for Arnold *in* the conflict, and

---

* *The Life and Correspondence of Thomas Arnold, D.D., late Head Master of Rugby School, and Regius Professor of Modern History in the University of Oxford.* By Arthur Penrhyn Stanley, M.A., Fellow and Tutor of University College, Oxford. London. 2 vols. 8vo. 1844.

as portrayed and developed by it, with a real, though unobtrusive equilibrium as to the sides of the conflict themselves. "*Mallem equidem cum Platone errare quam cum aliis vera sentire*," he thinks most justly not to be necessary to show the deference of a disciple, and the affection of a son. His neutrality has not thrown the least shade of coldness or insipidity on his portrait, while it has done much to engage the interest of opposite minds in it.

There is a congeniality often between a man's birthplace and his future tastes. The port of West Cowes in the Isle of Wight, then proud and flourishing in all the naval and military stir of the French war, was the birthplace and nurse of the earlier years of Dr. Arnold; and the noise and sight of equipments, naval and military, fresh arrivals and departures, weather-beaten visages, widespread sails and cocked hats, gave early a strong geographical and historical turn to his imagination, mixed with a considerable amount of pugnacity; which vented itself in the battles of paper fleets, and the combats of Homeric heroes dramatised from Pope's translation. A genuine love of the sea through life, and an amusing philosophical form of the true sailor contempt for "landlubbers," was a result of these scenes. The scenery, if scenery it was to be called, of the midland counties, affected him with sensations little short of disgust. "I *must* satisfy," he says, thirty years after, "a physical want in my nature, which craves after the enjoyment of nature, and for nine months in the year can find nothing to satisfy it. I agree with old Keble, that one does not need mountains and lakes for this; the Thames at Laleham —Bagley Wood, and Shotover at Oxford, were quite enough for it. I only know of five counties in England which cannot supply it; and I am unluckily perched down in one of them. These five are Warwick, Northampton, Huntingdon, Cambridge, and Bedford. I should add, perhaps, Rutland, and you cannot name a seventh; for Suffolk, which is otherwise just as bad, has its bit of sea-coast." The age of the Pisistratidæ would certainly have found Arnold one of the "Paralii," or coast party. For a considerable quantity of stupidity which came before him as schoolmaster of Rugby, he would very charitably account for from the circumstance that the poor boys had been pent up in those plebeian farm-yards of nature, the midland counties, and had never seen the sea. It was a consolatory reflection to him, however, that perhaps they were not quite so mischievous as they would have been with a wilder origin and more spirited natures. The reflection is a true one, and is capable of a large application.

"He was from his earliest years," says his biographer, "exceedingly fond of ballad poetry, which his Winchester schoolfellows used to learn from his repetition before they had seen it in print; and his own compositions as a boy all ran in the same direction. A play of this kind, in which his schoolfellows were introduced as the *dramatis personæ*, and a long poem of 'Simon de Montfort,' in imitation of Scott's Marmion, procured for him at school, by way of distinction from another boy of the same name, the appellation of Poet Arnold. And the earliest specimen of his composition which has been preserved is a little tragedy, written before he was seven years old, on 'Piercy Earl of Northumberland,' suggested apparently by Home's play of Douglas; which, however, contains nothing worthy of notice, except, perhaps, the accuracy of orthography, language, and blank-verse metre, in which it is written, and the precise arrangement of the different acts and scenes." "But he was most remarked for his forwardness in history and geography. His strong power of memory (which, however, in later years depended mainly on association), extending to the exact state of the weather on particular days, or the exact words and position of passages which he had not seen for twenty years, showed itself very early, and chiefly on these subjects. One of the few recollections which he retained of his father was, that he received from him, at three years old, a present of Smollett's History of England, as a reward for the accuracy with which he had gone through the stories connected with the portraits and pictures of the successive reigns; and at the same age he used to sit at his aunt's table arranging his geographical cards, and recognising by their shape, at a glance, the different counties of the dissected map of England."

At Winchester, Russell's Modern Europe, Gibbon, and

Mitford, succeeded to the task of feeding his historical cravings. It is remarkable, that when, in his professorial chair, he quoted Dr. Priestley's Lectures on History, it was from his recollection of the book, when he read it at eight years old. The child is father of the man. When we afterwards read of "my friends Herodotus and Livy, that I am reading now for the fiftieth time;" and the geographical zeal with which the editor of Thucydides announces the intelligence of his "six maps, all entirely original," we know where to go back to for his enthusiasm. The native, genuine, and almost poetical ground which the sciences of history and geography occupied in Dr. Arnold's mind, is indeed remarkable. The maps for Thucydides were "Aunt Delafield's cards" over again. There is something very characteristic in the toys and minutiæ, the $\tau\grave{a}$ $\dot{\epsilon}\sigma\chi\acute{a}\tau a$, to use the Aristotelian word, the hobbies of science. Maps were great favourites with Arnold. Maps, with their lines of latitude and longitude, their ridges of mountains, and ruggednesses of coast, are absolute pictures to some minds. They represent the terraqueous globe, and put before us, in one striking and definite shape, the great fact of the human race, and the whole idea of this earthly state. A map is the modern unclassical representative of the goddess Terra, and makes us realise, in the Lucretian sense, the ground on which we stand, the greatness of space, and the solidity of matter.

Arnold came up to Oxford just in time to be one of a clever and high-principled, High-Church and Tory set, which was then predominant among the undergraduates of Corpus Christi College. Judge Coleridge gives us his affectionate recollections of it:—

"There was his single-hearted and devout schoolfellow, who early gave up his native land, and devoted himself to the missionary cause in India; the high-souled and imaginative, though somewhat indolent lad, who came to us from Westminster—one bachelor, whose father's connection with the House of Commons and residence in Palace-yard made him a great authority with us as to the world without, and the statesmen whose speeches he sometimes heard, but we discussed much as if they had been personages in history; and whose remarkable love for historical and geographical research, and his proficiency in it, with his clear judgment, quiet humour, and mildness in communicating information, made him peculiarly attractive to Arnold;—and above all, our senior among the undergraduates, though my junior in years, the author of the *Christian Year*, who came fresh from the single teaching of his venerable father, and achieved the highest honours of the University at an age when others frequently are but on her threshold."—Vol. i. pp. 13, 14.

"He was a mere boy," continues Judge Coleridge, "when he first came to us, in appearance as well as in age; but we saw in a very short time that he was quite equal to take his part in the arguments of the common-room; and he was, I rather think, admitted by Mr. Cooke at once into his senior class. As he was equal, so was he ready to take part in our discussions: he was fond of conversation on serious matters, and vehement in argument; fearless too in advancing his opinions—which, to say the truth, often startled us a good deal; but he was ingenuous and candid; and though the fearlessness with which, so young as he was, he advanced his opinions might have seemed to betoken presumption, yet the good temper with which he bore retort or rebuke relieved him from that imputation; he was bold and warm, because so far as his knowledge went he saw very clearly, and he was an ardent lover of truth, but I never saw in him, even then, a grain of vanity or conceit. I have said that some of his opinions startled us a good deal; we were, indeed, for the most part Tories in Church and State, great respecters of things as they were, and not very tolerant of the disposition which he brought with him to question their wisdom. Many and long were the conflicts we had, and with unequal numbers. I think I have seen all the leaders of the common-room engaged with him at once, with little order or consideration, as may be supposed, and not always with great scrupulosity as to the fairness of our arguments. This was attended by no loss of regard, and scarcely ever, or seldom, by even momentary loss of temper."—Vol. i. pp. 11, 12.

His Oxford character is summed up in the same graphic way:—

"At the commencement a boy—and at the close retaining, not ungracefully, much of boyish spirits, frolic, and simplicity; in mind vigorous, active, clear-sighted, industrious, and daily accumulating and assimilating treasures of knowledge; not averse to poetry, but delighting rather in dialectics, philosophy, and history, with less of imaginative than reasoning power; in argument bold almost to presumption, and vehement; in temper easily roused to indignation, yet more easily appeased, and entirely free from bitterness; fired, indeed, by what he deemed ungenerous or unjust to others, rather than by any sense of personal wrong; somewhat too little deferential to authority, yet, without any real inconsistency, loving what was good and great in antiquity the more ardently and reverently because it was ancient. A casual or unkind observer might have pronounced him somewhat too pugnacious in conversation, and too positive: I have given, I believe, the true explanation; scarcely anything would have pained him more than to be convinced that he had been guilty of want of modesty, or of deference where it was justly due; no one thought these virtues of more sacred obligation. In heart, if I can speak with confidence of any of the friends of my youth, I can of his, that it was devout and pure, simple, sincere, affectionate, and faithful."—Vol. i. pp. 22, 23.

The warm-hearted, tender, affectionate, lively, sincere character soon comes before us in another connection. Arnold was born to be a *paterfamilias*, as well in the mere literal as in the larger sense of the word. He was made for the parental and didactic relationship to others. There is a great difference between first-rate minds on this point. Some have no natural taste or liking for the particular office of influencing minds; their hearts and intellects expand within themselves, spread over the earth, air, and sea of speculation, and pervade all metaphysical nature, before they definitely take up the notion of impressing their views upon any one being but themselves. The pleasure of getting their views received, seeing them take, and watching their entrance into other minds, is one which they do not feel or appreciate. It is just the reverse with another class: with them the very process of expansion in their own minds takes the form of communication with other minds; and they have no sooner a view at all, than they want to see it out abroad, and doing its work. The very life of an opinion, even as an inward one, is connected in their idea with its external power; and the internal and external go on together. This constitutes perhaps the very soul of the genuine *magister*. The teaching instinct carries a man naturally into what Archbishop Whately has called the heresy of the οἱ πέρι— into putting himself into the relation of guide and informant to others—into instituting the society and forming the school, or whatever other shape there may be of the active centrality of one mind amongst others.

Arnold became a married man and a tutor as soon as he could well be either, *i.e.* after a very short residence upon his College fellowship. College society, bright and captivating as it was—even Oriel, full of original thinkers as it was—was not the sphere for him: his instinct marked out a more insulated and independent line. He had soon his nucleus about him. He was of the latter class of minds that we have mentioned; and, as he used to say of himself, " could hardly live without tuition." His boyish vigour and spirits, his intuitive love of communicating and teaching, and the particular class of affectionate feelings which were so strong in him, all fitted him to deal with the young rather than the old, and carried him into the society of his inferiors rather than of his equals. The scene at Laleham soon rose up, under his care, into a perfect little garden and paradise of tutorial and domestic felicity. Children and pupils grew up under his eye; and his own stock of knowledge was rapidly growing too. He had time for his favourite pursuits; he had the full enjoyment of literary activity and literary leisure; and he had a beautiful river and luxuriant scenery to feed his eyes. Many a tutor has had exactly the same scene around him, but very few have been able to enjoy and appreciate it as Arnold did. And, in the meantime, he was insensibly observing phenomena, and collecting rules relating to his peculiar department. And the growth of a thorough tutorial experience was preparing him for a larger, more systematic, and more conspicuous field for its employment.

The state of Public Schools at this time is pretty well known. We need not say much about them. Any public-school man of some fifteen years ago will remember the routine which he went through, what he was taught, and what he was not taught. Good elegant and accurate scholarship was certainly encouraged; and grammar was well hammered into boys' heads. A still larger class of boys caught an air and style from the atmosphere of the place, and learnt gentlemanly manners; and, perhaps, in these traits we have the principal results which the public-school system, as such, aimed at. Many moral and religious boys, doubtless, came every year out of them; but morality and religion were hardly the aims of the system; and the notions of the latitudinarian and political economist respecting the relation of Church and State had almost found a counterpart in the relation of the master to the boys in our public schools. The instinctive feeling, though it would not have been formally confessed, was, that good scholarship, and not good morals, was the legitimate aim of the schoolmaster, as such: that much as the latter might have rejoiced, as a man, in seeing a good moral and religious tone grow up in his boys, still he had little to do, as a master, with the boys' consciences; that the particular uses of a school was to teach him Greek and Latin, and not religion; and that if the former only was learnt, that was the boy's and not the schoolmaster's look-out. What has the State to do with teaching religion? the political economist triumphantly asks. And what has scholarship to do with religion? was a question which many a good kind of man asked, who had the sincerest respect separately for both. Feeling had certainly changed since the time that the pious Dr. Busby listened with warm and affectionate ears to the prayers of anxious mothers, as they gave up their innocent children into his magisterial but truly priestly hands. We do not want to institute invidious comparisons; the faults of our public-school teachers have been the faults of the age, and not of the men: and the apparent Quixotic position which always attaches to any advance upon an established order of things, is one which literally cannot be carried off by common minds; and which may, therefore, be excusably not attempted by them. The old-fashioned schoolmaster of the eighteenth century was a useful State instrument for keeping up a gentlemanly and aristocratical standard of education. Methodical, strict, and upon a theory as much as his own inclination pompous, he regarded his office and dignity rather in its official light, as the headship of a department, than as involving a living contact with heads and hearts. A stiff barrier of form kept him at a distance from the real minds he had under him, and the abstract school intervened between himself and his scholars. He was a respectable functionary in the service of education, but was rather her bedel than her champion; and the dignity of the mace quelled the row, and silenced the murmurer, without much aid of the deeper and more refined reverential feelings.

Dr. Arnold was just the man for making an advance upon this old-school system, and an opportunity was given him of doing so. After a nine years' residence at Laleham, in 1828 the head-mastership of Rugby became vacant; he stood for it, and was elected. The genuine strong confidence with which he had inspired his Oxford friends in his talents for such a post, showed itself in their testimonials, and carried all before it. A wave of applause and bright predictions lifted Arnold into his new position; it was generally felt that something would come of it, and that a beginning was made of a great change in our school system, in the mere fact that he was made a head-master. He entered upon the work with spirit, zeal, and joyousness, which betokened an efficient future. A few regrets at leaving the quiet scene of Laleham, a little musing over reminiscences of nine pleasant domestic years over, and he was ready for his large task, and longing for it, like a horse for its gallop. "There will be a great deal to do, I suspect, in every way, when I first enter on my situation; but still, if my health continues, I do not at all dread it, but, on the contrary, look forward to it with much pleasure. I have long since looked upon education as my business in life; and just before I stood for Rugby I had offered myself as a candidate for the historical professorship at the London University, and had indulged in various dreams of attaching myself to that institution, and trying as far as possible to influence it. In Rugby there is a fairer field."

In the same tone he writes to Mr. Cornish while the election was still pending:—

"You have often wanted me to be master at Winchester, so I think you will be glad to hear that I am actually a candidate for Rugby. I was strongly urged to stand, and money tempted me; but I cannot in my heart be sorry to stay where both M. and myself are so entirely happy. If I do get it, I feel as if I could set to work very heartily, and with God's blessing, I should like to try whether my notions of Christian education are really impracticable; whether our system of public schools has not in it some noble elements which, under the blessing of the Spirit of all holiness and wisdom, might produce fruit even to life eternal. When I think about it thus, I really long to take rod in hand; but when I think of the πρὸς τὸ τέλος, the perfect vileness which I must daily contemplate, the certainty that this can at best be only partially remedied, the irksomeness of 'fortemque Gyan fortemque Cloanthum,' and the greater form and publicity of the life which we should there lead, when I could no more bathe daily in the clear Thames, nor wear old coats and Russia duck trousers, nor hang on a gallows, nor climb a pole, I grieve to think of the possibility of a change."—Vol. i. p. 72.

A public school was, in fact, just that mixture of the secular and religious which suited his character and fell in with his theories. The act of bringing religion into common life, and allying, according to his own sense of the word, Church and State, was his *beau-idéal* of Christian efficiency. Church and State, and religion and the world, come over again and again in his letters, as if his mind was never without the image of this coalition; and a school was just such a union in miniature—a little religious polity, or small Church and State, and the schoolmaster a form of the *Rex atque Sacerdos*. Arnold went to Rugby with the determination of making the school religious. In opposition to any separation of scholarship from religion, the aim of the school from that of the boy, he had conceived a levelling of demarcations, a concentration of energies, a union and solution, which fused the whole purposes of a school in one rich mellow religious intellectual glow.

One very remarkable idea especially penetrated his whole mind with respect to the scene he was entering on; and it continued with him throughout,—we mean the strong idea of an actual encounter, a fight with evil. The image of a great conflict with evil comes out repeatedly in his thoughts upon school, the state of parties, and the world in general. This is a rare quality of mind. Everybody has, of course, a distinction between right and wrong, but a particular class of warm characters are positively haunted by an image of evil as a definite bad thing and an enemy; it is ever catching their eye, and is a perpetual mark and butt to let fly their bolts at. The feeling is not necessarily connected with the highest perceptions of truth, or the highest form of character; statesmen and warriors, and many heroes of the world, have had it in their way. It is in its lowest shape, however, a divine impulse. It is the instinct of man, not in his animal or in his depraved aspect, but simply as man, and as he came from the creating hand. Other animals have their instincts of hatred and enmity; and the human creature has the highest, the hatred of evil.

Arnold had a notion of evil in a school as a sort of spreading blot and mercurial poisonous fluid running about everywhere, and infecting, with awful quickness, in so thick a hive of minds. The power that company and crowds give to the bad, in consequence of the cowardice of the good, and the shame which prevents resistance, the tyranny of a bad public opinion, of swagger and fashion, were positive eyesores to him:—

"I have just had," we find him writing to a friend, "one of those specimens of the evil of boy-nature, which makes me always unwilling to undergo the responsibility of advising any man to send his son to a public school. There has been a system of persecution carried on by the bad against the good, and then, when complaint was made to me, there came fresh persecution on that very account; and divers instances of boys joining in it out of pure cowardice, both physical and moral, when if left to themselves they would have rather shunned it. And the exceedingly small number of boys who can be relied on for active and steady good on these occasions, and the way in which the decent and respectable of ordinary life (Carlyle's 'Shams') are sure on these occasions to swim with the stream, and take part with the evil, makes me strongly feel exemplified what the Scripture says about the strait gate and the wide one,—a view of human nature which, when looking on human life in its full dress of decencies and civilisations, we are apt, I imagine, to find it hard to realise. But here, in the nakedness of boy-nature, one is quite able to understand how there could not be found so many as even ten righteous in a whole city. And how to meet this evil I really do not know, but to find it thus rife after I have been [so many] years fighting against it, is so sickening, that it is very hard not to throw up the cards in despair and upset the table."—Vol. i. pp. 161-2.

"At the very sight of a knot of vicious or careless boys gathered together round the great school-fire, it makes me think," he would say, "that I see the devil in the midst of them." "What I want to see in the school," he says again, "and what I cannot find, is an abhorrence of evil; I always think of the Psalm, 'Neither doth he abhor anything that is evil.'"

A rule which he very soon laid down for himself after his entrance on the office is a significant one on this subject. He found a general feeling existing abroad that "so long as a boy kept himself from offences sufficiently enormous to justify expulsion, he had a kind of right to remain in a public school." One of Arnold's first announcements was a set down to this notion—"Till a man learns that the first, second, and third duty of a schoolmaster is to get rid of unpromising subjects, a great public school will never be what it might be, and what it ought to be." He made up his opinion on this point very early in his tutorial career, and he adhered rigidly to it:— "Sending away boys is a necessary and regular part of a good system, not as a punishment to one, but as a protection to others. Undoubtedly it would be a better system if there was no evil; but evil being unavoidable, we are not a jail to keep it in, but a place of education, where we must cast it out, to prevent its taint from spreading." An educational war with evil was in short pictured upon Arnold's mind as he entered upon Rugby; his scope was a free, indefinite, and uncircumscribed one; his energies were tasked to the full, and he had to do everything because he had to do good.

There is a method of going to work which shows a man at home with his department. Arnold's plan and scheme for the management of his school was a clear and straightforward one. He selected for his lever and instrument the Sixth Form. The Sixth Form was his prætorian band, and surrounded the head master like the club-bearers of the Greek chieftains, and like the bodyguard which attends the queen bee. They were admitted into his confidence, to his most esoteric thoughts, to his favourite and finest theories. The head master saw comparatively little of the rest of the school. Twice a week a lesson was heard, and the forms of the lower boys passed in review at considerable intervals before his eye, to give him the opportunity of seeing that the routine went on properly, and of exercising a superintendence over the labours of the other masters. But he was visible to the mass principally through the veil of the Sixth Form. And, though as open as day, as far as his personal presence went, and constantly seen about in the playground, with respect to the school, as such, he leaned considerably to the Persian policy of shutting himself up in his palace; and the Tower Library, where he heard the Sixth Form, apart from the noise of school and the popular eye, was the Ecbatana of Rugby. The political and theoretic liberal was anything but a practical one in his own sphere, and the extent to which he made himself scarce was sometimes remembered with even bitter feeling by boys who left before they arrived at the stage of intimacy. Still the relations of distance he maintained—his occasional sternness and anger—his " ashy paleness and awful frown," when anything very bad happened, did not on the whole impede, but aid his popularity. He seems to have had the art—a great one with boys, and men too—to show that you don't care for them; that you care *about* them indeed a great deal, but do not care *for* them the least. Arnold had this happy mixture. He did not injure his school-popularity by wishing and aiming for it, the most certain way generally of not getting it. We see both men and boys detecting selfishness even on the tender point of gaining their own affections, and liking a superior the better for not showing it. "There grew up," says Mr. Stanley, "a deep admiration, partaking largely of the nature of awe; and this softened into a sort of loyalty, which remained even in the closer and more affectionate sympathy of later years." " I am sure," writes a pupil, who had no personal communications with him whilst at school, and but little afterwards, and who never was in the Sixth Form, "that I do not exaggerate my feelings when I say that I felt a love and reverence for him as one of quite awful greatness and goodness."

The Sixth Form, then, were Arnold's representatives and delegates in the school, the channel through which his influence was felt and his wishes known. He concentrated his personal interest, and all the peculiar feelings of master to disciple, upon them; he upheld their authority in the school with rigour, and he rebuked them the most deeply and indignantly when they behaved ill. They had the principal honour of his affection and his wrath.

"I do not choose," he says, on one occasion, when some vigorous measures in members of the Sixth Form towards the populace of the school had been called in question,—"I do not choose to discuss the thickness of Præpostors' sticks, or the greater or less blackness of a boy's bruises, for the amusement of all the readers of the newspapers; nor do I care in the slightest degree about the attacks, if the masters themselves treat them with indifference. If they appear to mind them, or to fear their effect on the school, the apprehension in this, as in many other instances, will be likely to verify itself. For my own part, I confess that I will not condescend to justify the school against attacks, when I believe that it is going on not only not ill, but positively well. Were it really otherwise, I think I should be as sensitive as any one, and very soon give up the concern. But these attacks are merely what I bargained for, so far as they relate to my conduct in the school, because they are directed against points on which my 'ideas' were fixed before I came to Rugby, and are only more fixed now; *e.g.* that the authority of the Sixth Form is essential to the good of the school, and is to be upheld through all obstacles from within and from without."

The fact that the Sixth Form was an instrument ready made for him—their prepositorial authority, as well as the fagging system, having been part of the old school plan, which he found going on when he came to Rugby—does not at all interfere with the credit due to him for converting it into such an instrument of government as he did. He showed the capacity of an able mind in appreciating the materials which his department offered him, and making them serve his turn instead of discovering others. The old-seasoned timber is likely to be stronger, and more serviceable too, than the green planks just cut from the wood. Arnold kept up the old system of the school to an extent extraordinary for a person of his very anti-

Tory sentiments. The keen practical insight which his tutorial genius and experience gave him in his own particular department,—the acuteness and solidity of the new schoolmaster, came round to the same point with the prejudices of the old one. Arnold gave life and strength to the machinery already existing, pointed and edged the tool, and turned it into the hole it was meant to cut. The Sixth Form was a definite instrument of his, and was made to act upon the school and reflect himself.

With the same practical view he kept up fagging, and he kept up flogging. On the latter *vexata quæstio* he was very clear and decided, though making a distinction between big boys and little ones. "I know well," is his criticism on the liberal dislike of that punishment, "of what feeling this is the expression: it originates in that proud notion of personal independence which is neither reasonable nor Christian. . . . At an age when it is almost impossible to find a true manly sense of the degradation of guilt or faults, where is the wisdom of encouraging a fantastic sense of the degradation of personal correction? What can be more false, or more adverse to the simplicity, sobriety, and humbleness of mind, which are the best ornament of youth, and the best promise of a noble manhood?"

And he liked old school associations as well as the old school system. Winchester and Oxford were historical places; he desiderated some associations of the ancient sort for Rugby, and felt painfully the contrast between it and Winchester in that respect. In their place, he had a scheme for getting a crown medal for Rugby, to give the school more of an old-established aristocratical air. However, he dwelt upon its antiquity, even in spite of these defects. "There is, or there ought to be," he tells his boys, "something very ennobling in being connected with an establishment at once ancient and magnificent, where all about us, and all the associations belonging to the objects around us, should be great, splendid, and elevating. What an individual ought, and often does, derive from the feeling that he is born of an old and illustrious race—from being familiar, from his childhood, with the walls and trees which speak of the past, no less than of the present, and make both full of images of greatness,—this, in an inferior degree, belongs to every member of an ancient and celebrated place of education."

A good, bold, systematic character thus stamped Arnold's whole school-scheme and basis. But his great forte, and secret of influence, after all, was *himself*. The system was nothing without the man: the man was at the bottom of the whole work; and "our great self," the school, was the portrait and impersonation of the master. "Whatever peculiarity of character was impressed on the scholars whom it sent forth, was derived, not from the genius of the place, but from the genius of the man. Throughout the whole, whether in the school itself, or in its after effects, the one image that we have before us is not Rugby but Arnold."

To take a look into the Library Tower, and see him at the head of the table, with his class before him. Mr. Stanley gives us the scene from his own vivid recollection, and calls upon his fellow-scholars to

"remember the glance with which he looked round in the few moments of silence before the lesson began, and which seemed to speak his sense of his own position and of theirs also, as the heads of a great school; the attitude in which he stood, turning over the pages of Facciolati's Lexicon, or Pole's Synopsis, with his eye fixed upon the boy who was pausing to give an answer; the well-known changes of his voice and manner, so faithfully representing the feeling within; the pleased look and the cheerful 'Thank you,' which followed upon a successful answer or translation; the fall of his countenance, with its deepening severity, the stern elevation of the eyebrows, the sudden 'Sit down' which followed upon the reverse; the courtesy and almost deference to the boys, as to his equals in society, so long as there was nothing to disturb the friendliness of their relation; the startling earnestness with which he would check in a moment the slightest approach to levity or impertinence; the confidence with which he addressed them in his half-yearly exhortations; the expressions of delight with which, when they had been doing well, he would say that it was a constant pleasure to him to come into the library."—Vol. i. p. 126.

"'You come here,' he said, 'not to read, but to learn how to read;' and thus the greater part of his instructions were interwoven with the process of their own minds; there was a continual reference to their thoughts, an acknowledgment that, so far as their information and power of reasoning could take them, they ought to have an opinion of their own; a working not for but with the form, as if they were equally interested with himself in making out the meaning of the passage before them; a constant endeavour to set them right, either by gradually helping them on to a true answer, or by making the answers of the more advanced part of the form serve as a medium through which his instructions might be communicated to the less advanced part."—Vol. i. p. 127.

The solicitude that boys should apprehend his meaning for themselves, and take it in with their own minds, and not with the master's—a common mistake, by the way, in teaching—this genuine tutorial sympathy established a kind of equality and reciprocity between the master and boys. He never concealed difficulties; was never afraid of confessing ignorance; and would appeal for help to the French scholars and Latin verse-writers among the boys. His own books even did not escape; and, touchy article as a printed book is in the eye of the author, the mistakes in his own Thucydides were acknowledged to his class with most creditable candour.

Arnold's warmth of heart was, in short, part, and the most effective part, of his talent. A stream of exuberant feeling carried him along, and carried the school along with him: they were taken off their legs, and found themselves floating and swimming, and enjoying their delicious bathe in the blue sunshiny lake. Arnold's school was his family: he had an overflowing fund of feeling for pupils, friends, family, and all; not one set of feelings for one class, and another for another, so much as a fund of large warm and luxuriant affectionateness for all. And this, though entirely sincere, was just of that easily excitable kind which most tells upon persons, and impresses most vividly. Always ready to bubble up, and find a vent in tone, look, the tremor of the voice, the tear in the eye; it was constantly giving life, warmth, and animation to what he said. Its very uncontrollableness, in the kindly and tender shape which it took, was a pleasing feature about it; persons were quite won over by the liveliness of his emotions, and carried away the little scene which it created as a tender picture in their minds. He burst into tears on somebody in his own family circle making a comparison, which seemed to place St. Paul above St. John, and begged that the comparison might never again be made. Such a lively unaccountable sally of emotion breaking in upon a religious argument is very characteristic. "He was sometimes so deeply affected in pronouncing sentence on offenders that he could hardly speak. 'I felt,' he said once of some great offence in a sixth-form boy, and his eyes filled with tears as he spoke, 'as if it had been one of my own children.'" "No thoughts were so bitter to him as those suggested by the innocent faces of little boys, as they first came from home. 'It is a most touching thing to me,' he said once in the hearing of one of his former pupils, on the mention of some new comers, 'to receive a new fellow from his father—when I think what an influence there is in this place for evil, as well as for good. I do not know anything which affects me more.' His pupil, who had, on his own first coming, been impressed chiefly by the severity of his manner, expressed some surprise, adding, that he should have expected this to wear away with the succession of fresh arrivals. 'No!' he said; 'if ever I could receive a new boy from his father without emotion, I should think it was high time to be off.'" In administering the Communion he bent himself down to the little boys with looks of fatherly tenderness, and glistening eyes, and trembling voice.

Even every-day school routine and repetition was not dry to him. He was asked whether he did not tire of hearing the same lessons constantly. "No," was his answer: "there is a constant freshness in them; I find something new in them every time I go over them." His "childlike enjoyment of Herodotus," and of "that fountain of beauty and delight," Homer, quite overpowered him. At the hundredth time of hammering it into a class, the story of Cleobis and Bito brought tears to his eyes.

We follow him into his house, and we see his children playing upon his knees, while he writes or reads rapidly in spite of that interruption, and that of constant visitors going in and out. "A stir of so many human beings greets him from morning to evening, that he sometimes feels that he should like to run his head into a hole." He goes into the playground, salutes the little boys cheerfully *en passant*, and watches the cricket. He is as fond of play as any one of them, and only does not climb his gallows in public at Rugby—a treat which he thought he could not as head master well indulge in. But he looks forward to the deprivation with some degree of gloom from Laleham :—" I want absolute play, like a boy, and neither riding nor walking will make up for my leaping-pole and gallows, and bathing, when the youths used to go with me, and I felt completely for the time a boy as they were" (p. 81). He was quite the "elder brother and playfellow" of his sons and pupils, but with the superior relation close at hand to fall back on when he thought fit. His pupils at Laleham are his walking, bathing, and jumping companions; and "he calls us fellows!" is the first exclamation of surprise from the little boys that come to Rugby. Moreover, he actually trusted their word; and, "It is a shame to tell Arnold a lie,—he believes one," was the current remark.

Next to children and pupils, his delight is scenery. "The enjoyment of nature is necessary to satisfy a physical want in his nature." The delight of living in mountains, "and seeing and loving them in all their moods," takes him to Westmoreland; and nothing satisfies him but he must actually build a house at Fox How, some three hundred miles from Rugby, where he retires for the holidays, out of pure love of fine scenery. Warwickshire, "with no hills, either blue or brown, no heath, no woods, no clear streams, no wide plains for lights and shades to play over, no banks for flowers to grow on," is only pleasant for the intellectual and moral enjoyments it supplies in the shape of pupils, which it gives in plenty. But at Foxhow the enjoyment is completed, and comes to a climax. There he has scenery, children, pupils, friends. His favourite boys often accompany him there for the holidays. He is full of invitations to persons to come and see him; and the society of Wordsworth is in keeping with lofty mountains, cataracts, and summer skies. Very fine weather could make even Rugby smile. "The deep green of a field of clover, or an old elm on the rise of a hill, or a fine oak," made him stop and admire; and the sight of "the blue depth of ether" elicited his philosophical preference of the modern idea of the "blue sky" to the "iron firmament" of the ancients. And there were "the happy walks by the side of his wife's pony, huntings for flowers in the fields and hedges, excursions to the neighouring clay-pit to look for coltsfoot, the mock sieges which followed," and all the fun and cheerfulness of the party.

The peculiarly domestic standard about which all these pleasures and excitements, moral and physical, gathered—the type of the *paterfamilias* which ran through them, was a thing to be observed. All persons have their whole and centre to which their tastes and feeling attach. Arnold's whole was the house, the οἰκία, the family. He was domestic from top to toe; his school a family—his family a school: the family type surmounted and headed the whole scene of his employment and his pleasure. A family was a temple and a church with Arnold,—a living sanctuary and focus of religious joy,—a paradise, a heaven upon earth. It was the horn of plenty, the sparkling cup, the grape and the pomegranate, the very cream of human feeling and sentiment, and the very well-spring of spiritual hopes and aspirations. He thought and he taught, and he worked and he played, and he looked at sun, and earth, and sky, with a domestic heart. The horizon of family life mixed with the skyey life above, and the earthly landscape melted, by a quiet process of nature, into the heavenly one. "'I do not wonder,' he said, 'that it was thought a great misfortune to die childless in old times, when they had not fuller light—it seems so completely wiping a man out of existence.'" "The anniversaries of domestic events—the passing away of successive generations—the entrance of his sons on the several stages of their education,—struck on the deepest chords of his nature, and made him blend with every prospect of the future the keen sense of the continuance (so to speak) of his own existence in the good and evil fortunes of his children, and to unite the thought of them with the yet more solemn feeling, with which he was at all times wont to regard 'the blessing' of 'a whole house transplanted entire from earth to heaven, without one failure.'"

The feeling extended itself into the past in his mind, and became a genuine patriarchal ancestorial taste. "When, in later years, he was left the head of the family, he delighted in gathering round him the remains of his father's household, and in treasuring up every particular relating to his birthplace and parentage, even to the graves of the older generations of the family in the parish of Lowestoff, and the great willow-tree. in his father's grounds at Slattwoods, from which he transplanted shoots successively to Laleham, to Rugby, and to Fox How. Every date in the family history, with the alteration of hereditary names, and the changes of their residence, was carefully preserved for his children in his own handwriting; and when, in after years, he fixed on the abode of his old age, in Westmoreland, it was his great delight to regard it as a continuation of his own early home in the Isle of Wight." And the vivid affection he entertains for all the scenes of his youth, comes over and over again in his strong Wykemist reminiscences, and in the "poor dear old Oxford, and Bagley Wood, and the pretty field, and the wild stream that flows down between Bullingdon and Cowley Marsh, not forgetting even your old friend, the Lower London Road."

We have seen Arnold at work, and Arnold at play; but the fact is, play and work were the same thing to him, with respect to telling upon his happiness. They were the Castor and Pollux, the delightful and happy variation of his existence. It was one down, another up; either he was at work and happy, or he was at play and happy. But work was his chief play, his charming, and most absorbing and satiating excitement : his meat and drink. He hungered for it; he looked forward to it with all the eagerness and sharpness of genuine appetite. Recreation was more pleasant, from the delightful termination it had in prospect, even than on its own account; and he seems to have had the power of taking long camel's draughts of it, which set him going for months, and upon a basis of strength which made no continuity of work a fatigue to him. "It is this entire relaxation I think, at intervals —such, again, as my foreign tours have afforded, that gives me so keen an appetite for my work at other times, and has enabled me to go through it, not only with no fatigue, but with a sense of absolute pleasure." His spirit carried him through his long half-years with a swing; and after a long morning's work in school, like the hunter that positively put his master into a rage because he could not be tired, and would come home fresh after the hottest run, he was as vigorous as ever, and ready to set to at his Thucydides, pamphlets, correspondence, or anything else on hand. "'Instead of feeling my head exhausted,' he would sometimes say, after the day's business was over, 'it seems to have quite an eagerness to set to work. I feel as if I could dictate to twenty secretaries at once.'" "My spirits," he writes, "in themselves, are a great blessing; for, without them, the work would weigh me down, whereas now I seem to throw it off like the fleas from a dog's back when he shakes himself." "I do not at all dread it —I look forward to it with much pleasure," is his remark when a candidate for Rugby, on the immense career of work that he was bringing down upon himself. The retrospect of labour is the pleasantest part of it to most people; the prospect of it was to Arnold. "I have nothing to do with rest here, but labour," he says; and he adds, "I can and do look forward to labour with nothing but satisfaction."

What with work and what with play, in short, what with pupils and children, and scenery and nature; with Thucydides, Herodotus, Livy; Fox How and the Lakes; leaping-pole, gallows, and bathing; above all, himself, his activities, feelings, emotions; his inexhaustibleness, perpetual motion, the intense and indomitable principle of life there was in him; what with his happiness and what with himself, who so thoroughly apprehended and imbibed it—Arnold's happiness made up as overpowering a whole as is often presented in the lot of man. "The very act of existence was an hourly pleasure to him." He dwells upon "the almost *awful* happiness of his domestic life." The "entire happiness that he tastes year after year, and day after day, is almost *startling*." He "never raises his eyes from the paper to the window without an influx of new delights." The "quiet hourly delight of having mountains and streams as familiar objects, connected with all the enjoyments of home, one's family, one's books, one's friends, associated with our work-day thoughts as well as our gala days—as a vision of beauty from one vacation to another"—represents a particular department of the enjoyment which he imbibed from inanimate nature, and is quite a picture.

Upon the character, of which we have just given a sketch, —and a vigorous, youthful, eager, intense, lively, affectionate, hearty, and powerful character it is,—we have now a remark to make. We find a deficiency—we want a something here. Energetic characters, of all others, need, and should have, the depressing balance in some shape or other; and an indefinite sensation to this effect rises like a vapour out of the rich glow and warmth of such a life as Arnold's.

Is there a Christian form of the dark rough-hewn idea of the old world expressed in the πᾶν τὸ θεῖον φθονερόν, the awful "Divine Envy," the disturbing Genius of this earthly life? A natural instinct, or a remnant of superstition, or something better, puts us on the watch for pain to counterbalance power, and sadness to relieve success; predicts all not right where things are too flowing, misfortune latent where it is not seen; makes fear the test of solidity, and melancholy an element of greatness? The touch which turns to gold, the eye that brightens earth and sky, the life which feeds and satisfies all sweet affections and intellectual activities, encounters this sad comment. Has not the success of the really great been paid for generally, as if by a law of nature, by the sting which has extracted the inward satisfaction of it; by the pressure, burden, cloud within; the grievance and the sore; the wound deep-seated at the heart, which knew no flattery, and defied the ointment? He who braved it out of doors wept at home, and felt in secret all the languor and depression of feeble nature, while a gallant show of strength and boldness rode over the outside world. This, indeed, is the popular theory of the interesting in epic, drama, and novel; to which even the child's story-book and strolling rustic barn-floor play appeals. It lies at the bottom, if we may say so, of the *science* of romance: and is applied and developed, rudely or with polish, simply or subtly, awkwardly or dexterously, as we may fancy a principle in mechanics, according to the hand it falls into. A hero is one who suffers; man, woman, and child expect it: they think themselves defrauded of their right if he does not: the luxury of pity was the temptation and the attraction. They did not want him to enjoy himself: that perfect harmony of life, and full reception, into the inner man and very heart, of outward nature's light and glow, makes a brilliant rainbow, but an uninteresting soul. There is one view of character, of course, which does not make this necessary—in which characters interest us as agreeable phenomena, and pleasant combinations, in the way that rich mixtures of colours please the eye. We may see this in many of the delightful characters in works of fiction. With all that is amiable and genuine in them, and which has doubtless a real claim to the interest due to goodness, the charm these characters possess does seem to approach more or less to the *physical*, and so far as it does, it differs in kind from the one we mean. Moral interest, pure and intrinsical, requires the other, the severer and sadder basis; it does not attach itself to the harmonious image of life: and the pleasurable state, whether sluggish and heavy, or sparkling and vivacious, is exactly not its object. We are speaking of the natural, rough, popular view, which the human mind takes. Pity is akin to love. We are very sorry when our friends are unhappy, but we do not like them less, but more—yes, more—for being so. And large mixture as these popular facts doubtless contain, in the concrete, of caprice, morbid sentiment and nonsense, they betray a principle underneath.

Arnold's character is too luscious, too joyous, too luxuriant, too brimful. The colour is good, but the composition is too rich. Head full, heart full, eyes beaming, affections met, sunshine in the breast, all nature embracing him—here is too much glow of earthly mellowness, too much actual liquid in the light. We do not discern the finest element of interest in Arnold's character; he is too full to want our sympathy, too happy to be interesting. The happy instinct is despotic in him; he cannot help it, but he is always happy, likes everything that he is doing so prodigiously—the tail is wagging, the bird whistles, the cricket chirps. This is not at all necessary in an energetic practical character; it is notorious that the very foremost of history's heroes have had a great deal of the sombre element in their constitution, and we all like it. In short, a great character of this class must have it or he loses caste. Arnold is without it; he is amiable and philanthropic, and his philanthropy is hurt and distressed at times. That is not what we mean. Philanthropy does not touch the centre; does not wound where wounding tells; leaves a man heart-whole, unhumbled.

Arnold's happiness is made almost part of his religion from its intensity. "Awful," "startling," "the very act of existence," a sort of deep mysterious language with respect to it seems to convert the sensation of pleasure into a positive religion (on the principle that religion is the deepest part of us), and give the intensity of eternal essence to present life. The light, superficial, transient, interrupted sensation of pleasure only plays upon the skin, and does not appropriate the man; but the deep, solid, glowing, and constant pleasure of life cannot be felt without an act of incorporation passing, and pleasure being converted into a spiritual substance and becoming a man's religion. A religious theory, in short, seems to lurk beneath these outward symptoms; and, without grudging Arnold the Elysium of his generous, amiable heart, we will call the theory by its right name. Arnold was a German; his ἦθος was that of genuine religious Germanism, and his life a most favourable, but still a real specimen and legitimate development of the Lutheran theory—not the Lutheran *theory* in him, perhaps, so much as the genuine Lutheran instinct, which came round to the same point. Let our readers go to Miss Bremer's novels. They will see a number of characters drawn in glowing colours, with feeling, sentiment, generosity, simplicity, disinterestedness, the poetical love of nature and of art, and manly power and talent attaching to them. They have all the richness and juiciness of the human heart and intellect about them. But there is an *hiatus* somewhere; they please our mental palate rather than our soul, and a deep sympathy and a moral yearning at the bottom of our nature is left untouched by them. They are the offspring of a religion that naturalises itself here; garden plants, fairy forms of the Lutheran ether. Lutheranism has its fine as well as its coarse side. It materialises a higher world, and so succeeds in anticipating it; and it is most successful in doing so when it exhibits most of the *spirituel*. Arnold, we say, belongs to this world of character; he is a *religious* specimen of it, but still he belongs to it. The Lutheran and the Catholic systems have been ever, under one form or other, fighting for the possession of man's goodness. His goodness is recipient of either form, and may be refracted into either atmosphere. Arnold's was German and Lutheran.

But we must pursue our history, and take him upon a wider field than we have yet seen him upon. We are afraid the show will not be quite so smiling a one, and we must prepare for the rough side of his character and his pen.

The year 1830 ushered in what was perhaps the most memorable and alarming struggle between the Church and her political and dissenting opponents in this country that had been seen for a century. The repeal of the Test and Corporation Acts, and the Emancipation Bill, carried in the animus in which it was, had so strengthened the hands of the liberal party that they seemed to have the world before them, and only to have to strike in order to destroy. The Church was naturally the object to which their aim was directed, and all eyes were instantly turned in that direction. A climax seemed to be at hand; the cry was raised; pamphlet and newspaper were loud about her enormous revenues, her antiquated forms, and her State monopolies, the tithes of her rectors, and the baronies of her bishops, church-rates, and every part of the Establishment. Her wealth was exaggerated tenfold by ten thousand mouths day after day, till people had a kind of magical Oriental notion of it, and the alliance of cupidity with revolutionary zeal threatened to be too strong for any opposition.

A party existed at the same time *in* the Church, who were quite ready to make use of such a hostile outward demonstration for the purpose of recasting her upon their own model. Their language to the Church was that of favourable and friendly revolutionism. You cannot go on any longer as you are, they said; if you resist you are sure to be overwhelmed. You must give way, and you had as well do so voluntarily and with a good grace. Take a more liberal and more comprehensive ground, a freer shape and dress. Suit yourself to the age, and keep pace with the progress of opinion. Only put yourself into our hands, and we will refit you in unobjectionable style as a solid and congenial institution of the age. In other words, they took advantage of the present opportunity to promulgate and commend their own particular theories to the Church; and a Church-reforming party from within began very soon to excite more attention and alarm than the one without.

Arnold had been ripe a long time for such a movement as this, and he naturally took his place in it. He had reached an age when men have generally formed and matured their opinions, if they ever mean to have any; he had withstood the *genius loci* of Oxford, the endearments of High Church and Tory friendships, and the intimacy of one especially, whom to know and to be a liberal was indeed the height of liberalism. He was the fellow-schemer and theorist of the Archbishop of Dublin, the Chevalier Bunsen, and others—an acute philosophical circle, to whom, however, his peculiar life and brilliancy was a great gain and addition as a practical stimulus. Here was a great nucleus of power formed. A speculative liberalism had been the growing element for some time, even in Oxford and in Oriel, under the fostering patronage of Dr. Copleston and Dr. Whately's vigorous and argumentative training. There was every look of a rising school that had its career to come, and a whole chain of youthful anticipations to run through. The formidable test of fashion had shown itself; it was beginning to be fashionable to be a liberal, and the intellectual tide was leaving the Church basis. That Arnold and Dr. Whately had great ideas of their strength, these volumes, we think, show. The old High Church school were partly gone and partly asleep; the Evangelicals had no ground of their own from which they might resist liberalism with any effect. There seemed to be an open field to the new reformers, every prospect of the Church falling into their hands in the natural progress of things, and they appear to have looked confidently to this result themselves. The feeling was much aided by their great opinion of each other, their great expectation of what must be the effects each other's talents would produce. Of the Archbishop of Dublin, Arnold writes—" He is a truly great man, in the highest sense of the word, and if the safety and welfare of the Protestant Church in Ireland depend in any degree on human instruments, none could be found, I verily believe, in the whole empire so likely to maintain it." " In Church matters they (the Whig ministry) have got Whately, and a signal blessing it is they have him to listen to, a man so good and so great," etc. Of the Chevalier Bunsen the same— " In Italy you meet Bunsen, and can now sympathise with the all but idolatry with which I regard him. So beautifully wise, so good, and so noble-minded!" "At this day," he says in the last year of his life, " I could sit at Bunsen's feet, and drink in wisdom with almost intense reverence."

A series of small restless moves at first showed Arnold's zeal and fertility in the cause more than anything else. The attempts themselves all died in the birth; but his solicitude about the state of things and the crisis that seemed at hand actually kept him at Rugby for the holidays—a strong evidence of anxiety and excitement for *him*. "I should not like to be away from my post," he says, " if there is likely to be any opening for organising any attempts at general reform. Heaven and earth are coming together around us. That *Record* is a true specimen of the party, with their infinitely little minds disputing about ' anise and cummin.' These are times when the dove can ill spare the addition of the serpent." The first scheme was that of " Tracts, *à-la*-Cobbett in point of style, to show people the real state of things." These tracts, or the " Poor Man's Magazine," or " Register," by which names the papers seem to have come out at last, met with a disheartening fate very soon. An article on the Tory party, in the third or fourth number, was thought too sweeping by some, too milk-and-water by others, and Arnold thought it no use going on. " You give a death-blow to my hopes of finding co-operation for the Register," he writes to Dr. Whately ; " that very article upon the Tories has been objected to as being too favourable to them, *so what is a man to do ?*" He changed his tack, and took to writing in the Sheffield papers, and thought "often of a Warwickshire magazine, to appear monthly, and so escape the stamp duties." A "Comprehensive Christian Commentary" was the call next. "Oh, for your Bible plan, or at least for the sanction of your name; I think I see the possibility of a true comprehensive Christian Commentary, keeping back none of the counsel of God, lowering no truth, chilling no lofty or spiritual sentiment, yet neither silly, fanatical, nor sectarian." These moves and feelers but just tickled his energies however, and did not satisfy them. "I cannot get over my sense of the fearful state of public affairs; is it clean hopeless that the Church will come forward and crave to be allowed to reform itself? . . . I can have no confidence in what would be in men like ———, but a deathbed repentance. It can only be done effectually by those who have not, through many a year of fair weather, turned a deaf ear to the voice of reform, and will not be thought only to obey it because they cannot help it"—*i.e.* by Arnold himself and his friends. His letters are a string of spirited hortatives to his friends on this subject, and nobody is quick and brisk enough to please him. "The ten who were sought for to save Sodom will be as vainly sought for now." "You are going," he tells Mr. Tucker, on his farewell for India, "from what bids fair to deserve the name of a city of destruction."

This subterranean noise and rumbling did not go on without an explosion; and before long Arnold went off and up into the air like a rocket in the shape of a pamphlet, which astonished and astounded his friends, all the world, and lastly himself: we allude to the memorable pamphlet on Church Reform. This was a premature burst for the movement. It scattered in one fell discharge the gathered advance and development of a century, and the consequence was that the explosion ended with itself and with the flash it made. The pamphlet, however, was a perfect harmonious and natural expression—the genuine child of Arnold's mind. He threw his whole soul into it, and gave to the world, in one bold leap of authorship, the darling religious theories of a life.

The first was the idea of the Church-State. German religionism has taken two remarkable lines against the Church—one against her corporate character, the other against her doctrines. It has subjected Church to State with one hand, and it has destroyed unity of faith with the other. The German idea of the alliance of Church and State does not make them two independent societies, each on a distinct foundation of its own, though acting in union, but merges them both into one common element, and makes one religious incorporation of the two. The result of this is what is called "national life." The State, by becoming religious, *ipso facto* becomes a Church. The king, as the concentration of the power of the community, is the head of the Church-State. The material corporeal State, the constitutional power, wherever residing, is in fact made to sit upon and occupy the Church's ground; and all that remains of the Church after the act of absorption is the materialised reflection of itself in the absorber and incorporator, the sanctity of the natural-religious sort, which accrues to the State from its usurpation. The tide of divine economy is sucked back again into the earthly vortex; the divine society is humanised. The Church, which was formed out of the original clay of our social humanity, is turned back into its clay again; and man, after being called by God from the natural into the supernatural bond of union, seems to declare that he prefers the natural, and retraces his steps. The result is that Christianity so far relapses into the religion of nature; and instead of being the apex and consummation of the natural dispensation, becomes a past and gone experiment, a visionary recollection, a theory, which was tried and did not answer, a cheat, which deluded the world for a time; and the discovery of which now sends the world, made wiser and sharper by it, to rest the more firmly upon her own ground again, and to rely, after the failure of her high-flying acquaintance, more than ever upon herself. She returns to the pagan theory. Before the Christian Church existed, the *State* was the church; heathen philosophy solemnly recognised it in that character. The Grecian *polis* was a human and divine society at once; its office divine, its descent human. The German system returns to the *polis* again; and well would it be for it if it could do that simply, and did no worse. But the Rubicon is crossed; nature cannot be what it was before without being worse than it was before. We cannot be either pagan, or patriarchal, or legal again; those were anticipations, they cannot be results; they were types, they cannot be substances. The man cannot be the child again, the plant the seed, the sculptured marble the native rock again. Time cannot retrograde; the dainty mouthful cannot be retasted; the old world cannot return; nature cannot be bare nature again. Unchristian she may be, but she cannot be classical again; she cannot return to her old eras without decay and dissolution in the act of retrograding. Reaction is fatal: Lot's wife looked back, and she became a pillar of salt. A distinct creation of a Church is undone in returning to the era before the Church, and paganism is no longer itself, but the unnatural fungus upon its own grave—the rotten fruit, and not the ripening seed.

Nevertheless, the ancient theory of a *Church-State* is, as a classical idea, truly captivating. And Arnold's mind had a peculiar leaning toward the classical; he was tenderly alive to that ideal which was the high and philosophical aspiration of his most favourite ages of the world. Greek and Roman history was his delight; he "threw himself with a glow of passionate enthusiasm into the age of Pericles;" with deep veneration into the "institutions, order, and reverence for law of the Roman republic." "How can I go on with my Roman history?" he said, upon some bad symptoms breaking out among the Rugby boys: "there all is noble and high-minded, and here I find nothing but the reverse." And his classical taste, it is to be observed, especially selected the purely classical or high pagan finish of the old world *as it was*, for his affections to rest on, rather than its rude and elementary yearnings after what it was not. He liked the historical and picturesque indeed of Homer and Virgil; but poetry was not his point: Herodotus, Thucydides, and Livy were his authors; he was historical all over. His whole aim on this head, his "intensely political and national turn of mind, his admiration for the Greek and Roman republics," amounted in him to a relish for the actual politics and moral basis of the Old State as such, to a real fancy and preference for the classical theory in parts where Christianity had directly superseded it. It is remarkable that that portion of ancient literature which went deepest in its anticipations of Christianity, which, if any such there were in the old world, was indeed a genuine oracular yearning from its very sanctuary for a higher system, that melodious heathen prelude of the Christian mystery—Greek Tragedy—was just the portion of it that he did not take to. The life and blood of the classical age, more than its shadows and anticipations, its present more than its future, was the fascination. Such a favourite point as the "Greek union of gymnastics and philosophy" showed the direction of his mind. The tendency is one which is brought out and developed broadly in the present state of German literature, light and grave. Miss Bremer adopts a pointed classical model, and is a worshipper of nature and Greek statuary; she converts the Swedish *salon* into an Ionic temple, and floods her domestic ether with all the floral fragrance and refined sensuality of classicalism. Milton, though not a German, adopted the mediæval antiquity of the genuine neologian, viz. pagan mythology. Different minds touch upon the circle at different points, and Arnold had decidedly his point of contact. The neologian attempts of modern times have indeed remarkably coincided with one or other sort of classical *renaissance*. Arnold's mind was fixed on one—the revival of the Grecian *polis*, and the substitution for the Christian Church of a Church-State.

Thus fostered and encouraged, this classical Church ideal became the substratum of a positive science of Christian politics—a Christian ἡ πολιτική, in Arnold's mind, which gave the centre to every thought and speculation upon religion. It was the point "round which were gathered not only all his writings, but all his thoughts and actions on social subjects," and the ground of all "the aspirations which he entertained of what Christianity was intended to effect." "If rightly applied," he thought, "it would effect far beyond anything which has been yet seen, or is ordinarily conceived, for the moral and social restoration of the world." "It was the vision which closed the vista of all his speculations; the ideal whole, which might be incorporated part by part into the existing order of society; the ideal end, which each successive age might approach more closely—its very remoteness only impressing him more deeply with the conviction of the enormous efforts which must be made to bring all social institutions nearer to it. It was still, in its more practical form, the great idea of which the several parts of his life were so many distinct exemplifications—his sermons, his teaching, his government of the school, his public acts, his own personal character—and to which all his dreams of wider usefulness instinctively turned, from the first faint outline of his hopes in his earliest letters, down to the last evening of his life, when the last thought which he bestowed on the future was of '*that great work*'"—that great work of his matured experience and wisdom, not Aristotle's but Arnold's ἡ πολιτική, which would base and adjust the Christian Church-State upon a new and final footing.

This ideal of a Church of course utterly *unpriested* it, and a priest, accordingly, Arnold could not tolerate. The idea of a priest was a real abomination to him, in the strictest sense of the word; it was an image horrible and unclean to his religious eye. To the abstract priest he had very much the sensations felt by the genuine Brahmin towards an impure reptile. He argues characteristically: "The Heraldic or Succession view of the question I can hardly treat gravely; there is something so monstrously profane in making our heavenly inheritance like an earthly estate, to which our pedigree is our title. And really what is called Succession is exactly a pedigree, and nothing better; like natural descent it conveys no moral nobleness,—nay, far less than natural descent; for I am a believer in some transmitted virtue in a good breed, but the Succession notoriously conveys none. The sons of God are not to be born of bloods (*i.e.* of particular races)." He felt, at the bottom of his heart in short, an utter distance and uncongeniality between a priestly religion and his own, and that if his religion was Christianity, the other could not be. He was not one to mince matters in expressing himself, and accordingly (indeed we do not see how he could do otherwise) he pronounced the idea of a priesthood to be positively "Antichristian;" a real *bona fide* form of "Antichrist." The "Priesthood, the Sacraments, the Apostolical Succession," were his "heresy," his "idolatry," his "schism and his anarchy." He had his idea of the Christian system in his mind, and the priestly distinction was a positive break-up to it; it made two where he made one; it undid a whole; it destroyed the visible form of Christianity in the world as he pictured it. The form of the "religious State" to him answered to the form of the Catholic Church to others; and the departure from this form was his schism. "Priestcraft" and "Priestcraft Antichrist," "the essence of all that was evil in Popery," "the idolatry of the Priesthood as bad as the idolatry of Jupiter," "the Church's worst enemy," "the false Church," most copiously express the entire contrariety he felt between his own principle of State Christianity and that of Church Christianity.

It was of course strictly necessary, with such a theory as this, that he should be prepared to unchristianise the whole framework of the Christian society from the first; and Arnold did not shrink from the conclusion. That he wanted "something truer and deeper than what satisfied, not the last century, but the last seventeen centuries," was a mild expression of his view. It was with the fact full before him of a priestly-governed Church of eighteen hundred years' standing that he pronounced "a priestly government transmitted by a mystical succession from the Apostles" to be "the great Antichristian Apostasy," "the deadly Apostasy which St. Paul in his lifetime saw threatening."

The very first era and movement indeed in the Church, from its commencement downwards, which he rested upon with satisfaction as affording any home for his principles, was the Reformation in the sixteenth century: and of the Reformation accordingly, both English and foreign, he was a most ardent, affectionate, loyal, devoted, enthusiastic and genuine disciple, admirer and son. He looked up to the Reformation as the first step that was made on the great point of State supremacy. There he saw the first dawn of a new order of things, the first blow struck to priestcraft, the first breath in the total absorption of the Church into the State. He disliked and condemned the individual instruments by which it was effected, the motives on which many acted, and the coarse and violent proceedings which accompanied it. But the movement, as such, had his unfeigned admiration and adhesion : the principle on which it was based, and which it set going, appealed to his very deepest religious sympathies and heartfelt aspirations. He saw, in the rude usurpation of a tyrannical king, the first stone laid of his Church-State ; and the precedents of King Edward VI. were the sacred model upon which, with jealous and loyal accuracy, he moulded the whole relations of Church and State in a country. They made the king the head of the Church ; and that, in principle, gave him all that he wanted : it only remained to consolidate and fill up the system which had been but just sketched in the outline, and then left ; and to develop a principle which an intervening reaction in the Church had stopped and thrown back. "The statutes passed about the Church in Henry VIII.'s and Edward VI.'s reigns, are still the ἀρχαί of its constitution," he writes, "if that may be said to have a constitution which never was constituted, but was left as avowedly unfinished as Cologne Cathedral." "The idea of my life," he says emphatically, "to which I think every thought of my mind more or less tends, is the perfecting the idea of the Edward VI. Reformers." He lamented that "a female reign was an unfavourable time for pressing strongly the doctrine of the Crown's supremacy." But "a doctrine vouchsafed to our Church by so rare and mere a blessing of God, which contained the true and perfect idea of a Christian Church—this peculiar blessing of our Church constitution" he did hope would ultimately "work out a full development."

It is remarkable, too, that with that peculiar acumen which a man has in detecting any attack upon a favourite theory, that critical sensitiveness which he feels for what is part of himself, and by which he recognises a real blow and stroke, which under any circuitous process, hits the mark and comes home— Arnold discerned in those times, which an ordinary mind would select as specially exemplifying the Church and State principle, the most positive reaction against it. He connects the Caroline era with the revival of the principle of Church independence, and the power of the priesthood; and he says—" viewing the Church of England as opposing the good old cause, I bear it no affection; viewing it as a great reformed institution, and as *proclaiming the king's supremacy*," etc., etc., he feels quite differently. He says the principle on which Archbishop Laud and his followers went, was " to reactuate the idea of a Church;" and that by the Church they meant " the clergy—the hierarchy exclusively." He mistakes them indeed here, but the mistake does not give the picture a more State colouring, but the reverse. So, again, on the subject of Church doctrine in general, he says : " Historically, our Prayer-Book exhibits the opinions of two very different parties—King Edward's Reformers and the High Churchmen of James I.'s time and of 1661 ; no man who heartily likes the one could approve entirely of what has been done by the other." The distinction is repeated over and over again ; and much in the same way in which he regards the whole Catholic Church as a departure from the first, from the Apostolical system, he also regards the career of the English Church as a departure from the genuine principle of the Reformation. "From *Elizabeth's* time, downwards," he says (a pretty early reverse of his bright side of the Church), " the clergy have been politically a party in the country, and a party opposed to the cause, which, in the main, has been the cause of improvement." Even ordinary, commonplace High Churchmanship, the lowest average Church principle among us, he carefully parts off from any Reformation connection. And the two parties in our Church have their respective shares in it thus apportioned to them : " The High Church party idolise things as they are: the Evangelicals idolise the early Reformers"—idolise, he means, as distinct from outstripping them, as he himself wanted to do. Arnold saw, we say, that his and the Reformers' movement had been stopped by an intervening school, and that the Church's actual career had been more or less a reaction upon it.

And this distinction gives us the clew to a good deal of Arnold's language about the English Church, when he speaks of her as a " motley" one, with much of good about it, and much of evil; and reprobates an over-fondness for "our dear mother the panther." The language in itself might proceed either from a discontented Catholic, or a discontented liberal; from one who saw too little catholicity in the Church, or one who saw too much. It is evident that, in his case, it is spoken in the latter character. The Church of the Reformation, as such, he liked. That particular spot in her history, the focus of Edward the Sixth's religionism, he thoroughly liked; and all but that he disliked. He liked the Church of England so far as it verged on the latitudinarian and State principle; he disliked it so far as it retained the dogmatic and the priestly one. He aimed at thoroughly expanding the former, and entirely extinguishing the latter. The most flourishing portions of her history to him were just those which her catholic son looks back to with the greatest shame and sorrow. He specially selects the Georgian period of latitudinarianism and State servility as a "noble exception" to the Church's general character, and a bright contrast to the unpleasant Laudian shades that have too much overspread her history. He lays his sharp finger on the shoots of the Reformation wherever they peep up to light: and he treasures them as earnests of a gladder day, when the Church shall be indeed thoroughly reformed on the Edward VI. model, and the dawning brightness of the sixteenth century become one flood of light over her.

We turn from the ecclesiastical to the doctrinal side of Arnold's system, and of the Church Reform pamphlet.

Arnold's notion of belief was the completely individualist one; there was no connection with the social principle in it. It clung to no church or sect, to no corporate mass or body of opinions whatever. Most persons, whether they are Churchmen or dissenters, are, in some sort, *social* in their belief. A man likes a chief point or two in Methodism, and he forthwith not only takes these, but swallows all the others for the sake of company: he adopts, that is, not only one or two Methodist opinions, but Methodism; he becomes a Methodist. He feels one part, and he takes the rest on trust. A society is faith's body; she does not feel herself alive except she is embodied.

A mass communicates its own solidity. The Wesleyan bosom lodges the Conference. A Quaker's faith reflects his garb in combination. Man supplies the conscious deficiency in his own apprehension by an appropriation of his neighbour's; he throws the social mass, good stone, or rubbish, as it may be, into the spiritual vacuum in his own mind; and then, what with himself and what with others, he feels himself full, and he believes. He extends over a sect, he covers so much actual ground, and is satisfied. It may not be a very large one, but, as one of the company, he is at home there, and he feels his right; his belief is his regular property, like his farm or estate; he is content to bargain for a little narrowness, if he can have the feeling of solidity; to be strait-laced and keep within the bounds of his sect, if he can feel what there is there his own. This is the *corporate* principle of belief. The ordinary sectarian, though he *is* one, likes belonging to a body. His faith is social. Individualist belief, on the other hand, prefers space and freedom to solidity; puts its foot everywhere, and is at home nowhere; picks out of every system just what it likes, and leaves just what it likes; combines all its spoils in some kaleidoscope pattern, and makes that its system. The slender packthread work straggles over the universe in skeleton fashion, touching and dotting where it goes; but including no territory, delineating no form. Sectarianism is narrow, but eclecticism is shadowy and unreal. And to throw one's-self into some whole system, and be a Methodist or a Quaker, has as much largeness about it after all, as their philosophy, who pick only what suits themselves; who only look over the world to discover the scattered images and reflections of the particular ideas which the chance or chaos of individual life has thrown up within their own minds; who are satisfied with the richness of their own internal soil, and who go on, never really enlarging their minds, but only illustrating them. The *reason* of eclecticism's choice is a narrow, though the *field* of it may be a wide one.

Arnold was a strong example of the latter class. His religious tastes extended far and wide, and had their spot, and point they touched on, in every religious body. He felt in himself a centrality, which seemed to prove the feasibleness of centralisation for all these bodies, and he wished to bring them all together. One large wall of circumvallation was to include them all. His very idea of religious unity took this form, and unity with him was not so much a corporate as a federal one,—not so much different individuals uniting in one body, as different distinct bodies in one large alliance. Independents and Methodists, Quakers, Baptists, Churchmen, were brought all together upon a common ground, and included in one national Church. He united, in short, his own favourite idea of a State Church with the more ordinary latitudinarian one of a union of creeds.

One difficulty there was, indeed, not of theory but of practice, which appeared to touch him now on the subject of Church and State. It arose out of a comparatively insignificant corner of the national material. All the Christian denominations were members, of course, of the Church; and as such, of the State; the identification of Church and State fully met their case. But what was to be done with the Jews? The broadest ecclesiastical basis could not include them: they were out of the Church and therefore out of the State too: not Christians, and therefore not citizens. "I must petition," he writes to Mr. Hare, "against the Jew Bill, and wish that you, or some man like you, would expose that low Jacobinical notion of citizenship, that a man acquires a right to it by the accident of his being littered *inter quatuor maria*, or because he pays taxes. I wish I had the knowledge and the time to state fully the ancient system of πάροικοι, μέτοικοι, etc., and the principle on which it rested; that different races have different νόμιμα, and that an indiscriminate mixture breeds a perfect '*colluvio omnium rerum.*'" He was anxious, at the same time, to make as ample amends to the excluded race as could be made, in consistency with the State ideal. And having secured the State's total abrogation of Judaism, he could afford to temper justice with mercy. He admitted the Jews to the rights of marriage, and of domestic life, though not to the supreme order of political rights. "I would give the Jews the honorary citizenship which was so often given by the Romans,—*i.e.* the private rights of citizens, *jus commercii et jus connubii*,—but not the public rights, *jus suffragii* and *jus honorum*. But then, according to our barbarian feudal notions, the *jus commercii* involves the *jus suffragii*." The barbarous mixture, however, of the two rights, commercial and suffragial, though feudal in origin, was not likely to be disturbed by the predominant feeling of the present age; and Arnold advocated some systematic encouragement of the Jews to emigrate.

We have come to the subject of doctrine. He had the ordinary latitudinarian theory here. He thought that "doctrine, in its practical and religious side, as bearing on religious feeling and character, not doctrine, in the sense of a direct disclosure of spiritual or material essences as they are in themselves, was all that could be found in the teaching of Scripture." This rationalist, or private-judgment theory of the interpretation of Scripture, is so well known and so common now, that we need not dwell upon it. Arnold wanted every individual and sect to draw their own conclusions for themselves, without censuring or separating from each other, if they come to different ones. We are afraid we even see (and we mention it now we are on the subject) a tendency in him—we will not call it more—to a still lower stage of rationalism. The form which the rationalistic theory has assumed in this country has allowed any unworthy or defective *application* of the Bible language, and sanctioned every religion which professes to be gathered from it. It has destroyed the one grand sense of Scripture, but there it has generally stopped: it has abstained from interference with the text itself; and the career of doubt and inquiry has not yet thrust home to the historical substance and matter of the sacred volume. The Germans have outstripped both their English and Genevan friends, and done this. They have crossed the boundary, and asked the awful question, What is the Bible? What does inspired writing mean? And distinction upon distinction, as to the sense in which, and the degree in which, the Bible, or different parts of it, are inspired, have led to a separation of the earthly and human from the spiritual particles, and into an analytical breaking up and solution of the mass, of which it is impossible to tell the consequences. The comparative escape of this country from the analytical contagion is a matter of daily and hourly increasing, though thankful surprise to us. We can hardly dare to face, or to contemplate to its full extent, the anomaly of the unhesitating, literal, dead assent of such an age as the present to the authenticity and infallibility of such a book as the Bible,—a book so *prima facie* legendary and mystical as the Bible must to this age's philosophy appear. One thinks, naturally, why be at so much trouble at explaining away?—why keep what you are always running against, and endure the perpetual difficulty of squaring to modern views the old structure of supernaturalism? Why encounter the crooked corners of the old mysterious labyrinth, when with one breath you might have an open area in its place.

We do observe *tendencies*, however, in Arnold, towards undermining this entire assent we speak of,—a suspicious liking for distinctions in inspiration, as a subject of speculation that his mind fed upon. Physical science is not taught in Scripture; then why should history be? It is quite possible to deny the historical inspiration, retaining the spiritual, which is all we have to do with. "He had a wonderful discernment," says Mr. Price, "for the divine, as incorporated in the human element of Scripture; and the recognition of these two separate and most distinct elements,—the careful separation of the two, so that each shall be subject to its own laws, and determined on its own principles,—was the foundation, the grand characteristic principle of his Exegesis." And this view of Scripture was "of slow and mature growth" in him. Having *begun* with, and "intended once to have preached a University sermon in *favour* of the verbal inspiration of Scripture," his mind developed slowly and steadily against the verbal inspiration. He had a peculiar wish to take up this line as an author. "He had a sharp struggle to choose between the interpretation of Scripture and the Roman history; and his choice was determined, not by the consideration of his peculiar talent, but by a regard to extrinsic matters, the unripeness of England for a free and unfettered discussion of scriptural exegesis." Is it a part of this theory that he appears to be so ready on one occasion to throw aside some particular chapters in the Bible which do not happen to harmonise with a view of his on prophecy? "I have long," he says, "thought that the greater part of the book of Daniel is most certainly a very late work, of the time of the Maccabees; and the pretended prophecy about the kings of Grecia and Persia, and of the North and South, is mere history, like the poetical prophecies in Virgil and elsewhere." His reason is—"Those chapters, if genuine, would be a clear exception to my canon of interpretation, as there can be no reasonable spiritual meaning made out of the kings of the North and South." But we will not pursue this more esoteric line of rationalism in him further.

Arnold had constructed his great national Church of all denominations—including both Churchmen, and all that are called "*orthodox dissenters;*" but then came the delicate question as to the admission of some to whom the title of orthodox was not allowed. Were Unitarians to be admitted or not? In spite of the haziness and perplexity of Arnold's whole state of mind and point of view on the subject of Unitarianism, so far is clear, that he had no objection to including sincere and earnest Unitarians in his church. And he arrives at this conclusion by the following process—a most painful one for us to follow; because, say it we must, it puts Arnold's own individual belief on this doctrine in a most unsatisfactory light.

We take his letter to Mr. Smith of Norwich. Mr. Smith had written to complain of him for making the act of "addressing Christ as an object of worship" essential in his scheme of comprehension. Arnold, in reply, explains what that phrase of Christ being an object of worship means, in his view.

Does he say that it necessarily means addressing Christ as God? He does not. He says that common Unitarians make Christ virtually *dead*, and that they ought to think of him as *alive*. That is not the same with thinking him God. Again, he says the fault of the Unitarians is, that they approach God "in his own incomprehensible essence;" whereas they ought to approach him through Christ: and that, whereas a direct communion with God is reserved for a more spiritual state of being hereafter, they anticipate it here. Here the fault of the Unitarians is referred to the *mode* of worship only—not to the *object* of it; and they are blamed, not for refusing to regard Christ as God, but for refusing to regard him as the medium through which God is worshipped. And so far from there being an essential and eternal difference in the two relations to Christ, which the Unitarian and orthodox side respectively suppose, he distinctly intimates that the very relation to him which the orthodox side supposes is only a function of our present earthly state of existence, and will not continue in our future spiritual one. A most painful expression of doctrine, by which he identifies the incomprehensible God with God the Father (" God the Father, *that is*, God as he is in himself"), concentrates but too clearly the line of idea throughout; viz., that the Unitarians and the orthodox, having both the same Being before their minds as the object of worship, only approach him in different ways, the mediate and immediate; that there is, therefore, no fundamental difference in their respective doctrines, and that such worship as we pay to Christ, as being the medium of the worship we pay to God,—worship *in this sense* to Christ,—is not inconsistent in principle with the creed of Unitarians, and need not be objected to by them.

The question, in short, with Arnold was one of feeling, not of doctrine; and regarded the affection of the man to the Being, and not the essence of Being himself. It is not easy, indeed, to see how the two can be separated; for our feeling towards a being must be affected by the consideration of what that being is. But we state the view as he seems to hold it. "The feelings," he says, "with which we regard Christ are of much greater importance than the question of his humanity or proper divinity." And if Unitarians would think of him as *alive*, and would love and fear him, whether they thought him man or God, he regards them as true Christians. The word "fear" comes in strangely: "I never meant to deny the name of Christian to those who love and *fear* him." Religious fear is a feeling which applies ultimately to the Divine Being alone; and the notion of the "fear" of Christ going along with the simply human idea of him is a perplexing one. Indeed, in the general tone of Arnold's mind on this subject, we see no cold Unitarianism, but what might be taken for the vague forshadowings of high uninstructed nature: and it is melancholy to see what would have delighted us so much as an aspiration toward revelation thrown into such a different aspect by the fact of its being a relapse from it. What are we to think when Arnold could say what he did, and yet absolutely imagine that he thought the "central truth of Christianity was the doctrine of our Lord's divinity"? We can only suppose that he partly did not know what his own view was, and partly did not know what the doctrine was. "There was a vividness and tenderness," we are told, "in his conception of our Lord, which made all his feelings of human friendship and affection, all his range of historical interest—his instincts of reverence, his admiration of truth—fasten on Him as their natural object." "He seemed," says one, "to have the freshest view of our Lord's life and death that I ever knew a man to possess. His rich mind filled up the naked outline of the Gospel history;—it was to him the most interesting *fact* that had ever happened,—as real, as *exciting* (if I may use the expression) as any recent event in modern history of which the actual effects are visible." We must own we look fearfully on the richness and warmth of that feeling toward our Lord which could tolerate the Unitarian view of Him.

A latitudinarianism, however, which embraced all sects, even the Unitarians, could gather also from Catholicism. Arnold ornamented and enriched his system with not a few flowers and external beauties of Catholic worship, its striking ceremonies and symbols, and even its institutions. With a philosophical dislike and contempt for metaphysical "questions between Homoousians and Homoiousians" ready to fall any moment from his pen, he yet regarded the creeds "as triumphant hymns of thanksgiving;" and the very Nicene Creed of the Homoousion was chanted, instead of being read, in Rugby Chapel, at his own special wish; and had imparted to it the sacred musical pomp which symbolised the deep dogmatic faith of the Catholic Church. He was for crosses and way-side oratories, daily services, religious societies of females, "commemorations of holy men of all times and countries," and religious processions. The former would have included

"Catholics, Arians, Romanists, Protestants, Churchmen, and Dissenters." The processions would have consisted of all the denominations. He was for confession, but not to a minister. Having extracted the Catholic and sacerdotal sting out of Church forms and institutions, his taste loved the beauty, and his common-sense the evident utility, of the exterior.

He carries on, we must observe, the same character into the political and poetical department: he is for the same mixture here. He is a vivid admirer of the picturesque, and likes the prestige of antiquity,—the churchyard at Oxford and Winchester, and the pedigree associations of Lowestoff,—but the feudal nauseates him. It makes him ill to see an old castle. The visible demolition of the French castles is the feast of his eyes in his French tour. A great charm of the Westmoreland lakes is that there are no feudal remains there to disturb him. He thinks Chivalry an Antichrist; but then he does not like Jacobinism: he thinks Jacobinism an Antichrist too. The three glorious days, however, were a "blessed revolution; beyond all example pure and heroic." He subscribes to the monument of those who fell. It is difficult to analyse; but we think it is due to this want of the old poetical associations, of which the order and rank are here deprived, that we do not like that reference to the "gentlemanly" which he is rather fond of, and which does not, somehow, come with grace from him. He exhorts his boys to be "Christian gentlemen;" and he wants an undermaster who must be a "Christian gentleman." We would rather see this combination implied than expressed. Expressed in this way, it seems to have a lowering influence on both characters—to tend to secularise the Christian and to puritanise the gentleman. There was a book published some years ago called *The Portraiture of a Christian Gentleman.* Arnold was a mixture in nature as well as religion.

The reader has been put in possession of Arnold's system, ecclesiastical and doctrinal, to the best of our power; and we have only to tell him now that he has been going through, in the last pages, what constituted the substance and matter of the Church-reform pamphlet. That pamphlet was a clear, striking, and utterly fearless exposition of these great theories, without concealment or reserve. The entire fulness of the author's own conviction, which armed them in his own idea, with the almost transparent self-evident irresistible force of truth, made disguise unnecessary : and the scheme of a national Church, to comprehend all sects, and to be under the control of civil functionaries, whether by the name of bishop, or any other, was, with the most ardent seriousness, submitted for *bona fide* acceptance to the Church and nation.

The effect of the burst was what might have been expected. The whole religious feeling of the country was roused and up in arms instantaneously against the aggression. All who had any vestige of Church instinct, all even who had any definite creed of their own, who thought themselves right and others wrong—Churchmen and " orthodox dissenters " alike—were astonished at this bold leap of latitudinarianism. Different persuasions were not prepared for the idea of finding themselves all together within the same walls. And even moderate, lax Churchmen were taken aback at the prospect of officers in the army and navy administering the sacraments,—for the pamphlet went the full length of the author's own conversational illustration of his principle. The theory had in fact come out before its time ; it was not a development, but a burst; the hypothetical work of a century was anticipated in it. It was fullblown mature Germanism, as a century of favourable growth would have made it, only put to the beginning of the period instead of to the end. The cart was put before the horse ; the building was begun at the frieze and cornice, up in the air, and the unnatural suspension could do nothing but come down. Aladdin's palace, the *polis*, the Utopia of Lutheranism, the reign of feeling over creeds, was an airy creation of magic, and not *terra firma*, so early. Never was there such an imprudent step, to speak politically of it, as a premature exposure which only reflected in the repulsive form of their ultimate development, the tendencies which were yet in the bud. The age started back at the exaggerated likeness of itself, and the Church, we trust, took warning. It was an impolitic disclosure. What Arnold should have done was to wait ten years ; and then construct, not a Reform pamphlet, but a

Jerusalem bishopric. That would have been wise caution; that would have been natural growth. His friend and fellow-theorist, the Chevalier Bunsen, has shown himself a less complete thinker perhaps, but a more practical manager. Mr. Stanley has alluded to the parallelism here with Arnold's view. He had a perfect right to do so.

His own friends remonstrated. We have a reply to a letter from Dr. Hawkins, a theologian professedly not of the deepest Church stamp, who, it appears, had passed sentence upon it, and passed it in a more *ex cathedra* style than the author thought quite legitimate. "You write with haste and without consideration," says Dr. Hawkins; "you write on subjects which you have not studied and do not understand, and which are not of your province." This, we must observe, is an unfortunate line of censure to take, because it simply subjects the censurer to immediate contradiction upon a matter of fact, without possibility of reply—a contradiction which, accordingly, Arnold gives flatly. "You cannot possibly know that I wrote in haste, or that I have not studied the question. I have read very largely about it, and thought about it habitually for several years." It is not, in fact, an appropriate line of objection to urge to the fundamental, the heartfelt, the primary idea of an enthusiastic religionist—that which has given the colour to all his thinking and reading—to tell him to go to his books again. He *may* go to his books again, and the only result will be that his additional reading will be coloured by the same primary idea which coloured his reading before. Let the idea be ever so extravagant, this only makes the case the clearer. To have told the founder of Mahometanism, for example, that "he had not studied the subject," and "that he acted with haste and without consideration," would have been simply not to the purpose; he would have answered, of course, that he had studied the subject and thought about it a great deal, and that all his speculation had confirmed the idea with which he started. All enthusiastic promulgators of theories and systems say this, and they say it correctly. Arnold had thought and had read about his subject a great deal, and these two volumes show it. To imagine that all error springs from not "studying" the question, and that if the question "is studied" the mind will right itself; to make the perception of truth the mechanical result of information and inquiry, is an assumption which in multitudes of cases only diverts attention from the real source of the evil. The fact, however, of such a criticism from such a quarter showed strongly the unripeness of moderate contemporary latitudinarianism for the contents of the Church-reform pamphlet. Arnold sounded his trumpet and then found himself standing alone; the blast had alarmed, or had shocked, or had fretted and annoyed respectively the whole English world. The pamphlet was stranded, and the very clearest and most copious evidence was given him, in the shape of criticism, public and private, in good taste and in bad taste, that society did not go along with him.

Arnold now showed a deficiency, a decidedly weak point in his mind. He stood the shock without giving way, indeed, an inch—nobody would expect him to do that—but he stood it also without understanding or appreciating it the least. He showed a complete want of sympathy and experience in his way of taking these demonstrations.

With the whole world out of breath at his proposed scheme, he stood as innocent and unconscious of having given offence to any one's notions as if he had proposed a new Vestry Act. He was quite hurt, perplexed, surprised, that people actually thought him a latitudinarian. He could not understand it, could not see what people meant. Latitudinarianism was just what of all things he disliked. He wished, indeed, Churchmen, Independents, Baptists, Quakers, and the good sort of Socinians, to be all comprehended in his church system; but was that latitudinarianism? Could any one be so blinded by prepossession as really to imagine that there was any latitudinarianism involved in such an arrangement? "It grieves him to find that some of his own friends consider the *tendency* of his Church-reform plan to be latitudinarian." Even this modified apprehension, and accompanied with the most courteous confidence in the absence of any such "*intention*" on his part, is unintelligible to him. Far from indicating any latitudinarian intention—how even any incidental undesigned consequences of that nature could, in the chances of things, shoot up from such a scheme he cannot divine. "My belief," he says, "is that it would have precisely the contrary effect." "If we were *only* to cut away articles and alter the Liturgy, the effect might be latitudinarian; but if, while relaxing the *theoretical* band, we were to tighten the *practical* one, then, I do believe, the fruit would be Christian union." That is to say, he embraces the full recognised latitudinarian idea of "practical" union amidst "theoretical" (*i.e.* doctrinal) differences, and this idea presents itself to him as just *the opposite* of latitudinarianism. This is his notion of latitudinarianism and its contrary, and he has no clew for discovering by what process of mind in other people their idea is just the reverse. He does not apprehend their view or mode of thinking on the subject the least, and therefore not their objections. The whole demonstration against his pamphlet is a dead wall to him; he looks hard and sees nothing. His own conclusions are so absolutely transparent to himself. "I was not prepared," he says, "to find men so startled at principles which have long appeared to me to follow necessarily from a careful study of the New Testament." And he proceeds accordingly to account —as account in some way or other he must—for the feeling against his scheme, by attributing it to hostility and prejudice toward himself. He says, "It is painful to think that these exaggerations, in too many instances, cannot be innocent: in Oxford there is an absolute ἐργαστήριον ψευδῶν, whose activity is surprising;" and he talks of the "constant and persevering falsehoods" which are circulated about him. The class of martyr-feelings follows. "If we oppose any prevailing opinion or habit of the day, the fruits of a life's labour, as far as earth is concerned, are presently sacrificed; we are reviled instead of respected;" and "every word and action of our lives misrepresented and condemned."

A more or less vague public opinion has been Arnold's antagonist and judge hitherto; but a more formidable opponent now comes upon the scene. A mere present state of feeling, a present impression in society, is not an insuperable barrier to the influence of a very active mind. Men start at opinions at first, and afterwards take to them. The Church-reform pamphlet was sufficiently stranded at the time; but the opposition of conventional feeling, of the noise of numbers, was not perhaps one in itself to have stopped and driven back Arnold's religious theory. That Church and State are one thing, and one thing only, is a definite idea; that of the union of hearts is a broad one. A positive downright theory of Church and State, a positive downright theory of Church union, cuts its way through a mass of opposition that has no definite weapon to oppose to it. An intensely active rich mind like Arnold's has an inspiriting stirring power among friends and fellow-speculators, though he may disconcert them by a too early demonstration; and there was a sufficiently strong nucleus of united liberalism in the Church to gather minds around it if no opposite one of another sort appeared. The opposition to Arnold wanted a principle infusing into it, and a definite ground given it to stand on. It wanted a pledge for the future as well as the demonstration of the present, a pledge that it would go on and not allow the aggression to outlive it.

It so happened that there was a party at hand to give this pledge. The systematic movement on Arnold's part just happened to be coincident with a most decided and systematic one from an opposite quarter. The Church of England had, after a century of growing laxity, just come to the point at which she must either retrace her steps into a stricter state, or go forward into a formal latitudinarianism. Arnold was for the latter course; the writers of the "Tracts for the Times" for the former. The two schools met at these cross roads as it were, and a remarkable contrast indeed they presented. The foremost characters in the Church movement, if they will excuse us looking at them so historically, were undoubtedly phenomena in their way, as Arnold was in his.

Of one of these we can speak: the death, that robs us of so much, gives at any rate this privilege. Singular it is that antagonist systems should so suit themselves with champions; but if the world had been picked for the most fair, adequate, and expressive specimens of German religionism and Catholicism—specimens that each side would have acknowledged—

it could not well have produced better ones for the purpose than Dr. Arnold and Mr. Froude. Arnold, gushing with the richness of domestic life, the darling of nature, and overflowing receptacle and enjoyer, with strong healthy gusto, of all her endearments and sweets—Arnold, the representative of high, joyous Lutheranism, is describable—Mr. Froude hardly. His intercourse with earth and nature seemed to cut through them, like uncongenial steel, rather than mix and mingle with them. Yet the polished blade smiled as it went through. The grace and spirit with which he adorned this outward world, and seemed to an undiscerning eye to love it, were but something analogous in him to the easy tone of men in high life, whose good-nature to inferiors is the result either of their disinterested benevolence or sublime unconcern. In him the severe sweetness of the life divine not so much rejected as disarmed those potent glows and attractions of the life natural; a high good temper civilly evaded and disowned them. The monk by nature, the born aristocrat of the Christian sphere, passed them clean by with inimitable ease; marked his line and shot clear beyond them, into the serene ether, toward the far-off light, toward that needle's point on which ten thousand angels and all heaven move.

Of living persons we cannot speak, but the reader has his ideas of them pretty well fixed by this time; they form a regular group in our Church's history; and they brought with them a system and a philosophy of a somewhat deep, stern, and mystical aspect to confront their antagonists'. The Catholic system, as it advanced from the worlds beyond the grave, came with some of the colour and circumstance of its origin. It contrasted strangely with the light, hearty, and glowing form of earth, that came from wood and mountain, sunshine and green fields, to meet them. And the unearthly, supernatural, dogmatic Church opposed a ghostly dignity to the Church of nature and the religion of the heart.

The commotion of the Church-reform pamphlet but ushered Arnold into a more formidable and esoteric struggle with this new opponent—a struggle which had shifted from the ground of invasion, with him, to that of self-defence. He was not, indeed, selected as any special object of attack by the writers of the tracts, or any of the Oxford school; rather remarkably, the contrary. Jacob Abbot was commented on, and he was left untouched. But the appearance of such a system as theirs made it not a question of waiting to be attacked. The fact itself was enough. A system like his was bound to expel and thrust out such an antipodist one, and, in order to have any chance of success for itself, could not allow the ground to be preoccupied by an opponent. It is remarkable, indeed, how completely a counter-aggressive movement to his own had turned the tables in this respect, and made the object of a negative success, a check to the rival, the chief and great point to gain with him, instead of the positive spread of his own system. The stop thus given to the progress of "Church Reform" is felt, and "their object is to provoke the clergy to resist the Government Church Reforms" is his complaint.

The matter, on Arnold's part, indeed, became from the first moment very serious. His first thing is to prophesy. He prophesies that the "Tracts" cannot take, that, though they may please a few of the clergy, the laity must scout them to a man. We may remark that Arnold is rather fond of prophesying, and prophesies with a kind of ocular certainty. However, the "Tracts" do take, and Arnold's argumentative pulse quickens. The religious naturalist saw in the new school a pernicious destructive species of theological animals that were simply bent on eating into the core of liberalism; and a religious blight and plague seemed to be the inevitable result of the swarm spreading. The Oxford writers were "idolaters," "Judaisers," maintainers of the "priestcraft Antichrist," schismatics to the Church, and "in principle traitors to the State." "I call this Judaising direct idolatry," he says. "In other men I cannot trace exactly the origin of the idolatry," but in them I do; "it is clear to me that Newman and his party are idolaters." "With respect to the Newmanites, I do not call them bad men, nor would I deny their many good qualities. . . . I judge of them as I do commonly of mixed characters, where the noble and the base, the good and the bad, are strangely mixed up together. There is an ascending scale from the grossest personal selfishness, such as that of Cæsar or Napoleon, to party selfishness, such as that of Sylla, or fanatical selfishness, that is, the idolatry of an idea or a principle, such as that of Robespierre and Dominic and some of the Covenanters. In all these, except perhaps the first, we feel a sympathy, more or less, because there is something of personal self-devotion and sincerity; but fanaticism is idolatry, and it has the moral evil of idolatry in it." Their insisting on the necessity of the Apostolical Succession is "exactly like insisting on the necessity of circumcision." And going upon his old favourite idea of there being no descent either of blood or order in Christianity, and of this being a positive antichristian element to introduce into the system, a really rude violation of the Christian's holy freedom, he took "schismatic," "profane," and the like terms, clean out of the mouth of the Apostolical Church towards the latitudinarian, and applied them, if we may say so, with the utmost *naïveté* and simplicity towards the Church herself.

The Regale was urged heartily, and the Church movement attacked from the Plantagenet platform. "In Elizabeth's time such a notion would have been reckoned treasonable." The notion of the Church being an independent body, and able to keep her own succession going on, apart from the State, is "all essentially anarchical and schismatic;" and he is only defending, he says, "the common peace and order of the Church against a new outbreak of Puritanism to oppose it." It appears a curious objection, at first sight, from a man like Arnold, to urge against a particular religious claim that it would have been considered treasonable in the reign of Queen Elizabeth. But this, as we have seen, is the period of English history to which he always goes for his ecclesiastical principles.

Another point of accusation, more of a moral one, does not come with peculiar grace from Arnold, viz. the charge of immodesty and impudence in persons daring to go so counter to received opinions in their views of things and persons. "I have read Froude's volume," he says, "and I think that its predominant character is extraordinary impudence. I never saw a more remarkable instance of that quality than the way in which he, a young man, and a clergyman of the Church of England, reviles all those persons whom the accordant voice of that Church, without distinction of party, has agreed to honour, even perhaps with an excess of admiration." Now, let it be ever so true that "the accordant voice of the Church of England" has taken one view of Cranmer and the Reformers, whereas Mr. Froude took another, Arnold was not precisely the person to found a charge of impudence upon such a fact. A man who, without a vestige of internal scruple or misgiving, unchristianised the whole development of the Church from the days of the Apostles, who made the very disciples, friends, and successors of the Apostles teachers of corruption, who made the Priesthood an Antichrist, and had just himself shocked the whole Church of England by the promulgation of a religious theory repugnant to the feelings and ideas of almost all her members to a man, was certainly not a person to be tender in requiring compliance with received views from another, or quick to call in another impudence what in himself was the necessary adjunct of philosophy.

The condemnation of Dr. Hampden by the Oxford Convocation in 1836 brought a powerful accession to these feelings. It was a vigorous demonstration in exactly the opposite direction to his own, and he felt it to be such. But on this subject we have a preliminary remark to address to Mr. Stanley: there is an assertion of his upon this subject which we should like him to explain. An amiable feeling, which we should be the last to blame him for, appears to have suggested a method of softening this somewhat rough part of Arnold's career, and he vulgarises the opposition to Dr. Hampden, in order to fit and accommodate it for Arnold's aversion. He says, "There is no reason for believing that the most eminent of Dr. Hampden's opponents had any sympathy with the conduct and feeling of the great mass of his supporters." Now all we can say is, that if "the most eminent of Dr. Hampden's opponents" had no sympathy with the general mass of opposition on that occasion, they were the most accomplished and the most audacious hypocrites that ever exhibited in public life. For they originated that opposition, they headed it throughout; they wrote, they spoke, earnestly and heartily, in public and in private, about it; they appeared at the very top of the movement; they collected, strengthened, and systematised the opposition, they sustained it, and they brought it to its consummation. If Mr. Stanley alludes to a more esoteric standard of sympathy than the recognised public one, we do not profess to be able to follow him. He may be right or wrong in asserting that the average inward religious $\mathring{\eta}\theta o\varsigma$ of a body of five hundred members of Convocation was not one in which Mr. Keble, Dr. Pusey, and Mr. Newman recognised the exact reflection of their own. But without deciding this question either way, it is as certain as facts can make it, that the feeling against a latitudinarian innovation on the Church doctrines,—which was real and strong in that convocational movement against Dr. Hampden, however political motives, in such a large mass, mingled with it,—was a feeling in which "the most eminent of Dr. Hampden's opponents" heartily sympathised, and with which they *bona fide* allied themselves and acted.

To proceed: Arnold's view of the question was soon settled, and very decidedly. "Hampden's Bampton Lectures" were to him "a great work, entirely true in their main points, and most useful." "Hampden only did what real reformers had ever done, what the Protestants did with Catholicism and the Apostles with Judaism." He instantly identified Hampden's system with the principle of religious march and improvement, and made it the natural development of the creed of the Reformation. "Hampden holds exactly the language and sentiments," he says, "which Cranmer and Ridley, I believe, would hold if they were alive now." The opposition to him, on the other hand, he identified with the line of Catholicism in the English Church from the first. The Oxford Convocation of 1836 "was a repetition of the scenes at the Reformation." The "Oxford High Church outcry" at Dr. Hampden, as Regius Professor, was an echo of the "Oxford Roman Catholic outcry" at Peter Martyr, as Regius Professor, in the reign of Edward VI. The censure of 1836 was "the condemnation of Burnet's Exposition of the Articles by the Lower House of Convocation," repeated a century later in another form. "The Nonjurors reviling Burnet, the Council of Constance condemning Huss, the Judaisers banded together against St. Paul," were all concentrated in the opposition of the University of Oxford to Dr. Hampden. Arnold's feeling on the Church movement now assumed more of a solid practical shape, more of a moral disgust than it ever bad. "Hampden's business," he says, "seemed to me different, as there was in that something more than theoretical opinions, there was downright evil acting, and the more I consider it the more does my sense of its evil rise. Certainly my opinion of the principal actors in that affair has been altered by it towards them personally. I do not say that it should make me forget all their good qualities, but I consider it as a very serious blot in their moral character."

An article in the *Edinburgh Review*, to which the title of "The Oxford Malignants" was attached, and which (though that was not, it appears, of Arnold's but the editor's putting) fully bore out its title, at last let out the full torrent of his indignation. "It is painful to dwell," says his biographer, "on a subject of which the immediate interest is passed away, and of which the mention must give pain to many concerned. But, though only a temporary production, it forms a feature in his life too marked to be passed over without notice. On the one hand it completely represents his own strong feeling at the time, and in impassioned earnestness, force of expression, and power of narrative is perhaps equal to anything he ever wrote; on the other hand it contains the most severe and vehement, because the most personal, language which he ever allowed himself deliberately to use." A more hearty, sincere, enthusiastic vituperation of an adversary indeed could not well have been penned. Arnold did nothing by halves. The opponents of Dr. Hampden were denounced, amidst a variety of names, specially as being the modern representatives of the "party of Hophni and Phineas." And Arnold could afterwards defend the expression with all the gravity of a logician. "Hophni and Phineas are recorded as specimens of the worst class of ministers of an established religion. I do not say or think that —— and —— are bad men" (a rather tame mode, by the way, of expressing a favourable opinion of the persons whom these blanks appear to represent). "I do not think that John Gerson was a bad man, yet he was a principal party in the foul treachery and murder committed against John Huss at the Council of Constance."

He now sets to his task in a regular systematic way; "having written once agonistically," he resolves "to go deeper to work with the root of error from which all this Judaising springs." A series of Church of England tracts suggests itself to him. "I want to get out a series of 'Church of England Tracts' which, after establishing the supreme authority of Scripture and reason against Tradition, Councils, and Fathers, and showing that reason is not rationalism, should then take two lines, the one negative, the other positive; the negative one showing that the pretended unity, which has always been the idol of Judaisers, is worthless, impracticable, and the pursuit of it has split Christ's Church into a thousand sects, and will keep it so split for ever; the other positive, showing that the true unity is most precious, practicable, and has in fact been never lost. . . . That all sects have had amongst them the marks of Christ's Catholic Church, in the graces of His Spirit and the confession of His name, for which purpose it might be useful to give, side by side, the martyrdoms, missionary labours, etc., of Catholics and Arians, Romanists and Protestants, Churchmen and Dissenters. Here is a grand field, giving room for learning, for eloquence, for acuteness, for judgment, and for a true love of Christ in those who took part in it,—and capable, I think, of doing much good. And the good is wanted, because it is plain that the Judaisers have infected even those who still profess to disclaim them. . . . I shall talk this matter over with Hawkins, who has behaved nobly in this matter, but who still, I think, contributed to their mischief by his unhappy sermon on Tradition." "Notes and Dissertations on the Three Pastoral Epistles (Timothy and Titus), to embrace naturally every point on which the Oxford Judaisers have set up their heresy, the Priesthood, Sacraments, Apostolical Succession, Tradition, and the Church," was another project.

As the antagonistic feeling however grows, the scheme of writing *at* the party from Rugby gradually gives way to the intense longing to be at headquarters at Oxford: "I should be of weight from my classical knowledge, and I am old enough now to set down many of the men who are foremost in spreading their mischief, and to give some sanction of authority to those who think as I do, but who at present want a man to lean upon." We may observe, generally, that his spheres of usefulness tend to lap over each other in his imagination. He has had hankerings after India; had once a notion of going to Ireland to "Christianise the gentry;" has a great fancy for New Zealand, and for founding a colony. And so with literary fields—" a complete ecclesiastical history ;" a Roman history ; the Scriptural interpretation line ; the Church and State science —captivate him one after another. A report of the promotion of Dr. Hampden to a bishopric opens out a prospect to him now : "I wish they would put me in his place in Oxford. I could do more good at Oxford. I should have a large promising body of young men disposed to listen to me for old affection's sake." And "his bad name" to be defended is another object which requires the Oxford arena: he even mentally courts a Hampden-war against himself to bring matters to a point about him. "He ought not silently to bear a sort of bad name, which to man or dog is little better than hanging." If there is a similar feeling against him that there is against Hampden, let it "be got up into some tangible shape."

Anyhow, he wants to be where he can confront the actual leaders of the party. The times are roughening. He feels an actual call to battle, to see whether the tract-movement is or is not to be checked. To him especially it spoke aloud : "You must not let these minds go on; you must come to close quarters with them; you are the man to do it; you must stand in the defile." An intensity of conviction on his own side of the question, together with the gallantry and frankness of his nature, made up altogether a sort of high pugnacious enthusiasm. He wanted fairly "to be at 'em," to use the pugilistic phraseology ; to try strength, muscle, and sinew with them; to feel himself in the encounter. His state of mind was in itself the loudest challenge. It said to all the world, Come and be knocked down; feel the force of intrinsic truth. "Magna est vis veritatis et prævalebit." The challenge was natural in him. "If any respectable man of *my own age* chooses to attack my principles, I am perfectly ready to meet him, and he shall see at any rate whether I have studied the question or no." His imagination was now peopled with Judaisers. The word is always at his tongue's end. An ignorant reader would be really perplexed by the perpetual recurrence, and form an almost bearded image of the school Arnold was opposing. And "Have at the Judaisers" was the internal watchword; "Shiver the Judaising idol in pieces;" "My spirit of pugnaciousness would rejoice in fighting out the battle with the Judaisers, as it were in a sawpit."

The striking feature of Arnold's mind—and we notice it as being literally a phenomenon, a remarkable specimen of that particular internal power—is his confidence; we mean a rare, esoteric intensity of assurance in his own views. He is *omnia magna;* has every quality that there is in him forcibly, and confidence among the rest. A firm faith is one thing; what we mean is another. A brilliancy of the whole chamber of the mind—a dance of light—a clearness which made his own view of truth to him an object of the keenest internal ocular demonstration rather than of faith, carried him into conflicts and controversies with a boldness that an evident warrant from the invisible world might produce. A phantasmagoric halo of truth accompanied him, and the flame played upon his helmet, as it did on that of Diomede; he was invulnerable; his armour was proof against sword-cut and thrust; a dip in the magical pool had achieved the same security for him that it had done for the hero of old. His courage was not tried and deepened by fear; it saw nothing to be afraid of; it went right forward without a misgiving to its object. The contest with other minds, and genuine argument, where truth is at stake and is to be lost or won, has something of the fearful character. It is a trial of strength; one mind struggles with another, and the invisible push and blow are felt within: nervousness and misgivings, mistrust of self, and sense of weakness, are the natural sensations, more or less, of him who feels the conflict, and knows what he has to look forward to. The highest human courage is compounded in a great measure of fear; it attains its triumph by its sensibility, and does not force the instinct but decide the heart. The air that we breathe is composed to a large extent of atmospheric ingredients, in themselves positively hostile to life, though, mixed with the crowning element, they support it. Take away these ingredients for the sake of an intenser support, and you have an air that volatilises life, and makes it evaporate in laughter and titillation. Air should not be all air; courage should not be all courage. Arnold longed to be in the thick of the conflict at Oxford, and imagined himself with vivid pleasure in the scene of danger and the struggle of mind; but he did not know what that really was which he was so ardent for; he did not appreciate the force of the minds he wished to encounter; he did not feel the evidences, whether they were great or small, on their side of truth. A torrent of internal, self-fed light, a dream of truth, carried him along, and displayed rather the animal courage of argument than the sobered mixture of human zeal and fear becoming the process. His courage saw no difficulties, and marshalled no nervous symptoms of mental distresses, doubts, apprehensions, weaknesses, in the prospect; a gallop and good hearty exercise of the intellectual muscles, a pleasant circulation of the blood was pictured; he saw his own "gallows" and "leaping-pole" in intellectual shape in the scene; he saw the field of thought and energy, and the development of the whole man before him. The prospect was full of delightful anticipation; and Bagley Wood, and Shotover, and Iffley, and Newnham, mingled their scenic tents and gaieties with the theological battle on the arena of Oxford. Fights on the Apostolical Succession, and walks to Bullingdon, youthful joyous associations, religious truth and the Cherwell, combined all in one captivating image. The view before him was a mixed and grotesque one, because every feature of it was so real; genuine religious polemics—genuine Bagley Wood. The genuineness and heartiness bind all together, and make a characteristic whole of it; the sombre arena and the mortal fight cannot resist the powerful transforming influence of the German mind; they go through the flowery metamorphosis, and breathe lightness, spirit, exuberance, and security.

The author of *Undine* has exquisitely symbolised, in the contrast of grave humanity and the soul, with fairy nature, two great classes of character. He describes a light transparent world of life to begin with; a heart all air, quick sense, and effervescing spirit. Brisk joyous beings sport aloft, or mingle with the stream, or colour the bank-side; grow, swim, fly, bound; are trees, fish, bird, or brook, or cloud, or sunshine, or green earth. Brooks walk, men flow, all mingle in one wild luxuriance; and earth and nature live and move, and weep and laugh in their own efflorescences and emanations. Sweet tears, rough merriments, and transient wraths—all simple tendernesses and picturesque excitements—flow, explode from nature's infancy and boyhood. A solemn gift descends upon this airy mixture, and it subsides; a weight is felt, and nature, she knows not how or why, is changed from what she was. "Moonlight hath in her sober livery all things clad," and shows an altered landscape to the heavy, burdened eye. The royal crown of reason presses the wearer down. The bright heart turns contemplative, and looks within herself; mistrusts, misgives, foretells. A sobering visitant works within, and impregnates the light exuberance with a sad serenity. The sympathetic reader grieves at the change, and feels inclined to reproach the soul with cruelty and hardheartedness. "Why spoil this fairy scene," he says, "and tame the life that sparkled with animation before you came and overspread it?" The change from vivid to serious in life's stages, the accession of depth to the soul in all its degrees, is the source of conscious weakness, undoubtedly, as well as of dignity; and self-mistrust and apprehension marks the grown man, as self-confidence does the boy.

We do not see the man absolute in Arnold. Manly in his own department, upon the broad basis and open field of life he is a splendid boy. His ignorance of the world around him, peculiar unreasonablenesses, surprises, complaints, indignation, the rush into the battle with the mixture of fun and fierceness, show the boy. Positive, eager, sanguine; his appetite of mental courage and joyous strength of nature lack the subduing, becalming sovereignty of soul.

We are approaching the end of our observations. Arnold's sudden death, in the midst of his philosophical and religious career, makes it unfair to draw any result as to his natural intrinsic influence, his inherent effectiveness as a philosopher, from the matter-of-fact event. One who has not had his full time to work in should not be judged as though he had, or be expected to have created his world and established his system. At the same time, we do not see any tendencies in Arnold's course in this direction, any signs or evidence of spread which only wanted time. As a proselytiser, a spreader of certain views, we do not see him so much advancing as receding, and his religious career seems to grow more and more solitary.

That this was the main effect of causes external to himself is indeed true; and yet that he contributed himself to it by a very positive deficiency in his character and mind we can hardly doubt. Arnold had but slightly that fundamental and all-important quality for a spreader of opinions, and a winner and gainer of minds, that great faculty of manhood—the power of intellectual sympathy, and of entering into other people's minds. With singular opportunities in this direction amongst the opposite minds he was thrown with at College, and the High-Church friendships of a life, whether from natural incapacity or from want of taking proper pains, he never seems to have learned this art and power. His "skirmishes" with Mr. Cornish, with Tucker, Coleridge, the Kebles at Oxford, were, as such contests naturally are in youth, pleasant exciting feats of intellectual skill: he delights in looking back upon them, as he would entertain any other pleasing reminiscences. But what is to be observed is, that neither the arguments nor the minds themselves of his opposite-thinking friends ever seem to have taken hold of him, and fairly gained an apprehension from his reason. The totally opposite views of men loved and known are, at any rate, a strong fact. This fact does never appear to have got a really deep reception into Arnold's mind. He does not embrace it, enter into it, try to put himself in his opponent's point of view and state of thought, and feel the force of the evidence on his side, whatever it may be. He applies his clearness and force to his own side of the question only. Lively and paradoxical in his conversation at College, speculative and self-confident in his letters afterwards, his argumentativeness throughout plays and expatiates within himself, and does not enter within the adversary's lines. His career is one of self-development; a philosophical growth from within entirely, and an expansion of a set of primary individual ideas. Highly communicative of principles, he does not imbibe them, and he impregnates inferiors without understanding equals.

The consequence is that distinction in him which we have already alluded to. At Rugby he is great, because at Rugby only the power of self-expansion and self-imparting was wanted. A school of boys is a great receptacle of ideas, and not a counter-stream; they lean upon the master mind, treasure up the thought, suck in the hint, but oppose no standard of their own to exercise and try the master's apprehension, and to be penetrated and surmounted by it. Arnold could watch with genuine tutorial sympathy every stage of the ingress of the idea from his own mind into the pupil's; and all the issues from himself were keenly and minutely seen. That answered perfectly for Rugby; that showed the accomplished schoolmaster. But the schoolmaster came out into the world, and then the scene was changed. In order to implant his ideas in men and equals, he had first to understand theirs, and be the learner and the listener that he might be the teacher; and that he could not be, or would not try to be. He came out into the world, and immediately spoke *ex cathedra*, as if he were in his school-seat. He pictured the world a large Rugby, a grand receptacle of his ideas, and did not think of it in any other light. But the world turned out to be no passive receptacle; it started back and was restive, and then Arnold could not deal with it. Then Arnold was a child. He saw that he had disturbed people indefinitely, but he saw no more. He could not explain, meet objections, soften, accommodate. He could not see why people objected; the mind without was a blank to him; and he could only stare and complain of the unreasoning mass. He was out of his element. Triumphant at Rugby, his exhibition in the world was a failure. His Church-reform pamphlet was a leap into a sphere for which he was unfit; and it let out a secret, which the world might not have discovered else, viz., that he was not a great man. A great man manages a department like Rugby with one hand, and has another as good for another. A corner of his mind is in the professional sphere, while he has the rest for the open field of life. But Arnold did not manage Rugby with a corner of his mind, or anything like it. He had the whole of his practical power invested there. He had none to spare for the world at large. And therefore, when he came into the world he was not at home there, and blundered. This accounts, by the way, for a few gentle pedantries that appear in the Rugby department. Able and successful as he is there, his ability is accompanied with rather more of a smack of the lips than sounds quite great—an indication ordinarily that the whole man is expending himself on his work, and is not adequate for a much larger simultaneous charge.

Upon the open world accordingly even the creations of Rugby begin to be independent of him, and slip out of his philosophical hands. When they cease to be passive receptacles, the main hold over them, we perceive, is gone; the mind that impregnated their intellectual infancy cannot deal with their intellectual strength, and as they advance to be equals they feel thoughts arising which the quondam master does not answer or pacify, nor indeed understand enough to cope with. The mass have "diverged more and more widely" from him. He has formed no school; he has produced no race of his religious opinions to perpetuate and multiply the parent stock. He has given a cast and a complexion indeed to the minds that were directly under his care, and he has scattered about historical tastes and classical theories, and he has left a delightful remembrance of himself in his pupils' hearts; but he has not made them think what he did, and the instincts which he put into them, the love of the real and genuine, do not go in his direction for the object of it. Arnold, in short, as his career advances, becomes more and more religiously alone in the world, and finds himself to be either a premature or an eccentric philosopher. His favourite theories are almost confined to his own breast; his Church and State ideal lives in himself; he must send his petition to Parliament alone. " I want to take my stand on my favourite principle, that the world is made up of Christians and non-Christians; with all the former we should be one, with none of the latter. . . . I want to petition against the Jew Bill, but I believe I must petition alone ; for you would not sign my preamble, nor would many others who will petition doubtless against the measure." He fails in Christianising the Useful Knowledge Society, and withdraws. The combination of rejecting and being rejected, of seeing faults in all schools which prevented him joining any, and being dissented from by all schools because his particular mixture was not theirs, has a melancholy effect on the reader as he advances through this book. He took, he told, he fascinated himself; but his system fell dead. He was admired, and what he said was admired, and the motive and the spirit were praised, and the idea was thought his own shape of some truth, but the idea as he thought it was not taken. The highest admirer subtly evaded the task of the disciple, and the teacher sat alone in the porch, while the man was surrounded.

Aristotle draws a distinction between *sophia* and *phronesis;* or, as we may translate them in one aspect, between the speculative power and moral tact or experience. He says young men and young minds are capable of the one and not of the other. Young minds can evolve their own ideas and be philosophical, but they cannot have experience before they have acquired it. Whether we have caught Aristotle's meaning or not, some distinction not unlike it seems to apply to Arnold. He evolves his own mind, but he does not enlarge it by experience, that is to say, by contact with other minds. Speculation is necessarily upon ideas that we already have. It is not its office to renovate and enlarge; it does not pretend to freshen and pour new blood into a mind. Contact with other minds does this, *i.e.* when it is genuine and real;

where the man feels his way about others, catches their meaning, gathers their point of view, exposes himself to the whole weight of another's mind upon his own, and receives, with the full embrace of a sensitive appreciation, arguments which he does not assent to, and the whole basis of thought which he cannot appreciate. It must not be a sham contact, a mock fight, a tussle for the sake of fun, a mere source of life and spirit to the communication of his own view, a mere stimulus to self-development. It must be the *bona fide* action of mind upon mind, where the blow is home-felt, and your adversary's thrust received into your reason's heart. You either survive the sword's point of your antagonist, and gain a most quick, lively, subtle experience of another man's power and form of thought, you appropriate a new sympathy and take home another mind, or you die under a nobler antagonist; and so much the better still, for you rise to his level, you enter upon his state of mind, and suffer a painful but glorious metempsychosis. In either case there is enlargement, either that of sympathy or that of transition. And both of these are more or less necessary to make up a real philosophical experience, such as fits a man for the conflicts of intellectual life, and enables him to understand and deal with other minds. It is astonishing indeed what an irresistible engine this power of sympathy and self-bending has shown itself to be in some great religious intellects of the Church. Ever flexible, malleable, fusible at its own will, overflowing with self-mastery, melting and embosoming, absorbed and absorbing,— the imperial element of liquid mind has lapped round its millions like a flood. Up comes the subtle water everywhere, and bathes a world. Invisible nets, impalpable soothing tendrils creep over human souls unconscious and delighted, and they are clasped and won. High alchemy and self-transmuting power of mind! Effectiveness of sympathy! of a nature ever ready to be what she is not, and throw off her own self for another. The mere faculty inherits the earth; she gains a thousand selves by losing one. Life becomes self-multiplying, and one mind is a million. An individual symbol of the empire of the Church Catholic over her children, her heavenly wiles, her awful sweetness, her iron endearments, the sympathy which earth cannot escape from though she would, and which makes her the confidant of all human hearts at once.

Arnold's career of self-development was attended by the natural accompaniment to himself of isolation. No keen trials had won him the field of experience and sympathy, freshness and enlargement, and the concomitant of such a basis of mind was that it had no domain and empire. As a religionist, he stretched along his own line and covered his own ground only, and we on our side are bound to think it fortunate that it was so. The truth is we had much rather not think of him as a religionist at all,—we had rather, much rather, think of him as the Master of Rugby only,—the reformer of education, the generous superior, the communicative teacher, the watchful guardian, friend, and trainer of boyish nature: we had rather think of the affectionate, ardent, domestic heart only. Would that Arnold had stuck to his natural department, and not left it for the open world,—for the public arena of theology! But he has not done so; he has entailed a biography upon his pupil which enters into the thick of religious controversies, and exhibits him in all the open undisguised fulness of the latitudinarian and rationalistic character. It has been no pleasure to us to view him in the antagonistic aspect, to touch on the tender doctrinal point, to notice how very deep Arnold's mind had imbibed the sad theory which undermines all truth. But the doctrinal point, the theory, was before us in all its obviousness. A published life is a fact which must be dealt with as it stands, and forces the inevitable duty on us of deciding and stating what a man is. We appreciate and understand fully the affection which Arnold has created for himself, and the love and gratitude of the Rugby pupil, now refined and heightened by his death. Any pain caused to any one of a circle of whose society and high tone of feeling the writer of these pages has long had the privilege and benefit is equalled by his own; but to have stated the plain truth as it appeared to him, though a pain, will never be a regret.

BLANCO WHITE.*
(October 1845.)

"I HAVE written a great part of my Memoirs, which are not to be published till after my death. Few, except men like yourself, will take an interest in them—the irreligious will despise me for most of what I have to state; the dogmatic religionists will conclude that I have ended in something little short of atheism, and will turn away from the history of my mind with horror. That history, however, *shall* be known. I consider it my paramount duty; if I had not lived for the purpose of attesting faithfully the facts of my mental experience, I have lived in vain. But I have better hopes; and the joy with which, at the close of my *mission*, I look at the instances in which God has enabled me to be faithful to it, is a pledge that I am not deceived. . . . I feel therefore that I have done all that was assigned to me by Providence in the world, and now I must wait for death in this perfect moral solitude—without a single human being near me to whom I may look up for that help and sympathy which old men that have walked on the beaten paths of life expect when their dissolution approaches. My only comfort is, that I have been true to my internal light; that I have not betrayed the *cause* of truth. My works (except the last) do not afford me any satisfaction, for they have been generally written under an imperfect light —a light thickly clouded by the large remnants of the enormous mass of religious prejudices which my education laid upon me. But I leave the result to Providence; such *gropings*

---

* *The Life of the Rev. Joseph Blanco White, written by himself; with portions of his Correspondence.* Edited by JOHN HAMILTON THOM. 3 vols. 12mo. London, 1845.

as mine, upon record, may be profitable to minds destined to shine in future on the way to improvement." Such is the view which Mr. Blanco White takes, near the close of his life, of his "mission," the object for which he conceives he was sent into the world. He was born to suffer a martyrdom in the cause of truth; to spend a life of acute and agonising intellectual self-examination; and, after clearing his own mind, step by step, of all the religious ideas which first Roman Catholic, and then Protestant, Christianity had fostered in it, to leave to the world, at any rate in his own internal system, one isolated, individual exemplar of rational piety. He speaks as if this mental analysis had never once been thoroughly done before, as if his own were literally the very first complete achievement of the kind, and were a distinct introduction of a new intellectual era.

Nevertheless, in spite of his deep feeling to this effect, in spite of self-analysis, determination, singleness of purpose, and clear-headedness, we do not think that nature intended Mr. Blanco White for a theologian: she gave prognostics of a much more simple literary, we may even say of a dilettante, line. So, as we happen to know, thought his friend Quintana, in talking to an Oxford acquaintance of Blanco White's, who went with a letter of introduction to him,—"A great pity," was his view; "a great mistake: Blanco White was a literary man, and should not have perplexed himself with theology." The autobiography, we think, strongly confirms this. We do not say that Blanco White's is not a deep mind—far from it; but a literary and a dilettante mind may easily be a deep one. There are different kinds of depth—of *real* depth. Blanco White has one kind, not the most solid. His mind is a penetrating, but not a large one. He perforates, but he does not spread; he grasps particular ideas very tight, but does not take in a field of balance and comparison. He dips under, and comes up again; he disappears, and comes up instantly in the same place; he brings up something solid with him from the metaphysical bottom, but he has not stayed there long enough to see its large and awful extent. He is content with seeing very clearly and pointedly what he does see, and does not feel the enlarging swell and movement of the inner mind, which suspects narrowness, and wants to have as many ideas under its eye at a time as possible —to think as many things at once as possible. We mention it more as a philosophical than a moral fault in him, that he is far too satisfied with the mere clearness of an intellectual view, and luxuriates in metaphysical point and local accuracy. The pleasure of clearness is a regular snare to the philosophical mind, just as the confined exertion of any of our powers of body and mind always is. It becomes soon comparatively easy to do one thing well, if we abandon ourselves to it; but mind and body become one-sided in the process. Clearness of idea is not the only object which a philosophical mind should have in view; largeness is quite as important. Blanco White handles and handles his idea when he has got it; he likes to feel himself handling it, to think to himself—I have it; I've got it; I've hold of it. This is the luxury of thought. It is effeminate to go on indulging in the enjoyment of the capture, after the act of capturing the idea has been performed. The mind ought to be going on to other things, and enlarging its field. Here Blanco White fails; and this is what is especially essential in the department of theology. Scientific theology is a regular chart, a map; it is a field of lines and sections, contacts, juxtapositions, comparisons, balancings. Take one of the philosophical schoolmen, and think what he had to do; what a vast expanse of intersecting intertwining ideas, of similarities and dissimilarities, he had to master and keep in order. We are speaking now simply of the power of mind shown. If Aquinas, for example, had real ideas in his head corresponding to his words, and it is probable he had, what a field his mind becomes! Blanco White had not the sort of mind to carry on such a process as this; it was not regular, not business-like enough, for there is such a thing as this latter even in metaphysics. His natural temperament enters into his philosophy. His is capricious and unmarshalled depth: he thinks deeply, but impatiently. With his real force of intellect a metaphysical form of the childish goes along; and the amiably fretting, peevish, querulous man, is the subtle, but impatient, metaphysician. He likes thinking in his own way, and putting down his thoughts as they occur. The album and commonplace-book have too great an intimacy with his theology, and he is a divine and a philosopher in the mould of a literary dilettante.

Notwithstanding this, however, there is a depth and force in this book which tells. Such a life as Mr. Blanco White's is, in a minor way, a blow struck at Christianity, and a blow which will not be unfelt, perhaps, in some quarters. Christianity has had many blows struck at it in the course of its earthly career, and more than one in this country within the last century. Hume's argument against miracles was a blow; Gibbon's Roman History was a blow. Christianity simply received them, allowed them to tell and have influence upon this or that portion of society, and went on its way. A feebler blow in the same direction is Mr. Blanco White's autobiography. His mind is a deep, narrow well, out of which infidelity springs up with wonderful genuineness and life. The infidel objection he raises has a clearness and transparency which can result only from the reality of the thought in his mind. It is surprising to see the old objection which Butler's Analogy has long ago dealt with, and which one thought had now had its day, springing up again with the freshness of life, and with as seemingly clear a sensation of its unanswerableness as if the fountain-head of truth itself were speaking. In this light the present autobiography is not an unimportant book. It seems to reflect, as in a mirror, the intellectual elements at work in the infidel mind in general. Defective in itself, it has weight and power as a reflex. The scattered sounds come from the true oracular hole, from the navel of the earth. He seems to hit off occasionally some deep principle of infidelity that we may expect to see coming out some of these days. As a reflex of this kind, it gives warning symptoms. For hints of approaching questions, a theological mind, we doubt not, could gain something from looking into it. There are signs in the political world which tell what questions are on the rise; and there are signs in the theological world of the same sort. The quick thrusts that we have here may be intimations of something more general. The English mind at large is not one to be much influenced by metaphysical reasonings, but a portion of it is; and upon that portion a theological cloud seems hanging.

These volumes consist of extracts from a journal and correspondence, mixed with his own reflections. The journal begins in 1812, starting with the second stage of his religious course. In 1834, a new course of self-review commences, a comment upon his own diary, and gives extracts. The process is continued at certain intervals up to his death; and his mind is altering as this very process of review is going on. The effect is almost puzzling to the reader. The strata of scepticism multiply and intertwine with each other. After commenting upon his own diary, he then comments upon his own comments. The very act of reflection is itself reflected on, and the tone of a former stage of review is too orthodox for a later. The autobiography becomes itself a kind of animal and seems to move; and the very narrative turns narrator. The extended trunk that we are sitting on begins to creep. We think we are stationary at last, when a little note at the end of the page transcends the text, and converts the ground we are on into an inferior and moving stratum. "I am struck with the absurdity of the expression, which I used from habit only two years ago," is a note which marks the progress which two years had made in his mind. The same advance goes on to the last; and where the writer does not himself observe it the reader may see a tone taken at one stage of review which is not in keeping with that further on. But we must turn to the contents of this history.

Joseph Blanco White was born at Seville in 1775. "Of the excellence of my parents' hearts, of their benevolence, of their sincere piety," he says, "it is impossible to speak too highly." They were true specimens of Catholic devotion, deeply attached to their faith, and fervent in works of mercy. His father's walk, after prayers on the Sunday, ended in "visiting the wards of a crowded and pestilential hospital, where, for many years, he spent two or three hours of the evening in rendering to the sick every kind of service, not excluding the most menial and disgusting. He was twice at death's door in consequence of infection. But nothing could damp his philanthropy." His childhood was a solitary one; and in his diary he recollects how, while his two sisters were receiving their education at a convent, and he was left alone, he "looked on the children of the poor, who were playing in the streets, and envied their happiness in being allowed to associate with their equals."

An ardent, affectionate temper, a fastidious taste, a busy intellect, a sceptical fancy, a dislike of mental checks, marked, in their measure, his boyhood, and even his infancy. A Spanish translation of Fénélon's *Télémaque* was among the small collection of books which constituted his father's library."

" I read it, indeed, so often, when only six or seven years old, that I knew it almost by heart. The effect it had upon my imagination was very powerful. Nor did it confine its influence to that faculty. It is a curious fact, that my first doubt of the truth of Christianity originated in that book, before I was full eight years of age. My recollection of every circumstance connected with that transient doubt is quite perfect; my delight in the descriptions of the sacrifices offered to the gods was intense. I felt, besides, a strong sympathy with the principal personages of the story; the difference between their religion and my own struck me very powerfully, and my admiration of their wisdom and courage suggested the question, why should we feel so perfectly assured that those who worshipped in that manner were wrong ? I dwelt upon this argument for some time, but when the day arrived to go to confession, and I had to look at the catalogue of sins which is contained in the book of *Preparation*, I perceived the necessity of accusing myself of doubts against the faith. At the moment I am writing, the place where the confessional stood is clearly before my mind, and I see the countenance of the Dominican who used to shrive me; his name was *Padre Baréa*, a fat, rosy, good-tempered man, who, nevertheless, held the office of *consulting Divine* to the Inquisition, and hated heretics from his heart, as in duty bound. In accusing myself I fairly stated my argument. The friar's astonishment made him fall back in the confessional-box; yet, using the kindest expression which the Spanish language affords for addressing a child,[1] he asked what kind of books I read. I answered him with great simplicity, that I read no books but *Télémaque*. On hearing this the friar smiled, and desiring me not to trouble my foolish head with such subjects, absolved me of all my sins, and did not even interdict the book

---

[1] " *Angelito, qué libros lees ?* Little innocent (literally, little angel), what books do you read ?"

which had been the innocent cause of my scepticism. I believe he would have been inclined to twist my neck, had he possessed any prophetic spirit, so as to foresee that the time would come when even the *Heretics*, whom he would have burnt with exultation, would find me too much a heretic for their taste."

A dream he had in his childhood was never forgotten, and is duly recorded as an "important mental fact about himself:—

"I remember that even in my childhood I had a fear of a future Life, and shrunk from all the Pictures of Heaven which abound in the Catholic Books of Devotion. I preserve a pretty distinct recollection of a Dream, which I had about my eleventh or twelfth year. In that Dream I felt disembodied and climbing up (it was a laborious Motion) through a dimly-lighted passage, at the end of which I found myself—as if I had been a Swedenborgian—in a House very like those to which I was accustomed in Spain, full of Angels such as I saw daily in Pictures, who welcomed me and told me I was really in Heaven. Though I had now nothing to fear from the Place of Torments, which I almost distinguished at the foot of a long flight of Stairs, the deepest Melancholy took hold of me, because Heaven appeared to me a very dull habitation, and I did not know what to do with myself through a long, long Eternity. I was relieved when, waking, I found that I was still on earth.

"'What a childish dream!" some people will say. I suspect that the charge of childishness lies at the door of those who make it. The child did not contrive the dream for himself: it was the pure spontaneous result of those pictures of Heaven which are supposed to have the greatest power to *bribe* mankind into virtue. Now, if such allurements had any real influence they would chiefly exert it upon such a being as I then was—a stranger to the passions and interests which bind men to this life. Yet the most glowing pictures of a future life had no attraction for me. The fear of an interminable, suffering existence possessed my soul, and, though I had never thought on annihilation, I remember that I preferred *not to be*, to the *chance* of living for ever with the angels, which I felt somewhat in the character of living in a church."

A quarrel with the Dominican Professor at College, when he was fifteen, was another epoch in his intellectual career. The Dominican was an adherent of the old Aristotelian school of logic; and the works of the Benedictine Feyjoo, a disciple of the French school, and maintainer of Bacon's experimental philosophy, had already settled deep in the young student's mind. And

"now the very sight of the friar, who lectured on logic at the Dominican College, became odious to me. One day he gave me a reprimand, before the class, for neglecting my studies. I rose from my seat, and told him plainly those studies were not worth my attention, and should never have it. I repeated a number of remarks against the Aristotelic Philosophy, which I had learned from Feyjoo. The friar was enraged: and I wonder I escaped a beating from the other students. Frightened at my own boldness, I ran home, and told my mother all that had taken place." He adds, "Nearly fifty years have elapsed, and now, more than ever, I recognise and rejoice in my intellectual identity with the boy of fifteen."

An ardent taste for literature gave the main direction and occupation to his mind for the whole first half of his life. At the age of fourteen he "was instrumental in forming an Academy for examining the beauties of Don Quixote in the style of Scholastic Theology." Some of the youths rather objected to the pertness of this process, but "he had the pleasure, through the exertions of himself and some able young friends, of seeing that prejudice nearly subdued." A "serious academy of Belles Lettres, to which he chiefly owed the original development of his mind," kept these young literary men together, "till they were all about the age of four or five-and-twenty." An intimacy with an accomplished literary friend gave him a still deeper bent in this direction. He and Arjona formed, out of their circle of acquaintances, a select and finished literary club, who met in Arjona's room and read papers, and discussed. An election to a fellowship in the *collegio mayor* at Seville, a secular and aristocratic foundation, finished his position, and furnished an unfailing passport into the best informed and most brilliant part of Spanish society.

A large part of his character, a favourable sphere for its development, tastes and friends to sympathise with them, reading in the morning and conversation in the evening, lectures, soirées, and clubs, thus combined and went a considerable way towards making a purely literary man of him. There is a difficulty in that phrase "would have been," in the conjecture what a man would have been had he lived in a different age, under different circumstances. Without troubling ourselves, however, to make such a conjecture, it is impossible not to observe the strong, pointed tendency to the purely literary man which Blanco White's whole picture exhibits. There are certain signs which show this particular class of mind, just as every class has its own signs. A genuine literary man evinces a sensitiveness to the details of his department, and sees charms in minutiæ, and ravishing graces in *quæstiunculæ*, which no other mortal does. Each sprig and tiny flower in his path is full of meaning, and reflects, in its narrow compass, the animation of a world. The soul of literature pervades and animates the universal body up to the extremest tips and finger-ends. Every wheel of the machinery of authorship, and every fact that proceeds from behind the scenes, delights simply from being *recherché*. A disputed authorship, reading, derivation, have a definite interest to his mind; and inquiry and decision pick up favourite materials everywhere with a tender embrace. The technicalities, in fact, of every department, to persons outside of it, are realities to those within. Blanco White is genially imbued with a love of the literary circumstantial, and shows it thoroughly. In the very thick of his theological metaphysics, up to the very last, the pages of his diary teem with literary matter. He puts it down for his own private pleasure, and as a part of his own intrinsic mental course, without any other object than this: he loves it for its own sake, and does not get it up for a purpose. Theologians have often and often been literary men; but their literary life becomes a past stage to them when they have once entered regularly the theological: they do not pursue theology and literature together, as twin pursuits. Blanco White does this. The literary man is the divine, and not the divine the literary man. On the same pages with the most abstruse and awful points of religious inquiry, and with metaphysics as to the Trinity and the Incarnation, appear, given with evident relish, and real depth, reflections on style, language, grammar; on Addison, Steele, Blair, Lindley Murray; or Goethe, Tasso, Le Sage, Shakespeare, Chaucer, Cervantes, Schiller; Mitchell's Aristophanes; on the respective characters of Gil Blas and Tom Jones; on Goethe's Bettine. He suggests new derivatives, new conjectural readings; a "subsume" as well as a "consume" in English; súppliance, and not suppliance, in the line of Hamlet,

"The perfume and (the) súppliance of a minute;"

he quotes "Biondo Flavio, the antiquary;" Ugo Foscolo, upon the origin of grotesque names for Italian academies, "Guingené, Leo, M. Antoninus," "the inscription on the Alexandrian Pharos." He is translating Fichte's metaphysics.

"The love of information, of which I have found an inexhaustible mine in the German language, attracts me almost irresistibly to the works which I see already on my shelves, and those whose valuable contents I know by report. If I open the treasures of literature which nourished my mind in youth—especially the Italian poets—I feel young again, and my mind feels transported to the region of love and beauty, which I can now better enjoy than during the fever of the passions. I am reading Tasso, after more than thirty years of neglect, with a far higher perception of the immortal beauties of his great poem, than I ever had in the period of my æsthetic self-instruction. How can I quit this elysium of the mind, to plunge into Stygian floods of controversy!"

Looking at the way, then, in which he threw himself into those tastes, and adopted them as his regular line as a young man, and kept them up with relish to the very last, he is not the person whom one would expect beforehand to become the founder and exemplar of a new theology. We can imagine him, under certain circumstances, having contented himself with his literary line, and lived and died in it. A strong natural scepticism is apparent in him, it is true; but many a literary man with such tendencies has, before now, finished a flowing and successful career without any positive quarrel with established religion. If religion lets him alone, he will let religion alone, and he is satisfied with the uninterrupted development of his own powers which is secured to him, and with the liberty to sneer. But Blanco White had another state of things to encounter; and in the Church domination of Spain a stimulus was felt, which sent him in another and far more dangerous direction.

The state of the Roman Catholic Church at this time in Spain exhibited that mixture of exuberant devotion in the mass, and suspicious despotism in the rulers, which is so striking at certain periods of that Church's history. The Inquisition still held its ground, and exerted its mediæval powers. In the midst of an universal change which had spread over the intellectual surface of the world, Spain alone was prohibited ground, and kept out the movement. People could philosophise freely everywhere else, but not in Spain ; and the intellectual Spaniard who had caught any portion of the continental " enlightenment," felt himself in a dark prison, and fretted under his total exclusion from the open air which the rest of the world enjoyed. He could not speak to a bosom friend, without risk, of any religious doubts that an active intellect had raised. He could not move, or speak, or whisper, without a danger of the sound reaching the Inquisition: even walls had ears, and thought betrayed its own workings. The very isolation of Spain in her Inquisitorial system compelled a more rigorous watchfulness in administering it, and the circumjacent liberties of the rest of the world sharpened suspicion about opinion at home. A general feeling of distrust spread downward from the "holy tribunal" into the mass, and penetrated into the very recesses of private life. Fathers and mothers were afraid of hearing a casual word from their own children, which might impose on them the duty of reporting them to the Inquisition. All sects and schools have in their day persecuted pretty vigorously, and the theory of persecution was the popular one for centuries; but now it had not that excuse. Public opinion over the world had declared against it. The Inquisition had outlived its natural term, and was keeping up a forced and artificial authority as useless as it was odious. It had, moreover, outlived the sanctity and earnestness of its first institutors. The course of things hands over institutions from genuine to hollow hands, and a twofold hatefulness attaches to what time, while it has unnaturalised, has also hollowed and corrupted. What a symptom it was, when the very tribunal that had condemned a miserable woman to be burnt, had not the courage to hear her confession, and with a base cowardice called in a stranger to face her! The ruling powers of the Church in Spain seem, with a trembling sensitiveness to the impending storm, to have been simply bent on keeping things going, and maintaining an established ascendency; and without the smallest sympathy or tenderness for the intellectual dangers of the age, simple, stifling prostration was the order of the day. The plan, of course, could not answer. They tried to keep out the whole body of continental literature, and the only result was a smuggled influx of the exclusively bad and infidel part of it. They threw intellectual minds into a hopeless self-consuming morbidness, and forced them into secret clubs and hotbeds. Scepticism could not be artificially stopped: it only went on in Spain under ground instead of above ground, and with almost more pollution and darkness than attached to it in other countries.

While a fierce mental struggle was thus raging in the upper circle of the Spanish mind, the mass below presented a warm and glowing picture of Catholic devotion and unsuspicious Church-submission. Churches were thronged, the priesthood ruled, young women left their homes and entered, moved by their simple aspirations after a high devotion, into the most austere nunneries. There were temporary spiritual retreats for those who wanted them; and crowds of penitents listened to favourite preachers, and responded with groans and tears to impassioned appeals which set their own sins and God's judgment, death and hell, in vivid horrors before them. At Seville the spiritual exercises of St. Ignatius went on in the oratory of St. Philip Neri, under the superintendence of Father Vega—a person of whose eloquence and great powers Blanco White was himself a witness:—

"His countenance, besides, was very striking. It must be an interesting fact to physiognomists, and, perhaps, to phrenologists, that an excellent bust of Oliver Cromwell, which I had frequently before my eyes during two years of my residence in this country, forcibly reminded me of my old spiritual leader. That this was not a mere fancy may be proved by the circumstance that a young

Irishman, whom I intimately knew at Seville, and who, through my father's influence, submitted to the Spiritual Exercises, told me that from the recollection he had of the portraits of Oliver Cromwell, he imagined he saw him alive when Father Vega stood before him. His voice was harsh and nasal; but in the private chapel, fitted up on purpose for the *Exercitants*, he could modulate its tones with a wonderful effect. During the performance of mass, he was daily affected to such a degree that a flood of tears gushed from his eyes, especially at the time of consecration. This may convey to some people the idea of perfect acting: but I knew the man very well, and having often reconsidered his character, I feel bound in candour to acquit him of that charge. The modifications of enthusiasm are, indeed, innumerable, and the manner in which the thought of things invisible, constantly dwelt upon with vehemence, can affect the nervous system, has never been thoroughly investigated. Indeed, in sternness and boldness he might be compared to Knox, the Scotch Reformer. . . .

"A large bell announced the first meeting in the chapel. That place was kept nearly dark. A lantern, closed on all sides but one, threw its light on a statue of Christ expiring on the Cross. As the object of the sculptor was to strike the senses, without any regard to taste, the statue was as large as life, with glass eyes, and the body so coloured as to represent flesh, sprinkled here and there with blood. After the congregation had taken their seats, in profound silence, one of Father Vega's assistant priests read the subject of *Meditation* for that evening. This reading generally lasted half an hour. At the end of it, all knelt. For about a quarter of an hour nothing was heard but the pendulum of the clock which was to measure a full hour for *Meditation*. Aware, however, that most of his spiritual patients would lose themselves in reverie, if left entirely to their own thoughts, Father Vega assisted them with what, in the language of asceticism, are called *ejaculations*. It seemed as if his thoughts, growing too big and vehement to be contained in his breast, broke out in spite of himself. At first these ejaculations were short, and came at long intervals; but they gradually grew more frequent and longer; till, near the end of the hour, and just before the congregation were allowed to rise from their knees, the monotonous chant of the ejaculations was changed into agonising screams, accompanied with a loud smiting of the breast, in which the congregation joined, as they were moved; most of them repeating the words of the Director, and loudly calling for mercy."

At Cadiz, the "Cave" of Father Santa Maria, a dark

dimly-lighted cellar below the street, presented scenes of an even more tremendous character :—

"Directly after the Sermon, two Priests, each bearing a large bundle of knotted scourges made of whip-cord, paced up and down the subterranean chapel, furnishing every one present with one of those instruments of penance. After this, all the lights were extinguished, except a small taper, which was concealed in a dark lantern. When perfect darkness had been produced, one of the Priests chanted in a wailing voice a short narrative of Christ's sufferings. The devotees were in the meantime removing that part of the dress which stood in the way of the lashes which they intended to inflict upon themselves. Previous, however, to the intended revenge on the sinful flesh, the pious self-tormentors interrupted their invisible stripping, to give themselves a sound slap on the face, when the singing priest mentioned a similar blow inflicted on Christ by the High Priest's servant. The narrative being ended, the *Miserere* was set up in a louder voice, and the whips, clashing quickly and loudly against the bare flesh, accompanied the melody with the strongest thorough-bass imaginable. The zeal of the flagellants waxed hot as the operation proceeded; I have, indeed, seen the walls sprinkled with blood in churches where this practice prevails. The noise of the lashes might be supposed to grow less as the Psalm (the verses of which are alternately chanted by the congregation and the Priest) approaches to the conclusion; but it is not so. I confess that at the recollection of that conclusion, feelings of scorn, pity, and indignation are strangely mixed in my breast. The frantic clamours raised all at once by two or three hundred voices, in such screams as the sight of the bottomless pit yawning before them might wring from the creatures who saw the first undeniable evidence of their eternal misery; the increased violence of the blows, the sighs, loud sobbing, and cries for pardon—all this wild noise re-echoed in perfect darkness by the walls and vaults of the chapel, surpasses in horror everything which the novelists have imagined for the purpose of terrifying their readers. A repeated loud clapping of the priest's hands puts an end to the flagellation. After a pause of about five minutes, allowed for clothing, the dark lantern is opened, and the lamps rekindled."

Whatever may be said of such scenes as these—morbid, fanatic, frantic they may be; and we are not going to set them up as the types of the highest kind of devotion—whatever they may be, they carry with them their own evidence of religious sincerity. There is a reality in them which shows that the Church in Spain, with all its corruptions and abuses, had also its practical side, and was a converter of souls; made people feel themselves sinners, and preached Jesus Christ and Him crucified to the miserable wandering crowds within its fold. A rude excited luxuriance of devotional feeling, somewhat answering to the Methodistical revivals in our own country, marked the popular religious mind of Spain, and showed the real Gospel element in its intermixture with the disordered human mass.

There are two ways in which such a state of things as this tells upon a sceptical nature. Either the scepticism thaws before the scene of devotion, or the scene of devotion irritates the scepticism. In Blanco White the latter took place. The popular religion, hollowed and eaten out in the first instance by the sceptical element in his mind, received but a superficial and treacherous glow from such displays, and his intellect pictured but the more intensely the internal rottenness of the painted corpse. Scepticism was first in the field. He had just those impressions from such scenes that a man has on seeing a false system "showing off," and putting on a face. He disliked it so much the more. He had also a natural repugnance to all impassioned devotion as such. A peculiar want of sympathy with any form of religious enthusiasm is a regular feature in him. It co-exists with that warmth of natural affection which would lead us to expect, *à priori*, the very contrary: but there it is all the same. He is warm in nature; cold in religion; has ardent human affections, and dry spiritual ones. Family, friends, and acquaintances; father, mother, and sisters; all the world, so far as it is nature's, has a power to fascinate and soften him. The tear starts to his eye, his voice falters, his heart beats—this is the sympathy of nature. But sensitive and impassioned nature sees her own reflection in God's Church; is at once cold, suspicious, and angry; and, proud in her tenderness, will not let herself be translated into religion. She gives to man and to this world the worship of the heart, and to God the worship of the reason. The strong affectionate principle and the strong rationalistic one go side by side in Blanco White. He cannot bear the religious affection, the devotional sentiment; it annoys him, pricks and irritates him. He thinks it so foolish, absurd, weak, empty, untenable. He turns from the kneeling knee and outstretched arms, from the *Miserere* and the *Gloria*, with an irritation almost like positive spite; and the serpentine intellect writhes under its own sting, as all its refined and piercing hatred of superstition rises up. He even dislikes it the more from having felt its impressions; impressions made hollow, in his case, by the antagonism of the counter element in his mind. "Though tears," he says, "flowed from my eyes, and convulsive sobs were wrung from my bosom, my natural taste recoiled from that mixture of animal affection (I do not know a more appropriate name) with spiritual matters, which is the very essence of mysticism." Its internal morality was equally offensive to him. A strict scrupulous religion was always a "*disease*," upon his theory. "The mixed disease, both mental and bodily, called Scruples, so common among nuns and recluses of both sexes, was, to my great surprise, here present in a Protestant clergyman,"—is the remark he makes in the course of his journal, upon an English clergyman of his acquaintance, who calls on him to ask some religious advice in a distressed state of mind. The whole religion that Spain presented was a phenomenon to him, an irritation, an eyesore, —a national distemper.

The religious hiatus in his mind thus handed him over a total and undivided prey to the fretting, gnawing disgusts which the inquisitorial system in Spain provoked. Without any sympathy with the devotional side of the picture to counterbalance the collision with the tyrannical, without any of those feelings of spiritual fellowship which actually do in multitudes of cases so console and tranquillise internally doubting and irritable minds, his refined fastidious intellect simply chafed under the bit, and felt in the religious system over it only a grinding and remorseless mistress, treating it as a slave. The Church was always dogging him, interfering with him. She would not let him read his *Don Quixote* as a child, except by stealth. "Concealing it from all the family, he devoured it in a small room allotted him that he might read his lessons undisturbed;" his father and mother would certainly not have permitted it if they had known. She hovered in threatening attitude over every rising movement of his opening intellect, and he could not even be alone in his own mind without the Church's ominous form stepping in and claiming to be there. Every avenue of thought led to the Inquisition, and the ideas of a naturally sceptical fancy no sooner assumed form and body than they appeared as the officers of the holy tribunal come to summon him. He felt that his own parents would become themselves his accusers there, at the very first overt expression of what was passing in his mind. His own mother was, in fact, made wretched by this fear, and avoided his presence from the apprehension of what might incidentally drop from him in conversation. His own favourite literature, even when most unconnected with theology, was pursued with the conscious guilt attaching to a forbidden pleasure. It was a *vetitum nefas*, a department that strict orthodoxy had proscribed; and an unreasonably suspicious, fettering, and vexatious system came, by the most unhappy fatality, just into contact with the most bare, sensitive, and blistering fastidiousness. The consequence was a perpetual wound and sore, which ran and would not heal. A feeling toward the Inquisition grew up, more resembling the hatred of a personal mortal foe, than hostility to a system. The strength of the hatred impersonated its object; and the Inquisition, with its subtlety and its mercilessness, seemed to call for the knife. It is impossible not to see how deeply this one great hostility enters into his very philosophy, and becomes a kind of basis. Hatreds, very akin to personal ones, are much more at the bottom of the history of many a mind than is generally thought. We mean hatreds experimental, as distinct from those of pure principle. A system that has actually and solidly galled a man is charged with all the odium of what it has *done to him*, over and above its hatefulness *per se*; and the former odium is often quite as fundamental a one in the philosopher's mind as the latter. Blanco White grasps a solid inquisitorial image in his mind, which no mere process of reasoning could have produced; he has deep personal sensations and convictions, of which ordinary argument is a poor unequal expression. "See me," he seems to tell everybody, "look at me and my state of mind. Am not I a fact in myself? How could I hate a Church system as I do if it was not what I tell you it is? I have known it, felt it, borne it; I have a certainty on the subject which you, who have not known it as I have done, cannot have." His censure here becomes invective, his argument gall: he cuts deep in the way a person does when he is aiming at a personal foe, and wants to wound. He almost hates his very country because it was the country of the Inquisition. "I never felt proud of being a Spaniard, for it was as a Spaniard that I found myself mentally degraded, doomed to bow before the meanest priest and layman, who might consign me any day to the prisons of the Inquisition." Even the Spanish language is odious to him when it touches on theology, and the very sounds themselves that so long clothed those hostile ideas are intolerable. He had rather, as soon as he has put foot in England, at infinite inconvenience to himself, think and reason *to himself* in broken English than in his own Spanish. "Why did I not carry on my religious inquiries, and arrange my thoughts in Spanish?— I answer, Because the religious phraseology of my native language had become *ludicrously disgusting to me.* When, some time after the period on which I am dwelling, I was requested to correct for the press a Spanish New Testament, I could hardly bear the disagreeable impression which I received from old associations." "Orthodoxy," under all shapes, always retains in his mind the original associations of its form in Spain; and allusions to its "poison," "tyranny," "*auto-da-fé's*," "frowns," "insolence," "disdain," "horrors," "fulminations," "anathemas," the "anguish of spirit," "unmerited degradations," the whole life "martyrdoms" which lay at its door, show at every page the smarting mind. "Every human error and infirmity should be treated by the Christian philosopher with tenderness, except when it assumes the character of sanctity. When *sanctified* by superstition and bigoted pride, error acquires such a poisonous and destructive nature, that whoever perceives it is justified in procuring its extermination as that of the most venomous reptile."

One or two cases where he came into actual contact with the mortal foe are recorded with bitter force. One was a case in which a friend was at stake. His confessor called upon him to give up a friend's name to the Inquisition. "He told me he could not absolve me unless I promised to accuse my friend of having lent me a prohibited book. I well recollect the sort of trembling yet resolute courage with which I told him that I would rather 'go to hell' than betray my friend." A much more trying scene awaited him at his last parting with his only sister on her entrance into a nunnery. Here, touched in the very tenderest part, and feeling all the overpowering arguments of an excited and glowing affectionateness, in their bitter contrast with the Church's severity, his mind turned into one black flood of thought, horrible from its very intensity. He could hardly restrain an outbreak :—

"When I recollect the circumstances of the melancholy transaction which I am recording, I am quite surprised at my having escaped without committing myself by the vehemence of my indignation. My sister's health was extremely delicate; that of my mother was in a state which absolutely required her only remaining daughter's company at home. Yet the poor deluded man (I have not the heart to call him harsher names) whom I have just mentioned, conceived that he was sure of heaven's approbation and favour by encouraging the enthusiastic feeling which had turned my sister's eyes towards one of the gloomiest nunneries at Seville. It was a nunnery where the rule of St. Francis was observed with the greatest rigour; where the nuns were not allowed a bed, and were obliged to sleep on a few planks raised about a foot from the ground; where the use of linen near the body was forbidden; where the nuns wore coarse open sandals, through which the bare foot was exposed to cold and wet; where the nearest relations were not allowed to see the face of the recluse, or to have any communication with her except on certain days, when, in the presence of another nun, and with a thick curtain close behind the double iron railing which separated the visitors from the inmates of the convent, the parent, sister, or brother exchanged a few unmeaning sentences with the dear relative whom they had lost for ever. I will not conceal that, even at this distance of time, my feelings of indignation choke me when the picture of Father —— sitting near my sister, about the time when her resolution of being a nun was announced, presents itself vividly to my mind. I see the room;—

I stand on a well-known spot, where, in the presence of my mother, I was betrayed into a burst of indignant disapprobation, which darkened the priest's brow into that threatening scowl by which even the most contemptible wretch convinces you that he is thinking of the Inquisition. He bade me hold my tongue, and not lend my services to the great Tempter. Oh, what man who has a heart, not deadened by vile superstition, would not be on the side of the Tempter, if his office were only to defeat the priests! But I am ready to rave! Yes, I have suffered these things in the nineteenth century; I have suffered them as the effects of Christianity; and they still exist *as Christianity*."

A man has often a unity and force of character thrust upon him from without, that he would not have derived from within. "Some are born to greatness, some achieve greatness, and some have greatness thrust upon them." Touched in some soft part, or galled by pressure, the tender luxurious mind has gone off at a tangent, and gained audacity from its smarts; and a bold line is the result of the doggedness and purpose which its very irritation gives. A wound is a strengthening thing. A soldier fights the more fiercely after he has been grazed. The spirit's heat gives real power. Not born to be a martyr or a champion, either for Christianity or infidelity, Blanco White is indebted to the Inquisition for having had a career, and attained an unbelieving greatness. A wounded sensitiveness gives him a strength of mind that he would not otherwise have had, and shoots him, possessed of an aim and purpose which he had not before, into that fearful vortex of speculation into which he sank never again to rise.

The history of Blanco White's theological course in Spain is short and summary. An intense disgust at the Church system there upset the whole Roman claim in his mind; and with the Roman claim went Christianity altogether. A period of several years followed, in which he officiated regularly as a priest, while he was inwardly an atheist. For some time conscience would not let him do this smoothly, and he lived in a fever. But conscience was quieted by the analogy of an ancient philosopher under paganism. "If they conformed to the external rites of their country, and worshipped God in their hearts, why should not I do the same?" He plunged into the thick of infidel

French literature; and the reaction from the restraints of the Church system threw him into an atheistical intoxication that drowned his moral sense. The mysterious freemasonry of sympathy introduced him to the same secrets going on in other minds around him that were in his own. The excitement of discovery, the closet disclosure of mind to mind, the secret talk and free vent of intellect and passion, which this clique communion supplied, kept up the spirits. There was the charm of a conspiracy, and each kept the other in countenance. An easy thought suggested that what was going on at Seville was going on elsewhere, and each secret atheist held imaginary society with a secret body of atheism all over, that was undermining the Spanish Church. A miserable state of morals among a large number of the clergy, and especially the more dignified class, the vows of celibacy producing their natural result upon the luxurious and undisciplined, and the systematic alternation of crime and confession, completed their justification, and seemed to show the whole Spanish Church sunk in that state of far-gone rottenness which naturalised almost any infidel or immoral position in it.

Upon this antagonism between Blanco White and the Spanish Church one or two questions occur. In considering the great influence which the Inquisition had in making Blanco White an infidel, it must not be forgotten that simple Christian dogmatic truth, standing by itself, has a tendency to produce that effect upon many minds. It is a melancholy fact that persons have been often driven, by the mere presence of the Church's teaching, into a worse infidelity than they would have had without it. The Church is not, of course, responsible for such an effect; but she is responsible for any tendencies in this direction, arising from unnecessary and narrow-minded intolerance. We do not acquit the Spanish Church of this charge upon her. She is chargeable with the offence and the folly of keeping up an obsolete theory of persecution, when the rest of the world had changed its ground. The Inquisition was instituted, indeed, in an age when all the world persecuted; and, therefore, its institution was no special fault in her: but she is chargeable with its obstinate continuance, amid a wholly different state of things. At the same time, we are aware of the great practical difficulties that always lie on the side of change. It does not appear to be the habit of institutions to dissolve on the principle of accommodation, and yield a voluntary and rational assent to the proofs of uncongeniality which the world around them presents to their eyes. They expect their dissolution under another form of approach, and they generally wait for that final evidence, good or bad, of incompatibility, which forcible overthrow supplies. The Inquisition did what all other institutions do; it went on till it was stopped. On the whole, we can only say that the continuance of such a system inflicted, undoubtedly, a harder trial upon Blanco White than a milder tone of Church-government would have done; though in what proportions his career of infidelity was owing to the simple presence of dogmatic truth, and to the local inquisitorial appendages of that truth respectively, may be difficult to determine, and must be left for a general survey of his life to declare.

How far, again, are we exactly to trust Blanco White's account of the immoralities of the Spanish clergy? It is, of course, the tendency of a person in his situation to exaggerate, and make out everybody, if he can, to be in the same condition with himself. We cannot trust such a person's general impressions as to what is the case: his general impressions are sure to be somewhat one-sided. At the same time Blanco White mentions individual cases, and those cases are miserably strong ones. They are cases, too, that fall naturally within his knowledge, and which he meets with among his own circle of acquaintance, formed in the ordinary course of things, and previously to his atheistical change: so that we cannot quite say that a particular clique, which his own infidelity introduced him to, supplies the only ground of fact he goes upon. It is impossible, on the whole, we think, not to believe that a vast amount of the worst corruption and immorality existed among the Spanish clergy. Only the point should be remembered—and it is too often forgotten in such cases—that a great mass of corruption in a body does not at all exclude the existence of a great mass of real and effective good; but may be perfectly coincident with it. Real evil and real good go on together in the Church—in particular Churches—all the world over. The evil is not nullified by the good, nor is the good nullified by the evil; but both co-exist. It often happens that each intensifies the other, and that the more active the bad principle is, the more active the good one is too. In the present instance the phenomena which present themselves are deep pollution in one part of the Church, deep fervour in another; here an infidel spirit, there an apostolic; the poison of French atheism working, and the Gospel working and converting too.

A new opening, and an escape from his wearisome position, offered itself in course of time to Blanco White. In 1808 the French entered Spain; and the general confusion and dismay allowed him to look out for himself, and decide on his future prospects. He resolved to quit Spain for ever. He was in Madrid, when

" the Spanish Government, no longer able to conceal that the French troops were advancing towards Seville, had consulted their own safety by flight. The consternation reduced the mass of the inhabitants to that state of mental torpor, that absence of all definite will, which leaves the few who can exert their own, at full liberty to act as they please. But I knew that the inaction produced by terror could not be of long continuance: I was persuaded that the mob would awake from its slumber with a determination to compel the upper classes to await the common fate of the city. Within the three days of stillness which preceded the popular storm I formed and executed my determination to quit Spain. The desire to leave that country had, for many years, been working in my inmost soul, and so identified had it become with my whole being that there hardly was a thought, a feeling, into which the wish of expatriation had not insinuated itself: but before this moment, it acted in the character of despondency, and like a poisonous root, its multiplied fibres conveyed a sickening breath to every perception and thought. Not so the moment that the light of hope shone upon it, in one full burst of immediate expectation."

He did not leave Spain, however, without one short but much-relished triumph over his mortal foe. The disorder which for some time preceded the French invasion had opened a variety of new political prospects to the country, and caused the appointment of new commissions to prepare for the changes.

Blanco White had signalised himself by a journal, the *Semanario*, which he and his friend Quintana conducted. Jovellanos issued circulars to the Universities, desiring their opinion as to the future constitution of the *Cortes*, and Blanco White was one of the commission of two appointed at Seville for this purpose.

'I went about my task without delay: but before I began I agreed with my colleague in forcing the Inquisition to let us have some of the prohibited books which at different times they had seized and thrown together, to be destroyed by the worms, in one of the halls of their odious palace. I suggested that in the present state of things public opinion would not tolerate any denial on the part of the Inquisitors. It is true that we had very little occasion for such books as we were likely to take out of their possession; but there was a kind of triumph in this recovery of books that were completely lost to the world. They indeed belonged to nobody. In a word, my scheme was hailed with applause by all my friends, and the success with which it was attended produced a rejoicing among us which no Englishman can conceive. My colleague and myself addressed a petition to the Inquisitors expressing our desire to have some foreign books, and requesting to have them from their stores. The *Holy Tribunal* authorised me to enter the place where the confiscated books had been thrown together, and take out whatever I pleased. It is quite impossible to describe the state of the room into which I was admitted. The floor was covered with large heaps of books in perfect confusion: the dust, which in the burning summers of Andalusia penetrates to the inmost recesses, had settled upon everything to the depth of more than a quarter of an inch. On moving the confused volumes for the sake of completing a few valuable works, the Secretary and myself were involved in a cloud. I succeeded in obtaining two copies, nearly complete, of the French Encyclopædia. That work must have been frequently seized by the Tribunal: the floor was covered with volumes of its various dictionaries tumbled in distracting confusion. I now forget what other works I was able to save from the worms, which, with a devouring power, of which people who have not seen their ravages in hot climates can form no conception, had reduced a great number of volumes to fragments. The liberated captives were shared equally between my colleague and myself.

"I cannot well express," he says, "the exultation I felt upon seeing the Union Jack hoisted as we set sail for Cadiz. My joy would have been complete if our course had been at once to England. Still there was a pleasure of anticipation which I would not have exchanged for the best bishopric in Spain. . . . The idea that I was going to be free was more than a compensation for all my troubles. I was under the British flag in the open sea, as the sun rose above the horizon. The beautiful town of Cadiz was sinking gradually behind the waters. A shade of melancholy passed over my mind, when I thought that I should never see those buildings again; and then I gave myself up to the sublime enjoyment of the solitary expanse before me. . . . It was about eleven o'clock on the 3d of March, 1810, when we anchored in Falmouth harbour. Until this moment I had felt no anxiety whatever. But eleven days at sea, in very uncomfortable circumstances, had produced a bodily indisposition, which could not fail to have a certain influence on my spirits. I had not thought of providing myself with clothing suited to the English climate. A chill, such as I had never experienced, seized my whole frame. I thought I was breathing in death with the fog. Thus I stood on deck in the midst of the confusion which attends all landings, especially where there is a crowd of passengers, all anxious to get on shore, all regardless of everybody else, all wound up to the highest pitch of peevish selfishness. Unacquainted with everything about me, and fearful to an absurd excess of that kind of ridicule and disrespect which a foreigner, especially a Spaniard, apprehends in England, I stood motionless, waiting for the last turn, and perfectly indifferent whether I passed the remaining part of the day and the ensuing night in the packet. A strong persuasion that the climate would kill me in a short time took possession of my mind; and I felt as if I were going to land into the grave."

The first five years of his English life passed in literary political occupations. Blanco White had grown a politician in Spain. His politics took a strong democratical direction. The monarchy in Spain was in close alliance with the Church, and a fast friend of the Inquisition; and when he turned infidel he turned republican too.

"My colleague," he says (speaking of the Seville University Commission), "in this Commission was a Doctor of Laws named Seoanes, an Advocate of great reputation; but he devolved on me the whole business, after having agreed on the principles which were to be recommended. A disregard of ancient forms and privileges, a mere *toleration* of the *Grandees*, and one Chamber, such were our democratical views and wishes." "I had for many years," he adds, " lived in an habitual detestation of political despotism, and of its main prop, the Church. During my residence at Madrid, the most pointed invectives against these two sources of our national degradation had given zest and interest to my daily intercourse with the *patriots*, to whom the rising of the country against Napoleon gave a prominent influence. My desire that mental freedom should spread over the world was neither limited nor qualified by political considerations."

He wanted something to employ and support him when he came to England, and, at Mr. Richard Wellesley's advice, he set up the *Español*, a Spanish journal. Working for a livelihood was a serious change for him.

" My life had been one of ease bordering upon idleness. Reading and writing had been always my amusement, never my regular occupation. Suddenly however the necessity of working many hours in the day came upon me, in a foreign country, without the least assistance, and under a vague and magnified impression of responsibility. But there was no time for reflection. I took a wretched lodging in Duke Street, Westminster, one of those shabby places in the neighbourhood of Downing Street which have entirely disappeared, and began to prepare the first number of the *Español*, of which I immediately published a prospectus. My plan was to give at least a sheet and a half of original matter, and to fill up the rest with translations of public documents, parliamentary debates, and military despatches."

Only two numbers were published, when the news of the first revolution in Spanish America arrived in England. "The honest joy which this event raised in me was greater than my readers can imagine. I knew that the Spanish Colonies had been cruelly wronged by the mother country, and ardently wished to see them legislating for themselves. Not a doubt occurred to me in regard to the feelings and views of the *philosophical* party with whom I had been connected. I flattered myself, on the contrary, that the article in which I hailed the dawn of liberty on our transatlantic brethren would meet with applause among the panegyrists of philanthropy, whose speeches upon that subject had often filled me with enthusiasm."

He was egregiously disappointed. The Spanish press was

upon him immediately, and with the greatest ferocity. He describes, with genuine pathos, his first introduction to the class of feelings which a regularly-peppered politician has. It was altogether a new experience; Spain had had her Inquisition but not her press before.

"To those who have grown up in a country where no public man escapes abuse, the feelings of an *unrevolutionised* Spaniard on the subject of honour must appear childish and absurd. Let my readers, however, endeavour to imagine a man educated in a town where the life of the better classes was regulated in most things by a kind of Chinese ceremonial, and imagine the writer of these memoirs as one full of these notions in an excessive degree, and they will understand how deep must have been the wound inflicted by the first violent attacks of the Spanish press. . . . One evening, as I was preparing to go early to bed, a parcel was brought to me from Lord Holland. It contained a file of the diminutive Spanish Journals which had begun to venture into light, and which, in spite of the censorship, availed themselves of the excitement of the country more for the purpose of venting the private jealousies and malice of the writers than to speak boldly and honestly in favour of reform. Lord Holland, being well acquainted with the Spanish notions, had the kindness to accompany the Journals with a note, by which he endeavoured to break the shock which he well knew they would give me. The note alarmed me, and I took up the papers in great agitation. I knew the editors of one or two, and had believed them my friends; the unjust and insolent manner, therefore, in which I saw myself treated by them was doubly painful, because they were the men whom I believed ready to stand at all times in my defence. I continued for some time in a state of wretchedness of which I had no idea."

The change from "the Chinese ceremonial" of Hidalgo society in Spain to the buffetings of the press is no small one certainly.

Blanco White was, moreover, unfortunate in the line he took; it was a line of his own, and pleased no side. The Spanish *patriotic* party were French in their tastes, Castilians in their nationalism; they felt like republicans, but like Spaniards too. In patronising the revolt of the Hispano-Americans, Blanco White inflicted a severe wound on Spanish pride, and they retorted with all the spleen they could muster;

he even tells us they seriously thought of getting him assassinated. And while he offended Spaniards, he got no thanks from the Hispano-Americans. The very party whom he had been patronising cruelly hoaxed him.

"One of the South American Deputies, with the knowledge of all the rest, forged a letter, in the name of Perez, as chairman of an imaginary committee of the Transatlantic Deputation. The forgery contained the warmest thanks for the liberal manner in which I was defending the cause of the Colonies, complained of the unfairness with which their claims were treated, and left me at liberty to publish the letter. To remove all possible suspicion, the authors of the hoax applied to the Count Pamela, then Portuguese Ambassador in Spain, requesting him to forward the letter to the Portuguese Ambassador in London. Under all these circumstances I thought it proper to acknowledge the letter, and I published it in my following Number."

The bait had taken, and the American Deputies enjoyed themselves at his expense. "Perez mounted the Tribune in a furious mood. He charged me by name with the forgery; while a titter went round, and the words, *the Mitre is gone*, were repeatedly whispered." The injured journalist appealed to the Spanish Cortes, the Cortes laughed at him, and the paper war was carried on by Blanco White singly on one side, against all Spain and Spanish America on the other. In this perpetual hot water one advantage, nevertheless, accrued to him from his Journal. The *Español* faithfully supported the English interests in Spain, and Blanco White was rewarded with a pension of £250 a year. "The publication of the *Español* continued till the total expulsion of the French troops from the Peninsula and the return of Ferdinand VII. It is impossible," he says, "for me to express the fatigue I underwent for nearly five years. My health was ruined to such a degree that life has ever since to me been a source of nearly unmixed suffering."

His party position in England partook of this ambiguous and fretting character. His whole personal history took him among the Liberal party, but his detestation of Rome was too genuine and furious for an English Liberal. Here was a collision. Blanco White could not forget his old scent; and the subject of Popery threw him into anti-Roman vehemence and earnestness far too theological and *outré* for the Parliamentary standard. He was a furious dogmatist on this subject, and could not be silenced; and the English Liberal, quite ready to patronise him in his negative character, did not care to hear him preach. Sir James Mackintosh thinks he wants candour. " The candour of Blanco White is remarkable, but his indignation at the necessity to dissemble, long imposed upon him, makes him not so fair as Grotius in his account of the opinions of his former fellow-religionists." He is thought too violent against priesthoods; and even his friend Archbishop Whately would caution him "against reviving early prejudices" and continuing his youthful "horror of bishops and priests."

His Oxford diploma was an unfortunate sufferer from this jar; its spotlessness was marred by an awkward little incident. We [1845] are giving the Oxford gossip of twenty years back, but we believe we can pledge ourselves for its truth in the main. Blanco White's diploma ought to have been a unanimous one; it was intended to be so. The panic in 1825 about the Roman Catholic Relief Bill had brought his book into favourable notice. The benevolence of the Oxford Tory party was secured by it, the Whigs were his natural friends, and Blanco White walked over the course. The diploma was prepared accordingly. Unluckily the then Vice-Chancellor, with that well-known briskness and zeal which has so distinguished his University course, but which operated unfavourably in this particular instance, inserted the anti-relief-bill services of Blanco White in the document, which alluded expressly to a certain "well-timed defence of the English Church" that had come from his pen. The Whiggery of a particular College took fire, and two Radical M.A.'s appeared in Convocation and opposed the honour. The consequence was that the word "unanimously" had to be struck out of the diploma, and a sad hiatus was left. If we are not mistaken, it was sent back to the Provost of Oriel, Dr. Hawkins, by Blanco White, on his becoming Unitarian, in whose possession we presume it is now.

The Roman Catholic Relief Bill pursues him again. The first occasion on which he had to exercise his vote was the

Oxford election in 1829. As a strong denouncer of Popery in his writings, he was expected, of course, by the anti-emancipationists to support them on that occasion; but he came into the Convocation-house and gave his vote for Peel. Still ardent in his conviction of the extreme danger of intrusting the Roman Catholics with legislative powers, he escaped the natural inference from it by a sudden act of strong faith in Sir R. Peel's declaration that a civil war was unavoidable without the measure. " On this (which is a matter to be settled by correct information as to the real state of Ireland) I have no reason to mistrust the opinion of the Government. I know," he continues, "that I shall be abused by those who have hitherto praised me. Let it be so. The laws of this country make me a British subject in the most ample and unqualified manner. The University of Oxford has given me a vote in Convocation. To shrink from the exercise of these privileges would be cowardice. In the name of God, therefore, I will do my duty." A somewhat magniloquent soliloquy on such a subject. Blanco White on this and other occasions is far from altogether disliking the horrors which he conjures up, and takes pleasure in his own flutter. All first votes are apt to be ponderous, to exult in awful responsibility, and defy indefinite consequences. We have heard of a precociously deep view in the mind of a young philosopher, who converted the fact of his becoming a ten-pound householder and voter for the borough into a sort of moral metempsychosis. Blanco White registers the step duly: "I succeeded," he says, "after a great many and unavailing efforts to get through the crowd, in giving my vote for Peel. The Vice-Chancellor (Dr. Jones), in consideration of my ill-health, allowed me to enter through the Divinity School. I was treated with the most perfect civility." A few days afterward he meets a gentleman at the Athenæum, whose mode of address to him on this subject, to the effect that he (Blanco White) should not have meddled with English politics, creates a storm of feelings that he can hardly keep in; and an imaginary letter "to the Rev. Mr. B.—," in his diary, vents "his full heart."

His situation as a stranger brought its own class of distresses. A foreigner, thrown all at once into the thick of English society, he was nervous and suspicious to the last degree. His foreign accent and want of knowledge of the language haunted him, and he was perpetually "apprehensive of awkwardnesses and gaucheries."

"The retired manner in which I was brought up had made me extremely sensitive to every apprehension of the ridiculous. Finding myself in perpetual danger of raising a laugh, I soon fell into the habit of being silent. But as while others were talking my mind was active on the subject of the conversation, the pain of suppressing my thoughts prevented my taking an interest in these frequent social meetings. Perhaps without this keen spur perpetually at my side I should not have devoted myself as fully as I did to the study of English."

A particular metaphysical constitution of mind increased this tendency :—

"I believe," he continues, "that I never was a fluent speaker in my own language. The reason seems to be that even upon the subjects most familiar to my mind I must repeat the original process of analysis through which I became originally acquainted with them every time that I have to speak or write upon them. Kant says that eloquence consists in making the work of the understanding one of imagination. That transfer from the one faculty to the other seldom or never takes place in my mind, or if it does, it is performed simultaneously with the act of thinking. Hence my delivery has at all times been laborious, and conversation seldom fails to exhaust me. . . . Among the instances of surprising knowledge of the human mind and heart in which Shakespeare's works abound, few, if any, have struck me so much as that contained in a passage (probably little noticed by readers not in my circumstances) in which he describes the magnitude of the loss which a man banished from his country has to endure by living among those who do not understand his native language. Mowbray, Duke of Norfolk, in *Richard II.* (Act I. Scene 3), on hearing the sentence of banishment pronounced against him by the King, is made to say :—

'A heavy sentence, my most sovereign liege,
And all unlook'd for from your highness' mouth :
A dearer merit, not so deep a maim
As to be cast forth in the common air,
Have I deserved at your highness' hand.
The language I have learn'd these forty years,

> My native English, now I must forego ;
> And now my tongue's use is to me no more
> Than an unstringed viol, or a harp ;
> Or like a cunning instrument cased up,
> Or, being open, put into his hands
> That knows no touch to tune the harmony.'"

There is an amiableness, mixed with weakness, in the excessive tendency of a mind to these sort of fancies : we mean when a person is always thinking himself doing things ill, and making mistakes, and fancying others are laughing at him. He naturally has our sympathies much more than the bolder and coarser character,—the one quite at ease, cool, self-complacent, and self-confident. A sense of weakness in a mind is a great charm where it is genuine. It is just that sort of charm, for example, which Dr. Arnold's character wants. Arnold is always gushing with a rude health and strength, inclining to the nature of what the Greeks call ὕβρις, and leaving no room for sympathy; and Blanco White's mind contrasts favourably with his in this respect. Its amiable sensitiveness, and perpetual tendency to view itself as in some unfavourable, some depressing, relation with respect to others, some relation in which others have the advantage of it,—he, in imagination, in the dirt, and others walking over him,—even his disgusts as he corrects his proof-sheets, tell for him. We have heard his intimate friends talk of him, and are sure that nobody could know him without feeling his attractions. His morbid, querulous temperament has a refinement of its own. We do not mean to say that Blanco White had thorough genuine humility; he had not. But there is a lighter phase of this character: nature has the good taste to imitate grace. Nature, though she is not grace, often catches some of the air and manner, the look and step, of her spiritual counterpart; and the imitation, though it does not and cannot go deep enough, has its own charms.

Part of his irritableness was of course constitutional; he felt it, and could not help it. "It was almost unmanageable." He says :—

"I remember the desperate effort which I was obliged to make before I ventured to knock at the door, and inquire whether the person I wanted to see was at home. Any sudden question upon the most simple and indifferent matter used to startle me, and put me into a state of trepidation which deprived me for some time of all knowledge I might possess upon the subject. I remember instances of this at Oriel Common Room. I do not know whether from modesty or pride, whenever I found myself in that situation I never made any attempt to correct the blunder, or to explain the cause of it."

He is positively and purely ridiculous, however, at times. The "hetairocracy" of Oriel Common Room stuck in his mind.

"I had no knowledge," he says, "for some time of the spirit which is not unfrequently found among fellows of colleges, who constitute a kind of aristocracy among the masters." "In the Oriel Common Room I met with great kindness. I now imagined I had found a home, but this was a delusion, which vanished as soon as I understood the constitution of the club (for the Common Room is nothing else) to which I had been admitted. I imagined that this admission had placed me upon an equality with the other members; but it was not so. I found that even a probationary fellow took precedence of me, whatever might be my seniority as a member of the Common Room. I was, in fact, only to be tolerated."

He acknowledges that he never saw the smallest symptom of assumption on the part of any single individual fellow; but the *system* he objects to. "I was in *a false position:* individual good nature could only relieve, but not remove, my uneasiness."[1] Really this is the greatest nonsense that was ever seriously written. An ordinary master, we can state from our own experience of that Common Room, is quite on a par with a fellow as far as all social purposes go. He goes into the Common Room, reads the papers, talks, and drinks his wine

[1] One of these probationers proposing to spend the long vacation of 1829 in Oxford, all unconscious of being a cause of offence, thus writes of Blanco White's conversational powers:—"I shall dine, I suppose, almost every day with Blanco White, whom this is a very good opportunity of seeing; as in term-time he is so continually either dining out or confined to home by illness or depression of spirits brought on by over-excitement that we do not see much of him. His conversation is really more amusing and informing than any I have heard. . . . He is an incessant talker, and if he thinks his companion understands him would rather have one a listener than a talker; especially when he is on any of his favourite subjects, as Plato, errors of scholastic divinity, or logic;—on any of these subjects he would willingly talk for ever."

after dinner, without the smallest suspicion of his own inferiority. Nobody tells him of his mistake, if it is one ; and there is no possibility of his ever practically discovering it.

A number of little tastes, predilections, refinements, fastidiousnesses, nervousnesses, suspicions, jealousies, imaginations, fears, and disquietudes of his own suggestion, are the complement and circumstance of one particular predominant element in Blanco White. Intellect and taste are sure to develop a morbid element in a character, where it exists; and one specimen of the literary man is always fancying people are laughing at him, and watching him; is sensitive to criticism in the last degree, and attributes a barbarism and atrocity to it when it at all touches him, which is only the creation of his own exceeding tenderness of skin. His mind and his ear keep pace with each other. He was a splendid musician, but his nervous sensitiveness of ear made music a source of recurring irritation. All but the best was a jar to him, and a note out of tune scratched him like a pin. A very tolerably good undergraduate fiddle playing in a corner of Oriel quadrangle, as he was walking through with a friend of our own, gave him, he declared, real solid physical torture. A quartett party, exactly to his taste, did not exhibit the liberal communicative side of music :— "We allowed no audience, because we could not even bear a whisper. The initiated in the mysteries of music can alone conceive the luxuries of such an entertainment." A peculiar appreciation of a particular class of personal comforts, good lodgings, good waiting and attention, all harmonises significantly with these traits. Without wishing to grudge an elderly person his conveniences and solaces, we can hardly avoid a smile when he alludes so feelingly to a fact of this class :— "Through the bounty of the Archbishop do I owe the advantage of keeping an excellent valet, whom I was going to discharge before I quitted Dublin, and who, from his good qualities and respectful attention to my comfort, has become almost indispensable to me." "I have not enjoyed," he says, in one of his letters from Liverpool, "a more quiet period in England than that of the last six months. I have had some little trouble with servants, but by the kindness of some Liverpool ladies I am now very comfortable, even in that respect. When I return from my daily walk to the Athenæum, and find everything quiet, the house perfectly clean, my plain furniture in the best order, and my books ready to whisper wisdom and peace to my mind, my heart expands with thankfulness, and I almost forget that I have ever been in trouble."

We must go back to more serious subjects. We have passed through one stage of Blanco White's religious life; another and a more trying one begins. The infidelity of his Spanish life was gained at a bound; it was now to be acted over again by slow lingering steps, and the summary death which he passed through once to be repeated in a process which, attacking him limb by limb, at last reached the vital parts, and left his Christianity once more and irrevocably dead. The web was respun, that it might be unspun again. A new scene, a fresh air imparted a hollow artificial reaction that just gave faith strength enough to sink again. Once in England, and with Spain and its Church bidden farewell to, he thought he had no more to go through; that his mind was set like a rock, and had done with religion for ever; that he knew what it was, saw through it, had got to the other side of it, was in the region of certainty and absolute fact—cold and barren, but still as solid as the ground. He had been a Roman Catholic, and he *was* an Atheist; that expressed the whole. It was not so. His change had been too summary to be complete, and was superficial compared with what it was to be. A mind cannot unchristianise itself in a moment; and infidel Rome is not built in a day. A closer struggle now commenced, and unbelief started on a fresh span of life.

The change from the old scene of irritation, the welcome which attended him, and the whole social atmosphere he found himself in in England, had the effect at first of thawing his Spanish infidelity. Blanco White speaks correctly of himself when he says that he is much influenced by sympathy; he is so in one sense; he feels the charms of a social circle warmly, he does not like shocking friends whom he loves; and estrangement is great pain to him. His sympathies are of the social, not of the deep or internal kind; but these social sympathies he has strongly. They operated upon him very naturally now. He liked the persons he was thrown amongst; he found himself agreeing in intellectual tastes with them; he was fond of conversation, and enjoyed all the flow of spirits, the humour, badinage, and vivacity of choice society. He had a circle of friends, too, of a more intimate and endearing cast than the general acquaintance at Holland House or the Athenæum. The Christies in London, Mr. W. Bishop, Dr. Whately, and one or two more at Oxford, formed a sphere of friendship for him, in which he was more than at home. Oxford particularly suited him in this respect. Its quiet mornings, social evenings, rest when he liked, conversation when he liked, calmed, soothed, and cheered. Spain had only formed his first case of infidelity, and it gave way to these genial influences. He had not solid reasons enough for disagreement, and his feelings preferred agreement.

In 1814, having given up the *Español*, and having been a lay attendant at the communion for some time, he signed the Thirty-nine Articles, and was admitted as a clergyman in the Establishment. "He now," he says, "gave full scope to his social feeling in regard to the English clergy. My desire to identify myself with the body was vehement." The first time he read the Church service—in St. Mary's Church—was an epoch, and his nerves were perfectly unstrung by the act. It was on a week-day, and only six or seven persons were in church. "My dear friend Bishop, who attended me to the church, seeing me so deeply agitated, offered to relieve me: but I would not give way. My voice must have been nearly inaudible. When I returned to my lodgings, my mind, free from the agitation which had kept it so long on the stretch, took a direction entirely devotional; but the feelings with which my heart was bursting were of that kind which, had they continued so as to become rooted, would have made me a confirmed enthusiast. Wanting to unburden my heart, I wrote immediately a letter to Mr. James Christie, of London, who among my friends would most sympathise with my state of mind." His "theological" notions now revive: he feels himself beginning to dogmatise, and "all the habits of his mind associated with his early belief in Christianity reappear." He "relapses into orthodoxy;" he gives "a *provisional* assent to the doctrines on which the generality of divines are agreed." It is now my "spirit of revived subordination;" "my ascetic submission;" "my forced mysticism." He slides unconsciously in his diary, "into the censorious declamatory style of professed theological writers." The "spirit of the pulpit" comes suddenly upon him. In the "controversy about the Lancastrian and Bell schools, he finds his clerical spirit revive," and is on the point of joining "the ranks of the most violent High-Churchmen." His feelings so far veer round, that a fear of being ashamed of his religion amid the society of Holland House begins to trouble his conscience. He adopts even an "evangelical" style in his diary, and reproaches himself for talking on common subjects, and not the Gospel, in society. The sincerity of his feelings now, viewed as mere feelings, is very evident. He lays down religious rules for himself, and even attends to the formalism of definite times and hours. He makes resolutions. He spends a particular day in particular meditations. He is afraid of his zeal for Hebrew occupying his mind too much, and he resolves to spend an hour every day in reading the Greek Testament, and praying over what he reads. He even wants to devote his life to missionary labours, and he solicits, at the sacrifice of all his intellectual tastes and English prospects, the creation of a new Spanish Protestant chaplaincy at Trinidad, for himself to fill; he is ready to retire from the world, and consecrate himself to religion.

Alas! underneath these religious emotions and sensibilities a canker was at work. He felt its progress. At the very time that he was fostering these genial sensations of belief on the surface, doubt was eating its way within. He grew alarmed, and settled it for a time; but it rose again, and only sank to reappear. At the very time that he was "trying to make himself an Evangelical and Pietist," and growing warm and enthusiastic, he had asked himself the fatal question— How is the Bible inspired? The *crux* fastened malignantly upon him, and kept its hold to the last. It was immediately after his admission as a clergyman, when he was most enthusiastic, and when a whole career of religious feeling, usefulness, and intercourse lay before him, that the thought struck upon him with overpowering clearness. "I remember," he says, writing years after, with the greatest vividness, "the dismay which I experienced when, having attentively studied all that could be said to establish this preliminary point, I perceived the weakness of the arguments on which such a mighty theory as that which makes the Bible *infallible* is made to rest."

And if the letter of the Bible was being undermined, *a fortiori* was its creed. A miserable argument against the doctrine of the Trinity appears, and goes on in his diary at this time; and while he was sincerely waiting to be an evangelical missionary, he was sincerely writing down Unitarianism in his commonplace-book. He could, while a Pietist in feeling, actually write—"Person, if it conveys any distinct idea, means an *individual*: if, therefore, there are three individuals, every one of whom is God, the language of these divines says,—'There are *three Gods*.' If their words do not mean this, they mean nothing. But I am sure," he adds, "that I should be set down as a Unitarian and disguised deist, if they were acquainted with these observations." He thinks the "difference about the word ὁμοούσιος a verbal one." The germ of the whole reasoning in the "heterodoxy and orthodoxy" now appears; and separating the words of the Bible from their sense, he rejects the very idea of one creed.

After three years of this mental progress, he becomes seriously alarmed, and says—"I hope there is no lurking self-confidence in my heart. My doubts seems to increase every day." He wants to stop, and he looks out for a position and for rest. "I feel tired and bewildered," he writes. "I did not intend to write controversy; I wished only to collect my ideas concerning my own circumstances, which I perceive to be very awkward and difficult." He still "adores the mystery of the Trinity in the *language of the Bible*." He prays to "be defended from the spirit of unbelief." "But what am I to do —am I to shut my eyes and abstain from further inquiry?" Thus agitated and alternating, towards the end of 1818 he puts down on paper a formal description of his faith—what he believed, and what he did not. He does it to have a safeguard for himself, a barrier against further assaults, and a *locus standi*. What is it? He commences—" I firmly believe in one God, the Creator of the Universe, etc. I believe that He has, at different times, made extraordinary communications concerning His own nature." He then proceeds—" I believe that the Old and New Testament contain the sense and substance of these communications; but I must confess that I cannot persuade myself that there is nothing in the Bible but what God has been pleased to reveal to mankind. I suspect that, together with *revealed truths*, there is in it a considerable portion of human error." He proceeds to another point— " I believe that Jesus of Nazareth is the Son of God *in the sense in which He claimed that title;* but I cannot say that Christ is *God* and *Man*, without a consciousness of a contradiction in terms."

From this state of mind he appears never to have receded. He never appears to have gone further in orthodoxy than this secret manifesto marks. It was a state of belief compared with the past and the future; compared with Spanish infidelity on the one hand, and with the Liverpool one on the other: it was a stop short of a lower state on which he felt himself verging. An ordinary eye would look on it as infidelity; with him it is that form of Christianity which saves him *from* infidelity. He does not consider himself an Unitarian; on the contrary, he congratulates himself that he did not *turn* Unitarian at this time, because he would have been a superficial one had he done so, a dogmatic, popish Unitarian. For some time, indeed, touched with a sense of his disagreement with the Church's theology, he abstains from the communion upon "a popish scruple" that had not left him, "as to the communion demanding unity of faith in its participators." But the feeling that he is "a practical disciple" gradually overcomes this scruple; and he goes on speculating as he likes in his inner mind; his outer mingling with the ordinary lax religious stream of sentiment in the English Church. He takes duty, he preaches occasionally. His sermons before the University attract great attention. He attends once or twice the meetings of the Bible Society. An interest attaches to his situation, and he is made a lion of. He comes out as an author; and his *Evidence against Catholicism, Poor Man's Preservative against Popery, Doblado's Letters from Spain*, tell on the public mind, and give him a regular position in the literary and religious world.

The society of Oriel Common Room gave Blanco White some friendships, which he valued deeply, on the simply personal ground; the theological difference being understood. Admired for his literary talents and tastes, Blanco White never carried away Churchmen. He was quite understood. He was regarded as what he was, a clever and interesting latitudinarian, and as a regular member of that school he held an understood party position in religion. The tone of his books, and we must add of his conversation occasionally, was offensive to many, and that license of profane sarcasm which sceptical literary men have such a tendency to, stamped him in many eyes. Mr. Keble was a member of the same Common Room with Blanco White, but avoided all closeness of acquaintance with him.[1]

We take a leap over fifteen years of this course of life and opinion, and find Blanco White in Ireland, domiciled in the house of his friend Dr. Whately, now Archbishop of Dublin. On going to his See the Archbishop persuaded him to accompany him, and the two left Oxford together. Time, that changes a man's social position everywhere, does so especially

---

[1] [The following note from Mr. Keble, in reply to an apology for having introduced his name here, bears on this statement :—

"*Hursley Vicarage, July* 14, 1845.

"MY DEAR MOZLEY,—I ought to have written directly to say that I believe what you say of my demeanour to poor B. W. is substantially correct ; but how far it was owing to any long-sightedness or right-mindedness on my part is another thing. I rather believe, as well as I can remember, that I was partly influenced by a slothful dislike of the trouble of new acquaintance, and partly (which *is* rather to the purpose) by a strong instinctive dislike which my father had somehow conceived towards 'Blank White' (as he always called him), though I don't remember his ever seeing him. But here is more than enough on so unimportant a subject. I certainly should be glad, for some *too* good reasons, to have had an opportunity of drawing my pen across that sentence in your article which mentions my name, but to you I can only be obliged for thinking too well of me.—Ever yours affec^{ly}, J. KEBLE."]

in a University; seniors retire, juniors come in their place. The loss of such an intimacy as Dr. Whately would have left Oxford a somewhat barren scene to Blanco White. The Archbishop's kindness prevented this trial.

It was in the Palace at Dublin in 1834 that a mind, for many years kept superficially within the orthodox pale, and struggling with deep-rooted doubts, fairly broke loose and made the avowal. The event was heralded. The answer to Moore's *Irish Gentleman in Search of his Religion* alarmed Blanco White's friends. A translation of Neander's pamphlet on "Free Teaching" produced a scene :—

" When the Archbishop came in I expressed my sincere regret that, owing to the desire of putting it in his power when I publish anything to say that he had not read it, and consequently is not answerable for any opinions expressed by me, I could not avail myself of his judgment as I used to do formerly. He answered, ' that there was no reason why I should keep my MSS. from him, for he had always maintained that the person who consults is not bound to follow the advice given to him.' And then he added, ' But of course I should not like you to publish anything too *radical.*' "

The chord struck upon his ear :—

" A dream had suddenly become a reality. Must I then reduce myself to publish only what may be allowed (with the utmost latitude of *clerical* liberality) to come out of an Archbishop's palace ? This is my present condition. My friend's liberality of principle exceeds very much the limits which his brother bishops can possibly allow. But must I spend the last days of a life devoted to mental independence under any such restraint ? Am I doing my duty ?"

The determination was made. A note soon informed the Archbishop that the change had come, that he had embraced Unitarianism. He was told to wait, but wait any longer he would not. " ' Wait !' said Dr. D—. ' Wait !—Where ? Upon what ground ? Upon yours ? or upon the Calvinist's, or upon the Roman Catholic's ? To which of these shall I give the advantage of my waiting ? Have I not waited long upon your catechism, which was forced word for word upon my infant mind ? Have I not waited long during my nursery instruction ? Have I not waited several hours every Sunday at church, hearing the Church Prayer-Book and your long, long sermons ? Am I to wait till I die ?" He made the sacrifice. He left the Archbishop's house and removed to Liverpool. "January 9th : Waiting in anguish for the hour of departure." —" January 10th, Liverpool, 1835 : My whole life has not moments so bitter as those which I have experienced within the last half hour. I awoke in a distracted state. . . ." A deep form of mental pain shoots up in him now. Intellectual minds twist their feelings into refined torture and breed curious scorpion subtleties. "The whole of what had passed through my mind with such irresistible power respecting my duty appeared like a delusion, a dream, with my present misery for all its reality. Has not some martyr, when already bound to the stake, been tried by the awful impression that he had been brought there by a delusion ?"

Now follow the usual pains that attend upon persons in such situations—remarks, reflections, remonstrances of friends —and he gives them the peculiar irritating twist which is so strong in him. "Kind and excellent friends seem to take a delight in saying to me that *I have given a mortal stab to my usefulness.* Secret feeling does not allow them to perceive that what leads them to say so is *the desire of giving me a stab;* for I have already taken a decided step, and that observation can have no effect but that of adding to my sufferings." At any rate "*delay your publication,*" the disclosure of your state of mind, it is urged on him—consult the Archbishop's feelings. All in vain. He will not give delay, and complains of their asking it, and retorts querulously but feelingly :—

" A breach between the Archbishop and myself would be worse than death to me. But unless he can see my circumstances in somewhat like the light in which I see them, I must submit to the worst. What a thing this kind of orthodox good fame must be when a breath may tarnish it like the honour of a maiden ! I believe that if I were in the place of the Archbishop I should content myself with my own consciousness of rectitude, and expose myself to such ungrounded rumours for the sake of a friend, who, old, weak, and in constant suffering, cannot bear an additional weight besides that which almost crushes him."

Blanco White now for the first time, in the Unitarian congregation at Liverpool, seems to himself to breathe a pure air and to have a worship to his mind. "He attends the commemoration of the Lord's Supper at the Unitarian chapel," and is full of "lofty satisfaction and internal peace." "A rational, a sublime ceremony!" he says.

"Its perfect simplicity is preserved, and every particle of the enthusiastic excitement, charm-like mysteriousness, which the Church of England still encourages, is removed." Sunday after Sunday he enjoys "the most sublime moral and intellectual treat which the purified religious principle can offer to man. I draw near to the presence of the living God, and I know that his nearness is not visionary. I am convinced that it is real, and that it takes place in the only sanctuary which exists among men—in the temple of the Holy Spirit, our MIND, our reasonable mind, the seat of the Divine Oracle for men. My faith increases, aided by an undisturbed development of the reasonableness of the great truths of religion. It grows without effort, and just as I believe in any other truth of reality, by a conviction with which the will has nothing to do except obeying it. I thank my God for this faith. I pray for its increase." "At no period of my life have I enjoyed moments of purer happiness than during the present."

Such is his religion in the first exultation of its freedom from Church bondage and mystery. Disease and imagination are over, health and reason are begun. "I *was*, indeed, acquainted with a religious excitement very like intoxication; an excitement which, similar to that produced by stimulants, brings with it a deep-seated consciousness that it cannot last—that it will gradually disappear, leaving us exhausted and low. *Now* I have reality." Nervous excitement, enthusiasm, fear, delusive poetry and churchyard gloom, the religion of sensations and the mind's slavery and prostration, are passed away. "Reason alone is followed—God's is a reasonable service." The constitution of nature, the proofs of the Divine Wisdom and Power in the construction of the material world, "invariable order" and physical law, supersede the world of spiritual phantasmagoria, and invisible charms and terrors. A calm contemplative worship is produced, as superior to the irregular movements of a religion of the affections, as order is above disorder, cultivation above nature, and pure elemental reason above the passions.

We have observed already, at an early period in Blanco White's life, a union in him of dry spiritual and soft human affection; nature tender, and devotion cold. This temper is now systematised and brought under a theory, and an anti-devotional philosophy is constructed. Deeper and deeper, more solid and subterranean, becomes his basis; the midway peg removed, he falls. There is a peculiar dream, of the nature of a nightmare, which represents sad unutterable descent; we are falling, falling down some cavernous hole, which seems to be taking us to the earth's centre; treacherous ledges just keep us suspended for a moment, and then let us fall and fall again down the dismal geological fissure, and we seem to have parted company with the earth's surface for ever. Blanco White is dragged along now by his own intellect through one form of scepticism after another, till, like some metempsychosis going on, embodying and disembodying in turns the poor tortured soul, and sporting with his victim, the process at last dissolves him. Form gives way to form more shadowy, till body becomes nebula, and seems to mix with rolling cloud and thickening air. All is dissolution; the mind's stays giving way and scattering the loose particles; the fabric breaking up; the chain unwinding to its last link. An emptying exhausting operation draws out the mind's last drop. All is in motion of irresistible descent, and, like some machine which when once set going won't stop itself, intellectual unbelief with a miserable pertinacity works itself out, undoing as it goes. Unhinged, unstrung, disorganised, he follows his mind into the extremest developments of rationalistic purism, where, in the regions of rarefaction and space, a Siberian exile from the world of passion, the pure intellect looks around and worships the First Cause, the Origin of motion and Soul of the Universe.

There is a doctrine of Christianity upon which ultimately

hangs the whole of that awful and insurmountable difference which separates the two great *genera* of religions that we see in the world—the two that Blanco White denominates respectively philosophical worship and devotion—from each other. One doctrine there is which gives devotion its proper and irresistible basis against the religion of pure reason. It was one which Blanco White never entered into, felt, or apparently really believed. It now rises up with terrible energy against him, and with an awful retaliation consolidates and systematises his unbelief. His born dislike of Catholic devotion, and the sense of hollowness and delusion with which it always inspired him, making his devotions mere superficialities and conscious outsides, carried in them the latent and embryo denial of this one doctrine. The doctrine we mean is that of the Incarnation.

Two great mediums present themselves, from which we form our ideas of God, viz., Nature and Man. Nature, or the material world, contains evidences of design and intelligence in the creation of it. Its order, harmonious and complex machinery, vastness, systems, worlds, motions in earth and heaven, production, growth, nurture, bodies of men and animals—all present one with the irresistible idea of some first great Central Cause working in the wide realms of matter, arranging, adjusting, and producing these manifestations we see. Borrowing one idea from another department, and going upon a mixed ground, we call these—proofs of the benevolence of the Deity. Strictly speaking, however, this is a borrowed idea: looking purely and singly to the department of nature itself, and to no other, all the idea we get of Deity is that of centrality, origination, power: he is the spring of a great machinery, the centre of a world of physical movements and harmonies. His dignity here varies from the very lowest and most material idea that philosophy can entertain of a Cause, from being hardly higher than mere matter itself, up to positive intelligence, and mind. But higher than this latter point physical science, in its reasonings about the Deity, does not take us. A *moral* Being is not proved by these manifestations; that idea does not reside within the limits of this science: so far as we have gone as yet, we are not beyond that idea of a Deity, which the *anima mundi* philosophy puts forth. The bee constructs its hive; the bird its nest; the ant its hill. From the material world we gain an idea of contrivance and design—of some intelligence or instinct, by whatever name we may call it, residing at the centre of the Universal Machine. We do not gain a higher idea than this. Mind, we are not speaking of the idea which, with the teaching of our natural feelings, we extract from the view of the physical world, but only of the idea which pure physical science imposes. That science does not draw any other necessary conclusion about its Deity than this one; it does not present us with an object of love and worship; it does not disclose to us a moral Deity.

All that view of the Deity and religious contemplativeness that takes its rise from this quarter betrays this great hiatus. The religious feeling that surveys nature simply, is weak. It does not give God a character. The sky is large, the sun is warm, the earth is green: the eye looks over the material expanse; a notion of a benevolent Deity arises; but the benevolence is the impersonation of the material expanse itself, rather than any really moral idea in us. It is too superficial a thing to constitute what we mean by character. A characterless Deity spreads over the scene an hypostasis of atmosphere, light, and warmth, nourishment, fertility, resources. How wonderful, harmonious, large, and pleasurable!—the round arch, the horizontal plain, the solar system and its orbits, the earth revolving on its axis; space, magnitude, motion!—this is the character of the Deity of pure philosophy. He takes his colour from the scene that represents him. The mind expands, and has an idea of a large pervading Being; but this Being has not a character.

But through the medium of man God appears as a very different Being. Nature is not a moral medium—man is. Man has an image of a character within him; he ascends through that to God, and clothes the Divine Being with those moral attributes that he finds belonging to himself. Those intense affections, those greatnesses, those admirations, that moral love and hatred, that he finds within himself, he transfers to God; he transfers them, not, of course, in their literal matter-of-fact form, as he himself has them, but in a transcendental supernatural and incomprehensible one. Still he makes God the perfection of that goodness that he sees within himself, and assigns to Him his own character. Through the *medium* of man, God is not an animation and a principle only, but a Personal Being, as much as a man is, and with a character like man's. There is an awe attaching to man. We see it in the way in which deep minds look into themselves to find out what they are ; in the trembling sensitiveness with which any new discoveries in themselves or others are hailed; the acuteness to traits, symptoms, intimations ; the interest with which they push into the *terra incognita* of their nature. Hence the admiration and curiosity with which we dive into the history of great men, and trace their thought and feeling, sensibility and emotion. Every trait is caught that comes up from the bottom, and shows what man is. A vast idea of some richness rolling at the bottom of human nature, some well of character indefinitely far down and deep, takes us with interest in the direction of any communications that speak to us of man. They are like oracles, like revelations. Man is the great object of curiosity. What he says and does, and how he feels, his secret impulses and movements within, chain the attention like a spell. The region of character has a mystery more overpowering than that of nature. What does the drama do but picture man ? What is the interest we take in the representations, greatness, and height, that we meet with there, but a symptom of that inborn reverence for man which, even in his fall, is ever directing us to him ? We want him to be unfolded to us; we want to get near him. The arcana of the substance and the viscera of a great nature draw us on, and we go through dark avenue and winding cavern. It is like following an awful rite and ceremonial; the drama is an Eleusinian mystery, and courts us with the charms of initiation and secret knowledge and enjoyment. It promises disclosure ; it hints, it alludes, it throws spells into the air ; it is usher and conductor to the unknown : it goes with pomp and procession, and solemn march and dirge, to the secret shrine ; it elevates and stimulates us with hopes, and whispers, and sensations that go and return, and half-sights, and approaches. What is all this about but man? Man is the hero of the tale, the centre of the plot. How great he is! is the music which murmurs in the ear along the way. And man is the image of God: that truth is seen in the distance all along; thither unconsciously tend the avenues of thought; and all we see is deepened by it. Every new revelation of man's greatness throws light on the Divine. We see God through it. His omnipotence, omnipresence, immateriality, and freedom from passion, cause Him to have this human character, in that incomprehensible and infinite way in which a Divine Being must; but thus translated and spiritualised it is His.

It may be said that human *character* is too solid, too human, too earthly-poetical, too dramatic a medium to the Deity; that we rather take only certain primary *ideas* of goodness with which our moral nature presents us, which primary ideas we then pursue, not in connection with their human manifestation, but upon their own abstract ground; and that a purely ideal path conducts us to the knowledge of the Divine character. But this is not true. We do not part company with human nature so early in this process; we never part company with it. It is human *character* or developed humanity, as distinguished from the mere elementary moral ideas which our nature acquaints us with, that conducts us to our notion of the Character Divine. We do not know what those ideas really are till we see them worked out and developed in actual states of mind and individual life. It is their dramatic issue, their ultimate appearance in the shape of character, that manifests what they are. The ideas are little more than superficies to our mind at first; it is this process which cubes them, deepens them into substance. To reason simply on the superficies is a Barmecidal proceeding. Take the idea of the moral element— love, and pursue it on the naked elementary ground; it appears to issue in that weak purism, the contradictory of justice, which some schools of philosophy have made their basis. But see it brought out in the shape of actual character, and you see it a rich, solid, complex quality, doing things which appear beforehand contradictory; tender, indignant, pitiful, severe.

The truth is, it was a superficies before; it is a solid thing now. The life actual consolidates the elementary idea, and puts it in its true and real meaning before us. Food must be eaten, air must be breathed, the moral idea must come into the experimental world to be understood. In the shape of high human character it does so. It becomes a reality then, a substance, and the mind embraces it. In morals we cannot develop mathematically, because we have not a stationary basis to proceed on; our moral perceptions themselves advance and change as we go along. Here we take hold of a hand; we look every moment to a model. That model is man himself. High humanity we cannot part a moment from in representing to ourselves the character Divine; and, in proportion as the mysteries of man's goodness unfold themselves to us, in that proportion do we obtain an insight into God's.

The Bible uses this medium. The Bible reveals to us, from first to last, the Divine character through the human. It throws itself (we say it reverentially) with the most unreserved freedom into this accommodation, and describes, with the boldness of inspiration, a transcendental human character in the incomprehensible Nature. It portrays a God with human feelings in their utmost intensity of love, pity, anger, jealousy; it describes those feelings as working with all that noble excess, to use the common term, that we encounter in them in high human characters. There are the same apparent contradictions, the same inexplicableness, mysteries, obscurities, the same flights, and what seem wildnesses and extravagances; the same unutterable piercing movements in the Divine character, that the human in high dramatic development assumes. A history is thus gone through; scenes pass before us, a plot unrolls; the Bible unfolds, like some awful drama, a Character—the Character of God. Throughout the great succession of movements which take place in it, from the world's fall to its restoration, one Chief Person comes out, and comes out Personally. Not a principle—a cause—an essence, but a Being Personal, with a character of His own as much as one of ourselves, and inspiring a love and fear analogous to that which human character does, is the Deity of the Bible.

"There is wrath gone out from the Lord; the plague is begun." "The Lord is a man of war, the Lord is His name." He kindles with jealousy; He deeply feels ingratitude. One awful sentence discloses to us what He felt when His creation forgot Him : " And it repented the Lord that He had made man, and it grieved Him at His heart." " The Lord long-suffering and of great mercy, forgiving iniquity and transgression, and by no means clearing the guilty, visiting the iniquity of the fathers upon the children unto the third and fourth generation"—such is the God of " Abraham, Isaac, and Jacob," the " God of Israel," the " God of their fathers,"—" who had done so great things in Egypt, wondrous works in the land of Ham, and fearful things by the Red Sea." A holy pride and boasting fills His people's hearts as they think of their God, and compare Him with the gods of the nations, the impersonations of nature and the elements that formed the divinities of the pagan world. An exultation, a disdain, an inexpressible scorn scatters such deities to the winds. Miserable blinded people, whose gods are no gods. Let them bow down to stocks and stones, and worship idols and phantoms. " These are your deities," they tell the heathen. " They have mouths, and speak not; eyes have they, but they see not. They have ears, and yet they hear not; neither is there any breath in their mouths. They that make them are like unto them, and so are all they that put their trust in them." But, " Praise the Lord, ye house of Israel; praise the Lord, ye house of Aaron; praise the Lord, ye house of Levi; ye that fear the Lord, praise the Lord." Not a law, not a delusion, not an impersonation is He, but a real and true God, whom we are not ashamed of; the natural Sovereign Lord of human hearts. He is not nature, but the Lord of nature; wielding her like an instrument, and making the whole world the mere dumb material engine of His own personal absolute will. All the motions in the firmament, all the wonders of the deep, sun, moon, and stars, the heavens, and the waters beneath the heavens, animal life in earth, and air, and sea; the very depth and occult unfathomable realms of nature, where she is most powerful, most mysterious, most originative,—not even is all this God; infinitely below all, and deeper than the very foundation, is the invisible absolute Being whose empire this is. "Praise the Lord upon earth, ye dragons, and all deeps, fire and hail, snow and vapour, wind and storm, fulfilling his word. Mountains and all hills, fruitful trees and all cedars, beasts and all cattle, worms and feathered fowls; kings of the earth and all people, princes and all judges of the world; young men and maidens, old men and children, praise the name of the Lord; for His name only is excellent, and His praise above heaven and earth."

Now pass away the types and adumbrations of the old Law; a deeper mystery arrives. God has hitherto only exhibited Himself under the human character, but now He takes upon Himself human nature. God the Son is born, lives, and dies upon earth. He takes our own whole and perfect nature upon Him, and reveals His character, not through a metaphorical but through an actual manhood. The human medium is now a mysterious reality instead of a symbolical expression, and humanity has an absolute basis in theology which it had not before. All the condescensions of the Old Testament are completed and consummated in the New, and the Incarnation substantiates all that human medium through which God was represented before. God is man: God's character is literally man's. Through all the compartments of a perfect humanity has God made human nature His own. Our humanity is now in a special way, in which it was not before, God's image and manifestation. All its high tendencies, aspirations, affections, now speak to us more than ever of Him; we see Him in them all: those nameless graces, depths, refinements, those ideas not caught, those hints that just come like far-off scents and are lost again—all take us to God. *Mite et cognatum est homini Deus:* God is, in a sense transcendental, incomprehensible, and divine, all that man is.

To the original idea of God as a moral Being are we referred throughout this whole view of Him. The question is, whether we are to regard Him as a moral Being or not. If we take the moral view of Him we are thrown at once into the whole human development of goodness as our exemplar. Not an elementary superficies of moral ideas, but high humanity itself worked out and consolidated, is our guide. Of the two great divisions of philosophy, the physical view reduces God to a mechanical principle; the moral raises Him into a Person and Character.

Two different modes of worship are suggested by these two views of the Deity, and the mediums of nature and man have their respective systems. The worship termed "rational," consisting in a calm consideration of the effects which have proceeded and proceed from the first great Cause, in a contemplation of the beauty and harmony of the universe, and in various intellectual and benevolent regards, form the worship of the physical deity. He does not require any other, and it would be an absurdity to give it him. A simply intellectual homage suits him; and in proportion to the extent to which such a view obtains, worship must become necessarily unimpassionate and unadoring. The medium of man, on the other hand, establishes a God adorable. His character through this medium is awing, prostrating, and jealous of His creature's devotion; it demands and is the legitimate object of the genuine affections of our nature. The symbolisms of earthly Headship, and the expressions of human love,—the folded hand, the bended knee, sighs, tears, and groans,—mingle with His worship, and man's whole nature energises in the act of adoration.

It is the diametrical contradictory to this latter view of a worship of God that Blanco White brings accurately out and systematises. He utterly banishes the human from God and His worship. This particular insinuation of the element of human feeling into the worship of the Deity is what he puts his absolute veto on. He pursues it into its most refined and spiritual seats, uncovers its most intellectual guises, and ejects it. He detects its real "grossness" and materiality, in spite of its illusions, and will not allow the adulteration of a purely mental worship. His technical term for it is the $\psi\nu\chi\iota\kappa\acute{o}\nu$, the "sensuous." "External religion addressed to the senses, and using the body as an instrument of devotion," he says, is "what St. Paul calls carnal—*i.e.* confined chiefly to the flesh, the body, or animal part of man, and to the ψυχή, the seat of sentiment or feeling." All "flattering devotion," as he calls it, "all that method of praying and addressing the Deity which supposes Him to have all the habits and feelings of an Oriental despot, who likes to hear the people approaching Him call themselves Dogs, dead Dogs,"—all impassioned religion, whether of fear or love, he puts under the head of ψυχικόν, or "sensuous." The "Imagination," as the great *fautor* of this spurious worship, he rigorously excludes. "Is Imagination," he asks, "to be banished from practical religion?" And he answers—

"It is my conviction that the *spirituality* of our Religion depends on that exclusion. Are we to banish *feeling?* All feeling arising from imagination should also be excluded. I am not an enemy to the sublime emotions which arise in our bosom at the contemplation of ourselves and this wonderful universe with reference to God. They constitute the most blessed moments of a rational existence. But I consider the Imaginative Faculty—that faculty which clothes every idea in matter—as the arch-enemy of those truly spiritual enjoyments. Cleanse the internal sanctuary from idols if the Deity is to take his seat within it."

The whole system of external worship that results from this "sensuous element" is termed θρησκεία, "service," and is altogether put aside, and Christianity is pronounced to be neither a "science" nor an "occupation."

The reason he states plainly in his own fashion. The "sensuous" worship, or "*service*," he says, implies a Deity with something human about Him—a Deity in some way "embodied," "localised, circumscribed," to the mind. All this "refined idolatry," this "devotional restlessness," that he so much objects to, supposes, he says, such an object. "The idea of service to a master *represented as a human being, must* give real uneasiness to the sensitive mind;" and of this uneasiness "a real θρησκεία (service), in which the zealous servant must always be in doubt whether he has done enough," is the natural result. But the original hypothesis overthrown, the result is overthrown too; and therefore this service he altogether repudiates as inappropriate, and meant for a wholly different Being from what God really is.

"Service," "Religion," "Devotion,"—he pronounces a clear and dogmatic condemnation upon them all :—

"Is Christianity properly called the Christian RELIGION ? Is the Gospel a RELIGION ? We do not find any word equivalent to *Religion* applied to the Gospel in the New Testament. Appellations of that kind originated with the Christian writers as soon as the true character of Christianity began to be obscured in the minds of those who professed it. Εὐσέβεια, θρησκεία, would be ill adapted to a revelation, the very object of which is to remove all notions of means by which men may *worship well and properly*, or become θρῆσκαι, according to a regular method. The Christian θρησκεία is benevolence and purity, according to the Apostle James ; and true worshippers, according to Christ, are those who worship *in spirit*—*i.e.* mentally, not according to *worldly* or fleshly elements (directions, instructions)—and *in truth*—*i.e.* without symbols and emblems. In my opinion, Christ came to liberate mankind from *all religion*, that great source of the worst human evils ;

'Tantum Religio potuit suadere malorum!'

All men devoted to *a religion* are slaves, servants, θρῆσκαι. Christ came to make us *free*."

We thus come round to the human medium—to the Bible-revelation of God, as the one great source of the Christian world's superstition ; and the argument of Blanco White rolls back its deadening weight on the doctrine of the Incarnation. Upon human nature, quite independent of any sculptured representation of the human form—upon human nature, as simply conjoined with God and believed by the worshipper—upon human nature itself, singly and alone, he fixes as that circumscribing, discolouring medium of the Deity, which constitutes essentially the Christian idolatry.

"A religion which presents an *incarnate* God as the supreme object of worship is essentially idolatrous. Idolatry does not consist in worshipping *material figures*, but in reducing the Deity to an object of the *imagination*. If God is made Man, it signifies little whether you worship the *image* within you, or whether you represent that image in wood or stone, according to the Roman Catholic practice. It is childish to make the evil of idolatry consist in the materiality of the idol; that evil arises from the inevitable degradation of the Deity when conceived as *a Man*. All spirituality disappears in that case ; and whatever you do, the association of human passions and feelings with the idea of God (an association to which we have a most decided natural tendency) will take place in a higher or lower degree, according to the power or weakness of every individual mind."

"The Deity conceived as *a man*," and worshipped, not in a dead image, His likeness, but in a living soul and body, His assumed nature, is an energetic living idolatry to him, and the most pernicious one of the two. A mere image does not do what the Incarnation does. It may allow the mind to throw it aside, and wander from it into the world of pure intelligence and formlessness: the Incarnation never can.

Effacing real character from the Deity, however, and sentiment and feeling from worship, Blanco White's system is not atheism, his deity not simply mechanical. His is a formless *anima mundi* theo-philanthropism. Between the medium of nature on the one hand, and of man on the other, a diluted physical ground exists, which borrows from the moral world an elementary benevolence, and colours the mechanical principle with it. A characterless benevolence just preserves the airy universal soul from being a mere physical influence. His effusions to this deity have feeling and power, warmth and beauty in them: sometimes a small catholic surviving element seems to be melting in the wide vacuity; and Deism has in him an eloquent mouthpiece, that expresses all the sentiment and idealism of old philosophy.

"I had opened my window, and seated myself in view of the heavens, to collect my mind for the daily tribute of adoration to my Maker. The mere act of directing my mind to Him in the presence of His glorious works filled me with an inexpressible, though tranquil and rational, delight. I said to myself, What a glorious gift conscious existence is in itself! Heaven must essentially consist in the absence of whatever disturbs the quiet enjoyment of that consciousness—in the intimate conviction of the *presence of God*. . . . Oh thou great Being, who from the dawn of my reason didst reveal Thyself within my heart, to Thee I may venture to speak humbly but freely in the sanctuary of my soul. It is *there* that I obtain the nearest approach to Thee; there alone I know Thee face to face, not in the figure of a man, not in the coloured shadows of Imagination, but in the truly spiritual character of Knowledge, Power, Will, Consciousness."

But a grotesque jar goes on even here. Every other sentence in his prayers is a protest against the last being supposed to be meant in an orthodox sense. He is afraid even of philosophy. He tells his deity that he is not to suppose himself worshipped in the strict sense of the word, and that he abstains "from addressing him in complimentary language." He is perpetually lecturing him on the subject of orthodoxy, creeds, and established churches. He tells him, at least once in every prayer, how exceedingly little he believes about him. "It is long since I have renounced the (to me) superstitious practice of falling on my knees and formally addressing to Thee either praises or petitions. I am, however, uninterruptedly in a praying state."

Nature, however, from her capricious wayward depths, seems sometimes to utter oracles which she cannot help; and a sort of wild Christianity, the conception of a mind that seems to be working upwards from infidelity, meets us. Are such gleams the forced expressions of a rebellious nature, and torn out of a man in spite of himself, or do they show religion still surviving? Even Saul prophesied, and was seized with a spirit that he could not resist. What is Blanco White's view, when he says, "If abstract argument could so bewilder me as to lead my understanding to deny a Creator, I should still kneel before Christ, as the true God of the moral world"? He seems to be longing for the doctrine of the Incarnation sometimes. One wonders he does not see it: he gropes like a blind man, and seems just on its edge. "I want to feel *sympathy*," he says, "with God," and adds, "How blasphemous this will sound to some! how they will start!" Then he is off again, and makes the language which might be truly noble, pantheistic. His mind has vivid breaks of truth upon it, like gleams from a dark-lantern, or phosphoric lights; but its solid course goes on, and makes illusions of them.

This course of speculation inevitably led to another; the question how he was to deal with the Bible came on. What was he to do with it? From first to last it stood in his way. It put forth one view of God, he another; it had one system of worship, and he another. As it stood, it was a vast erection exactly antagonistic to his own. How were the two to be brought into harmony? Two courses are open in such a case. The more natural one is, that of giving up the Bible altogether, and leaving the philosophical area free. This is the summary method that a Hume and a Voltaire would take, and it is less revolting than the one Blanco White takes: he undertakes the task of remodelling the Bible. The process is a miserable one indeed. A summary effacement does the act in an instant; this prolongs it and destroys piecemeal. Blanco White haggles at the Bible; tears, mangles, and dissects, with a minute and torturing impiety, the holy victim. He puts himself into the body, and cuts out bit by bit, till he leaves nothing but a case; and only does the same that other infidels have done in a more shocking way. Even the very notice of such contact with Holy Writ seems to carry a contagion of profaneness, and it is painful to be forced upon it.

First in order, in such a speculation as this, stands, of course, the fundamental question of the Infallibility of Scripture. It is one on which Blanco White has long ago made up his mind. Even the days of his orthodoxy decided that "the mighty theory which makes the Bible infallible" was simply a phantom, an unreality. The Bible is not an oracle, is his dictum. "God never intended to dwell miraculously among men as in a BOOK, as in an oracle, from which we might obtain infallible answers. . . ." Such an oracular infallibility must have an infallible medium through which it came. If the medium is uncertain, then that of which it is the medium is uncertain too. Of the communications which are made in the Bible, *language* is the medium—a necessarily fallible one: it follows that the issue cannot be infallibility. "If the language which conveys inspired thoughts is human, infallibility is at an end."

This argument may be valid, taking the Bible to stand entirely by itself. Of course the answer to it is, that the Bible does not stand by itself; that a general current tradition, going up to the times of the Apostles, asserts that, as a matter of fact, the Christian doctrine, as they delivered it,—the real sense of Scripture—was such and such. The fact of that doctrine rests upon historical grounds of exactly the same certainty that other acknowledged facts in history do. One general tradition over the world speaks historically to it; the historian looks in vain for any similar tradition the other way. In the year 325, out of a general council of all the Bishops of the Catholic Church, all except thirteen declared for a particular interpretation of Scripture, as having been, as a matter of fact, always held in their churches; the remaining thirteen, for the most part, not meeting that fact by a counter one, but only arguing against it on grounds of logic. A fact supported by one general line of testimony, and not contradicted by another, is what is called historically certain.

Exposed and unguarded, however, in Blanco White's system, the Bible now yields, step by step, to the intellect's inroad. A human medium of revelation is discovered to be subject, not only to uncertainty, but to corruption. The stream of truth is discoloured in its passage from the fountain-head, and gathers all kinds of turbid and base matter. What has to pass through the distorting human mind, with all its feelings and passions, cannot be taken for granted as that pure effluence from the Divine Mind that persons think it to be. It mingles instantly with a whole mass of popular ideas and prejudices of the day, and the Bible becomes a confused heap, to Blanco White's eye, of good, bad, and indifferent; a small element of Divine truth every now and then just appearing occasionally amid a world of legendary matter and supernaturalism. "The massacre of the Priests of Baal, the horrible destruction of the last remnant of the family of Saul, never failed to fill him with horror." The miracles of Elisha revolted him; the "history of Samson exhausted his patience," and that of "Balaam appeared to him a mockery of the Deity." The one cemented whole now exists no longer: whole masses of literal interpolation appear; genuineness gives way; and the composition of the Bible breaks up, and crumbles into pieces.

At one speculative touch, thus fell the whole system of Biblical religion. It had no basis. The "mighty theory" was gone. This is a tender and an awful subject to us at this day. It suggests wide consequences and connections. On what does the popular religion of the present day rest? On the

Bible, and the Bible alone, we are instantly answered: the Bible, without note or comment; without tradition or the Church. But on what does the authority of the Bible itself rest? is then asked; and no answer is given. There the matter stops. A dead stagnation locks up every avenue of rational thought. Persons have no answer, and do not see that one is wanted;—they see a printed book: that book is the Bible. That volume is inspired, is infallible. Did the Church tell you that? No; I never asked her. Then who told you it? No one. Then why do you believe it? There is no answer. We should be the very last to insist on any formal logical reason for a belief where there was any latent unconscious ground upon which the mind could be supposed to go. We have no doubt many and many minds among us have this ground here. But on what ground those who make the denial of Church authority the very distinctive principle of their religion, and whose distinctive principle thus destroys the only channel of evidence that exists for the canon of Scripture, —on what ground they receive and implicitly adopt that canon we do not understand.

The truth must be stated: there is a belief in the Bible which is a "Bibliolatry," and of which nothing can be said, but that it rests deadly in a mere book, which it has no reason (for its own part) to think comes from God. It is an artificial, material, fixed and set, negative belief without life in it. It is not belief, it is unbelief. It stands like a wooden thing, without nerve or sinew or pulse to support it by its mere weight. It does not bend, or open out, or mingle with the Bible: it looks *at* it; it sees a book simply; it stands on the outside. It exists by inertia, by indifference, by negation; action is madness to it; motion is death. Would that it were a solid hearty belief, however illogical. But what does it do? Instead of imbibing the supernatural from the Bible, it uses it for the very reverse purpose, for locking up the supernatural in it. The Bible becomes not so much a revelation of the world invisible, as its prison. Within a close wall of circumvallation the miraculous influences work: there they are kept and not allowed for an instant to come outside: at the first symptom of egress a jealous eye drives them in again, and fixes them in their enclosure. There the supernatural is safe; there it does no harm; it interferes with nobody. The past is over and gone; we do not see it, feel it, hear it: it does not disturb us; it did exist once, but it does not exist now; *we* exist now: there is no interference; a past miraculous can be admitted. Is it felt as a difficulty, that if mysterious supernatural agencies went on once, they may do so again?—a convenient wall of distinction is at hand in the Bible to meet it. That enclosure receives all the supernatural that ever was or is, will or can be : all is disposed of, shut up, got out of the way. It is the one receptacle of all that need trouble and annoy the human mind; and, relieved from the fear of living antagonists, the intellect is comfortable. How little does it signify that something once took place! How little do we feel the past! On flows Time, the great unrealiser, and we are in his stream. The world has floated down and down, lower and lower, and left the supernatural behind it; Eden, Babel, Egypt, Sodom and Gomorrha, Goshen, Canaan, Jerusalem, Babylon, the Wilderness, Nazareth, Capernaum, the localities of the miraculous, it has long passed by; the age presents an order of nature, a system of policy, a machinery of its own to our eye; and this is our truth; and we say, Since the fathers fell asleep, all things continue as they were from the beginning. We pass by the burning bush and see it not. The mysteries, miracles, lives of prophets and saints—how legendary would they be to many, if they but one single moment realised what they are! But all simply passes by them. They do not enter into the contents of the book *positively*. The Bible stands for the negation of the Church rather than for what it is itself, and has an empty contrasted and not a *per se* existence. They do enter into it sufficiently to reject it. The blood does not come from a dead belief. Numbness is calm. Yet what an edge does such a faith rest on! The state of mind of a large number in this country, the dead-lock of mute acquiescence, which keeps a mass of energetic antagonism to the supernatural adhering to the Bible, is an extraordinary phenomenon in religion, equal to any which any age has produced.

One thought on this subject. This Bible is read every day, Old Testament and New, morning and evening, in our churches. The Church receives with humble faith all these, that the froward reason calls, legends; and recites them in regular liturgical order, to her children, as the simple truth, the history of what has been upon this earth. Blessed privilege to hear them! Amidst a jarring world those disclosures of the supernatural strike deep into the heart that wants to realise God's presence. There He is: He lives and moves as a real God; He loves and concerns Himself for His creatures; He breaks forth from the veil of nature, and uncovers Himself to us. Every day we hear those Gospels which tell us what He did, when He lived upon this earth; His compassions, and divine sweetness, His humility and majesty supreme in mortal shape. What untold depths lie in those simple accounts which the Evangelists have written, and in those acts of pity to the blind, the lame, the deaf, the dumb, the sick, the dying, and the dead! What an image do they raise in our mind of our Blessed Lord in His earthly form! Great privilege, indeed, to hear these holy narratives read! May they go on, forming and deepening an image of Him, which will stay in us and never go away. That sword of the Spirit, may it drive away the rationalistic shapes that throng and threaten at the Church's door, and mock her worship as it goes on! Would our popular religion, of itself, take up those parts of Scripture that the Church obliges it to use? It would not. It does not. It picks its favourite epistle, and explains and spiritualises upon it; but in the oblique process the Bible field, as a whole, is forgot; and human inference and feeling take their one-sided course, and spin their own webs far away from Holy ground.

To this mixed confused mass, in his opinion, of truth and falsehood, fact and fable, Blanco White applies his canon of restoration. He talks of the plan just as he would of restoring the Hesiodic or Orphean fragments:—

"The original picture must be restored, as artists of genius restore an ancient statue, by means of its incomplete fragments; the work is not difficult, provided the love of the miraculous does not disturb the moral sense. Would you wish to have a test by which to try the genuineness of passages in the New Testament? Observe the consequences which they have produced, taken as rules of conduct, especially as rules of *perfection*. All those which, in the most direct manner, have been the origin of monachism—in a more general term, of *asceticism*—must be excluded."

This is his canon. The rational element, wherever seen, is carefully to be separated from the superstitious, and the pure portions, thus cleared, to be collected together and formed into shape. He instances such passages as the one against making vain repetitions; not used by divines, he says, because they are rational; but which are *the* true, genuine, original Bible in his opinion, and which should be extracted by the critical restorer. The New Testament comes quite as much as the Old under this process. You cannot reconcile, he says, the Gospel morality of almsgiving with the discoveries of political economy. Dr. Whately endeavours to do this, but fails. As the Gospel books stand, they teach a completely different duty from what the demonstrations of that science allow; and it is glossing over things to try to reconcile the two. A restored Gospel, on his principle, can alone meet the difficulty. It can alone meet the difficulty again of the doctrine of Counsels of Perfection, which, with all its developments, may be gathered straight from the Gospel as it at present stands. "The Messianite expectations of a numerous Jewish religious party, that seem to have existed since the Maccabees," which have mingled with the simple account of the events of our Lord's life, may be separated from the Gospels; and Stoicism, "the main source of the Pauline philosophical fragments," from the Epistles. But we really cannot extract more of these shocking dicta.

Isolated and alone, occupying a ground far in advance even of the sect he has joined, and looking back on Socinianism in the distance as a system faintly struggling, at an immense interval, to follow him; the rest of the world not yet seen even on the verge of his horizon; with wide shoreless space before him, a Deity of air, a worship of reason, a Bible in process of discovery, Blanco White can only refresh his philosophical solitude by a hollow prospect of some large illumination yet distant, some indefinite advance of the human intelligence, and disenthralment of the world yet to come. "When the light of philosophy shall have spread itself sufficiently among those whom Providence appoints everywhere to take the *rational* lead—when the painful, and it may be horrible, destruction of existing obstacles shall have cleared the way for the operations of rational influences, then will the change be." But the prospect is hardly real enough to be consoling; the distant scene is felt, in the very act of reposing on it, to be illusory; and the phantom throws back a sickly pallor on a lone philosophy. He has not real hope. He does not really think the world ever will be right, that religion ever will come round to him; he is a fragment amid overpowering brooding systems that have spread over the earth. Strange and melancholy is the idea that atomises truth; strange to come to such a pass, as really to think that truth narrows and narrows till it becomes a mere point amid a universe of error; and that the final issue of things is against it. It is an upsetting of the whole moral basis of things; and yet philosophy, in some of its moods, seems able to face the thought that, truth being real *bonâ fide* truth, it is quite compatible with its being so that it should never succeed; that truth may pine and die, and yet be truth; and error flourish in eternal universality, and yet be error. This is the real *feeling* in some infidel minds; they will not acknowledge it; they have a theoretical reign of truth before them, but they do not really expect it. Seeing the whole world in error, according to their view, their religion is defective in the only quality that could bear them up against such strong existing phenomena; they have not faith enough, even in their own system, to weigh any indefinite development of it against the matter of fact present, and the whole counter system of established opinion. Buoyed up by a sanguine temperament in some, infidel philosophy is more commonly a hopeless one. It sees human nature against it; it despairs of the mass. It feels itself an alien in God's world, yet it holds up. An envy, shall we call it, that feels its own hollowness, and sticks to it; a deep, subtle contradiction; an internal mystery of unbelief, that enables them really to disbelieve, and know what they disbelieve to be true, is the slavery of the proud. The antagonistic will sees what is Divine, but hatred repels the contact of belief, and a hopeless struggle against Divine Fate consumes them. An obstinate acquiescence in its own uncatholic nature is the resignation of their philosophy. Despair is the devotion of unbelief, its ethical state of mind, the counter and rival one of Christian hope.

We do not forget—it would be unfeeling to do so—the real natural causes of dejection which pressed on Blanco White; but can we mistake his tone?

"January 1st, 1838. I have a Hope that this will be the last Year of my Life: to wish it otherwise would be extreme imbecility. I cannot expect any sound Improvement in my Health. The Slow Fever which has uninterruptedly been upon me for more than twenty Days must proceed from a total derangement, which, though it will not kill me, must increase my general Debility and Helplessness. Every Year must deprive me of some remnant of Activity. My Solitude, combined with the Necessity of being idle, renders my Life intolerable. All Hopes of Usefulness have died in me. Bitter indeed has been the Disappointment which the clear Perception of some men's Minds—men in whose Love of Truth I trusted, has brought to my Soul. All have made their Peace, at least a long Truce, with established Error. They are miserably afraid of following it up to its Sources. What chance then is left for positive Truth? None on the part of Man's honest Exertions. The Course of Things will probably shake these monstrous Structures of Superstition by indirect means; but till that Crisis arrives, even the most clear-sighted men are agreed to let them be undisturbed, except when some external Advantage may be snatched out of the Hands of those who manage the Interest of the grand Delusion, by Law established.

"Yet, in spite of this Despondency, I do not wish that my own course had been different. I have laboured in vain, but I have laboured in the Field of Truth: my Wages have been Pain and Misery, but I love them infinitely above the Wages of Dishonesty. I thank God that I have been able to endure so much for that which *is* and *must* be eternally true. Let the Grave close over my Sufferings, my Weaknesses, my involuntary Errors. I feel that Death will give a sort of Consecration to my imperfect Efforts. This is a most consoling Anticipation."

"I can hardly control my impatience. . . . Sooner or later, the end cannot be distant. . . . How can I convey in words the utter misery into which I am sinking deeper every day! Nothing but a firm persuasion that self-destruction would be criminal in me prevents my putting it into execution. But my will is fixed: I am determined not to do wrong. In this horrible distress I still wish to conform to the will of God; but it seems to me impossible to continue much longer in this state, preserving my Reason. I have scarcely any power of self-government against this despondency."

Accompanying his intense adherence to his own isolation, we see in the unbeliever a tendency to envy the social belief of the world around him. Abandoning real dignity and self-repose, solitary truth bites venomously at gregarious error. A kind of jealousy arises at the very sight of communion, extension, systems that keep people together; and the stupidity and quiet of the large unconscious masses excites positive spleen; a feeling of which not supposed wrong opinion simply, but that opinion as social and uniting, is the object.

"Every Church Establishment is a mighty Joint-Stock Company of error and deception, which invites subscriptions to the common fund, from the largest amount of hypocrisy to the lowest penny and farthing contribution of acquiescence in what the conscience does not entirely approve. Yet these last contributors form the true strength of the Establishment."

The splenetic force of his language is quite miserable:—

"There is a reality in English bigotry as keen, as cutting as the north-east wind, which blasts the young spring at this moment. The *practical* temper of the nation is seen here most clearly." "The names of the Corpus Committee at Oxford compound such a horrible idea in my mind that I can hardly endure it; it is made up of mental light rendered, by mixture, so lurid and hellish that it might be conceived to be of the same kind as that which some divines think was set as a mark on Cain's forehead."

It is remarkable how all company as such, how the Established Church as such, jaundices him. All social established religion is an eyesore; the fact of its existence an insult to him, which he feels as a reproach upon his own tenuity, and retorts upon with sarcasm.

Some sort of union in this way, even division itself desiderates; the principle feels itself so much at a disadvantage without it. Blanco White, with his peculiar natural love of sympathy and connection, wants to bring those of his persuasion under some head and name. They should call themselves something.

"I wish that the few Christians who profess the Gospel in perfect independence of a human confession of faith or creed,—that is, without a fixed standard of scriptural interpretation, settled at some particular period according to the notions of certain individuals,—would agree to call themselves by some name unconnected with any disputed point of interpretation. I have no other objection to the name *Unitarian* but that it is *dogmatic*. . . . If the scholastic system were better known, anti-scholastic Christians might be a very good denomination for those who are now called Unitarians and Rationalists. I wish some word expressing individual independence from any self-constituted interpreter of the Scriptures could be found. Perhaps *anti-sectarian* (understanding the word sect in its original meaning, of a philosophical system or school) or *un-articled* Christians would do. The latter has a smack of vulgarity,—but it would be understood by John Bull."

He is a proselytiser, and one convert is a treasure,—some one to agree with. His solitude makes him even rapacious, and almost persecuting, when a convert is the prey. The letters to a "Miss L.," with a prying pertinacity pursue an amiable female mind from the last holds of her old religion. She clings to a shred, and he takes it from her. "You appear to me to cling too much to the acknowledgment of certain usual assertions respecting Christ. . . . You are afraid. . . . Give up these old prejudices. . . . Follow God into the sanctuary of your heart. . . . Be on your guard against the fear of religion being too simple. . . . What I recommend requires a most painful effort." Make that,—you are yet only half-way. You have vestiges of the "devotional" spirit about you. Denude yourself; throw off old notions; accept my deity. Half-afraid and hesitating, and still looking back with longing, lingering eye on her old religious feeling, he drags her on to take the plunge; and weakness, in search of companionship, is eager, bold, and ravenous.

A latent consciousness of moral inferiority is another stimulant to the sarcasm and bitterness of infidelity. The jealousy of a felt superior appears in the way in which such minds talk of high religious attainment. How the mere fact seems to sting them, that there is such a thing! They want to get rid of it. They will invent any name to fasten on it, and cover it to their own and other eyes. And when they can really pick any hole in such characters, and unsubstantiate them, what a pleasure it is! How will they, on the mere mention of goodness, slip in the insinuation, the innuendo! What cleverness they show in doing this! This is weakness. An animal bites because he is afraid of you, not from too much spirit. Sadly infected with this temper is Blanco White. There is no mistaking the sarcastic pleasure which he feels as he alludes to "that *extinct* generation of men whom an impending mitre drove with affright into the fastnesses of the desert." Now, what is it he says here? He *knows* there was once this generation of men; that pains him: he sees it almost extinct; that pleases him. He is really pleased, that is, at thinking that men are worse than they were, and that there is not so much good in the world as there was. "Charity rejoiceth not in iniquity, but rejoiceth in the truth." This does just the reverse. Throughout Blanco White's writing this tone runs. Such profaneness, blasphemy, bitter scoffs at saintliness, as pervade the *Evidence against Catholicism,* and other writings, what do they betray but this? He joins the common herd of infidels. Degradation, indeed, of man, grovelling and cleaving to the ground from whence he came! he will not be raised and lifted up, and only sees the held-out hand to relapse more proudly into his own fallen nature again. Earth and clay are in love with themselves; persist in being themselves, and nothing more; and rot in their own grave with satisfaction. "Now we are going," they say, "falling." "Slow and sure is the progress of the world downward. Nature is retracing her aspirant steps, and getting wise and material again. Light is fading; virtue is a dream; darkness is growing; elasticity is spent; earth is settling; the Fall is completing; receive us, O lowest residuum of matter, into thy impenetrable hold, where dust has finally parted with spirit, and is solid and eternal. Shut out for evermore the realms of sky and air; they are illusions; we see through them. We have got into our cave; the mouth is stopped, the stone is over us." An image of the world in their minds, soberly lowering, systematically subsiding into itself, a slow, sure, even fall, which takes all down together, is their miserable solace.

On the subject of the immortality of the soul it is the same. One might suppose that mere philosophical dignity would make them stand up for their own nature, and save it from being an evanescence. But the horrible disease which preys on them, the unnatural appetite for descent, makes them suicidal. Their nature likes destroying herself. A demoniacal refinement of philosophy takes them to a more inaccessible theory of annihilation than the ordinary one, and makes them separate the soul's immortality from its identity: live on, it says, but do not be so sure that you will be the *same* soul. As if it were not the bitterest mockery to say that you are immortal—I mean not you, but some other being. The soul clings with inspired strength to the fundamental abyssal rock of its own personality; to its own identity, as the very essence of its immortality; to the one eternal line of self that penetrates the future infinite. Take that away, and you undo her; and life becomes a galvanic action or meteoric show. Driven to extremities, philosophy becomes treacherous, insidious, and assassin-like. It tampers and plays with the vitality that it kills. A subtle glassy absorption, under the name of a future life, sucks in evanescences; being is inveigled, and lost in a solution of identities; and an immortal annihilation calls itself immortality. The hollow levity of such views is marvellous. Sir James Mackintosh it is, we believe, who makes immortality lie in succession of beings; as if it were quite an indifferent thing so long as there *was* life, that it should be the same life. Blanco White has passages in much the same spirit. He makes the personality of souls the function of the state they are in. The state goes: the personality goes with it: a succeeding state rearranges and redistributes it.

"Were it shown," he says, "that Personality consists in the Limitation, the shaping of the inferior Soul by the circumstances of each person's condition in this life, I believe that all the difficulties against the Immortality of the Soul would vanish. They arise, in my opinion, from making the word *Soul* express a multitude of things, which cannot be reduced to one predicament. This is, however, the effect of the Imagination—that treacherous faculty to which men surrender themselves, in all subjects connected with religion. P. P., Clerk of the Parish, must be the identical individual throughout Eternity : the same as every one of his Neighbours wishes; against which wishes there are difficulties which every reflecting man must find insuperable. 'Alas! You will take away our Personality.' And who will mourn for the loss? Some distressed *Impersonal!*"

Nec miserum fieri, qui non est, posse; it is the argument with which Lucretius tries to persuade men into the idea of the soul's non-existence after death.

Unhappy man! His mental miseries, his doubts, fluctuations, hopelessness, bodily disease, make death at last welcome. He prepares for it with the fortitude of an ancient philosopher. He thinks the position of a human being waiting calmly for his translation into the unknown state a dignified one. But philosophy cannot regain now the same tranquillising power that once it had. It does not protect the mind that apostatises to it. He cannot sustain the effort, and gives way; and his death, as his life, is a tragedy. "The agony of despair threatens him."

"The only check to it is a deeply felt horror of such a state of mind." He recovers and inspirits himself. " I am weak, and therefore my feelings overpower me. I have contributed my mite to the liberty of mankind. It is cast into God's treasury. I stand upon a rock. God's providence is carried on by the struggles of reason against the passions. I have no doubts. I came from God, and I go to Him." Pain then overpowers him, and he cries out to God with the voice of nature, checking it immediately with the rationalistic protest—" Oh my God! oh my God!—But I know Thou dost not overlook any of Thy creatures. Thou dost not overlook me. So much torture—to kill a worm! Have mercy upon me, oh God! Have mercy upon me! I cry to Thee, knowing I cannot alter Thy ways. I cannot if I would—and I *would not* if I could. If a word could remove these sufferings, I would not utter it!" " The night after, to several members of the family collected around him, he spoke of the state of his mind in what he knew to be the presence of death, and, aware that the power of distinct utterance was failing, added—'When the hour shall come, let it be said once for all, my soul will be concentrated in the feeling, "My God, into Thy hands I commend my spirit." God to me is Jesus; and Jesus is God—of course not in the sense of Divines.' He remained some days longer, chiefly in the state of one falling asleep, until the morning of the 20th, when he awoke up, and with a firm voice and great solemnity of manner, spoke only these words —'Now I die.' He sat as one in the attitude of expectation, and about two hours afterwards—it was as he had said."

Blanco White is of the French school of infidelity. He has not the calmness and weight of the English school. He takes more after Rousseau than Hume, and more after Voltaire than Gibbon. He impersonates acute, fastidious, tender, and refined nature's scornfulness, that sees in the devotional sentiment a rival to itself, and hates it. Higher perceptions, and a sense of duty and conscience, make him what these infidels were not; but an internal grossness, so often the plague-spot of the refined literary man, comes out in him. Rich in affection, ardour, and sweetness—nature in herself breeds horrible moral disease. There is no use trying to make her out; she is a consistent inconsistency; why should she be anything else? Blanco White pleases; Blanco White disgusts. Miserable and shocking as he is, he has, and retains to the last, the amiable phenomena and sensibilities in a refined form. This is a mystery. We know not what fine feelings are, and what they depend on. We do not know how far the goodness which we have now has moral root in us, or is the physical phase and fluid of the mind *pro tempore.* A day will come which will manifest what every one is; but, doubtless, many a man is better here than he deserves to be. Whatever charm of character accompanies evil, it has by a dispensation; it is in a particular *state* now, and partakes of the benefits which attach to that state; it enjoys the sweet influences flowing from God's spiritual bounty through the world of mind. The question is, whether it appropriates these influences, and unites them to a moral basis within itself. If it does not, the soul's meteoric borrowed atmosphere may disappear in a moment, when God wills, and leave essential evil in naked forlorn ugliness. We neither apply this remark to

Blanco White, nor withhold it: it is a caution which his and many other characters lead us to.

As a philosopher, a rejection of mediums is his system. He had it in the germ in early life; he unfolded it systematically in his later. His believing Roman Catholic life intoned his philosophical. Some forms of mind do not tolerate mediums in religion. They demand truth, bare of all introductions, expositions, and economies. They want the naked soul of truth; they penetrate through form and exterior to pluck it out; they are impatient of interval as such; they put aside all covering to get at the core, the solid divine particle itself, of truth. Dogmas are husks, creeds are distortions. Everything is seen through; nothing is final: truth is always ulterior; it is contrasted to the form in which it is presented to them, instead of being apprehended in that form. They want a truth bodiless: they cannot have it. Nothing is without a body here; and truth is not. Resolve to have it without body, a hopeless work is before you. Can you separate man from his body? The man, soul and body, is one; and the latter is part of himself; his soul mingles with the minutest veins and arteries. Pierce and penetrate as you may to formless truth, it flees from you. The sceptic rejects the outside; he peels off coating after coating to come to something solid: he never finds the solid particle; everything is coating to him: he peels away and away, and throws aside, and still finds nothing but peeling. He will not look at doctrine through the Church medium; he will not look at God through the human. All those creeds and statements, that whole body of teaching, the product of the Church's collected intelligence, the simply expositional and interpretative form of the original revealed truth, as it came from the Apostles' mouths—all this is thrown aside because it is a medium. The mind of the Church is considered not a mean to truth, but as an obstruction in its way. The bare ulterior thing, behind all, beyond all, residing beyond the whole system of the human mind, beyond the very first operation of Christian intelligence, is aimed at; and the inquiry presses on to an ever-retreating fountain-head. In the same way, the human character is no exponent of the Divine. The human medium—that body of feelings, affections, sentiment, desire, that we are composed of,—is thought simply to corrupt our idea of God; to be an obstruction which the philosophical mind must especially clear away in forming its idea of Him. A purer Deity than that seen through our gross nature, and worshipped with its feelings, is aimed at—an essence, a First Cause, an intellectual permeance, an *anima mundi*. It wants a God clear of the human medium, a truth clear of the dogmatic; and it objects as much to the very expositions of moral nature as it does to those of the Church. It will have no expounder, no medium, no voice speaking to it. It places itself outside of system and fact, and resides in the primordial nakedness of the vacuum beyond the moon.

" Every spirit that confesseth not that Jesus Christ is come in the flesh is not of God, but is that spirit of Antichrist, whereof ye have heard that it should come; and even now already is it in the world." Most wonderful prophecy and surpassing test! Man will believe anything rather than this. That mysterious line of intimate conjunction where God becomes man and unites Himself to our nature is where men stumble. Fallen man dreads so near a neighbourhood, and trembles at the doctrine which makes the Divine Person become connatural with him. He will worship Him beyond the stars willingly, but not on earth below—not in the flesh. There he feels God invading him on his own territory, and appropriating nature, feeling, human affection to Himself; he feels himself occupied, seized by an all-powerful force, and a metamorphosis proceeding. He resists it. He says to God, " Enjoy Thy kingdom, and let me enjoy mine; be Thyself God only, and let me be pure earthly man. I will worship you in your own Divine sphere, but my nature and feeling you cannot have; they are my own, my especial enjoyment; the world is the congenial object of them; you cannot have them without stripping me of myself." "Grant the Incarnation," says Blanco White, "and the whole devotional system of life follows from it." He was miserably consistent, and proud Nature's jealousy and scorn of the life devotional grew into a denial of the Incarnation and simple Deism.

Throughout this life there is one feature that we can never forget; it haunts us like a perplexity and a mystery; it is a difficulty more apparent than real; but it is one. Blanco White lived, undoubtedly, a life of pain. Disease of body, misery and laceration of mind, were his lot. We look for the religious effects of such a state and see them not. Infidelity was not in his case the system of fat-hearted and insensible nature. He was not a Hume, to see phenomena around him and be perfectly satisfied without explaining them. He was singularly without the temperament of comfort in mind and body. We assign a moral cause for infidelity; but one great moral cause is singularly wanting here—pain, and not comfort, meets us. We expect, on Christian grounds, pain to do people good, —to subdue and chasten them, and kill the inward carnal stimulus to unbelief. Alas! it is not always so; pain is no panacea for moral evil. It depends on the man what effect it has, and does not operate apart from the will. Pain is sometimes disciplinarian, and sometimes simply inflictive.

But there is another reason for noticing this point; and that is, that a life of pain gone through in pursuit of truth, and the consequence in part of that pursuit, seems to give a man authority, creates interest, and attaches a character of heroism to him. An infidel tells us in his justification that his unbelief gives him much pain; that he has followed his doubts at every stage with reluctance and uneasiness; that he has got nothing by the course his mind has taken, and is a disinterested witness; he requires confidence and trust on that score. The fact of the pain he informs us of we do not doubt. Man is naturally a believing creature. Unbelief violates a real part of his nature, and unbelief is therefore pain. But this pain is neither a voluntary nor a self-mortifying one. He pains one part of his nature to gratify another. The intellectual element, imperious, proud, and aggressive, is mistress, and he humours her at the expense of better feelings. There is pain when instinct rises and is quelled, and when the heart yearns and has to be corrected. But the eager diseased pleasure of the intellectual stimulus carries him along in spite of the necessary pain which a soul impaired in health is in.

Other circumstances come in. A man does not like separating from friends, and unbelief does this to him; and Blanco White had more than the ordinary amount of pain from this quarter. This does not undo what is taking place on the other side of his nature; *that* is in a course of gratification. When Blanco White is saying, as he is constantly, that his scepticism was positively resisted and checked by him, and only reluctantly given in to, he alludes we doubt not to one real fact on one side; but he omits another on the other. All that such assertions come to is that mental processes are mixed ones, and that, while a gratified part of the mind is in pleasure, a violated one is in pain. It is a miserable reflection to make, that even bodily pain, protracted and agonising as it appears to have been in Blanco White's case, seems rather to stimulate than subdue the intellectual principle at work in him. His mind is sharpened and irritated into greater unbelieving acuteness by it. The fatal cordial is applied to the more eagerly, and pain of body and counter stimulus of mind excite, agitate, and emaciate him, mind and body and all. In no fatalist sense, of course, but in the simple conventional one we say it, Blanco White was a natural sceptic. Bishop Butler mentions a class of minds whose probation arises not from a sensual but an intellectual quarter, and in whom evil assumes the form of a strong sceptical appetite in them, to be chastised and kept under. Blanco White is one of these; he allows it to dominate, and it works itself out.

This is the aspect in which Blanco White is put forward by the Unitarian school in these volumes. This is the one ground of sympathy which is to concentrate every class of liberal thinkers, however much they differ from him positively, in his favour. They may all meet on the ground of his martyrdom for truth. That the Unitarians of this country can be putting forward such an infidel mind as Blanco White's as an exemplar at all is a striking fact. They cannot profess actually to agree with him; they do not professedly reject the Bible —Blanco White is very far in advance even of them; he positively laments often over their prejudiced and superstitious creed as compared with his own. Then why do they put him forward? Because he is a martyr to truth, because he pursues his own ideas of truth fearlessly in spite of all difficulties. This standard gives a wide field of sympathy, and as if truth itself were nothing, and the search after it the only reality, that process of restlessness and difficulty which any inquirer, be he what he may, goes through, is made an ultimate virtue. Superseding all other considerations whatever, the simple exertion of the intellectual powers is beatified and glorified as such, and canonises the man.

We are unable to see, for our part, on what such a view as this, when pushed to its legitimate basis, can rest but the assertion of this principle, viz., that the intellectual part of human nature is no department of human probation. Every one allows that man is tempted, and is capable of sinning through the flesh; but it seems there are some who deny that he is capable of sinning through the intellect. The idea of human trial and sin admitted, it stops according to this view with the outer and does not go on into the inner sphere. This is a question, of course, of simple moral perception and conscience. There have been, and are, very rude savage nations who do not seem to have perceived the fact of a probation even in the department of the flesh, and sensual acts that would excite the horror of any informed conscience seem literally not to have been regarded as wrong by them; they really do not appear to have seen the evil there was in them. As God's law enlightens the human conscience, however, this gross darkness disappears; it is perceived that the flesh is capable of sin, and the awful distinction of good and evil comes to light, and is established at any rate in this lower and more palpable region. This is the first, and it is a mighty step in the progress of morality; but the moral perception wants still further enlightenment to meet the more profound and subtle departments of our being as they unroll, and a powerful intellectual nature residing underneath the solid body, conversing with abstractions, penetrating depths, and having a world and empire of its own, has still to be dealt with. Here also sin enters. The intellect appears in some ancient philosophies as a sort of metaphysical fluid, and its existence is realised by materialising it. We may realise its full substantial liability to sin without any such supposition; no reason is to be alleged why a simple spiritual nature may not sin as really as a corporeal; the distinction is altogether irrelevant to the subject. As a further stage of enlightenment then comes on it is perceived that the intellect is capable of sin as really as the flesh is, and its spirituality no longer preserves it from suspicion; evil is seen in its operations—in neither, of course, it being the intellect itself or the flesh itself that sins, but the personality of man that sins, in the one case through the intellect, in the other through the flesh.

The Gospel dispensation has mainly introduced this deeper, larger, and more searching morality. It conducts man to a more ample development of his moral nature than he ever enjoyed before. The Church watches anxiously over the department of the human intellect, and cautions man against his dangers there. She tells him, You may not see so clearly sin here as you do in the bodily instance; it is not so palpable as ocular tangible sin is, but it is as real. Look into yourself; do you not feel an excitement, a stimulus, a pungency in pursuing an intellectual process? does not a particular movement, accompanied with pleasure, carry you along? Examine this, and see if it has not the same substantial liability to sin that an operation of animal nature has. Is not this movement, whatever it is, a something which may *become* sin, just as a movement of the sensual appetite may? Even the sensual movement is not *itself* sin, it only may become such; it has an inherent tendency to do so. Has not this intellectual movement the same? Reflect how you think, and how you are internally influenced while you are thinking and following out a speculation. As you go along do you not, independently of their bare truth, or supposed truth, acquire a partiality to your thoughts because *you* think them? And does not this partiality act very deeply? Will not this deep subtle pleasure in your own ideas tempt you to prefer them to truth if truth comes in their way, and so, denying truth, to adopt a falsehood? If so, everything has taken place that takes place in a sin of sense; there is a sinful tendency, and that tendency has reached a climax and an act. The process of pure speculation is capable of sin. So speaks the Church. The intellect, in her view, exhibits on inspection all the circumstances and phenomena as a field of sin that the flesh does—pleasurable sensation, stimulus, excitement; only having them invisibly, and not visibly. The conscience perceives, as an absolute internal fact, a sinful tendency in this department. And as the undisciplined bodily appetite rushes into grossness, so the undisciplined intellect abandons itself to a lie—the former issues in carnal sin, the latter in the sin of heresy.

It is nothing to the purpose here to say that we are not agreed as to what *is* truth. This argument makes no assertions about truth itself, but about that part of the mind that investigates truth. That part, the intellectual part of the mind, is capable of sin. A large number of persons absolutely do not see any sinful tendency at all in its operations; they do not connect their ideas of sin with that department. The intellect, with them, has no more to do with sin than physical law has; and it seems as absurd to talk of it sinning as to talk of any air, or gas, or chemical solution sinning. They see in all its movements pure rational influence at work, and moving with the same simple propriety and extra-moral innocence with which a tree grows out of the earth or a planet performs its orbit.

Upon a view then, we say, that first extra-moralises the whole of intellectual nature, and then elevates and enthrones it, it may be quite logical to canonise the fearless speculator as such, but on no other supposition is it so. We say it in no spirit of caricature,—that state of misery, doubt, and inquietude which a certain intellectual course brings on, does not in itself prove any more moral a martyrdom than the martyrdom of emaciation and disease that accompanies a licentious life. If the intellect can sin, its excesses must produce mental misery, as the natural consequence of a violated nature, and the use of a morbid internal stimulus. Infidelity points to a ghastly and sepulchral crown, to a career of doubt, hollowness, and restlessness, as an heroic life, as so much pain gone through in the great cause of truth. It compares such a course with the calm course of faith, as if it were comparing activity with torpor and sensibility with indifference. This may be quite true if the intellect is sinless. If it is not, then let such thinkers take care that they are not comparing disease with health, and attenuation with vigour; then let them be sure that they are not exposing themselves to another view of the case. True, the sceptical intellect has its crown, and has its martyrdom; it is the enemy of strength and health; it emaciates, it unnerves, it unstrings; it destroys the soul's balance; its serpentine stimulus, like the fiery liquors, becomes the more necessary the more it is taken, and it leaves the soul dry and anatomised. This is a martyrdom in a sense, and who would pray for it?

Amongst the ideas that have been abused, and that have been distorted, this one of the search after truth stands foremost. A splendid and majestic phrase has covered a process that will not bear inspection. The notion of seeking after truth carries a front of austere impartiality, serene candour, and enlarged vision. The mind wants truth, and nothing else; not what it likes, or has fancied, or has conjectured, or pictured; but what is true; what *is*, as distinct from what is *not*. On that account, and on that account only, not as being amiable, or fair, or bright, but as being truth, she seeks it. The pure, colourless appetency of the philosophical mind simply reaches towards its object—the essential intelligence proceeds towards its goal. Truth, simple, glorious, denuded, attracts by the one fact of itself; and the devotion of candid inquiry addresses itself to that one fact.

Such is the simply intellectual passion for truth. The cold, unlovely material, however, throws the whole interest and charm connected with it into the search rather than into the discovery. "If God offered me with one hand truth, and in the other search after truth, I would choose the latter," says a German philosopher. The sentiment is bold and complete, and is just what many unconsciously feel. It cannot but be so. This whole philosophy of search does tend essentially to make truth nothing, the search everything. Truth is a tenuity, an exsiccation, a misty vacuum in the distance, while the human engine is working with all its powers, and mind occupies the universal field, and is truth's investigator—truth and all. Nothing appears but mind. The world of truth ceases to be objective, and is brought within the mind itself, and subjected to it.

Here is the point. The fact is that the love of truth in fallen man is a corrupted affection, just as natural love is. It betrays the selfish element. His mind annexes truth to itself, and not itself to truth. It considers truth as a kind of property; it wants the pride of making it its own; it treats it as an article of mental success; it does not reverence truth as an object, but appropriates it as a thing; it loves it as its own creation, and as the reflection of itself and its labours. The merchant sees himself in his capital, the parent in his child; every one has the image of himself in the shape of some issue from himself; and there is a philosophy which sees such an issue in truth, and makes it, in its sphere, the very embodiment of that of which truth divine is the extinction,—the principle of self.

Not as the function of his own activities, the triumph of his own penetration, the offspring of his mind, not in the subterranean regions, where nature's fallen machinery and emulous exertion is at work, and the begrimed intellect labours in its own smoke and exults in its difficulties, does the disciple of Christ search for truth. He searches and he penetrates, but not in this way. Truth penetrates into him, rather than he into Truth; Truth finds him out, and not he It. He looks out for Its approach, waits for It, prepares himself for Its reception. He knows the signs of Its approach, and can tell Its features through the distance; he is alive to the slightest stir of the air, to a whisper, to a breath. But he looks on It all the while as something without himself, as something to advance and act upon him. The tender wax expects its impress, the air its motion. Upon all his activities sits an awful passiveness, and the mind adores with pure devotion an Object above itself. From the invisible realm above us a Form comes, too vast for our eyes' comprehension, majestically slow the heavenly clouded weight descends, and bears an impress with it. The soul awaits in stillness the awful contact and embrace; and while, with meekest pliableness and unresisting faith and trust, she commits herself to it, she fears it too. Safe and unformidable an idol truth may be; not so Truth living and divine. Ah! who can guess at all beforehand the power of that clasp, its subtlety, its penetration; may it not do anything, do everything, we think; and we shrink from the unknown. Change is awful; Truth changes us. It is not a mere discovery, and then over and done with, a goal reached, a prize won; but a power that reacts and operates upon ourselves. It is a new visitant that we are introduced to; we know it not at first; we get to know it after we have become acquainted with it. It is a new world that we are admitted into; what is in it we see not before we enter, but then we see. It is a new state of being, a higher life, into which a transition, a metempsychosis, and death conducts us. This is an awful aspect which Christian Truth has, and which mere intellectual truth has not. Let those who make it a dead thing and a philosophical reflection deal with it lightly, and let *them* be not afraid of it; let them repose with calm and pleased security on an intellectual success and ultimatum; he who really deifies Truth cannot. He sees in it no plaything, no invention, no curiosity of science, no mineral from the mine, but a living Omnipotent and Heavenly Form. All nature sobers at Its faintest step; the very skirt of Its robe turns all things cold; the distant hills look iron; the horizon hardens, and repels the gaze; nature is treacherous, her colour fades; this blue concave is but a sepulchre; "the earth mourneth and languisheth, the world languisheth and fadeth away, all the merry-hearted do sigh, the mirth of tabrets ceaseth, the noise of them that rejoice endeth, the joy of the harp ceaseth." The mighty form of Truth that the heavens just dimly disclose is spectral to our earthly eye, and a veil must be pierced through before we get within Its genial home and sanctuary. Sad and sepulchral in Its omnipotence, weak helpless nature fears Truth while she invokes it; and as the mountain moves, and the overshadowing form bends over, and the arch of heaven closes in upon the human soul, she breathes, not without a touch of mortal tremor, her mute prayer:—Oh! Image Omnipotent, Eternal

Pattern, fain would I love while I secretly dread Thee. Thou art that mould that makest Thy slow irresistible course through the world that Thou hast formed. Thou didst work at the beginning, and Thou workest hitherto. To thee all souls, all reasons bow; the world is clay before Thy path; man awaits his fashioning from thee, his change, his renovation; Thou informest, and fashionest all minds that love thee. Through earth's rebellion, through the disorder of human wills, Thou marchest on, and dost all that Thou wilt, and formest Thy spiritual world. Come down upon me, and be my living Mould. Yet not without some tender condescension, some mercy and unutterable love, impress Thy awful stamp upon my poor and trembling being. I am weak, and Thou art mighty; I am small, and Thou art Infinite. Crush me not by Thy force, Thy magnitude divine, but come in gentleness, in pity. For Thou art "kind to man, steadfast, sure, free from care, having all power, overseeing all things, and going through all pure spirits—holy, one, only, manifold, subtle, lively, clear, undefiled. Thou being but one canst do all things, and remaining in Thyself, makest all things new; and in all ages Thou enterest into holy souls, and makest them friends of God." Thou hast appeared upon earth, and man has seen Thee in visible form; and we know that Thou art the Way, the Truth, and the Life; the Door and the Shepherd; Thy sheep hear Thy voice, and Thou gently leadest them, and carriest them in Thine arms. Thou didst suffer for them; and now, being made higher than the heavens, intercedest for them; an High Priest that art touched with the feeling of our infirmities, Jesus Christ our Lord.

DR. PUSEY'S SERMON.*

(April 1846.¹)

[As a record of an occasion of extraordinary interest, it is felt allowable to give the large letter of the author's article on Dr. Pusey's sermon delivered at Christ's Church, February 1, 1846, while omitting ten pages consisting almost entirely of extracts from the sermon and Dr. Pusey's other works. It may assist the modern reader to a clearer understanding of the circumstances under which the sermon was preached, to preface the article upon it by some passages from a pamphlet by the author, entitled *The Plea of the Six Doctors*, written two years before, on occasion of Dr. Pusey's suspension.—Ed.]

The pamphlet begins thus :—

"The character of the proceedings against Dr. Pusey is now fixed and settled. An address, presenting in the most quiet and respectful form the simple request that the University should be informed of the grounds on which the sentence was passed, has been summarily answered in the negative ;"

and concluding as follows :—

"To come to the present matter: it so happens that, within the last few weeks, 'Tractarian' views have attracted, in a very marked and definite way, Parliamentary notice. For the first time since their rise they formed, during the discussion of the Educational clauses in the Factory Bill, the subject, as we may say, of a debate in the House. The speakers on that occasion were mostly unfavourable to these opinions; among the rest,

---

* *Entire Absolution of the Penitent: A Sermon, mostly preached before the University, in the Cathedral Church of Christ, in Oxford, on the Fourth Sunday after Epiphany.* By the Rev. E. B. Pusey, D.D., Regius Professor of Hebrew, Canon of Christ Church, and late Fellow of Oriel College. Oxford and London, 1846.

an honourable member for one of the divisions of Kent complimented the Premier on the recent appointment of one of the Oxford Hebdomadal Board to a bishopric, on the express ground that the person selected had taken here a decided line against them.

"The Right Hon. Baronet apparently received the compliment with satisfaction; indeed, such a remark could hardly fail of being gratifying, both to the Right Hon. Baronet who made the selection, and to the respected body from whom the selection was made. There could be no doubt whatever now what line of conduct on this point that body should pursue to be most in harmony with the sentiment of a Conservative Government, and the tone of the political world at large. The only question was about the particular measure. Convocation was tried last year and found unmanageable. What else? There is in the Statute-Book a statute *de evitanda offensionis et dissensionis materia*, a very little, short statute, but extremely to the purpose, highly convenient, serviceable, practical—rather imperious, perhaps, gives us all our own way, but that is just what we want—an energetic, spirited little statute, $\sigma\mu\iota\kappa\rho\grave{o}\varsigma\ \grave{a}\lambda\lambda\grave{a}\ \mu\alpha\chi\eta\tau\acute{\eta}\varsigma$. To be sure, it is rather antiquated, it must be confessed; it has not been acted on for some hundred and fifty years, but never mind that. If it has not been, it shall be with a vengeance. About this time, runs our narrative, Dr. Pusey preached, in the course of rotation, in Christ Church, before a large audience of the University. The audience listened with the attention it always does to Dr. Pusey, and then the audience went away. There were the usual effects of edification and admiration produced. The remarks upon it were pretty much the same as usual: it was pronounced a useful sermon, an eloquent sermon, a striking sermon, a beautiful sermon. Some said it was a long sermon, others that it was not longer than usual. It was, of course, said to contain high doctrinal views on the subject treated of; but as all Dr. Pusey's sermons contain high views, there was nothing to draw attention in this remark. In short, it was one of Dr. Pusey's sermons; the audience recognised that fact, went home, were perfectly at their ease, thought nothing more about it,—the reverential impression excepted, of course, which that preacher's discourses always leave on the mind,—when all on a sudden comes, like a clap of thunder on the ear, the news that the Board of Heresy is summoned to sit on Dr. Pusey. Board of Heresy? asks the dubious inquirer; what heresy has there been? However, the Board of Heresy meets, Dr. Pusey is suspended, and the little statute has done its work.

"So much for the revived statute. However unobjectionable such a recurrence to old law may be in itself, the remark is forced upon us—these are not exactly the persons to commence it. The mantle of a stern theology hardly sits well upon their shoulders; the rough garb of old dogmatism, the 'lion's hide,' hangs awkwardly upon their modern limbs. The old theologians who framed the statute, framed it on a bold, straightforward view; they brought a definite fixed system, a unity of belief, to bear upon the accused, and, confident of their ground, were not ashamed to exhibit it in the face of day. But the present proceeding displays the form of the old system without the spirit, the absolutism without the authority. An undecided, discordant theology dare not state its grounds for fear of exposing its weakness, and creeps underneath the shelter of statute-letter. The armoury of a former age is used, and degraded in the usage; and the sword, become the stiletto of justice, preserves not the University orthodox, but the judges safe."—*Plea of the Six Doctors*, p. 10. (1843.)

To any one who was within the walls of the Cathedral at Oxford when this sermon was delivered, the scene must have been an arresting one. When a voice speaks for the first time after a long silence, there is an interest added simply by that fact. Any long interval naturally throws the mind into a meditative state, and gives of itself an importance and a character to what it gradually brings upon us. A long interval at Oxford has, moreover, a serious effect in another way. There the generations of men come and go very quick; the academical body is not a stationary but a moving one, and three years are an undergraduate's life. The majority of those who heard Dr. Pusey on the 1st of February must have heard him for the first time. They had heard of him, had seen his name in newspapers, had heard his theology talked of in this or that spirit, had had him presented to their mind in one or other colour, but they had never actually had him before them, or come into contact with him. They now saw him; and there is something in the mere circumstance of seeing and hearing for ourselves that often relieves apprehension, and puts us into a new relation toward the person in our minds. The *omne ignotum* is not seldom a great part of that atmosphere of unfavourable prepossession and colouring in which our minds are with respect to persons of whom we have only heard by report. We do not say that a University audience would come as a whole with such prepossessions to hear Dr. Pusey; as a whole it would not, but probably some would. There was, of course, on such an occasion a number of minor circumstances which served to stamp an image on the minds of those present. There was a crowded church; nave, aisles, and transepts full; there was a procession unable to perform its march, and doctors unable to get their robes. And, from the small quantity of seats which the place supplied, the scene exhibited the, to English eyes, rather unusual exhibition of a crowded church standing to be taught.

But the circumstance distinguishing this particular sermon was, of course, the fact that it was preached after a suspension. It was the end of a kind of imprisonment. Dr. Pusey had been under a ban, and he was now so no longer; he was in his proper place again; he was teaching again in person, and not by pen only. And this was felt the more from the fact that the memory of the suspension was not allowed gradually to die away, but received a sudden revival only a week or two previously. It was doubted, as the time when Dr. Pusey would have to preach approached, whether some impediment would not be raised; and University statutes were talked of, which seemed, on a *primâ facie* reading, to arm the Vice-Chancellor with irresponsible control over the University pulpit. But a letter from that functionary, which appeared in the public papers, put an end to these doubts. Dr. Pusey was allowed to enter the University pulpit unopposed, but with the accompanying hint, that if any objectionable matter appeared in his sermon the delator's charge would meet with neither an uncandid nor a reluctant reception in the University council.

There is something in Dr. Pusey's tone and manner of preaching especially calculated to meet such an occasion as this. It may be asked how a preacher, who has none of what we may call the arts and accomplishments of preaching, who has not pliability of voice, or command over accent, time, or tone; who does not change from fast to slow, or pause, or look off from his pages; who, instead of facing an audience, in the way in which extempore preachers can do throughout a sermon, and which most preachers try to do more or less, keeps his eyes fixed down, and sustains an unvarying note throughout a long period of delivery; can impress, or raise feeling, or keep up attention? But the question would not show much depth of insight into the real avenues to people's minds, and the real causes which operate in moving feeling and deepening attention. What keeps a congregation fixed and absorbed is a preacher's feeling what he says, and being himself, as it were, in the words which come from him. Reality is the powerful and moving element on such occasions. Reality is of itself always striking, always effective. There is a sympathetic impulse always felt, as soon as ever the mind recognises the fact that the person speaking is in earnest; he is immediately the centre of all minds around him, when this is seen: there is life and intentness in the whole scene of thought, just as when a wire vibrates, or a spring leaps and fastens the stray material that comes near it. The wandering, scattered, restless images of human fancy are stayed; the thoughts that go in and come out, and come near and are lost again, the flitting shadows of ideas, the imperfect, half-formed, and ever-changing scenery, which goes on within every ordinary human mind, are then for once in a way stilled and fixed. A difficulty is mastered; and a great difficulty too. A common undisciplined human inside is a confused and scrambling scene indeed. How few are there who, walking, sitting, standing, taken at any time when they are not forced by some dire necessity to fix themselves on some one subject, retain any thought for half a minute together upon their minds? We go from place to place: we stand, we sit: objects are before our eyes, images of some sort or other are within our minds: sometimes a stray object catches the eye, sometimes a casual idea comes over the brain: a succession of momentary, uncontinuous, fragmentary impulses, ideas, and feelings; conjectures, reminiscences, sadnesses, jokes, wearinesses, disgusts, hopes, consolations, apprehensions, reasonings, all of the very smallest possible description, and the greater part of which any one person would be ashamed to acknowledge to any other, compose an ordinary unemployed human interior. It might seem, at first sight, that it was absolutely impossible for any natural power to subdue this chaos, and get hold of these slippery multitudinous activities. A large number of persons, with their several mental interiors, assembled in one place, reminds one of the Lucretian world of atoms, where the original particles of the universe are going direct and aslant, forward, backward, curving, shooting in the infinite vacancy, meeting one another, and making endless and multiform combinations. But there is one power that can conquer this difficulty. It is the power of earnestness. There is an instinct by which persons feel when the mind, from which the thoughts are issuing, is a real one; one not wanting to unfold itself, but to do them good, one that is absorbed in a task, and identified with a purpose of love. This is seen and felt by the internal sense, as much as any outward object is by the external. And when it *is* seen and felt, the effect is immediate. This temper comes into solid contact with their souls, in a way in which no other can. It touches and it calms them. Intensity is *the* want which human nature feels. She is right glad to enjoy it by substitute, though it be for an hour. She has no pleasure in the wanderings and disturbance of her own inward domain: she tolerates it only because she is weak and frail, and cannot stop it; she has not resolution to master her own disorders and inconstancy, and therefore she carries them about with her. But let any come and do this for her; let any power come forward which only requires her passive acquiescence, and she will sit and give it gladly. Let any one arrest her attention, and she is obliged to him for it.

We will not apply these remarks more pointedly than is necessary to the present case. For it is very difficult, in speaking of an individual, and especially of one like him of whom we are speaking, to be quite clear, and at the same time to maintain that delicacy which is necessary. Nevertheless, those who have had the fact before them will be able, without much difficulty, to test these comments of ours. It may be said, without venturing beyond those strict bounds of decorum which ought to limit such observations, that Oxford has had, and has, a voice within her, that speaks in this tone and with this power, to her sons; a voice which, without art or manner, or any of the advantages of oratorical discipline or nature, is powerful by intensity, and impressive by the single-minded force of love and a penetrating purity of will; a voice which always speaks amid the perfect silence of arrested and subdued thoughts; which is allowed always to still and fix, for the time that it is speaking, the waywardness, dissonance, and wanderings of inward nature: which imparts to its hearers, for the time, somewhat of that serenity, awe, and singleness, out of which itself issues; and which creates, amid the confusions and bustle of the mind's commonplace intellectual life, a temporary calm; during which ideas, hopes, and longings, which were never entertained before, find an entrance into many a mind, to produce their living and permanent fruits afterwards.

It is not our purpose, at the present, to enter into the particular subject of the sermon before us, or to follow out the line of thought which it offers to the members of our Church. That line of thought, when once naturally, earnestly, and in harmony with the course of events in our Church, begun, is, upon ordinary principles, morally certain to go further. A political eye sees an idea come in, and gain just a standing-room in the political world; the statesman argues, that if it has got there, it will do more than merely stand still there; that the fact of its getting there shows some strength; and that if strength more or less exists, it will be more or less productive. Thus he predicts changes, movement, progress in this or that direction, in a country. It is the same, though in a more quiet and less sensible way, in the religious world. A

Church gets into a certain state. A particular average standard of opinion prevails; people think on a level with that standard, and neither much higher nor much lower. Religion presents itself to their minds, in certain accustomed shapes, and imposes the duties and imparts the consolations which the standard sanctions and authorises. There is, in short, commonly existing, with its own degree of goodness, effectiveness, and depth, whatever that may be,—the religion of the day. Persons go on, for the most part, in that train of thought on which this religion puts them. Other ideas do not come into their heads. Even very obvious ideas, ideas, *i.e.* that appear very obvious afterwards, do not at all suggest themselves in this state of things. If they exist at all, they do not exist in practical form; they are not considered living and real ones; they are not part of the existing religious sentiment. A person may go on for a whole life in this way, without the propriety and suitableness of some acts of religion ever even occurring to him. He has, perhaps, no definite reason to allege against them, but he does not, in fact, think really enough of them to have such hostile reasons. The act lies out of his world—and that is everything. But there is such a thing as an established religious sentiment having a new or revived idea thrown into it, just as a new virtue may be imparted to a soil. The new chemical ingredient, which the agriculturist throws into his land, mingles with it, and the soil becomes a different one from what it was before. A new or revived idea, in proportion as it stands its ground, alters the established religious sentiment in its own direction. And in this altered stage of thought, a class of actions, which was unreal before, becomes real. It comes as a new thing upon us, that such an act is a real one to do, if we can muster strength of mind for it. It no longer presents itself to us as a nominal or impossible thing, nor can we blame the religious atmosphere in which we live, if we do not do it, but ourselves only. The change, so far as the former is concerned, has taken place, and the effect of it is felt; the idea is no longer an unreal, but a natural idea to us. And if it is a natural idea, then it enters, according to circumstances, into our natural and approved sphere of duty.

It is by an idea first gaining admittance, getting an introduction, that such a change as this, in the tone of opinion, takes place. And, putting ourselves into the position of spectators, we seem to see a revived idea coming in, by a solid and natural way, in Dr. Pusey's present sermon. If this is true, we may reasonably expect that, like ideas in the political, or the scientific or literary world, having come in it will do something; that it will penetrate into particular minds, and through them into others, and so produce its results. We may reasonably expect, upon natural principles, that it will have a course; and we will not interfere with those auspices under which that course has begun.

We shall concern ourselves now, not so much with the particular duty and doctrine themselves which Dr. Pusey puts forward here as with the course of mind by which he seems to have been brought to them. Dr. Pusey is not a teacher who has gone on by chance, or irregular will, in the course he has pursued. On looking back at his publications, and retracing his line of thought and teaching, we find it exhibiting much unity and singleness of purpose. In saying that it exhibits unity, we do not mean to assert that he has held exactly the same opinions always; or that a former stage of his teaching would not be found to omit what a later has supplied, and would not have to be modified in its theological tone by the latter. That is, indeed, the very fact that we wish to point out; and it is a fact which, so far from proving an irregularity or inconsistency in his course, shows its regular, continuous, and successive progress. A former stage did, more or less, omit what a later has supplied; but then the later has supplied it. And, in taking a retrospective view of Dr. Pusey's teaching, we seem to have a steady and natural course before us, not deliberately preparing its steps, but going through them with as much continuity as if it did, and making a whole by the unconscious consistency and unity of truth.

The first observation, then, that will naturally suggest itself to persons on comparing some of Dr. Pusey's present with his past works, is the greater severity of the former, which the latter have softened. Without any literal opposition between the two in doctrine, the former exhibit certainly a more unqualified view than the latter do. There is a perceptible superinduction of not an opposite but a new tone, in his later sermons, and especially in the one before us. The change is not so recent a one. The sermon "on the Holy Eucharist a comfort to the Penitent," was cast in a mould of thought, softer, if we may say so, and more lenient, than that in which his first Tracts were cast. And in Dr. Pusey's teaching the severe has prepared the way for the mild. There was something of what appeared, to many, over-austere in his first religious works: his last show anything but this. Here is then a difference before us which some will be inclined to call an inconsistency; others only a natural consecutiveness. Some will say the teacher's mind has altered, and that he has changed his ground; others, that he has only first given one side of the truth and then the other. So far however may be allowed, that, when one side of the truth is first given, the omission does give a *primâ facie* appearance of opposition to the other, when the other comes out. But whatever we may call this change or this modification in Dr. Pusey; that it has taken place on a most natural principle, and has been in him only the legitimate development of one line of thought, is quite clear. There has been essential unity, consistency, sequence in his course of teaching, though that unity has come out in successive sides, and not appeared at once as a whole. It has only unfolded itself, in agreement with the religious wants of the times, in having a former as well as a latter stage: and it has been the more serviceable and effective from having come out thus successively and by parts.

Dr. Pusey has devoted himself to one main line of thought in his religious teaching. He has devoted himself to the consideration of Sin; its awful nature; its antagonism to God; its deep seat in our nature; the remedy provided for it by our Lord's meritorious sufferings and death, and the application of that remedy in the ordinance of Baptism. The subject of Baptism winds up the line of thought. "We are buried with Him by Baptism unto death; that like as Christ was raised up from the dead by the glory of the Father, even so we also should walk in newness of life." Baptism is a new birth, an entrance into a new world, the communication of a new nature. And Sin is in Baptism pardoned: we are washed and made clean; and the evil is met and provided for. So far is clear, and the subject appears to close. But then comes the fact that men live after Baptism. Sin comes up again, and has to be dealt with again. Deadly sin after Baptism has the guilt and misery of a relapse over and above that of sin simply, and those sad and fearful thoughts come over us which are suggested by the passage in the Epistle to the Hebrews: "It is impossible for those who were once enlightened, and have tasted the heavenly gift, and were made partakers of the Holy Ghost, and of the powers of the world to come; if they shall fall away, to renew them again unto repentance." There is no absolute renewal provided after that of Baptism has been received and has been fallen from. Here the easy way to peace ends, and a rough and difficult one begins. The first state is past, and any subsequent state of favour must be a hard-earned one. Innocence is over, and repentance follows. True, the mercy of God has not left us desolate even in this last and most forlorn state. For His Church is endowed with a power, though not an absolute and complete one, of restoration; and the sinner is allowed, after sincere repentance and a course of self-mortification, after much self-revenge and humiliation, to enter into the re-enjoyment, though not so entire a one as that which he has lost, of baptismal privileges. But that repentance must appear in solid form; it must have proved itself to have gone through difficulties, made real sacrifices, and shown itself in deeds, and not in words only. Till this is done the judgments of God are alone before us, and we have no right to be easy or comfortable. Here then is a stage in the progress up to spiritual life in which we are upon indefinite ground, and have no fixed standard to go by. Some minds will be more severe, others more lenient, in their view of repentance. One age of the Church has given a harder, another a milder standard. Repentance is essentially an indefinite thing, and when a subject-matter is indefinite there will be room for shades of feeling, variations, degrees, all within one main circle of doctrine, and all on one agreed and acknowledged religious basis. Different tempers will more or less differ, and the same person will have a different feeling on the subject at one time of his life from what he had at another. Nothing is more natural, more certain, we may say, to happen than this. It is what does and what must take place in such a region of religious thought, and that especially where there is reality and seriousness.

It is true, then, that Dr. Pusey's first publications do exhibit a more severe and less qualified mode of dealing with the sinner than his later ones do. But he has followed in such a course the natural progress of thought in a real spiritual mind, and taken those successive steps which the religious atmosphere around him naturally and fitly called for and elicited. He has followed, we say, in the first place, that line which the earnest mind naturally does in its own internal feeling. In the progress of the sense of sin within the mind simple pain comes first, the consolation next; first comes self-revenge, then hope; first severity, then relief; first abasement, and then ascent. When the heart is first under the sense of its own wickedness, and is fresh stung by the recollection of past sin, it thinks of its sin, and of that only. It is fit that it should do so. Guilt is fastened on its feelings, as if it were irradicable and eternal. Conscience strikes on the same spot with continuous and unvarying force; the evil carries a sense of perpetuity with it; and the guilt of an act seems an essential and immovable consequence of it, to follow us with illimitable power and force of adherence through all time. With the first sense of sin the sense of pardon does not mix, the soul is weighed down, and simply oppressed. We do not say there is an absolute and definite feeling of unpardonableness in the mind, or that the soul with conscious intention excludes the idea of God's mercy from itself. For that would be an heretical feeling, and no heretical feeling is natural to us. But negatively it does this. It does not think of God's mercy, because it thinks only of its own guilt. It is under a dark cloud, a vague oppressive weight of pure grief. But out of this cloud and this oppression the sense of the Divine mercy proceeds, and then arises that other aspect of truth and that other side of the spiritual world. The sense of the Divine mercy as naturally springs out of the sense of guilt as a plant grows out of the soil. The sense of pardon and the sense of sin are correlatives; the former cannot be produced without the latter. It can only be after such real unmixed humiliation as the full sense of sin naturally inflicts that the idea of the positive infinity and unfathomableness of God's attribute of mercy can be admitted. An unreal, oblique, hollow, superficial sense of guilt in the man makes a poor, weak, and finite mercy in the Deity. On the contrary, a deep and real sense of guilt makes an infinite mercy. But then the one sense must be had before the other comes; they do not arise simultaneously, but successively. It is the fault of a popular religion that it makes them simultaneous. The sense of pardon, sanctioned by a popular religion of the day, comes in before it ought, and an original amalgamation of the two feelings destroys from the first the depth, refinement, and solidity of both. A man brings the sense of pardon to the sense of sin in the first instance, and he confesses, not like the Publican, who would not so much as lift up his eyes unto heaven, but like a pardoned and beatified man already. This ought not to be. There are two stages in this business, which, if we are true to ourselves, we must go through. Dr. Pusey as a public teacher has by a natural sympathy gone through these two stages. He has in following his subject been a preacher of humiliation and of pardon successively, and he has given, though not designedly, that line and sequency to his thoughts which the real subject-matter of them itself takes.

We turn from this inward ground to an outward and public one, to the general state of religious opinion among us, the peculiar wants of the times in which Dr. Pusey has written; and we find that they have been such as naturally to impose such a course of teaching upon him. He has given the age what it wanted, and given when it wanted it. Persons know what the strong tendencies in our Church were at the time when Dr. Pusey began to write; what had grown dead and wanted especially reviving. The idea of the reality of Baptismal privileges appeared to be getting more and more faint. One large party in the Church totally denied them: another made them very nominal and external. There was wanted a restoration of the doctrine of Baptism. It had to be brought out afresh, and put strongly before people's minds; the whole current language about it had to be deepened and enriched; a whole sentiment had to be awakened. Dr. Pusey did this work. He was exactly the person to do it. The patristic language was one with which he felt instinctively at home: he had been an early disciple of the Fathers; he dwelt with a congenial love upon their mysterious intuitions, their dark sayings, their awful windings of thought, their large field of spiritual analogies, their lights, their shadows, their oracular hints, their sacred fancy, their force and their feeling. He had a sympathy with all this; and all these features in their writing came strikingly to bear upon the subject of Baptism. The Fathers are deep and powerful, if on any subject, especially on that of Baptism. It is one which brings out all that holy poetry which so peculiarly belongs to them: their thoughts gather around the fountain-head of Christian life, as instinctively as memory reverts to early scenes, and streams flow into their parent ocean. Dr. Pusey brought all this to bear with genuineness and life upon the restoration of the doctrine. The consequence was that the deep view of Baptism received a remarkable impulse,—such an impulse as perhaps no other mind in our Church could have communicated to it. Dr. Pusey's tone, style, and whole inward taste and bias did justice to it. But then followed the necessary corollary to this doctrinal view. The immediate consequence of the idea of Baptism being deepened was that sin after baptism was deepened too. The greater the privileges of the new birth the greater the fall from them. There was not so much in falling away from a form; in falling away from a nominal state: but to fall away from a new life, to undo a new nature, to defile the temple of the Holy Ghost, was a serious and awful thing. Thus in close connection with the explanation of Baptismal privileges went the intensifying of post-baptismal sin. That is to say, the sins of all Christians were brought out, and put in their strong appropriate light, and made to appear indeed exceeding sinful. Their position after baptism suggested their intensity rather than their relief at first, and the fact of sin being viewed in connection with such a subject attached necessarily peculiar strength and severity to the view of it. . . .

THE BOOK OF JOB.*

(JANUARY 1849.)

WE notice elsewhere the scholastic part of Dr. Umbreit's book. Of the introductory essay, we need only say that it is a specimen of modified German thought, and gives a somewhat German colouring to the character and reflections of Job; and that, while it does not appear to us to grasp the argument of the book sufficiently clearly to afford any great help to the theological student, it yet creates a general idea of the deep and interesting nature of it, which has its preliminary use.

There is one important difficulty which readers of the Book of Job at first feel with respect to it; the difficulty, viz., how that holy man acquired his proverbial reputation for the virtue connected with his name. The patriarch Job is held up in the Bible as the great example of patience,—" Ye have heard of the patience of Job, and have seen the end of the Lord." We therefore not unnaturally come to the Book of Job with the expectation of finding there an uninterrupted expression of acquiescence in the justice and propriety of the providential visitation under which he is suffering. But it is unnecessary to say that these expectations are not fulfilled. One or two remarkable expressions of resignation meet us at the opening: "The Lord gave, and the Lord hath taken away:" " Shall we receive good at the hand of God, and shall

---

* 1. *Morals on the Book of Job.* By S. GREGORY THE GREAT. Translated with Notes and Indices. Oxford.

2. *A New Version of the Book of Job, with Expository Notes, and an Introduction on the Spirit, Composition, and Author of the Book.* By D. FRIEDERICH WILHELM CARL UMBREIT, Professor of Theology in Heidelberg. Translated from the German by the Rev. JOHN HAMILTON GRAY, M.A. of Magdalen College, Oxford, Vicar of Bolsover. Edinburgh.

we not receive evil?" But those mute seven days and seven nights produce a change, and in the very reverse direction from what we should have expected. As he dwells upon his adversity, he sees more and more reason to be dissatisfied with it; meditation, instead of its ordinary result of suppressing anger, disorders tranquillity; and from the womb of that awful silence issues such vehement emotion, such a flood of poetic wrath, mingling with the beauty and the tenderness of grief, that we seem to be introduced to the feelings rather of an ancient epic or dramatic hero than of an Old Testament saint.

Warburton saw this difficulty, and took advantage of it for the support of that extraordinary theory of the Book of Job which appears in the *Divine Legation*. Warburton formally professed to adopt as the ruling aim of his theological labours, discovery; misapplying, for his motto, the words of Pascal,—" Ceux qui sont capables d'inventer sont rares." He asserted the Book of Job to be an allegory, written after the return from the Captivity, and representing the feelings of the Jewish nation upon entering that stage of their history, at which a special providence ceased; and, from a dispensation of temporal rewards and punishments, they found themselves thrown back upon the ordinary inequalities of this present state of things. Job represents the Jewish people: his three friends, Eliphaz the Temanite, Bildad the Shuhite, and Zophar the Naamathite, who vexed him in his adversity, stand for Sanballat the Horonite, Tobiah the Ammonite, and Geshem the Arabian, who vexed and hindered the Jews at the rebuilding of the temple. For this allegorising theory of the Book of Job, he prepares the way by noticing the difficulties which attach to the ordinary view taken of the book, as an account of the real person of that name. " As the person Job," he says, " was so greatly famed for his exemplary patience that his case became proverbial, we can never on common principles account for his behaviour when we find him breaking out ever and anon into such excesses of impatience as border nearly upon blasphemy. . . . The writing and the tradition being so glaringly inconsistent, we must needs conclude—1. That the fame of so great a patience arose not from the book; and, 2dly, that some other character, shadowed under that of Job, was the real cause of the author's deviation from the general tradition." There is no occasion to comment on a view which, not content with separating the real Job from the scripturally portrayed one, positively contrasts the two; which supposes the author of the book to impose a character on the Patriarch exactly contradictory to his real one; and from which it would follow that when St. James alluded to the patience of Job, he made no allusion to, but drew attention from, the Book of Job. But the fact of such a view having been taken is worth notice, as showing that there is some apparent contradiction in the Book of Job, to the character of Job, which has excited attention, and given rise to explanations.

Such perplexities and obscurities, though they may only lie upon the surface, are enough to suggest the advantage of some inquiry into the general argument and design of this book,—an inquiry, we may add, which may be conducted without any particular reference to chronological or philological questions connected with the book, or to the various and numerous types contained in it, of the Christian dispensation or Church. To those who would pursue the latter line of research, great facilities have been recently afforded by a new and translated edition of St. Gregory's *Magna Moralia*, or Commentary on Job. But such advanced researches may legitimately be preceded by the more domestic consideration of the substance of the book itself; its argument, apparent design, and lesson.

All commentators agree, and it is abundantly clear upon the surface, that one particular argument forms the substance of the Book of Job, the argument, viz., as to the justice of this present visible dispensation,—the order of things established in this world in which we live. In this argument Job's friends take the side favourable to, and Job himself the side unfavourable to, this visible system. Such being, in brief, the argument of the book, before going any further, a question arises upon its very statement, which must be considered, in order to understand fairly the object and the position of the arguers. For it is to be observed that the argument relates solely and exclusively to the justice of the order of things established in this world; and it is natural immediately to ask, Why this should be made so important a question? The religious argument is only really concerned with the justice of God's administration upon the whole and eternally; and therefore why discuss so intently (whether the result be a favourable or unfavourable judgment) the justice of that particular portion of it which is exhibited here? As disciples of the new dispensation, it would never occur to us to make the justice of this visible order of things so critical a point in the religious argument. What is the difference, then, between us and the disciples of the elder dispensation, which would make this difference in arguing on this subject? The difference must certainly lie in the view respectively entertained by each of a future state. The Christian does not think the question of the justice of this present order of things an important one, because he has a definite belief in the existence of a future world, in which all the injustice of the present, if there be any, will be rectified. If the disciple of the patriarchal or Mosaic dispensation, then, made that question an important one, it can only have been in consequence of some uncertainty, or some indefiniteness of belief, on that point. We are thus obliged, on the very opening of the argument in the Book of Job, to devote some words to the old and much-discussed question of the belief in a future state, as held by the faithful under the old dispensation.

The opinions of the Warburtonian school on this subject are well known. Warburton secured, as he thought, from the supposition of the absence of the belief in a future state under the Mosaic dispensation, great additional strength and completeness for the proof of the Divine authority of that dispensation. The licentiousness of human nature, he argued, indulges freely in the crime for which it apprehends no punishment; and the only conviction which has been able to restrain it and keep society together has been a belief in a future state of rewards and punishments. But one nation is an exception. In the creed of one nation there was no reference whatever to a future state, and yet social order was for hundreds of years preserved in it. That nation was the Jewish —that creed the law of Moses. The Mosaic dispensation was therefore against the order of nature, or miraculous. With this argumentative object, the author of the *Divine Legation* boldly asserted the entire absence of belief in a future state amongst the Jews, insisting for his proof, first on the negative ground that such a state was not alluded to in the Mosaic law, and, secondly, on the force of a number of texts in the Old Testament which appeared positively to exclude it.

On this subject, then, we think a middle ground may fairly be taken, and the belief of the ancient Jew vindicated from carnality, without denying its imperfection. It is true, indeed, and a remarkable circumstance it is, that no allusion is made to a future state in the Mosaic law. And the ancient Jew showed remarkably, in the attitude of his mind on this subject, the absence of that allusion. He had no definite image or delineation of a future world before his mental eye. He shows to disadvantage, indeed, even by the side of the Pagan, in this respect; and the faith of the peculiar people of God appears curter and more barren than that of the idolater. The idolater was, indeed, far from being badly off here; he had even a luxuriant imagery on the subject of a future world. He saw Tartarus and Elysium, a burning gulf and shady groves; the great tyrants, murderers, and blasphemers of history were punished with curious and horrible tortures; the righteous souls wandered up and down their pleasant retreat, and enjoyed immortal leisure. This place had been visited by living men, and the dead had been seen and conversed with, in appearance and voice the same as they had been when they were alive. This was a definite picture of a future state. The Jew had no *picture*. He looked out of this visible world upon a void; the surface of futurity reflected no scene, and offered no invitation. But, in drawing the conclusion which he did from these omissions of the old law, Warburton took no account of that kind of belief in a future state which is compatible with having no definite image of it in the mind. Strictly speaking, a true believer in a God does *ipso facto* believe in his own immortality; as our Lord himself signifies in those words, "As touching the dead, that they rise: have ye not read in the book of Moses, how in the bush God spake unto him, saying, I am the God of Abraham, the God of Isaac, and the God of Jacob? He is not the God of the dead, but the God of the living," "for all live unto Him." From the moment of our belief in a God we must connect ourselves inseparably with Him; and the idea of this connection must have the effect of prolonging, to our minds, our own duration. For it will immediately follow from it that the merest thought of Him will raise as its natural correlative the thought of ourselves as existing through Him. Through all the worlds unknown to which our thoughts introduce us our being goes safe, because that Being is there. The Eternal Source insures the continual derivation of life; and because He lives we live. This sense of security as regards the continuance of life, which the true belief in a God imparts, is very perceptible in men in the case of loss of friends, and nothing is more striking than the distinction between the temper in which religious and the temper in which earthly love takes the removal of one who has been precious to it. Who can express the insupportable load of utter deprivation under which that love, which rested exclusively in the earthly object, sinks when that object is snatched away? Before the absolute unqualified idea of death Nature bows down and cannot lift up her head again; she feels herself irremediably desolate and forsaken; "the silver cord loosed," "the golden bowl broken," "the dust returned to the earth as it was," a departure and a vanishing away of one that delighted her are all she sees, and no solace can meet the final farewell and the eternal void. All this hopelessness is felt because affection never advanced beyond its earthly object, and, therefore, in losing it, lost all. But religious love, which loves the creature in the Creator, has that on which to fall back when its earthly object is removed. It reposes in the consciousness of One in whom all live and none die. Within the bosom of the Eternal Being no soul is lost. All are in that part, visible or invisible, of His universe in which He places them. When they leave one part they are transferred to another; they stay where they are while He permits them; they go when He summons them; but whether they stay, or whether they go, they are somewhere in Him. A marvellous security as to the departed and unseen, as if we had the possession of some secret pledge, is thus the result of the one idea of a God; and the believer in Him, like a swimmer at home in the water, feels all around him safe.

This true belief, then, in a God the Jew had; and with it he had that practical belief in a future state which is contained in it. A disputant may demand definite texts from the Old Testament, proving his belief in the continuance of his existence after death; but it ought rather to be asked, How he could possibly believe in its termination? Put before you a religious Jew, of the character of those holy men, actors in the Old Testament history, of whom we are told that they lived in constant communion of thought and prayer with God, referring to Him every purpose and act, and owning Him every moment as their source of life; and suppose him, with this deep belief, going to die,—it is evident that, as he had never referred to this material system in the smallest degree as the cause of his being, he could not think that being endangered by his separation from it. Had he supposed the one, he would have supposed the other; but, in the midst of all the influences and operations of the visible world, his recognised source of life had been an Eternal, Incomprehensible, Immutable Essence, Who was neither seen, nor heard, nor felt; a self-existent Substance absolutely distinct from all created ones; that is to say, something as totally distinct from this world as thought can conceive. Thus, habitually locating himself out of this world, he could not consistently think that he could perish by going out of it at death; having based his existence on the invisible all along, he had the same invisible to depend on then. Without entering, then, into the consideration of any incidental direct allusions to the existence of the soul after death, the great fundamental doctrine of the Jew's creed furnishes legitimate proof of such a belief. In the dogma of One Eternal and Supreme God, he had, however naked and unillustrated, a far truer and more practical doctrine of a future state than the

Pagan with his definite and local imagery. Every act of adoration to that one God was an acknowledgment by the soul of another and spiritual world, to which it really belonged in life and in death. Different portions of Scripture contain direct allusions to another life in different degrees of frequency and clearness, but all teach it equally, in so far as all proclaim Him. That unceasing praise, that joy, that love, that whole peculiar feeling toward the Supreme Being which pervades the Bible, and which no other book but the Bible and those which it has formed show, is really a belief in eternity.

But, besides the omission of the doctrine of a future state in the Mosaic law, attention is drawn to a number of texts in the Old Testament, which seem, as far as language goes, positively to exclude it. Thus we read in Job: "As the cloud is consumed and vanisheth away; so he that goeth down to the grave shall come up no more." "Man lieth down and riseth not; till the heavens be no more they shall not awake, nor be raised out of their sleep." In the Psalms: "For in death no man remembereth thee; and who will give thee thanks in the pit?" "Shall the dust give thanks unto thee, or shall it declare thy truth?" "Dost thou show wonders among the dead, or shall the dead rise up again and praise thee? Shall thy loving-kindness be showed in the grave, or thy faithfulness in destruction? Shall thy wondrous works be known in the dark, or thy righteousness in the land where all things are forgotten?" "The dead praise not thee, O Lord, neither all they that go down into silence." In Ecclesiastes: "The dead know not anything, neither have they any more a reward." In Hezekiah's hymn: "The grave cannot praise thee, death cannot celebrate thee, they that go down into the pit cannot hope for thy truth." But it is evident, upon a slight consideration, that these texts, and other similar ones, only describe after all the phenomenon of death as it presents itself to our eyes, and do not enter into the question of the reality which takes place under it. All the results which these texts attribute to death are, as phenomena, perfectly true and undeniable. The dead, who lie before us, cannot praise God; for the departure of the rational soul has left a simply material form of clay before our eyes, which cannot feel, or understand, or speak; and therefore cannot praise. It is equally true that the dead, in the visible order of nature, do not rise up again, but are dead for ever. It is further true that the dead are in darkness and silence; for we see nothing of them, and we hear nothing of them. The whole phenomenon of death is undoubtedly gloomy, and man is, as far as our eyes are concerned, indisputably a loser by dying. He goes for ever from the light of the sun and the freshness of the air, the earth and sky, life, action, and society, and enters a state of apparent negation. Thus, in various innocent forms of speech, even Christians express their pity for the dead, and feel towards them, as toward those who have suffered some irrecoverable loss, and deserve special tenderness. And thus men forgive their enemies who have died, as if it were ungenerous to pursue them with their hatred beyond the threshold of that deep calamity and grief. Before the image of departed being, human nature, in her sternest forms, gives way; that last appeal of a suffering state of being prevails, and from their hard spring, tears, which would have answered to no other form of evil, appear. But all this is concerned with the phenomenon of death simply. In enlarging upon this aspect of death, the writers of the Old Testament are not stating the real condition of the soul after death, but only its apparent one, as deprived of this life which we are now enjoying; and, so far as that one aspect goes, in a miserable and pitiable case.

Indeed, we cannot but observe, upon reflection, with what religious humility the minds of holy men, under the elder dispensation, seem to have fitted themselves to that exact amount of revelation, on this subject, which they had. Two revelations, so to speak, appealed to them, as they appeal to us; one upon the surface of things, and addressing the senses; another underneath the surface, and addressing faith. The order of nature is a melancholy revelation on the subject of death, placing one sepulchral picture before our eyes of generation after generation of men entirely disappearing, and being heard of and seen no more. On the other hand, Scripture is a consolatory revelation, telling us that we are spiritual beings, with a spiritual source of life, independent of this material system. Now, in the case of the Jew, the appeal of nature was as strong as it is now, the opposing one of Scripture much weaker. The consequence was, that the order of nature, an order intended to affect the mind in a particular way under all dispensations—for God does not make even appearances for nothing, but intends that joyful ones should duly gladden, and mournful ones duly depress us—affected the Jew more strongly than it does the Christian. As such was his lot, he bowed meekly to it, and received the whole of that melancholy impress upon his passive soul. He did not relieve himself, as the Pagan did, by raising a fabulous imagery, and inventing a definite future of his own, but confined himself to that consolation which his revelation gave him, that assurance of immortality which he had in the doctrine of one supreme God. Fixed upon that spiritual ground of life as upon a rock, he felt himself secure, come what might; amid all the changes and decay of nature, constant and enduring, he placed his future in Almighty love, and reposed, with a serene content, upon an indefinite eternity. Amid all the superior brightness of a more perfect hope, we can still allow its own peculiar beauty to the faith of the Jewish saint, believing with an obedient and resigned vagueness, and prepared in God to go he knew not and asked not whither.

So much on the side of a belief in a future state under the Mosaic dispensation. On the other hand, it must be acknowledged that the absence of that definiteness which the later dispensation gave to the belief in a future world was a great want; and that it is not said without meaning, that immortality was brought to light by the Gospel. The Gospel first gave to a future world clearness and distinctness, shape and outline; the Gospel first made it a positive district and region on which the spiritual eye reposes, and which stretches out on the other side the grave with the same solidity and extension the present world does on this side of it. A future life was not an image before the Gospel: the Gospel made it an image. It brought it out of its implicit form, and from its lower residence within the bosom of the great fundamental doctrine of true religion, into a separate and conspicuous position as a truth. This was a bringing to light, and a species of birth, compared with which the previous state of the doctrine was a hidden and an embryo state.

A balance of arguments thus issuing in the existence of a true but indefinite doctrine of a future state, under the old dispensation, it is obvious how this indefiniteness would affect the minds of those who lived under that dispensation, with regard to the question of the justice or injustice of this present state of things. We Christians feel no particular anxiety about establishing the justice of the order of things in this world, because we have quite definitely before our eyes another. The distinct image of a world beyond the grave reduces this world into a mere fragment of a large system, the most extensive portion of which is wholly invisible to us; in which case, whether it presents us with justice, or presents us with injustice, is not of the slightest consequence as affecting the character of God's moral government as a whole, because the larger portion may rectify what is defective in the smaller. But the ancient Jew had no distinct image of another world, and therefore the fragmentary character of this world was not clearly brought out to his eye. To persons standing on a plain, the distant parts, though in reality many miles in extent, appear nothing, and the few fields which immediately surround them seem the whole of the landscape. The absence of any positive extension beyond this world necessarily gave this world a sort of completeness to the eye of the ancient Jew. It was not that he positively thought this world the whole of the universe—positively thought there was no world beyond it; but this world was, the other was not, formally placed before him. The consequence was, that he felt a general disposition to expect whatever characteristics the Divine government possessed, to exhibit themselves in this world. In the absence of a definite invisible, the visible was great in his eyes. This world was a positive place, standing forth, from amidst the unknown and unconceived all around it, as the one formed universe, God's one creation. In the midst of darkness and vacuity here was substance and here was light, here was a perfect circumference, wherein were beasts of the field, and fowls of the air, and fishes of the sea; sun, moon, and stars; and man the ruler or end of all. A sort of religious affection for this earth, a general disposition to regard it as a favoured place, and the intended scene for the display of God's great attributes, his fundamental one of justice especially, thus arose, and gained hold of his mind; joined to an apprehension that unless it was found to present such a display, the justice of the whole Divine government must suffer, inasmuch as no definite room existed in his idea beyond this world, wherein any injustice in its administration could be rectified: a conclusion very unsatisfactory and very melancholy to a religious mind.

In this state of the case, then, the argument in the Book of Job opens. The friends of Job appear to represent that line of thought which has here been described—that too fond and exclusive regard to this world which the elder dispensation tended to produce in a class of minds, not the highest ones, by which it was too literally understood and interpreted; they belong to a school who are anxious to maintain that this world is a scene of satisfactory Divine justice.

The case of Job himself is what occasions and elicits their defence of this favourite doctrine, presenting, as it does, a most striking contradiction to it. Job had been, to all appearance, a righteous man; he had been conspicuously and preeminently devout, holy, and charitable, all his life, and yet he had been singled out for the greatest combination of misfortunes which could befall any human being. Strong in their favourite truth, the friends are ready with an explanation of this fact, and proceed to reconcile it with their system. They suppose some secret iniquity in Job, which has been cherished amidst all the goodness of his outward life, and they refer his misfortunes to it. They exhort him to repent, and promise him, if he does, a return of prosperity, at the hands of a just overruling Providence. Bildad the Shuhite speaks: "Doth God pervert judgment? or doth the Almighty pervert justice? If thou wouldest seek unto God betimes, and make thy supplication to the Almighty; if thou wert pure and upright, surely now he would awake for thee, and make the habitation of thy righteousness prosperous. Though thy beginning was small, yet thy latter end should greatly increase." Zophar the Naamathite speaks:—"Oh that God would speak, and open his lips against thee. He knoweth vain men: he seeth wickedness also; will he not then consider it? If thou prepare thine heart, and stretch out thine hands towards him; if iniquity be in thine hand, put it far away, and let not wickedness dwell in thy tabernacles. For then shalt thou lift up thy face without spot; yea, thou shalt be steadfast, and shalt not fear: because thou shalt forget thy misery, and remember it as waters that pass away." It would seem at first, indeed, almost incredible, that a pre-eminently good and holy man, having fallen into extreme misfortunes, under the pressure of which he was sitting on the ground in deep sorrow and affliction of heart, his three most intimate friends, having travelled from a great distance, and at great trouble and inconvenience, for the professed purpose of consoling him, should immediately on their arrival begin to reproach him with his iniquity, and successively inform him that they considered his calamities, however heavy, to be fully deserved. But it is evident from the first that an argument is carried on in the book, and that Job is not reproached upon any personal ground, but because a great general truth is concerned in the question of his guilt. It is necessary that he should be guilty, if this present visible system of things is to be just; and it is quite necessary, in the eyes of Job's friends, that this visible system should be just, if they are to feel sure of the justice of the whole Divine government of things. Under such a conviction, it becomes not a cruelty, but a charity, to tell any one who has met with affliction, that he deserves it. To let him know that he deserves it, is to give him the first step toward obtaining relief for it. For the same just system which awarded evil to him upon ill desert, will, upon his amendment, change its line towards him, and reward him with a return of prosperity.

Such is the argument on the side of Job's friends; and it is at first difficult to see how such an argument could be seriously maintained: how, in the face of such obvious facts as the course of this world presents, men could be bold enough to assert, that this visible system was just, rewarding and punishing all the moral agents in it in exact accordance with their desert. It is true, indeed, that there is a course of justice to be seen in its working. The system, on the principle of self-preservation, rewards those virtues, and punishes those vices, which tend respectively to its own maintenance or dissolution. Thus nature rewards sobriety with health, and punishes intemperance with disease. And thus the social system rewards the prudential virtues, because they are necessary for its administration; courage, because it is necessary for its protection; and even, to a certain degree, honesty; because honesty is necessary, as the foundation of credit, without which the system cannot go on. Nor can we fail to see much that is grave and imposing in this judicial side of the system of the world. There is, however, great irregularity to be seen, even on this side; for though honesty, to take one instance, is declared by the proverb the best policy, dishonesty has unquestionably often amassed fortunes, founded families, established dynasties, and the results have shown no want of substance or stability. Nor, were there ever so much regularity, would the success of one particular class of virtues—and that class not all involving perfection of character—show really, or show what Job's friends meant by, a system of justice here; for they mean, and mean properly, by such a system, one which rewards true moral and religious goodness—the whole character of the righteous man—according to its deserts. It is ridiculous to assert that the world is under such a system as this latter, for the whole state of things shows the contrary. And though, as the author of the *Analogy* proves, we have enough before us to serve as a sample of such a system, and so bear out our belief in a true moral government of the world, the sample of the system is not the system itself.

It is argued, indeed, by Warburton and his school, that there really was such a system in operation under the old law, supplying the place of that belief in a future state, of which he supposes that law to have been entirely devoid,—a system, to the positive fact of which at one period Job's friends could appeal: that, while the rest of the world was in its natural state of disorder, a special Providence did, in the one land of Judea, for the space of time between the promulgation of the law on Mount Sinai and its beginning of decay on the return from the Captivity, maintain a visible rule of distributive justice, did visibly reward all people according to their deserts. But not to argue about the chimerical and puerile character of such a conception in itself, the fact is untrue; for in no one part of the Bible history does such a state of things appear. We see the righteous under the old law suffering just the same trials and persecutions that they have done since, and as far from their reward in this world as they are now. They "were tortured, not accepting deliverance; and had trials of cruel mockings and scourgings, of bonds and imprisonment. They were stoned, they were sawn asunder, were tempted, were slain with the sword; they wandered about in sheepskins and goatskins; being destitute, afflicted, tormented (of whom the world was not worthy). They wandered in deserts, and in mountains, and in dens and caves of the earth." Did the days in which this was the lot of God's holiest servants exhibit that rule and dispensation just mentioned? Yet such is the power of a bold and positive author, in pushing his idea, that a considerable body of theologians have, since Warburton's time, insisted greatly on this alleged peculiar feature of the Mosaic dispensation; that it ruled those under it by the distribution of temporal rewards and punishments. If, indeed, they mean only to say, that the Jews had national prosperity and national adversity sent them, according as, in their national capacity, they obeyed or disobeyed God, the assertion would be more or less true. But how little way does it go toward proving a system of temporal rewards and punishments! Men are really rewarded and really punished, not when their nation is, but when they themselves are; and the individual Jew was obviously not rewarded and punished by this rule. Indeed, Warburton confesses, that from the first there were exceptions to it; which exceptions increased as time went on, and the Gospel era approached: which is very like an admission that his fact, upon examination, evaporates.

The truth is, men who have to maintain an hypothesis are bold staters of facts. It was a matter of religion with Job's friends to maintain that this visible system was just. They wanted the fact: they therefore made it. This is not an uncommon form of proceeding with schools of thinkers. Much of ancient philosophy, for example, was devoted to supposing certain facts: that is, imagining them as true, when they had really no place in nature. The Stoic felt a difficulty in that disorder in the system of the world which brought pains and miseries, bodily and mental, upon the wise and good: and he answered it by supposing that the wise and good did not care about pains and miseries, bodily or mental. He invented and described a particular personage, called the wise man, who was wholly indifferent to, nay, completely happy under, the loss of friends, reputation, property, or limbs. Were such a personage indeed real, he would have solved the difficulty, and have proved the union of virtue and happiness beyond dispute; but the defect was, that no such personage existed. Or, to go nearer home, a particular school maintains the moral and religious progress of society, a continual advancement of it toward some ultimate point of perfection. Such a theory has necessarily to suppose a whole state of fact, which does not really exist, for its support. The events of the real world show, every day, exactly the same vices and passions in mankind that there always have been. Revolutions and political commotions are stained by the same criminal excesses. But these being the real facts, the maintainers of moral progress suppose the contrary of them. They colour the state of the world to suit their theory, and overlooking what contradicts them, exaggerating what favours them, create a state of facts for themselves. In the same way the friends of Job suppose a perfectly just visible order of things. Zophar the Naamathite, addressing the righteous man, says: "Thine age shall be clearer than the noonday; thou shalt shine forth, thou shalt be as the morning. And thou shalt be secure, because there is hope; yea, thou shalt dig about thee, and thou shalt take thy rest in safety. Also thou shalt lie down, and none shall make thee afraid; yea, many shall make suit unto thee. But the eyes of the wicked shall fail, and they shall not escape, and their hope shall be as the giving up of the ghost." Eliphaz the Temanite assures the righteous man: "He shall deliver thee in six troubles: yea, in seven there shall no evil touch thee. In famine he shall redeem thee from death: and in war from the power of the sword. Thou shalt be hid from the scourge of the tongue: neither shalt thou be afraid of destruction when it cometh. At destruction and famine thou shalt laugh: neither shalt thou be afraid of the beasts of the earth. For thou shalt be in league with the stones of the field: and the beasts of the field shall be at peace with thee. And thou shalt know also that thy seed shall be great, and thine offspring as the grass of the earth. Thou shalt come to thy grave in a full age, like as a shock of corn cometh in in his season. Lo this, we have searched it, so it is; hear it, and know thou it for thy good." Putting aside the typical sense, with which we are not concerned at present, here is a beautiful picture drawn of a just visible Providence, an administration awarding in regular course good to the righteous, evil to the wicked. But the defect is, that the picture has no warrant in fact. It is not true that every righteous man lives in peace and dies in full age, like a shock of corn in his season: some do; others do not. It would be equally untrue to say that all wicked men led troublesome lives, and met with early deaths: some do; others do not. It is not perhaps easy for us Christians to realise what a desideratum on the religious side, where there was no distinct revelation of a future state, a just, present, visible providence would be: and what a stumbling-block an irregular and confused world would be, on the other hand; what power it would have as a standing memorial against the truth of religion, and suggester of melancholy doubts and fears. Such, however, is the argumentative fault of Job's friends. They suppose a state of fact, to suit what they think the necessities of religion, and make themselves mentally comfortable at the expense of truth.

On the other hand, Job maintains that this visible system is irregular and unjust. Standing up for facts, and demanding their recognition, whatever difficulties may ensue, he asserts this to be the fact—seen with his own eyes, in the whole state of the world around him, and brought specially home to him by his own adversity. He adheres resolutely to it, and will not allow truth to be tampered with and disguised. To this are owing all those justifications of himself, and assertions of his own righteousness, in which the book abounds, in answer to his friends, who try to persuade him that his calamities are judgments upon his sins. He makes these assertions, not on his own account simply, though firmly conscious of their truth, but for the sake of that argument which those assertions were the necessary medium of maintaining. Had he yielded to the persuasions of his friends, and confessed himself an offender, he would have allowed the conclusion they wanted; for his friends had simply inferred his guilt from his suffering, on the notion of the justice of this visible system. He therefore asserted his own righteousness; and from that fact, combined with that of his affliction, drew the very opposite conclusion to the favourite one which they maintained.

Such is the process by which the Book of Job opens at length upon that great question which has grieved, perplexed, and embittered men from the beginning of the world. We find ourselves upon popular ground, and listening to an old familiar line of thought. The sentiment against the course of things here is no strange one to human minds: it is, in fact, so popular, that it may be called hackneyed. It is one that has vented itself largely in poetry, in proverbs, in philosophy, in satire; and, in connection with this book of Scripture, it demands some consideration.

It is obvious, then, that the human soul is created with a desire for justice: a desire not entertained upon a mere sense of duty, but a real love of it. The popularity of courts of justice as places of resort, the whole construction of a large part of popular literature, the policy of governments, the history of revolutions, show this. The crowds that fill the law courts enjoy the scene because it is judicial; they see the representative of justice on the bench, and feel happy in his presence; they vibrate with each turn of the evidence or the argument with the pleasing confidence of a perfect adjustment to come in the shape of the sentence; and they repose in that conclusion, when it comes, as in something good and pleasant for its own sake. The romantic, and much of the historical, parts of literature give pleasure on the same principle; they excite the longing for retribution by pictures of wrong; which longing they gratify either directly by the fact of punishment, or indirectly by leaving on the mind an indefinable expectation of that event; a strong desire which seems to prophesy its own fulfilment, and converts even the backwardness of justice into an argument that it must be working more surely and deeply. The Roman and English empires are both instances of a government policy using the same principle. The court of law has been in both of them the successful atonement for the most unscrupulous conquest; and in the enjoyment of civil and domestic justice, the tributary has forgot his dependence, and been tranquil and contented. The Roman law quieted the world; and the English has just the same effect now upon the native Hindu, who sees his own or neighbour's wrongs repaired, and goes away satisfied. The great empires of the world have imitated, in earthly fashion, and for their own purposes, the government of the Most High, " who shall judge the world in righteousness, and minister true judgment unto the people;" and are thus witnesses, in their department, to the supremacy of the sense of justice in our nature. Revolutions do the same. The stimulus to them has ordinarily been that of indignation; the sense of injustice at being deprived of certain advantages, rather than the desire for those advantages themselves. Governments go on neglecting the interests of the people for long periods: their temper becomes more and more selfish and contracted: court statesmen hand down a traditional policy to one another: officials play into one another's hands; and established power breeds security and insolence. Large classes thus feel themselves defrauded of what is their due, and that idea torments and agitates them till they appease it by rebellion. Working in undisciplined minds, that feeling then produces dreadful and enormous acts, as in the French Revolution, and unregenerate nature's appetite for justice becomes more hateful than the injustice which excited it. Still the wild feeling is only a perversion of the true moral one; and even the worst revolutionary excesses witness, in their own miserable way, to the supremacy of the idea of justice in our nature.

How largely, again, does the idea of justice mingle with many other feelings not at first sight connected with it. An integral part, for example, of the love of praise, is the pleasure of being appreciated, of having justice done us. There is a mercantile element in the feeling; as if we had received the full worth for some article of property, and had not been defrauded. There is the same element in the pleasures of ambition. The mere gratification of vanity would be a hollow pleasure, were there not something of the idea of desert with it. The bread which is earned is sweet. Men throw themselves therefore into situations in which they do great services for others, and have a right to expect their acknowledgment of them. Leaders of parties go through long years of toil and anxiety for a cause; and that they are henceforth looked up to as leaders, and live upon an eminence, is their delight, because it is their due and proper compensation. The man has worked, and he is rewarded; and the marks of honour, and voices of friends and followers, bring the evenness of the balance sensibly home to him. In this way all the affections accompanying the different relations of man to man are connected with the idea of justice. The fidelity of soldiers is their justice to a commander; so is the enthusiasm of clans to their heads, the love of children to their parents, the gratitude of clients to their benefactors, and the respect of tenants to their landlords. And men like the positions of leader, parent, benefactor, and the like, for the sake of this return. They make debtors in order that they may have the pleasure of being repaid; contrive the void, that it may be filled again; and deserve of others, that others may be just to them.

Indeed, it is evident that the sense of justice, apt as we are to contrast it with the warm instincts of our nature in this respect, is not a merely rational quality, which we cultivate upon principle, but one which moves and excites the mind, as a feeling and an affection does. It stretches forward towards its object with longing and devotion, uneasy in the absence of it, and resting in it, when attained, with delight. It expresses the fundamental idea of right and wrong in our nature, and it has that depth and power which such a function demands. Shall it be called the love of order, harmony, fitness in moral things, which are perfected when good and evil get exactly their due, and violated when they fail of getting it,—a constant longing to see the balance struck, and things made straight? Certainly we do attain, in absolute justice, a kind of *acme* of content, as if all our wishes met there, and nature found its centre and was settled. And to the idea of justice there attaches a distinct beauty, as there does to that of love—the beauty of perfect measure and proportion—which captivates us, and excites emotion, as other beauty does. So that we rejoice in every, even the smallest, manifestation of justice in the world, as necessarily as the ear likes music or the eye form, and bodies like warmth and nutriment. And as in the case of love the end is absorption and rapture, in the case of justice it is satisfaction; satisfaction, as at the attainment of perfect correctness; the feeling of marksmen who hit from a long distance the exact point they aim at. Such is that passion for justice which, sometimes lofty, sometimes trivial in its subject-matter; sometimes fretful and vehement, sometimes patient and meek, according to individual character, lives on in the minds of men; expecting some day its final rest and fulfilment, and ever pressing toward it. Scripture appeals to it throughout, and represents the world, with that whole course of events which forms its history, and all the exhibition of character which has taken place in it, as tending, like some drama, or some trial, to a great judicial issue at the day of judgment. A universal gathering then is seen of all that have lived beneath the sun; the books are open, and the whole human race, high and low, rich and poor, as the sand which is on the sea-shore innumerable, appear before the Throne and Him that sitteth thereon, to hear their final sentence. And to man himself is promised an active part in this decision, for it is said that " the saints shall judge the world."

Such being the fundamental love of justice in our nature, next follows the fact of what this world is; and thence a certain feeling toward that world, in human minds true to their own nature and constitution. For whereas it is their nature to desire justice, and therefore their first wish to live under a system in which such justice is administered, they have no sooner attained to faculties of discernment and reflection, than they discover that this world is no such system. Ancient philosophy made a distinction between a state or polity in which law and one in which will governed, and ruled it to be a violation of our nature not to live under law. Looking simply to the state of facts, apart from the religious theory which explains them, the system of the world is that "lawless" polity which they condemned, and results in the same scandal to the moral nature of those who live under it. An antagonistic feeling toward the "world," as it is called, has accordingly been always strong in the poetry, philosophy, and popular maxims of mankind, and a number of common phrases and forms of speech, such as "the way of the world,"—" always is so,"—" must be so," and the like, have pointed to some established order of things, out of which injustice is supposed to be always proceeding, in one shape or another. The world in its collective capacity has never, indeed, come into contact with anybody; nor is it an agent, nor is it a real thing at all. Everything which is done in it is done by individuals in it. But the same may be said of country, or cause, or party, or any other of that class of abstract objects which occupy so conspicuous a place in our sphere of thought. The mind does plainly take cognisance of abstractions, and has a power of entertaining feelings towards them.

To turn to the department of poetry: In this department a considerable number of minds seem to have specially devoted themselves to the expression of this sentiment against the world, or this visible order of things. It is indeed a lamentable fact that all have not spoken as they should do. There is a strong line of distinction observable; and while some have used their poetical powers on this subject wisely and religiously, others have abused them, and gone into wild excess and profaneness. Of the religious class, two poems of a philosophical type occupy a prominent place. We refer to the

Hamlet of Shakespeare, and the *Prometheus Vinctus* of Æschylus.

Of *Hamlet* first. It is evident, to begin with, that Hamlet is a person disgusted with a particular state of things which has risen up in his own family and the Danish court. It is a peculiar source of offence when that which is a matter of intense grief to us is viewed with indifference by others, who, we think, ought to sympathise with us in it. And this source of offence is greater in proportion as the indifference is grosser, and contrasts more inexcusably with the whole circumstances of the case. This is Hamlet's grievance. A father whom he loved, a splendid and majestic prince, has just died, suddenly, and in the flower of life. The event is a shock to him. But from that most trying, because sudden void, which it has produced within his own heart, he looks upon the court of Denmark, and sees all going on as if nothing had happened. A whole new state of things—his mother married again, and married to his father's brother, and that father's brother seated on the throne—has immediately supplanted the old; and a round of courtly business and festivity, continued without a break, has simply ignored the event. Dante could, under the sensation of recent loss, even of the necessary indifference of unconscious passers-by, write :—

> "Pilgrims and strangers, here who thoughtful stray
>   With mind intent, perhaps, on other care,
>   Come ye, indeed, from climes remote so far
> As this your semblance and your haste would say?
> You do not weep while passing on your way
>   Among our streets, but hurrying onward, fare
>   As those who know not and who nothing share
> Our city's grief, in this her sorrowing day."

But in Hamlet's case this indifference was a wrong, because those were indifferent who ought not to have been, and he feels disgust :—

> "That it should come to this!
> But two months dead: nay, not so much, not two:
> So excellent a king; that was, to this,
> Hyperion to a satyr; so loving to my mother,
> That he might not let e'en the winds of heaven
> Visit her face too roughly. . . .

> And yet, within a month—
> Let me not think on't. . . .
> A little month ; or ere those shoes were old
> With which she followed my poor father's body,
> Like Niobe, all tears ; why she, even she—
> O heaven ! a beast, that wants discourse of reason,
> Would have mourn'd longer,—married with my uncle,
> My father's brother."

In this state of mind he receives from his father himself, who appears from the dead, the real explanation of that sudden fate which had carried him off. The cold indifference of his mother and uncle is now turned into atrocious guilt, and the feeling of disgust, with which he had hitherto stopped short, changes into that of stern religious vengeance, which will be satisfied with nothing else but the blood of the murderer.

> " O all you host of heaven ! O earth ! What else ?
> And shall I couple hell ?—O, fye !—Hold, hold, my heart ;
> And you, my sinews, grow not instant old,
> But bear me stiffly up. Remember thee !
> Ay, thou poor ghost, while memory holds a seat
> In this distracted globe. Remember thee !
> Yea, from the table of my memory
> I'll wipe away all trivial fond records,
> All saws of books, all forms, all pressures past,
> That youth and observation copied there;
> And thy commandment all alone shall live
> Within the book and volume of my brain,
> Unmixed with baser matter."

So far Hamlet's character is only the simple one of an avenger; he has the vivid sense of a particular wrong which has been committed, and he vows, as a religious task, its punishment. But now comes in the philosophical element in him. It occurs to him that, after all, this dreadful act, carried out with such successful artifice and self-possession, is but a sample of a vast system of wrong and injustice in this visible state of things. The King and Queen represent to his mind a great evil power, or tyranny, resident in the system. The court of Denmark, the scene of their crime and prosperity, is the world; its business and festivity, in which his father's fate is forgotten, the world's stir and bustle burying thought, and covering up wrong as soon as done ; its courtiers, the idle and careless mass of mankind, who look on as spectators of injustice, and do not concern themselves about it. Now all things expand to his mind's eye, and no one wrong deed retains him; he rises from the single to the generic, and from the concrete to the abstract; and he thinks of system, and a wholesale scheme of things beneath the sun. He can think of nothing, but he instantly thinks of the whole world. Denmark is a prison, and the world is a prison. If the world is grown honest, then is doomsday near.

> "The time is out of joint;—O cursed spite
> That ever I was born to set it right!"

In all his soliloquies he deals in generals, and harps upon the discords and burdens in the order of things here as a whole. Upon this generalising vein, an unsettlement of will with respect to his task of vengeance immediately follows. For, after all (he seems to say), what is the good of it, when it is done? This deed of violence is only one out of a thousand. You may adjust a particular case, but the wrong system goes on: it is out of your reach: do what you can, you cannot touch it; and true evil, impalpable and ubiquitous, still mocks you like the air. To set one case right is only to commit yourself to do the same with respect to others *ad infinitum*, and to enter upon an impossible task. Thus the work of vengeance lags; he takes it up and lays it down again according to his humour; he plays with it, and, when he might easily execute it, puts it off for an absurd reason, which, had he been practically earnest, would not have weighed a feather with him. Upon the basis of the philosopher he erects the child again: an assumed volatility, waywardness, and indifference express the hopelessness which a large survey of things has produced in him. The lofty ruminator within exhibits himself as a jester and an oddity without; and, not content with levity, he assumes madness, as if to enable himself to enjoy a fantastic isolation from the world and human society altogether, and to live alone within himself. And when at last he does execute his work, he seems to do it by chance, and from the humour of the moment more than from any constancy of original purpose.

Such appears the explanation of Hamlet's weakness and irresoluteness. So true is it that a mind may easily be too large for effectiveness, and energy suffer from an expansion of the field of view. The first effect of the mind's expansion, in ascending from the individual to the class, is an indifference produced by the perception of the law of similarity and uniformity in nature to which that expansion introduces us. The same form of mind or body which arrested us in a single object makes less impression upon us in a series—when we see that it is only a cast from some common mould. The effect of an enlargement of acquaintance is often the same, and for the same reason, viz., that one circle of acquaintance is very like another, and that the social world goes on repeating itself. The same disadvantageous effect upon our spirit and interest in things is produced, again, by largeness simply acting as largeness upon us, and throwing insignificance upon all particular or smaller compartments of the field. The first inference which childhood draws from an enlargement of its ideas upon education, is an idle one—Since its object is so large, it cannot signify my doing this particular thing. And, in maturer life, the vastness of the whole field of action and science which larger intellects realise has a great tendency often to depress them in their efforts; for, do what they can, they know they can do so little. Too deeply embraced, the idea damps not only the ambition, but the energies of nature, its intrinsic love of self-exertion and self-development; and produces that low opinion of itself which Aristotle calls $\mu\iota\kappa\rho o\psi v\chi i\alpha$, and rightly, inasmuch as what it practically amounts to is often little short of indolence and cowardice, an indisposition to all undertakings, and a shrinking from all venture. For success in action a certain narrowness and confinement of mind is indeed almost requisite. If a man is to do any work well, he must be possessed with the idea of that work's importance. He has this idea of necessity strongly, so long as the particular scene in which he is, is the whole world to him; and, therefore, while he thinks this, he is effective; but, once enlarge his vision, and show him that his field of labour is only the same with a thousand others, and that he himself is one of a class containing thousands,—make him, that is to say, realise this world and its vastness,—and he ceases to be absorbed in his task, and is tempted to unconcern and disrelish for it. And thus the class of what are called able men, in the departments of public business or trade, may be observed, as a whole, to have the idea of the immense importance of their several departments even to excess, and advantageously so, a wise providence securing by the exclusive pretensions of each department of the world's business a most effective pledge for the safe and careful administration of the whole, and converting the ignorance and narrowness of mankind individually to their great benefit as a body.

The stimulus of narrowness, then, being requisite for vigour in action, Hamlet wants vigour, because he is without it. His want of vigour does not proceed in him from a want of passion, for he has plenty of that, but from a disproportionate largeness of intellect. He has not too little feeling, but too much thought. He is never satisfied with, never rests in, feeling, however strong, but carries it up immediately into the intellectual sphere. The quickest impulse, by some twist in his mind, takes immediately the expansive form of some general contemplation. He is always thinking of the whole of things, and any one work seems nothing. As the air we breathe is not all air, and true courage has an ingredient of fear in it, the intellect should part with something of its own nature to qualify itself as proper human intellect. It should yoke itself contentedly with a wholesome narrowness in a compound practical and intellectual being. Its largeness tends, without such check, to feebleness. The mind of Hamlet lies all abroad, like the sea—an universal reflector, but wanting the self-moving principle. Musing, reflection, and irony upon all the world, supersede action, and a task evaporates in philosophy.

It is, however, by the very imperfections of such a character that the great poet who draws it succeeds in his object, and impresses upon us the more strongly a deep view of his own, as to the character of this visible system, or the world. For, as has been justly said, one of the strongest and most successful modes of describing any powerful object, of any kind, is to describe it in its effects. When the spectator's eye is dazzled, and he shades it, we form the idea of a splendid object; when his face turns pale, of a horrible one; from his quick wonder and admiration we form the idea of great beauty; from his silent awe, of great majesty. Of a temper originally, not high and noble only, which it never could cease to be, but vigorous, energetic, and practical, "the courtier's, soldier's, scholar's eye, tongue, sword," Hamlet is made, by the force of circumstances conspiring with his own acuteness and intensity of thought, to realise very vividly what this visible order of things is; and upon this an instantaneous and a palpable change comes over him. He goes about dizzied, as if from the effect of some blow; unnerved and unstrung; from a strong man, weak; and from a complete whole, loose and wandering; and we see that the fabric of his mind has suffered. The Psalmist informs us of an effect nearly produced upon himself, upon his realising in some such strong way the facts of this system, viz., that "his feet had almost gone, his treadings had well-nigh slipped;" alluding evidently to some injurious power, of whatever kind, which such a disclosure was apt to have. Nature, by various symptoms, shows when she has seen too much, and had some revelation made her to which she is unequal; as the stories of persons who have never got over the sight of an apparition, and the old fables of the basilisk's eye and the Medusa's head teach. By these effects, then, which follow Hamlet's keen realising of this world's system, the poet makes us feel what the system is; for we argue what that must be, the contact with which could distort and paralyse such a person; that utter opposition to the type of justice within his mind which could create such a jar.

The situation of the hero in the *Prometheus Vinctus* is an extreme one, of a sufferer under injustice; and it is described with much revolting detail and circumstance, and strong pictorial effect. The scene is a Scythian desert, a vast and dreadful solitude; the ground which the *dramatis personæ* occupy, just under one of the precipitous rocks of Mount Caucasus. Two demons, who, under the names of Might and Force, impersonate brute power, and whose horrible appearance upon the stage is alluded to in the dialogue,

ὅμοια μορφῇ γλῶσσά σου γηρύεται,[1]

[1] Like to thy shape the utterance of thy tongue.

lead in Prometheus. Vulcan, with chains and irons, screw and hammer, attends as executioner. The process of fastening him to the rock then commences, which is given step by step. First one arm is chained to its post, then the other; then one foot, then another; and a nail driven through his breast makes him finally secure. The speech of the two demons all the while is appropriate to their nature, and doubtless the poet took care that it should possess all the physical asperity also which stage artifice could supply. It consists of savage admonitions to Vulcan, at each stage of the process, to do his work well: such as, "Hammer again," "Strike harder," "Drive it in," repeated till an absolutely final tightness has been achieved. And with this stringent watch over the executioner there mingles insolence to the victim; the chain is riveted with the remark, "That will teach you discretion;" and, the whole process over, the two demons take their leave with loud scoffing. The reader will perceive, amid the undoubted grandeur of the scene, not a little grotesqueness. With his constant allusions to a deep philosophy which none but the few could appreciate, Æschylus mixes appeals to the many; and the opening scene in the *Prometheus* seems to have been constructed with the view of fixing a strong and palpable image of unjust power upon a popular audience.

Meantime we discover, as the real author of all these wrongs,—the superior at whose bidding they are done, and of whom these demons are the mere ministers and agents,—a much higher personage. Jove is the malignant and implacable inflicter of these tortures upon Prometheus; and he inflicts them not only undeservedly, for acts of mercy and benevolence on Prometheus' part to the human race, but in the highest degree ungratefully, after Prometheus has done him the most important services in fixing him on his throne, endangered by the formidable conspiracy of the Titans. Jove is represented as full of jealousy of the human race, and desirous of keeping them in a miserable and degraded state; and Prometheus has offended by his zeal in elevating and improving them; he is also a newly-seated monarch, and he has the instinct of persons newly risen to power to suspect and dislike those who have been instrumental in raising them. By these well-known traits—familiar especially to a Greek audience—Æschylus fixes upon Jove the character of a tyrant, and exhibits his government as a tyranny—

νέος γὰρ καὶ τύραννος ἐν θεοῖς . . .
ἅπας δὲ τραχὺς ὅστις ἂν νέον κρατῇ.[1]

The question then follows, who this personage is who is called Jove, and to whom this tyranny is attributed. As far as the name goes, he is the Supreme Governor of the universe; for Jove, or Zeus, was the name of the Supreme Being in Greek worship. But though the vituperation with which Æschylus assails one who, at least, bears that name, is sufficiently bold, and has an appearance even of that spirit which modern infidel poetry has shown, the religious temper of the poet, in the first place, and the very description which he gives of this personage in the second, precludes us from supposing that this name carries with it here that high meaning. For, as we have seen, he describes Jove particularly as a "new" monarch. And just as he assigns him a beginning, he proceeds to assign him also an end of his government: a liberty which the jumble of ancient mythology allowed him; for the poet is only following a portion of ancient fable here.

ΠΡ. νῦν δ' οὐδέν ἐστι τέρμα μοι προκείμενον
μόχθων, πρὶν ἂν Ζεὺς ἐκπέσῃ τυραννίδος.
ΙΩ. ἦ γάρ ποτ' ἔστιν ἐκπεσεῖν ἀρχῆς Δία;
ΠΡ. ἥδοι' ἄν, οἶμαι, τήνδ' ἰδοῦσα συμφοράν.
ΙΩ. πῶς δ' οὐκ ἄν, ἥτις ἐκ Διὸς πάσχω κακῶς;
ΠΡ. ὡς τοίνυν ὄντων τῶνδέ σοι μαθεῖν πάρα.
ΙΩ. πρὸς τοῦ τύραννα σκῆπτρα συληθήσεται;
ΠΡ. αὐτὸς πρὸς αὑτοῦ κενοφρόνων βουλευμάτων.[2]

---

[1] And harsh is every one when new of sway.

[2] *Pro.* But through all time no limit to my woes
 Is set, till Zeus from sovereignty be hurled.
Io. How! can Zeus ever be from empire hurled?
Pro. Thou wouldest joy, methinks, such hap to see.
Io. How should I not who suffer ill from Zeus?
Pro. That thus it shall be it is thine to learn.
Io. By whom despoiled of his tyrannic sway?
Pro. Spoiled by himself and his own senseless plans.
 The Dramas of Æschylus,
 tr. by Anna Swanwick, pp. 160-193.

A power like this, which has a beginning and has an end, cannot be really Supreme ; for that is necessarily without beginning and without end. Of such a power, however, not supreme really, inasmuch as it is not eternal, but supreme *de facto* and at present, and governing the world, one explanation remains. There is a sense in which power simply stands for and impersonates facts. We use it in this sense when we gather all the phenomena of the physical world together under one head or power, which we call Nature. And by a poetical license we use it in the same way also to impersonate the facts of the social world. We talk of the genius of a party, a nation, a school, meaning by it some power which we suppose to form and direct them. And, to take the largest instance, and the one which concerns us at present, we talk of a power working in this whole state of things, and making it to be what it is; moulding society and producing events :—a power or system of things, moreover, which is practically supreme while it lasts, inasmuch as nothing interferes with it or stops its course. Such appears to be the power which Æschylus refers to, and which he dresses in this mythological shape. And Jove is, to his mind, the god or genius of this present order of things ; and his temporary supremacy impersonates the world.

Such is the medium by which the poet succeeds in expressing a great idea in his mind of this world, as a system of things irregular and unjust. A tyranny had the conventional meaning, among the Greeks, of a government which ruled by individual caprice and self-will, instead of law ; and was consequently the great type of an unjust system to Greek minds. Any one who wanted to impress a Greek with the idea of any administration as unjust, would exhibit it under that form to him ; and, therefore, by exhibiting the whole present system of things to him under that form, Æschylus exhibits it under the strongest aspect of injustice which he could give it.

Under the severe pressure, then, of this unjust power, Prometheus is portrayed with deep sensibility and tremendous determination. He feels acutely—the wrong rather than the pain—the fact, that, having devoted himself to deeds of mercy to the human race, he is punished like a criminal ; and having conferred the greatest benefits on Jove himself, he is oppressed like an enemy; and invokes the compassion of all created things :—

> ἴδεσθέ μ' οἷα πρὸς θεῶν πάσχω θεός.
> δέρχθηθ', οἵαις αἰκίαισιν
> διακναιόμενος τὸν μυριετῆ
> χρόνον ἀθλεύσω. Τοιόνδ' ὁ νέος
> ταγὸς μακάρων ἐξηῦρ' ἐπ' ἐμοὶ
> δεσμὸν ἀεικῆ. . . .
> ὁρᾶτε δεσμώτην με δύσποτμον θεὸν,
> τὸν Διὸς ἐχθρὸν,
> διὰ τὴν λίαν φιλότητα βροτῶν. . . .
> . . . .
> μή τοι χλιδῇ δοκεῖτε μηδ' αὐθαδίᾳ
> σιγᾶν με· συννοίᾳ δὲ δάπτομαι κέαρ,
> ὁρῶν ἐμαυτὸν ὧδε προυσελούμενον.
> καίτοι θεοῖσι τοῖς νέοις τούτοις γέρα
> τίς ἄλλος ἢ 'γὼ παντελῶς διώρισεν;
> ἀλλ' αὐτὰ σιγῶ· . . .[1]

The proud inflexibility of a being more than human follows, as his friends and counsellors, the chorus of Oceanides, with the best intentions, acting the part of Job's comforters, try to persuade him to bow to this present power which is oppressing him, to confess himself in error, and ask for a remission of his sentence. Æschylus now seems to compress his lips, as he condenses the powers of language into absolute solidity, to describe a stubbornness like that of the round world itself, a perfection of just pride, an unbending moral will. Sustained by

[1] *Pro.* Behold what I, a god, from gods endure.
　　See, wasted by what pains
Wrestle I must while myriad time shall flow!
　　Such ignominious chains
　　Hath he who newly reigns,
Chief of the blest, devised against me.
. . . .
　　A god ye see in fetters, anguish-fraught;
　　　The foe of Zeus, . . .
　　For that to men I bore too fond a mind.
. . . .
Pro. Think not that I through pride or stubbornness
　　Keep silence; nay, my brooding heart is gnawed
　　Seeing myself thus marred with contumely;
　　And yet what other but myself marked out
　　To these new gods their full prerogatives?
　　But I refrain.—*Ibid.* pp. 164, 169-178.

an unerring foresight, which resides like reason in his nature, Prometheus sees far too clearly the day when Jove shall bend to him, to think of any other course than simply waiting where he is, and living out the time. He fulfils the transcendental type of Oriental rather than the natural one of Greek legend, and is, ideal man, independent of circumstances, true to himself, and unconquerable.

> πρὸς ταῦτ' ἐπ' ἐμοὶ ῥιπτέσθω μὲν
> πυρὸς ἀμφήκης βόστρυχος, αἰθὴρ δ'
> ἐρεθιζέσθω βροντῇ, σφακέλῳ τ'
> ἀγρίων ἀνέμων· χθόνα δ' ἐκ πυθμένων
> αὐταῖς ῥίζαις πνεῦμα κραδαίνοι,
> κῦμα δὲ πόντου τραχεῖ ῥοθίῳ
> ξυγχώσειεν· τῶν τ' οὐρανίων
> ἄστρων διόδους, ἔς τε κελαινὸν
> Τάρταρον ἄρδην ῥίψειε δέμας
> τοὐμὸν ἀνάγκης στερραῖς δίναις·
> πάντως ἐμέ γ' οὐ θανατώσει.[1]

This invincible strength of character is made to come out the more boldly by the introduction upon the scene of Io, who stands in such striking contrast to it. Io and Prometheus are the perfect types in juxtaposition of the two great kinds of grief, the magnanimous and the plaintive. The grief of Io is wonderfully beautiful of its kind; simple, transparent, and confiding; feminine, and full of utterance; most pathetic and appealing; but not without an element of selfishness. She comes suddenly upon the stage, flying from a malignant phantom with "a crafty eye," who is ever behind her, and pursues her over the face of the globe, wearied, but afraid to stop. She

---

[1] *Pro.* So 'gainst me now be hurled amain
　　Curled lightning's two-edged glare!
　By thunder and spasmodic whirl
　　Of savage gales be upper air
　Madly convulsed! Let hurricane
　Earth from its deep foundation rend,
　E'en from its roots. Let ocean's wave,
　Surging aloft, tumultuous rave,
　And, foaming, with the courses blend
　Of heavenly stars! ay, let him hurl
　This body to the murky gloom
　Of Tartaros in stubborn whirl
　Of fortune caught! Do what he will
　　My death he may not doom.—*Ibid.* p. 208.

enters with plaintive voice, and quick touching exclamations, like some tremulous and shrill but sweet music, and catches all at once the sight of Prometheus, suffering under a different, but quite as severe, an infliction as her own; whom she immediately asks to befriend her, and help her to some way of extricating herself from her troubles; apparently forgetful, that if he were a selfish person, he had enough to think of in his own.

> ποῖ μ' ἄγουσι τηλέπλανοι πλάναι;
> τί ποτέ μ', ὦ Κρόνιε
> παῖ, τί ποτε ταῖσδ' ἐνέζευξας εὑρὼν
> ἁμαρτοῦσαν ἐν πημοναῖσιν; ἒ ἕ . . .
> ἅδην με πολύπλανοι πλάναι
> γεγυμνάκασιν. . . .
>
> . . . .
>
> ἀλλά μοι τορῶς τέκμηρον
> ὅ,τι μ' ἐπαμμένει παθεῖν·
> τί μῆχαρ, ἢ τί φάρμακον νόσου,
> δεῖξον, εἴπερ οἶσθα, θρόει,
> φράζε τᾷ δυσπλάνῳ παρθένῳ.[1]

One or two brief inquiries about the unhappy situation of Prometheus are only a preface to further solicitations about herself.

> ΙΩ. καὶ πρός γε τούτοις, τέρμα τῆς ἐμῆς πλάνης
> δεῖξον τίς ἔσται τῇ ταλαιπώρῳ χρόνος.
> ΠΡ. τὸ μὴ μαθεῖν σοι κρεῖσσον ἢ μαθεῖν τάδε.
> ΙΩ. μήτοι με κρύψῃς τοῦθ' ὅπερ μέλλω παθεῖν.
> ΠΡ. ἀλλ' οὐ μεγαίρω τοῦδέ σοι δωρήματος.
> ΙΩ. τί δῆτα μέλλεις μὴ οὐ γεγωνίσκειν τὸ πᾶν;[2]

---

[1] Ah, whither on earth do these far-roamings lead?
What trespass canst find, son of Kronos, in me,
  That thou yokest me ever to pain?
    Woe! ah, woe! . . .
Enough hath outworn me my much-roaming toil.

. . . .
            But now by clear sign,
Reveal what for me yet remaineth to bear;
What cure for my plague. If such knowledge be thine,
Forthwith to the sad-roaming maiden declare.—*Ibid.* pp. 184-5.

[2] *Io.* Then further of my roamings tell the goal.
    What time to me, poor outcast, yet must run?
  Pro. This not to learn were better than to learn.
  Io. Yet from me hide not what I needs must suffer.
  Pro. Not chary am I of such boon to thee.
  Io. Then why delayest to make known the whole?—*Ibid.* pp. 184-186.

The grief of wandering Io, flying and lamenting, lamenting and flying, eagerly catching at any chance of relief, and full of her own misfortunes, even in the presence of greater ones; and that of the fixture of the rock, stubborn and self-controlling—

ἁρμοῖ πέπαυμαι τοὺς ἐμοὺς θρηνῶν πόνους,[1]

and able with majestic pity to soothe another's pain from the depths of his own, show respectively the poor mortal and the godlike sufferer, and produce just that difference in our feeling which there is between the simple kind of pity and that with which awe mingles—the pity for an equal, and the pity for a superior being.

In comparing the *Hamlet* and the *Prometheus*, we see the difference between the mythological (or, so to call it, theological) mind of Æschylus and the human sympathies of Shakespeare. Æschylus is above the clouds, in the region of supernatural characters and intelligences, and he describes the position of such a character and intelligence toward unjust power. Shakespeare is on this earth, and he describes the effect of injustice and disorder upon one of earthly mould mingling loftiness with frailty. He describes, in contrast with the Æschylean type of strength and determination, a musing, moralising, large-minded perplexity, a mixture of depth and weakness; seeming to sympathise genially with it, too, as he portrays it. Hamlet is a man, Prometheus is a god. The one is a critic, and the other a combatant. Hamlet gazes on present difficulties, and Prometheus penetrates them.

The stimulus, then, which has produced both of these great philosophical poems is obvious; but, besides her philosophical and direct teaching on this subject, Poetry has had her indirect. A very marked department of it has taken in hand the subject of ingratitude; and such stories as that of *King Lear* and of *Coriolanus* have been highly popular as subjects of dramas. We may almost include the *Iliad* in this class, so much of the interest in it has relation to this subject. Achilles is the ablest warrior and chieftain of the Greek army; he has worked hardest in the cause, and has been always victorious;

---

[1] Scarce have I ceased singing my dirge of woe.—*Ibid.* p. 186.

the expedition owes its success to him : and Agamemnon, as the leader of it, is under special obligation to him. But Agamemnon, so far from acknowledging the obligation, quarrels with him on some trivial matter, treats him with the greatest indignity before the whole council, reminds him contemptuously of the immeasurable interval between the rank of a petty chieftain of the Myrmidons and that of the Lord Paramount of Greece; refuses to allow that he has been of any use to the cause, telling him he may go as soon as he likes, as he can dispense with his services ; and, finally, actually sends his officers to his tent, and forcibly seizes and appropriates some of the inferior chieftain's hard-earned spoil. Achilles, in inexpressible indignation, retires from the council and the field, and shuts himself up in his own quarters. The battle with the enemy meanwhile goes on as usual, for Agamemnon is determined to show that he can do without Achilles ; and various heroes perform various achievements. The reader, however, never forgets the injured hero ; and the poem is so constructed, that, while the tug of war is going on, the chariots rushing, the trumpets sounding, the bows clanging, the spears whizzing, on the field of battle, the image of Achilles is ever seen in the background sitting in his tent, or wandering listlessly on the sea-shore brooding over his wrong; consoling himself with his lyre, or praying to his mother Thetis to come to help him. The contrast of the melancholy chieftain with the activities of the battle-field acts insensibly on the reader throughout, and he is ever borne to the position of Achilles as that which makes the poem what it is, and provides the interest. The great master, however, of this subject is our own dramatic poet. In the whole department of sensations, connected with the sense of ingratitude, Shakespeare is quite supreme and without a rival. His words pierce like swords, and the popular legend he has chosen at random out of the general heap, and developed into the scenes of *King Lear*, is the great model and exponent of this portion of the feelings of the human race.

Such poetry then, though only concerned immediately with individual cases, has a strong indirect bearing upon the system of things here, and glides by a natural and easy process into that general sentiment of which we have been speaking. Ingratitude is not only a species of injustice, but the highest species, and, as it were, the model and exemplar of it. For the obligation of giver to receiver results immediately from the very first relation in the constitution of things, that of cause and effect: the giver being the cause of that enjoyment or that advantage which the receiver has in the gift; and therefore ingratitude is the violation of the primeval relation in the constitution of things, and, in it, of the whole scheme and law of justice. So fundamental and normal a species of injustice is naturally suggestive of the whole genus; and the poet, in drawing out dramatically the personal wrong, is insensibly reminded of the system, and slides into general hints and reflections. In *King Lear*, for example, it is worth observing how soon the ill-used old king begins to implicate the world in the ingratitude of his two daughters :—

> "And thou, all-shaking thunder,
> Strike flat the thick rotundity o' the world!
> Crack Nature's moulds, all germens spill at once,
> That make ingrateful man!"

And by and by, as his madness becomes milder, trains of thought something like Hamlet's appear, and his wandering head runs on in a mock-philosophising way upon the world and all its proceedings,—

"What, art mad? A man may see how the world goes, with no eyes. Look with thine ears: see how yon justice rails upon yon simple thief: change places, and, handy dandy, which is the justice, which is the thief? Thou hast seen a farmer's dog bark at a beggar?"

> "None does offend, none, I say, none; I'll able 'em:
> Take that of me, my friend, who have the power
> To seal the accuser's lips. Get thee glass eyes;
> And, like a scurvy politician, seem
> To see the things thou dost not. Now, now, now, now:
> Pull off my boots:—harder, harder; so.
> *Edgar.* Oh, matter and impertinency mixed!
> Reason in madness!
> *Lear.* If thou wilt weep my fortunes, take my eyes.
> I know thee well enough; thy name is Gloster:
> Thou must be patient; we came crying hither.
> Thou know'st, the first time that we smell the air,
> We wawl and cry :—I will preach to thee; mark me!"

The use of the fool in Shakespeare is a good deal in connection with this vein of thought in the poet. Levity is a medium to a philosophical effect. It is remarkable that the gravest things obtain a conventional ridiculousness as soon as ever there attaches an idea of commonness and uniformity to them. The grave offences of cheating, lying, and drunkenness, are thus popularly ridiculous because they are large established classes of offences, and belong to a very prolific common mould; and thus the unquestionably grave affair of death has collected a world of jocularity around it as the result of its undeniable universality. As commonness then has a natural alliance with the ridiculous, so, *vice versa*, ridicule becomes an instrument to raise the idea of commonness; and as the fool wanders on with his laughter and jests, his absurd parodies and irrelevant reflections, the idea is unconsciously imbibed of some large type to which these griefs and evils belong, some order of things out of which they proceed.

But we have alluded to another and a very different class of poets, whose poetry also has been strongly marked by this sentiment against the visible course of things. This school may be said to be more full of the subject than the religious one; more exclusively and eagerly occupied with it. The obliquity of this visible system is the one great stimulus of the whole poetical thought of such writers as Lord Byron and Shelley; the one theme, which is ever drawing them magnetwise, and round which they work as round a centre. Loose and undisciplined themselves, these men feel an undoubted disgust for the looseness and disorder of the world in which they live. Their poetry cannot be set down as words; they mean what they say, and have an idea in their heads; and they swell the general body of sentiment which runs in this direction: while at the same time they must not be allowed to take their place side by side with the sacred poets and religious contemplators of the scene, as if their feeling and that of the religious class were the same.

The general subject of that common ground of feeling and taste, which good and bad men have, would be too large a one to enter upon here. It is obvious, however, that they have one; that bad men are capable of possessing affection, friendship, generosity, courage, zeal; and that just as they have intellect and imagination in common with the good, they have also moral sensibilities, and even refined and delicate ones, in common with them. The feeling against the injustice and disorder of this visible order of things is part of this common ground, and bad men and good men can both have it. We may ask what minds in themselves loose and immoral can see in such injustice to offend them, and why they should not feel perfect sympathy and content with a world like themselves, on the principle of the proverb in Aristotle, that " Like loves like, and potter takes to potter." But the answer to such a difficulty is easy. Bad men are capable of feeling disgust at evil without them, though they may have no such feeling toward it within them. There is all the difference between external and internal: men are annoyed with bodily uncleanness as a spectacle, who have no objection to it as a companion. Admitted within us, in the shape of some bad passion, evil is part of us for the time, and being part of ourselves is not felt as evil, and therefore does not raise disgust; but let the same bad passion be situated outside the soul,—that is to say, be apparent in some other person,—and it will raise disgust. The bad have a moral nature, in spite of their immoral acts; and they allow that nature to work where there is nothing practical or painful in its working, but on the contrary an agreeable irritation and excitement. Thus proud, unjust, and selfish men, will be fully alive to pride, injustice, and selfishness, in others: and the same with respect to any system or order of things external to themselves: if they see injustice in it, it will offend them.

In this way good men and bad men are alike capable of entertaining the sentiment against this visible order of things; the only difference in this, as in other feelings which they have in common, lying in a certain fundamental state of mind in which they respectively entertain it. Scripture points to a particular fundamental state of mind in which good men entertain all feelings whatever; which it calls " in the Lord." Good men entertain this, as they do other feelings, upon this basis. But this basis bad men want, and the whole line which this feeling takes in them, shows it. The moral ingredient in it, though it does exist, exists but as a small particle in the midst of a vast body of wounded pride and self-love. The feeling of religious minds towards the world is judicial; theirs is retaliatory. Good men would be heartily glad if the world got better, and would sincerely welcome a state of things in which virtue and innocence prevailed. But the bad do not wish the world to change, however they may rail at it. They know that a better state of things would be a witness against them, and they had rather have the worse state, and accuse it. Thus, retaliating on the world's injustice, and enjoying its laxity, they form the proud, misanthropical, and at the same time licentious school of poetry : in the wake of which follows that crowd of busy satirists, and describers of fashionable life, who unfold with such cleverness and vivacity, in such unwearied detail, the vices and selfishness of society, showing all the time that they secretly relish what they profess to expose, and glory in their real or assumed intimacy with it.

But after all, the injustice in this visible system is not the sole or the main object of complaint with this class of poets. And here lies the most striking point of difference between their feeling and that of the religious class. The religious class confine themselves to the phenomenon of injustice, that is to say, to the spectacle of undeserved pain and triumphant evil in this visible system : but the other class take the universal line of objecting to the existence altogether of pain and of evil. This is a widely different ground from the other. A spectacle of injustice offends the moral sense, and throws, though of course negatived by our certainty of there being a solution of it, a *prima facie* appearance of injustice upon the power that permits it. But there is nothing immoral in the simple fact of pain: it is mysterious to our intellects, and discordant with our senses, but it does not come into collision with the conscience. Nor is there anything immoral, as regards the Author of nature, in the fact of the moral evil or guilt which resides in us; for He is not the author of it. These minds, however, brood querulously over the fact of simple pain, especially pain of mind, disappointed love, wounded self-respect, weariness, satiety, terror, melancholy, doubt; as if these were in themselves grievances and scandals. And they proceed even to regard the moral evil within them in the same light, and to complain in the same way of "this life," which is "a false nature," and is not in

> "The harmony of things—this hard decree,
> This uneradicable taint of sin,
> This boundless Upas, this all-blasting tree."

The great fact of the fall of man and the corruption and disarrangement of our nature is acknowledged; they acknowledge their own particular sin and corruption; but the fact does not produce self-condemnation, but only makes them accusers; by a determined twist of mind they regard the very sins which they themselves commit as so much injustice committed upon them; and so far from feeling self-abasement, are positively elevated in their own eyes as victims. Such a view is of course self-contradictory, for why does sin pain them at all, except on the idea that they themselves are responsible for it, and are the authors of their own wrong acts, and not any other power? And yet, by an ingenuity of attack, they turn the very contradiction to their accusation into matter of accusation itself, and of all the effects of the fall and corruption of man, specially single out the pains of conscience for complaint; protesting against the "self-disapprobation" and "self-contempt" resident in human souls, as the greatest wrong of all done them, because it penetrates deepest, and turns the man himself against himself: the complainer seemingly forgetting that the judge must agree in his own sentence, and that therefore the self-disapprover cannot, except by the most ridiculous inconsistency, complain of the injustice of that disapprobation. In this way, then, they treat all pain and evil, all suffering and all sin, and with them the whole system of trial and probation which exposes us to them, as grievances;

> "To the last in verge of our decay
> Some phantom lures, such as we thought at first,
> But all too late; so are we doubly curst:
> Love, fame, ambition, avarice:"

thus, besides the difference in the subject-matter of feeling between them and the religious class of poets, differing also in the impatient inference which they draw; and, where the former simply assert a fact which comes before their eyes and there stop, proceeding to an immediate judgment upon the constitution of things, and making the order of nature a stumbling-block to their faith. Two such lines of objection as these come under the distinction which Butler makes in his *Analogy*, where he allows reason to judge of morality, but not of expediency. He would allow men to decide upon the justice or injustice of the system of the world as it stands before them, because that is merely deciding upon a fact of which our moral nature makes us proper judges : while to objections against the construction of this whole system, on the ground that it is productive of much actual evil and misery, he answers: "There could be no stopping (in such objections) till we came to such conclusions as these : that all creatures should at first be made as perfect and as happy as they were capable of ever being, that nothing of hazard or danger should be put upon them, some indolent persons might think nothing at all. . . . But we may see beforehand that we have not faculties for this kind of speculation."

In a general body of popular sentiment, then, and in the voice of constitutional, and even corrupt and extravagant poetry, enough has appeared to show the large place in human thought which the injustice and irregularity of this visible order of things has occupied. It was to be expected that the Bible, being a book intended for the instruction and consolation of the whole human race, should in due course touch upon this feeling. It is part of the office of such a book to show large sympathies, and spread over a wide ground of human feeling; on the rule that every instructor who undertakes to direct and discipline feelings should first show that he understands them. And, accordingly, the Bible does take this feeling in hand in one book, which is devoted specially to it. In the Book of Job it shows sympathy with it in the first place, and supplies its due correction in the second.

The form under which this sympathy is expressed is the same as that which the great poets, ancient and modern, have used. The character is real in one case, fictitious in the other; but in both cases a character is drawn. The Book of Job draws the character of the patriarch Job. Under the influence of one great idea—a sense of the injustice of this visible order of things, he pursues various trains of thought, and gives way to various emotions; he is argued with, and he argues; he is reproached, and he defends himself. His character thus comes out, as it were, dramatically, and it comes out as an extraordinarily intense, and, in the unobnoxious sense of the word, passionate one. It would seem almost as if it were the intention of Scripture to show to all generations of mankind how thoroughly it understood this vein of thought, and, however watchful over it, felt with it; and how it was resolved to leave no excuse to the most sensitive to say that their case had been overlooked and unprovided for. One look into this book should satisfy the most vehement, melancholy, and indignant natures of the existence of a religion which understands them, and would direct them if they would let it. They are anticipated there perfectly; they must see themselves there, and their keenest thoughts reflected. Scripture is beforehand with its sympathy, and they cannot escape it but by violence. And that whole school of morbid poets, who disbelieved it because they never chose to consult it, and never chose to consult it because they took it for granted that it did not understand them and could not instruct them, are simply proved guilty of the folly of hasty persons in worldly matters, who refuse the offers of experienced and sympathetic guides, on the mere indefinite dread of being interfered with, and meeting with the slightest check to their will.

The character of Job, as the book represents it, may be brought substantially under two heads,—his language about himself, and his language toward the Deity.

We have noticed already that the argument in the Book of Job requires him to take a high line about himself; but it is obviously not a satisfactory explanation of such a line of feeling to say that the argument requires it; for, however the argument may require it, the question still remains, whether it is in itself right and proper. It does appear at first sight singular audacity in a human being to assert, in the presence of God, that he does not deserve a particular train of calamities with which, in the natural order of providence, he has been visited. And yet this is what Job asserts and persists in maintaining. No argument, entreaty, or reproach can pull him from this ground.

Aristotle has given a famous definition of the magnanimous man : " one who thinks himself worthy of great things, being worthy :" ὁ μεγάλων αὑτὸν ἀξιῶν ἄξιος ὤν. It is obvious that this is the character attributed to the Supreme Being in Scripture. He is specially represented as "jealous," that is to say, aware of the great honour due to Him, and claiming it. He deserves great honour at the hand of His creatures, as well on account of His bounty to them, as on account of the ineffable goodness and greatness of His own character. He expects them to pay it Him :—" Thou shalt love the Lord thy God with all thy heart, and with all thy soul, and with all thy mind, and with all thy strength : this is the first and great commandment." Here is the character of the μεγαλόψυχος. From the Supreme Being, who is the type of it, this character descends in a subordinate sense to man, as made in the Divine image : he has it so far as he retains that image ; though so far as he has lost it he has another, and must simply abase and annihilate himself in his own ideas. We call it self-respect. A man, by the constitution of his nature, stands in certain intimate relations to himself, which it is his duty to maintain, just as it is his duty to maintain his relations to others. Thus he adopts certain general lines of action on the idea of it being due to himself to adopt them, and that any lower ones would not be just to himself; and he desires what is due to himself also in the actions of others toward him.

This temper, referring, as it does, the mind entirely to a standard and a voice within, stands in marked contrast to pride, of which, as St. Augustine says, the fundamental characteristic is " a certain swelling," that is to say, a " going abroad and out of doors, out of the world within into the world without."[1] There is indeed a species of pride, sometimes confounded with self-respect, which seems to keep a person wholly within and attending to an internal judgment; and which is, on that very account, considered a deeper and more intense kind of pride, and is unfavourably opposed to vanity, the very obtrusiveness and transparency of which is thought after all to indicate a simpler and more venial form of the sin. But this pride will not be found, on examination, to do what it seems to do. There is a chamber within the human mind, in which the whole external world, transferred from its external and material site, is lodged; and where, gathered to a point, are reflected all the influences and the eyes of society. In minds of a certain power this image of the world is so deep and strong that they are able to act under it as under the eye of the real world itself, and are not obliged, as the vain or weaker class of minds are, to be perpetually realising the stimulus and support of society by actual applications to the material body. But still it is the stimulus of the world's approval, reflected from without, under which they act, and not the genuine praise of the native judge within. That pure praise has no particle of pride in it, but is the act of simple original truth, measuring and weighing the moral being, defining what is his due, and authorising him to claim it at the hands of all creatures. Beneath this inward measuring eye of truth high moral natures live, and they claim what it awards them, not for the purposes of self-flattery, but of justice. And this freedom from selfish aims gives them confidence, nor are they ashamed of the sentence of their own hearts, as proud minds are, who, with that mysterious consciousness which evil has of its own shame, veil their self-exaltation under an outside of retirement, and hide the unseemly disease from the public eye; on the contrary, they express it, if occasion requires, freely and openly. True self-respect has nothing to

---

[1] Superbia intumescere, hoc illi est in extima progredi:—progredi autem in extima, quid aliud est quam intima projicere: id est longe a se facere Deum, non locorum spatio, sed mentis affectu.—Aug. lib. vi. *de Musica*, c. 13.

conceal, and is, like childhood, a plain-spoken claimant. And on this principle Homer gives his hero pre-eminent freedom of speech and openness in claiming his due, and, at the beginning of that great speech which is devoted to this object, puts that sentiment into his mouth,

$$\dot{\epsilon}\chi\theta\rho\grave{o}\varsigma\ \gamma\acute{a}\rho\ \mu o\iota\ \kappa\epsilon\hat{\iota}\nu o\varsigma\ \dot{o}\mu\hat{\omega}\varsigma\ \text{'}A\ddot{\iota}\delta a o\ \pi\acute{\nu}\lambda\eta\sigma\iota\nu,$$
$$\ddot{o}\varsigma\ \chi\text{'}\ \ddot{\epsilon}\tau\epsilon\rho o\nu\ \mu\grave{\epsilon}\nu\ \kappa\epsilon\acute{\nu}\theta\epsilon\iota\ \dot{\epsilon}\nu\grave{\iota}\ \phi\rho\epsilon\sigma\acute{\iota}\nu,\ \ddot{a}\lambda\lambda o\ \delta\grave{\epsilon}\ \beta\acute{a}\zeta\epsilon\iota.^1$$

And to go to inspired models, St. Paul uses great freedom of speech, and is remarkably open in this claim. So little cause is there to suspect this principle as if it were of the nature of pride, and were to be suppressed like a strong unruly appetite. Indeed, so far from it calling for suppression from being too strong, it is evident that the principle is much too weak in the generality of human minds; that the mass are ready to rest upon any respect whatever sooner than their own, and live upon the approval of the external circle, social, intellectual, or religious, to which they may belong, far too much; and that a diseased human race craves the artificial stimulus of the world's eye, either actual or reflected, and cannot appreciate that high form of honour which their own moral nature, as God made it, supplies.

Indeed, the exercise of self-respect, so far from being allied to pride, is in many cases, which will easily occur to any person who thinks on the subject, a positive exercise of humility. It is so in the kind of case with which we are now concerned. The first instinct of self-respect in a man is to see injustice when it is done him; and this very perception is at the same time humiliating. Injustice is of the nature of contempt; and it is humiliating to be despised. And therefore, though a class of minds who are sustained by the unnatural strength of pride and evil passion, counterbalancing and negativing that humbling result, will even take pleasure in brooding upon real or imaginary injustice done them, in the minds of good men who have no such counterbalance, the thought brings no pleasure, but simple pain. They would avoid it if they could, and refuse to see

---

[1] Him as the gates of hell my soul abhors,
Whose outward words his secret thoughts belie.

the fact. There is a well-known form of character occasionally met with in society, that allows the possessor to see no slight: the most obvious and palpable does not touch him: he will never believe in the possibility of any such intention toward him; he imagines, as a matter of course, all men always thinking well of him, and this determined previous view colours every act, or word, or look which he meets with, however unsusceptible in itself of such an interpretation. A secret indisposition to that kind of humiliation which injustice, either real or supposed, inflicts, produces such a character; the trial is too unpleasant a one, and he goes through life thrusting it away from him by the propelling force of this previous view. For the same reason, good men would avoid the sense of injustice done them if they could, and would refuse to see it, from the natural distaste for what is humiliating. Indeed, it is not paradoxical to say that, with respect to the mere question of comparative pain, they would rather have the sense of deserved wrong to bear, than the sense of undeserved; and that, after dwelling with the feeling of a person ill-used upon any piece of ingratitude, or contumely, or neglect, from any individual or body, the idea, could they persuade themselves of the fact, that they had done something to them to deserve it, would come quite as a relief. For then the wrong is accounted for, and, being accounted for, is removed. They stand on equal ground with the injurer, and the position of a victim shifts to that of give and take. Thus, had it suddenly occurred to King Lear, in the extremity of his distress at his daughters' ingratitude, that he had done them some or other great wrong, which he had till that moment forgotten, the fact would have been welcomed with consummate and indescribable joy, and his mind would have felt instantaneous rest. Unquestionably there is something in the situation of a simple recipient of injustice which must be said to stand quite pre-eminent in its repugnance to nature: and St. Peter alludes to this when he says, "What glory is it, if when ye be buffeted for your faults, ye shall take it patiently? but if, when ye do well and suffer for it, ye take it patiently, this is acceptable with God."

The character of Job is the "magnanimous one," according to the Aristotelian definition; that is to say, he is worthy, and he knows himself worthy. He is a righteous man, and he claims what is the righteous man's due. That this claim is made upon Providence in his case, and not upon a fellow-man, is no difference to the purpose; for if a man does not get his due, the fact is exactly the same, from whatever quarter he fails to get it. It may be objected, indeed, that there can be no such due or right, in the first instance, to be urged by a human being upon Providence, inasmuch as no creature can possibly know beforehand what his due from the Creator is. To enter upon such a question seems to be entering upon a task of measurement where we have no rule whatever of measurement, and no proportion to go upon, and therefore to be the height of folly and presumption. True; but Job is not claiming anything as his due absolutely and intrinsically, but by comparison. If the constitution of things does as a matter of fact supply a certain amount of happiness and well-being, the righteous certainly deserve this happiness more than the wicked do, and in this sense the righteous man can regard himself as having something due to him even at the hand of Providence. The impression is a sound and legitimate one as a first impression, however subsequent considerations may come in to correct and qualify it. Job claims this due then, and not having it, does not hesitate to say that he is treated with injustice. But this temper of self-respect carries with it those characteristics which accompany it in the minds of good men; that is to say, it is not a proud but a humiliating feeling. He would be ready, could he do so really, to make the discovery that he deserved his punishment and so had no occasion for that feeling, and the repeated efforts of his friends to extort from him some acknowledgment of ill desert appeal to one quite willing to be convinced, could he be so genuinely and reasonably, for he wants as much as they do to have the feeling of living under an equal Providence which deals justly with its subjects, and this conviction of his own ill desert would be, with reference to this want, a relief. But he will not feign an assent which he does not feel. As he cannot make that discovery he voluntarily submits himself to the full impression of injustice done him, and faces with strong endurance its humiliating and mortifying results. He pursues the idea long and continuously, unfolds it in all its vexatiousness, and drinks the bitter cup to the dregs. A long period of mute unbroken meditation, during which "none spake a word unto him, for they saw that his grief was very great," first puts this whole visible system of things in strong and vivid light before him. Thought gathering strength, and feeling pent up, then make their way into words, and Job opens his mouth and speaks. The hero of the *Iliad* had one burden of complaint when he delivered himself of his great protest against unjust power, the single sentiment contained in that line—

$$\text{ἐν δὲ ἰῇ τιμῇ ἠμὲν κακὸς, ἠδὲ καὶ ἐσθλός.}^{1}$$

Job has the same. The apparent fact that God "destroyeth the perfect with the wicked," nay, "shines on the counsel of the wicked," and "laughs at the trial of the innocent," absorbs him. And just as the hero of the *Iliad* reviews his own past course of action for the purpose of contrasting it with his reward, justly and frankly magnifying himself, and, according to the standard which his religion has given him of what is great and noble in man, proclaiming his great exploits and demonstrating his high desert; just as he says, I have taken so many cities by land and sea; I have fought for you, and spent nights of watching and days of toil and danger, and this is what I get for it! so Job, with another standard of man's true greatness and virtue, says, "When the ear heard me, then it blessed me; and when the eye saw me, it gave witness to me: because I delivered the poor that cried, and the fatherless, and him that had none to help him. The blessing of him that was ready to perish came upon me: and I caused the widow's heart to sing for joy. I put on righteousness, and it clothed me; my judgment was as a robe and a diadem. I was eyes to the blind, and feet was I to the lame. I was a father to the poor: and the cause which I knew not I searched out. And I brake the jaws of the wicked, and plucked the spoil

---

[1] Like honours gain the coward and the brave.

out of his teeth." And adds, "But when I looked for good, then evil came unto me: and when I waited for light, there came darkness. He hath cast me into the mire, and I am become like dust and ashes. My harp also is turned to mourning, and my organ into the voice of them that weep." And he concludes with a form of protestation, in which he makes his whole past life appear as in a public court and witness against an unjust punishment. "If I have walked with vanity, or if my foot hath hasted to deceit: if my step hath turned out of the way, and mine heart walked after mine eyes, and if any blot hath cleaved to my hands: If I have withheld the poor from their desire, or have caused the eyes of the widow to fail; or have eaten my morsel myself alone, and the fatherless hath not eaten thereof: If I have seen any perish for want of clothing, or any poor without covering: If I have made gold my hope, or have said to the fine gold, Thou art my confidence: If I rejoiced at the destruction of him that hated me, or lifted up myself when evil found him: If my land cry against me, or the furrows thereof complain: if I have eaten the fruits thereof without money, or have caused the owners thereof to lose their life: then let me be weighed in an even balance;" let my unrighteousness be known; let every portion of myself and my substance to which the sin attaches suffer : let the arm which was lifted up against the fatherless "fall from the shoulder-blade," and on the field which refused its bounty "let thistles grow instead of wheat, and cockle instead of barley. The words of Job are ended."

The language of Job toward the Deity is another remarkable feature of the book. This language is a startling carrying out even of that bold ground which he takes about himself; for he positively, as far as words go, accuses the Deity of injustice. He complains of Him, remonstrates with Him, protests against His course of government. This language the more calls for explanation because in reading Scripture we find it to be the type of a whole line of language toward the Deity which we meet with there. The language of complaint and remonstrance, more or less modified in addresses to God, is not unfrequent in Scripture, and that from the mouths of God's holiest and most zealous servants, of prophets and inspired men. Thus we meet with it occasionally in the addresses of Abraham and Moses to God, and oftener in the Psalms and in the Prophecies. The Lamentations of Jeremiah, indeed, seem to borrow their language largely from the Book of Job, so as to give the impression that that book supplied the recognised exemplar of that kind of language; the one to which the holy men of old looked when they wanted to express the extraordinary class of feelings which affliction imparts.

It is obvious then at first sight that this language cannot really mean what it literally means. No religious man, no reasonable man, no man in his proper senses at all, can really mean to accuse the Deity of injustice; for the very idea of a God implies the idea of perfect goodness, which idea would be contradicted by such an accusation. The literal meaning therefore being excluded as an impossible one, it remains to see what such language as a mode of speaking can mean; for modes of speaking have real meanings, though not literal ones.

The saint of the Old Testament had a very different idea of the Divine Being from that which the Pagan had; as in the point of the unity of God, so in other very important points. In particular, on the subject of His omnipotence there was a great difference. The Pagan had not a clear and consistent idea of the omnipotence of the Supreme Being; he attributed absolute omnipotence to Him on one side, and modified it again by imagining some distinct power running parallel with it on the other. This power figures in ancient systems sometimes as Fate, sometimes as Chaos, sometimes as Matter, sometimes directly as Evil. The old Greek mythology spoke of Fate, and pictured it as some positive and active force which produced events independently of the will of the supreme God. The Egyptian mythology taught, under the name of Typho, the existence of a primeval principle of disorder in things which would persist in interfering with and spoiling the operation of the Divine laws in the world. The Oriental philosophies held that matter was coeval with the Deity, describing it as an unmanageable substance, with obstinate lusts inherent in it which would be satisfied; or they were directly dualistic, and taught two independent original principles of good and evil. Thus, in one way or another, the omnipotence of the Supreme Being was limited. He was not the true Creator of the world, for Chaos and Matter were coeval with Him, and therefore He was the Creator of the world's form only, and not the Creator of the world's materials. He was not the true Governor of the world, for these original independent substances of Matter and Evil had power, and produced results independently of Him. But the Bible taught a God who was truly Almighty, the absolute Creator, and the absolute Governor of the world: " In the beginning God created the heaven and the earth : and the earth was without form and void." He created the formless matter, as well as the world which He made out of it. And having thus absolutely created the world, He is represented as the absolute Master of it afterwards, directing and controlling all its affairs.

It followed naturally then from the idea of God which the Bible revelation inculcated, that, as power creates responsibility, there would be a disposition in the true believer, on the appearance of things going wrong in the world, to interrogate the Deity upon it. The God of the Pagan was weak, and could not help himself; the original powers, which ran parallel to his own, took off the edge of his responsibility, and received the blame. But the Jew had no Fate, or Chaos, or Matter, or Original Evil on which to throw the blame; his God was almighty, and the whole weight of the government of the world rested upon His shoulders. So far, then, as he looked to the one attribute of power in the Deity exclusively, he would feel a disposition to make the Deity responsible for the evils of a disordered world, and to accuse him of injustice in his administration. It is true that this idea would, as soon as it occurred to the mind, be met simultaneously by the recollection of the other attribute of perfect goodness; and the character of the Deity, regarded as a whole, would instantaneously refute this inference from one particular attribute taken singly. But there is this difference between refuting an idea from without and by the authority of a superior consideration, and refuting it from within and upon its own ground; that though the former is quite as certain a mode of refutation as the latter, it yet leaves the idea refuted externally standing. The image remains though the substance is gone, and makes a particular impression, as a mere image, upon the mind. Thus the vivid appearance of a departed friend meeting our eyes, though we knew it was simply the effect of a particular medicine taken, which had the property of causing such ocular delusions, would still affect the mind; and we could not wholly get over the impression of somebody's presence. And thus an apparent falsity or inconsistency makes an impression on the mind while it lasts, even though we are sure it will be explained the next minute, and have perfect faith in the veracity of our informant. In the same way this idea of injustice in the Deity, which arises from the consideration of His attribute of power, though completely refuted by the attribute of His goodness, makes an impression as a mere image upon the mind. Such power and such results the mind repeats to itself, not believing in reality that the irregularity of the present system of things is the result of any fault in that power, but only regarding the two facts in combination, and allowing that combination to make an impression upon it. Thus arises an illusive language of complaint against the Deity, and beneath the shelter of a perfect faith in His goodness and wisdom, the soul feels itself secure in using an outward freedom with Him. With the consciousness of His true intentions really sovereign in its thoughts, it protests against His supposed ones; and it pleads the cause of justice forcibly against One presumed to neglect it. "O Lord, thou hast deceived me, and I was deceived: Thou art stronger than I." "My God, my God, why hast thou forsaken me, and art so far from my health and from the words of my complaint?" "Lord, why abhorrest thou my soul, and hidest thou thy face from me?" The holy men speak as if God were hard and unjust upon them, all the while feeling the fullest and most penetrating conviction of His goodness. Indeed, just as, in the case of ordinary irony, feeling expresses itself by contraries, and delights in urging the charge, and fastening the epithet, in order that the seeming accuser may feel the more vividly, by the contrast, his real love, and more consciously appreciate what he appears to deny, so in the adoption of this tone to the Divine Being. It betrays its own contrary meaning. The apparent doubt only expresses more strongly the real faith; the protest against injustice and harshness, the sense of absolute goodness and ineffable mercy. Amidst the disorder of the earthly scene the mind takes refuge in the position of accuser of, and pleader with, Divine injustice, as a mode of reminding itself of that Supreme justice which is that disorder's ultimate and certain remedy. Indeed, all prayer may be said to partake in some measure of this irony. The earnest and intense supplicant seems to himself to be addressing a Deity whom it is hard to gain, and who requires the utmost pressing to grant what he wants, even though the subject of the prayer be most reasonable: otherwise, why should he use such urgency, and adopt so pressing a tone at all? The very posture of supplication reflects a character of resistance upon the object of it; even though we know that character is no reality, but only the reflection of our own act. Heaven must be taken by violence, and the Unjust Judge won by importunity. Thus the piercing tone of the prayers in the Psalms, as if the Almighty were indeed a "hard" Master, and it were all but impossible to get any favour or mercy from Him. We may observe much of this species of irony in the poetry of our own George Herbert:—

> "Broken in pieces, all asunder,
> Lord! hunt me not,
> A thing forgot,
> Once a poor creature, now a wonder,—
> A wonder tortured in the space
> Betwixt this world, and that of grace."

Or—

> "Come, Lord! my head doth burn, my heart is sick,
> Whilst thou dost ever, ever stay;
> Thy long deferrings wound me to the quick;
> My spirit gaspeth night and day.
> Oh, show thyself to me,
> Or take me up to thee!"

Or—

> "Lord, didst thou leave thy throne
> Not to relieve? How can it be,
> That thou art grown
> Thus hard to me?"

Or—

"Whither, oh, whither art thou fled,
　　My Lord, my love?
My searches are my daily bread,
　　Yet never prove."

Or—

"Oh, take these bars, these lengths away;
　　Turn and restore me;
Be not Almighty, let me say,
　　Against, but for me.'

Of this compound character, then, is the complaint of angry Job, charging the Divine government of the world with injustice. He sees a world in disorder, and, looking simply to the responsibility of Absolute Power, he lays the blame of it upon the Divine Possessor of that power. When the perfect and the wicked are punished alike, it is He that does it; when the trial of the innocent is laughed at, He laughs. The earth is given into the hands of the wicked, and He gives it; He covereth the faces of the judges thereof; He shines upon the counsel of the wicked; and He despises the works of the good. But simultaneously with this charge comes a recollection of God's absolute goodness. He thus alternates from anger to love, and from blame to adoration; with fiery quickness the indignant complaint darts from him, and immediately he is a tender suppliant, according as his single idea of responsible power, or according as his whole religious conviction, including the belief of God's absolute goodness, is expressed. Nor,—and this is a further point to observe,—do these two lines of feeling alternate only, but intertwine; and by some remarkable interchange of results this very Power, in its turn, elicits love; this very Goodness, accusation. Thou tearest me, thou gnashest upon me, thou sharpenest thine eyes upon me, thou huntest me, thou breakest me, thou slayest me, thou scarest me, thou terrifiest me, thou plungest me in the ditch, thou settest thy bow against me, thou hedgest me in, thou watchest me, thou hast set me as a mark against thee, are Job's addresses to the all-powerful Being, while he thinks only of unjust power. "If I speak of strength, lo, he is strong; and if of judgment, who will set me a time to plead? He is not a man that I should answer him, and we should come together in judgment." But this power itself, the pure and simple attribute, in its turn completely subdues and softens him. And, just as the captured on a field of battle, expecting death, fall down and embrace their conqueror's knees, or clasp his hands, rushing into all the external expressions of the strongest love, not feignedly and for an object only, but because in very truth mere power wins by subduing, and the intense consciousness that some one has the absolute power to do what he will with us, puts us into the position of love to him; making us imagine him as our benefactor and friend, because we turn beforehand his absolute choice, of saving or destroying, into the alternative most favourable to ourselves: just so the power of the Almighty Maker and Governor of the world impresses Job. Such amazing power softens him. Many chapters in the Book of Job are devoted to the description of this power. For this purpose the great original act of creation is strongly insisted on, that incomprehensible act of power by which matter was brought out of void, and spiritual substances, which had not been, were made. The solid world, and all that therein is; the animals and vegetables upon the earth, the minerals beneath it, the heavenly bodies above it; the horse, leviathan, behemoth, hawk, vulture, eagle; the veins of silver and gold, brass and iron; Arcturus, Orion, and the Pleiades, all bear witness to a tremendous act of power, exerted at their creation, and maintained ever since, of which the very thought is overpowering. "Where wast thou when I laid the foundations of the earth? declare if thou hast understanding. Whereupon are the foundations fastened, or who laid the corner-stone thereof? Or who shut up the sea with doors, and said, Hitherto shalt thou come and no further, and here shall thy proud waves be stayed?" As he contemplates, then, that absolute Power which the idea of creation involves, and feels himself within its grasp a poor and feeble creature, to be dealt with just as that Power pleases; the thought of a Being on whom he is so absolutely dependent turns him with softened feeling towards Him, and draws out tender and supplicating love. And he says, "There is none that can deliver out of thine hand," and makes that his tie to Him. Thou art Almighty, therefore I love thee. Out of the eater came forth meat, and out of the strong came forth sweetness; honey out of the rock, oil out of the flinty rock; thy power is itself mercy; thy greatness is itself love. I am thy creature, thy property; thou canst do with me whatever thou wilt; I am thine; therefore thou art mine: I have a claim upon thee which thou canst not resist: thou must be my friend and my preserver. "Remember, I beseech thee, that thou hast made me as the clay; and wilt thou bring me into dust again? Hast thou not poured me out as milk, and curdled me like cheese? Thou hast granted me life and favour, and thy visitation hath preserved my spirit. Wherefore hidest thou thy face, and holdest me for thine enemy? . . . Though he slay me, yet will I trust in him." On the other hand, the idea of the goodness of God seems to embitter him, and stimulate accusation; for why, being so good a Being, should he treat him thus? The goodness of the punisher makes in one aspect the case of the sufferer worse, for it is more painful to suffer at the hands of the good than at the hands of the evil; as also the act of the punisher himself more inexcusable, for he is violating his own nature in it. Underneath the complaints of Job there is perceptible the feeling of the peculiar hardship of suffering under a good Being, whom he was bound to honour and reverence. And just as children by a certain fantastic inconsistency of feeling which some particular severe act of their parents, seen in discordant combination with general parental love, produces, are angry with their parents because they have done the act, *being* so good and loving, and make their very goodness an additional grievance because it gives a sting to their severity: so in Job's complaints of the Deity. He shows the inconsistency of perplexed love, keenly alive to the goodness of its object, and quickly susceptible on that very account of anger toward it. Thus, what with the original alternations of feeling in Job, and what with those alternations intertwining, such a deep and touching intricacy in his whole feeling toward the Supreme Being arises, as perhaps no dramatic poetry has ever yet described toward any object of love. Such quickness of transition and sharpness of contrast, and such invisible slidings of one feeling into another, appear. "The wind goeth toward the south, and turneth about unto the north; it whirleth about continually, and the wind returneth again according to his circuits." Yet all these alternations and contrasts have one solution; he confesses the absolute goodness of God in conjunction with the mystery of present injustice and disorder. Love in the heavenly state sees God face to face, and moves directly toward Him; but its movements upon earth are often inflected and circuitous, according as the various incongruities in the present system of things blamelessly affect it. In Job all is motion and change; he exhibits the innocent restlessness of the affection in its earthly stage. "When I was a child, I spake as a child, I understood as a child, I thought as a child; but when I became a man I put away childish things." Love in its earlier or earthly stages shows many of the inconsistencies and irregularities of childhood; but it will one day put away childish things, and its motion be clear, constant, and uniform, proceeding straight and direct towards its great Object.

We have endeavoured under two heads to exhibit what seem to be the main features of the character in which Job is presented to us in the Book of Job.

With this whole exhibition of character, then, Scripture does undoubtedly in substance sympathise; for at the close of the book, in passing judgment upon the whole discussion between Job and his friends, it definitively declares that Job "had spoken the thing that was right," whereas his friends, who had taken the opposite line to him, had offended. Without pressing this decision too far, or interpreting it as a sanction of the whole of Job's language and every outburst of emotion from him, it must be understood to convey an approval of the substance and groundwork of them; and to pronounce that his argument was true, and his feeling legitimate and right in the main. It must be remembered that there is a wide distinction between that movement of natural passion which has a reason, and that which has not; and that exactly the same amount of temper which is fretfulness in one case is natural or constitutional anger in another. Job is not angry at the simple sense of pain and misfortune, which would be unreasonable anger or fretfulness, for respecting that he simply says, "Naked came I out of my mother's womb, and naked shall I return thither: the Lord gave, and the Lord hath taken away; blessed be the name of the Lord." But he is angry for a totally different reason, derived from consideration and reflection; from long silent thought and meditation. That period of deep silent thought through which he passes, before the argument of the book begins, convinces him that there is injustice in the present system of things, and that he is suffering under it. Feeling proceeding from such a cause as this is reasonable feeling,—anger upon a natural and legitimate ground. He may fall occasionally into the excesses incident to human frailty, and allow his thoughts too free a scope; he may be too vehement, ardent, and bold in his manner of expressing himself; but his feeling itself is reasonable and just, and he speaks substantially "the thing that is right." We connect indeed a particular difficulty at first sight with his case, from the consideration of the fact that his sufferings have proceeded immediately from the providence of God, and that therefore when he complains of suffering unjustly he is complaining of the injustice of a providential dispensation, and not of any mere treatment from fellow-men. There is a difference between the two kinds of visitation which shows at first sight unfavourably for Job. "Let me fall into the hands of the Lord," says David, "and not into the hand of man," as if that was the particular difference between a providential visitation and the action of human force; that whereas in the one case you had a punisher who, however he might be a scourge in the hand of Divine justice, was unjust in himself, and his castigations revengeful and proud, in the other you might be sure that all was calm and judicial, and might have the feeling of simple resignation under it. But this difficulty is removed by Scripture itself at the very opening of the Book of Job. Inspiration there draws aside the veil, and lets us see that Job's pains and calamities, which we might have supposed to have been inflicted by God on some judicial ground, were really inflicted by Satan out of spite and malignity; and therefore it appears that Job was perfectly right in characterising his punishments as he did, and insisting on their injustice in spite of their providential appearance. The fact bears him out. They *were* inflicted by a tyrant and persecutor, and not by a righteous judge and governor; and they were only providential in the sense of being permitted by God, not in the sense of being awarded by Him. It is true this permission ultimately involves the Deity in the responsibilities of the case, but that is an ulterior part of the question to be considered and solved, if it can be, in its proper time; meantime the infliction itself is, as Job maintains, unjust, and proceeds directly from an unjust power. Scripture declares in favour of the freedom of Job's attitude toward an apparently providential dispensation, and sanctions the view that not only men but events may be unjust; and that what takes place in this world may proceed from a latent evil power, even where the system or order of nature alone visibly operates, and no individual agent can be fastened on. In David's case, the justness of the visitation is specifically secured, for God comes forward in the first instance as its inflictor; but in Job's it is otherwise. In this way, at the opening of the Book of Job, and at its close, inspiration undoubtedly declares itself in favour of Job's argument, and pronounces what he says about this visible order of things to be true, and Job himself right in asserting and maintaining it. And thus one great purpose of the Book of Job is clear and transparent.

And here we have a clew given us toward ascertaining what is a not unimportant point to consider in connection with it—the peculiar place and position of the Book of Job in the Bible. We may readily suppose that such a book does not stand by itself, but has relations to other parts of Scripture, and was meant to fulfil a particular part in the general scheme of revelation.

The nature of the expectations which the Jews entertained as to the Messiah is a feature of Jewish tradition, which it is not easy at first to enter into. It appears so much more natural, so much more agreeable to common sense, to suppose that an extraordinarily good person would rather meet with trouble in the world than with prosperity. "The majority are evil," said even the heathen proverb: the evil are necessarily jealous of the good, and jealousy naturally seeks to gratify itself by persecution and oppression. The instinct of moral nature thus clearly presages sorrow and affliction for the eminently good who come to perform their appointed part in an evil world; and Plato has a remarkable passage, bearing almost the appearance of an inspired prophecy, to the effect that when a perfectly just man ever did appear in the world he would be put to death. The writer of the Wisdom of Solomon speaks more fully and more clearly to the same effect in describing the feelings of the mass toward the righteous man. "He is not for our turn, he is clean contrary to our doings: he upbraideth us with our offending the law, and objecteth to our infamy the transgressions of our education. He professeth to have the knowledge of God, and he calleth himself the child of the Lord. He was made to reprove our thoughts. He is grievous unto us even to behold, for his life is not like other men's, his ways are of another fashion. We are esteemed of him as counterfeits: he abstaineth from our ways as from filthiness; he pronounceth the end of the just to be blessed, and maketh his boast that God is his father. Let us see if his words be true, and let us prove what shall happen in the end of him. For if the just man be the Son of God He will help him, and deliver him from the hand of his enemies. Let us examine him with despitefulness and torture, that we may know his meekness and prove his patience. Let us condemn him with a shameful death." And such presages of natural and higher wisdom were confirmed only too forcibly by facts. The system of ostracism was dominant in the classical republic; and among the Jews it had been exactly as the parable said, that the king had sent his servants, and the husbandmen had beat one, and killed another, and stoned another. Of the fact that the prophets and forerunners of the Messiah had been persecuted, imprisoned, and slain, the Jew had even his own confession before his eyes, in the sepulchres which he had built them, as a sort of compensation for his fathers' injustice. The Jew had no encouragement then, either from reason or fact, to suppose that his Messiah, when He came, would be an externally magnificent and successful personage; yet so obstinately was he impressed with the necessity of His being so, that he could positively think of no other character for Him, and would have a brilliant and prosperous Messiah, or none at all.

The reasons of this deep prejudice are to be found in those tendencies connected with the old dispensation which have been remarked upon in this article. The peculiar defect and the peculiar superiority of that dispensation both worked together and assisted each other in producing a strong idea of this present world as a scene of Divine distributive justice. The absence of a distinct doctrine of a future state, which was its peculiar defect, necessarily gave a greater wholeness and finality to this world as a field of Divine administration; and the doctrine of God's unity and omnipotence, which was its great superiority, necessarily gave an infallible pledge for the goodness and justice of that Divine administration, wholly and finally. The very truth of his system thus put the Jew to a disadvantage with respect to the particular view he took of this world; one truth, as is often the case, leading astray when not seen in connection with other truths. The Pagan was enabled to take a more natural and genuine view of this world as a wild irregular scene from the very circumstance of the erroneousness of his creed; for he started with believing in certain original powers of evil and confusion, independent of and coordinate with his deity. Error gave him freedom, and allowed him to take the facts of this world as they stood, without squaring or varnishing. But the Jew was trammelled by partial truth, and was thus tempted to varnish. The doctrine of one Omnipotent Deity, held without a sufficiently distinct conception of a future world, only put upon him the apparent necessity of making out this world to be, however facts contradicted it, a fit reflex of such a Deity, a scene of real distributive justice. It is evident what idea this whole line of thought must lead to of what the Messiah was to be when He came. He supposed for certain that so heroic and Divine a personage would have some signally exalted and triumphant career in this world. Greatness and success were His due, and therefore He was to have them; and the law of Divine justice imperiously required that goodness should be rewarded in the person of its great Exemplar and Pattern. That while the foxes have holes, and the birds of the air have nests, the Messiah should not have a place where to lay His head; that He should be despised and rejected of men, a man of sorrows and acquainted with grief, and die an early and ignominious death, would be at once a disproof of His mission. The cross was an offence to the Jew, in a real argumentative sense. The pertinacity with which the Jews of our Saviour's time connected adversity with ill desert, is evident in the question respecting the blind man,— "Hath this man sinned, or his parents, that he was born blind?"—and in the opinion, which our Saviour refutes, that the Galileans, whose blood Pilate had mingled with their sacrifices, were sinners above all the Galileans; and the eighteen upon whom the tower in Siloam fell, sinners above all men that dwelt in Jerusalem,—instances in which it is curious to observe how they were, without knowing it, prejudging the case of our Lord Himself.

When such an idea, moreover, as this was once entertained with respect to the Messiah, it is obvious how the whole language of prophecy about Him would fix and confirm it. For, as far as language goes, the prophets certainly exhibit the Messiah as a magnificent and successful prince, the conductor of a great national restoration, and raiser of the Jewish people from an oppressed condition to empire and glory. "Unto us a Child is born, unto us a Son is given: and the government shall be upon his shoulder: and his name shall be called Wonderful, Counsellor, The mighty God, The everlasting Father, The Prince of Peace. Of the increase of his government there shall be no end, upon the throne of David, and upon his kingdom, to order it and to establish it with judgment and with justice from henceforth even for ever." "It is a light thing that thou shouldest be my servant, to raise up the tribes of Jacob, and to restore the preserved of Israel: I will also give thee for a light to the Gentiles, that thou mayest be my salvation unto the ends of the earth." "Behold, I will lift up mine hand to the Gentiles, and set up my standard to the people: and they shall bring thy sons in their arms, and thy daughters shall be carried upon their shoulders. And kings shall be thy nursing fathers, and their queens thy nursing mothers: they shall bow down to thee with their face toward the earth, and lick up the dust of thy feet." "Arise, shine; for thy light is come, and the glory of the Lord is risen upon thee." "Because the abundance of the sea shall be converted unto thee, the forces of the Gentiles shall come unto thee. The multitude of camels shall cover thee, the dromedaries of Midian and Ephah; all they from Sheba shall come: they shall bring gold and incense, and they shall show forth the praises of the Lord." "The sons also of them that afflicted thee shall come bending unto thee; and they that despised thee shall bow themselves down at the soles of thy feet, and they shall call thee, The city of the Lord, The Zion of the Holy One of Israel.". The literal meaning of such prophecies was in exact accordance with the notion of a Messiah who was to enjoy upon earth the due rewards of His heroic virtue and nobility. They gave Him apparently a successful earthly result of His labours in a magnificent earthly headship, and the glory of a whole nation restored and elevated by His own hand. And the hopes and aspirations of the Jew in behalf of his nation and race combined with his previous prejudice in favour of present rewards, in committing him to the confident expectation of a visibly prosperous and glorious Messiah.

It is evident that to resist such a traditional notion of a Messiah, some book would be serviceable, which would specially resist that view of this world upon which such a notion was founded. If the Jew was to accept a Messiah who was to lead a life of sorrow and abasement, and to be crucified between thieves, it was necessary that he should be somewhere or other distinctly taught that virtue was not always rewarded here, and that therefore no argument could be drawn from affliction and ignominy against the person who suffered it. The Book of Job does this. It devotes itself to the enunciation of this injustice and irregularity as a law or principle of the present order of things. However the mass might cling to the idea of a visibly successful Messiah, such a book would insensibly direct the minds of the better sort into another channel, and prepare them for the truth of the case. It spoke things φωνᾶντα συνετοῖσιν, in describing the afflictions of one, whom when the ear heard, it " blessed him, and when the eye saw, it gave witness to him; who delivered the poor that cried, the fatherless and him that had none to help him." And thus it stood in a particular relation to the prophetic books of Scripture—a kind of interpretative one; supplying a caution where they raised hopes, suggesting suspicions of apparent meaning and conjectures as to a deeper one, and drawing men from a too material to a more refined faith. By the side of a long line of prophecy, as a whole outwardly gorgeous and flattering, and promising in the Messiah a successful potentate, and opener of a glorious temporal future for the Jewish nation, there rose one sad but faithful memento, and all that appearance of approaching splendour was seen in qualifying connection with other truths.

Accordingly, all the Fathers agree in declaring that Job prefigured Christ: that, as David typified the conqueror, he typified the victim; and that, put before us in the one special character of an undeserving sufferer, he foreshadowed the great undeserving Sufferer of all, the Sufferer upon the Cross. All cases of innocent suffering that are, or have been, or will be, are in a sense the shadows and reflections of our Lord's, the true pattern and exemplar of such suffering; and the afflictions of Job and the elder saints were shadows of it beforehand. For whereas goodness in the degrees it had here attained to had provoked, in all ages of the world, the jealousy and hatred of fallen man, and the husbandmen had everywhere beat one, and killed another, and stoned another, that had been sent to them; whereas the Jews had imprisoned or slain their prophets, and the Greeks had slain or banished their wise men, and, according to the dispensation they were under, intended guides and teachers; and goodness had no sooner presented itself to either Jew or Greek than it had excited, as if by a law of nature, the outrageous desire to expel and get rid of it, as a troublesome and noxious thing, a plague and torment; in

Him the world's ostracism was completed, and Supreme and Divine goodness encountered a perfect and consummate injustice. For then the "Beloved Son" himself, "the Heir," was slain, of whom the lord had said, "It may be, they will reverence him when they see him." Doubtless, according to the rule of justice, there was no honour which the world could give which was not due to our Lord in the flesh : that every knee should bow, and all heads do obeisance. Satan's own offer of all the kingdoms of the world, and the glory of them, was but His due : for universal empire is the natural property of absolute virtue, which, whether it be honour, or pleasure, or power, deserves all good that is. "But the light shined in darkness, and the darkness comprehended it not;" and the true Exemplar of goodness was cast out of that world which He came to inform, with hatred and contumely. Poetry has dwelt much upon the crime of man's ingratitude to man, and imagined cases in which children have made cruel returns to the parent, and persons rescued to the deliverer, and the befriended to their benefactors, for the purpose of raising emotion, and possessing our minds with the acutest sense of injustice ; but what is to be thought of the case of Him of whom it is said that "the world was made by Him, and the world knew Him not;" that "He came unto His own, and His own received Him not;" of the Creator of all things put to death in the flesh by His own creatures, the Redeemer of all men by the world He came to save? All other ill returns which have been made to good men, parents, friends, deliverers, in this wild irregular scene, are but faint types and reflections of this great one ; and the Crucifixion is the one consummate act of injustice to which all others are but distant approaches.

Of such injustice, moreover, our Lord, in accordance with the magnanimity of a perfect nature, feeling its own worthiness, had due sense ; which the Gospels manifest in various allusions made by Him to the unjust sufferings of the prophets, His forerunners, specially coupled with prophetic announcements of His own. Thus the parable, already quoted, of the Lord's servants, and the Heir of whom the husbandmen said, "Come, let us kill him, that the inheritance may be ours." Thus the allusion, so expressive of the sense of unjust power, to the fate of John the Baptist, that "they had done unto him whatsoever they listed;" immediately succeeded by the announcement, "Likewise shall also the Son of Man suffer of them." Thus the message to Herod: "Go ye and tell that fox, Behold, I cast out devils, and do cures to-day and to-morrow, and the third day I shall be perfected." Thus the reproach to Jerusalem: "Thou that killest the prophets, and stonest them that are sent unto thee;" coupled with the solemn declaration that He himself must die there, as "it could not be that a prophet perish out of Jerusalem." Thus the holy irony: "Truly ye bear witness that ye allow the deeds of your fathers, for they indeed killed them and ye build their sepulchres." Thus the fearful malediction: "Fill ye up, then, the measure of your fathers;"—"that the blood of all the prophets which was shed from the foundation of the world may be required of this generation; from the blood of Abel unto the blood of Zacharias, which perished between the temple and the altar." Thus the argument: "If I had not done among them the works which none other man did, they had not had sin, but now they have both seen and hated both me and my Father." Thus the protestation: "Are ye come out as against a thief, with swords and staves, for to take me? I sat daily with you teaching in the temple, and ye laid no hold upon me." Thus the rebuke to the traitor: "Judas, betrayest thou the Son of Man with a kiss?" Thus the parting admonition to the faithful disciples: "The servant is not greater than his lord: if they have persecuted me, they will also persecute you:" "if the world hate you, ye know that it hated me before it hated you." And to such expressions may be added the very particularity of His prophecies respecting His own death, its form, circumstances, and mode of bringing about: the betrayal, the trial, the condemnation, the mocking, spitefully entreating, spitting on, scourging—all so wonderfully undue to Him. Our Lord's character, in these respects, as portrayed for us in the Gospels, is in perfect keeping with His prophetical one in the Psalms, and He speaks there what He spoke beforehand by the mouth of David: "They that hate me without a cause are more than the hairs of my head. They that are mine enemies and would destroy me guiltless, are mighty. And why, for thy sake, have I suffered reproof? shame hath covered my face; I am become a stranger unto my brethren, even an alien unto my mother's children. For the zeal of thine house hath even eaten me, and the rebukes of them that rebuked thee are fallen upon me. I wept and chastened myself with fasting, and that was turned to my reproof. I put on sackcloth also, and they jested upon me. They that sit in the gate speak against me, and the drunkards make songs upon me. They gave me gall to eat, and when I was thirsty they gave me vinegar to drink." He says in the Gospels, as in the Psalms, "I have spied unrighteousness and strife in the city. Day and night they go about within the walls thereof; mischief also and sorrow are in the midst of it. Wickedness is therein: deceit and guile go not out of their streets. For it is not an open enemy that hath done me this dishonour, for then I could have borne it. Neither was it mine adversary that did magnify himself against me, for then peradventure I would have hid myself from him. But it was even thou, my companion, my guide, and mine own familiar friend. We took sweet counsel together, and walked in the house of God as friends." Such is the character which the Bible, as a whole, one part aiding and unfolding another, gives our Lord; the attitude in which it places Him toward the world. In the Gospels actually, and the Psalms prophetically, one view of His own sufferings and death comes from Him; viz., as the climax of a long hostility, on the world's part, to the good and righteous seed: the consummation and completion of the injustice and dominant evil in this visible order of things.

And upon the cross the full weight of this sense of evil, and its dominance, descended upon our Lord. Before the Last Supper, indeed, His soul was troubled; and in the garden of Gethsemane He was exceeding sorrowful, even unto death: but the Gospels record one final agony upon the cross, when, to express His burdened spirit, He used the opening words of the twenty-second Psalm, most awful from His mouth, yet most fitting and in place. For then, of all the apparent victories which he has had since the world's beginning, or will have to its close, Satan had the greatest; then, evil seemed positively triumphant and supreme, and the world given up to it; then, Perfect Goodness Itself was, to the eye, prostrate and conquered, with no more power left, and no more effort in reserve; then was "the hour and the power of darkness;" then the nearest of all approaches, which Truth could permit, to the appearance of all things having been made for nought, and the whole Divine scheme having failed at last. For expressing the weight of that hour, therefore, the extraordinary resources of Scripture were applied; the type of language laid up and reserved in it for extreme occasions,—that sacred and touching irony, which, when all regular modes of expression failed from inherent weakness and insufficiency, expressed the last and sharpest sense of evil,—was used; and words significative of utter desolation, and the total departure of the world's Sole Good, expressed our Lord's sense of that absolute triumph and victory of evil which was then, to all appearance, taking place, embodied in His own crucifixion and death.

To return to the Book of Job: Thus much for the sympathy which Scripture, in the Book of Job, exhibits with the sentiment against the injustice in this visible order of things. But there is another part, besides that of sympathy, which it fulfils, and that is, of correction. The feeling of Job, while it plainly receives the sanction and approval of inspiration in the main, and is pronounced in substance legitimate and right, has yet with equal plainness a check and a rebuke given to it; and Job is told that he has been excessive in it, and must take a calmer and more subdued view of things. "The Lord answered Job out of a whirlwind, and said: Shall he that contendeth with the Almighty instruct him? he that reproveth God, let him answer for it." Job had not sufficiently taken into account the ignorance of man respecting the Divine purposes— his perfect incapacity for judging of, or probably even understanding, were they revealed to him, the reasons why God permits all the evil which prevails in the system of the world; and he is reminded of that omission. And upon this a retractation takes place on Job's part, and he says: "I know Thou canst do every thing, and that no thought can be withholden from Thee. I uttered that I understood not, things too wonderful for me which I knew not. I have heard of Thee by the hearing of the ear, but now mine eye seeth Thee. Wherefore I abhor myself, and repent in dust and ashes."

This retractation on the part of Job is an important part of the book to consider, with reference to Job's character. The difficulty which was noticed at the beginning of this article, as arising from the apparent incongruities there were between his character as exhibited in the book, and his scriptural one as an exemplar of patience, has been met more or less in various places as we have gone along. Still, what has been said has been more in a negative than a positive direction—been more in the way of explaining and giving reasons for apparent impatience, than of showing a character of patience. Nor has it been possible to deny, because the fact speaks for itself on the very surface of the book throughout, and the rebuke to Job at the end decides it beyond dispute, that, with all the substantial justice of Job's argument and feeling, there has been excess. And therefore it may still be asked what there is in the book to make Job a special exemplar of patience to us. Here is a great and noble character, it may be said, one of extraordinary depth, power, and passion; but is it not more like one of those fine characters, as we term it, which dramatic poetry draws, than a scriptural one at all—a scriptural pattern of patience especially? Patience is specially a sober and quiet virtue, but here is anything, apparently, but sobriety and evenness of feeling; and were it not that we were particularly told that patience was Job's great virtue, we should certainly have thought that impatience was his great defect.

But, in urging such objections, it is not sufficiently considered that Job, after all, removes his own incongruities, and that the book itself restores the equilibrium of character which the book has unsettled. A temporary suspension of a particular grace is quite compatible with the person in whom it takes place being a special exemplar of that grace; and no one doubts that Abraham is the pattern of faith, and Moses of meekness, and David of generosity and the kingly virtues; though all three sinned at one or other stage of their lives from particular defect respectively of these virtues. And, if this is the case where a grace is wholly suspended, and a saint is allowed to do some act of positive contrary sin, much more may it be so where there has been no positive sin; where feeling has been right and legitimate in substance all along, and only gone too far. This is Job's case. His habitual state of mind is, for a time, unsettled, and he loses for a time his perfect equilibrium; but they return again, and he is the same as ever. Were the state of mind, indeed, thus described in Job, a permanent one, lasting for the whole of the rest of his life, there would be considerable difficulty in reconciling it with his being such an exemplar of patience as he is pronounced to be. But, though the Book of Job does, for a particular purpose, mainly put Job before us in such a state of mind, it is not his permanent one; and, between its being his permanent one and not, there is all the difference. Indeed, the matter of time, as regards the operation of natural anger and passion, not only makes a difference as to the quantity of the fault, but as to the quality of it, for the time. "Be ye angry and sin not," says St. Paul, "let not the sun go down upon your wrath; neither give place to the devil;" as if the anger which went on to the morrow was worse even yesterday than that which stopped short, and time were the test of innocence or guilt in the substance of the feeling itself, and acted retrospectively upon the case. And thus, with reference to the subject before us, there is an obstinate and gnawing anger against which the Psalmist warns us when he says, "Fret not thyself because of the ungodly, neither be thou envious against the evil-doers;" an anger which is not only worse than another sort, because it lasts longer, and there is more of it, but because whatever there is of it is worse. Such is the anger of morbid tempers; but such an anger Job's is not. We see him into his anger, and see him out of it. It is duly transient, and admits its check when the time comes. There is a temper of undoubted and signal patience at the commencement of the book; there is the same temper at the close; and the too strong and vehement feeling which occupies the book itself is only a short break in the midst of regular and habitual states of mind on each side of it, which enclose it, and favourably explain and interpret it at the same time. Upon a particular disclosure, which his own deep reflection and contemplation make to him, of the disorder and injustice of this visible system, he is moved and excited; and he passes through a particular phase of mind, in which indignation at evil too exclusively and intensely absorbs him; a state in which his mind, wrought up to a very high pitch of acuteness and force, an extreme vividness of perception as regards the character of this visible system, a sort of inspiration and supernatural degree of intelligence and realising of the truth, has, by that very intensity and power, its balance somewhat unsettled, so as to exceed the due limits of feeling and language. But, as such a phase of mind was produced by reflection, it yields to reflection again; Job receives the check given him with humility and a ready will; he sees that, in his view of this order of things, he omitted some considerations which would have calmed and modified his feeling; he acknowledges his own ignorance and the Divine wisdom, and with that confession abandons his complaints, and resumes his former resignation. Nay more—and it is very important to observe this,—he rises to a higher and maturer patience even than that with which he started, and his return to his original and habitual state of mind is a return with increase and advance. He now becomes an example of that particular kind of patience which St. Peter pronounces to be the very highest of all; the temper which bears not only inflictions, but unmerited inflictions, calmly; and acquiesces in evil, even with that most trying character, fully realised and embraced, attaching to it,—that it is not evil only, but injustice. "What glory is it if, when ye be buffeted for your faults, ye shall take it patiently? But if, when ye do well and suffer for it, ye take it patiently, this is acceptable with God." Job does this. He has realised the injustice of his punishment, and, realising it, submits to it. The phase of mind he has passed through has provided a harder trial for him, and he surmounts it. He overcomes his own acute perceptions and intelligence, and reduces a whole body of intense feeling which they gave him over and above his previous difficulties to surmount, to order. Before any change has taken place in his condition, or any external cause has been afforded for composure, this change takes place from within. The subtler class of temptations overcome, he thus issues the higher saint; and the hardest and finishing trial of patience surmounted, he becomes the great scriptural example of patience to all ages.

The corrective side of the Book of Job, then, first impresses on us a fact that injustice and disorder are a regular part of the system of things here, permitted by God for wise ends, with which we are unacquainted; and secondly, as a natural consequence of such a view, enjoins a particular temper of mind with reference to such a system.

It is remarkable, if we examine at all accurately the state of mind of the mass, how imperfectly they embrace the idea of the world's disorder as a regular and fixed characteristic of it. They acknowledge it in words, and when the time comes that they have any result of it actually to bear, they show that they have not really felt what they said. Let any piece of injustice be actually committed upon them, and the first and natural impression of nine persons out of ten will be to think it something quite extraordinary and unaccountable; something exceptional and contrary to the natural order of things. They think it so impossible that it can be justified, and therefore so wonderful that it should be done. They are affected with genuine surprise, and call attention to the curious event. It is repeated again and again, and still the same notion remains and occupies a deep and hidden corner of their minds; they fancy the world's basis right, and look upon each awkward result, as it turns up, as a mere accident. And as nobody, however quietly he might take its ordinary working, likes to be the object selected for the extraordinary caprices and eccentricities of any power, they are proportionally angry and vexed. Such a habit of mind is seen in all degrees in men, according as their general characters are more or less perverted. In some it produces only a comparatively harmless kind of fretfulness, which is ordinarily criticised with more pity and amusement than severity. In others it produces dreadful and monstrous effects; and necessarily so. If God has laid any one form of trial upon the human race, and a man obstinately and determinately refuses to undergo it, there is no limit to be assigned to the excesses into which that part of his mind may run for which that trial was intended. In this instance the temper has refused the one great trial designed for it by God, and it becomes like any other wild unreasonable thing in nature which has escaped its proper yoke. It sees no distinction between what is its due and what is not, and so thinks everything its due; it becomes insatiable, and therefore ferocious. Thus arises the class of imperious and savage characters in the world. Beginning with rejecting the yoke of injustice, they end in rejecting that of justice too. Those that would not be oppressed become oppressors, and those that would not bear persecution end in persecuting. The material of which the whole active injustice in the world is composed is the original impatience under injustice inflicted. Indeed, it is curious to observe how the proudest and most aggressive men seem to make this their trial, and put to their own minds even their most wanton acts of injustice to others under the form of resistance to others' injustice to them. A link is discovered, and we see that minds that began with not bearing real injustice are punished, in the natural course of things, with the haunting presence of an unreal and fictitious injustice, which they seem to themselves to have to bear, and against which they struggle at every turn; an injustice which is the mere correlative of an overbearing will, making right coincident with its own desires, and, therefore, stamping with injustice all opposition to those desires. We wonder, at first, how human nature, having the moral ground it has, can do the acts it does; but this is the way. It first forms an unbounded notion of what it has a right to, and then regards even the passive dissent from that as so much wrong to it. Thus tyrants and persecutors drive their stings into the poor passive masses beneath them with the spirit of zealous judges and avengers; and even the highway robber will regard, for the time, the harmless traveller as an unjust foe, and have, for the moment of assault, the retaliatory feeling towards him. There is no limit to the extravagant and fictitious standard which proud minds will raise of what is injustice to them, and what, therefore, is on their part simple resistance to injustice. Such is the unconscious witness which human nature, even in the most extreme cases, bears to the fact of what its one great trial, in the department of temper, is; and the aspect, however fictitious and absurd, in which it puts its own acts to itself, exhibits a great truth.

The indisposition to regard injustice and disorder as a regular and fixed part of this visible system of things has sometimes even gone beyond those practical symptoms by which the mass show their defective realising of the truth, and has taken a systematic and scientific form. A theory is maintained by some modern schools of philosophy, which does formally convert the injustice and disorder which has existed in the world from the beginning into an accident, of which the removal is feasible, and to be literally accomplished some day by the united efforts of governments and people. The theorist looks forward to this as the natural result to which social progress tends, and sees in all the improvements and advances of the age, in every new movement of thought, and every new modification of civil polity, symptoms of approach to it.

The sentimental philosophy—for this is the name commonly given, and very suitably, to a philosophy which fondles this material world, and expects perfection to issue out of it—took its main rise in Europe towards the close of the last century, under the teaching of Rousseau. Rousseau was a believer, or professed to be, in the absolute purity of human nature at the bottom. He pronounced man's original tendencies to be all good, and the evils found in society to be only the results of bad systems of education, which had gained a hold over it. His *Emile* provides a remedy for these evils by the removal of these bad systems. A plan of education of his own constructing, highly elaborate, and framed with great attention to detail, secures the negative ground in the first instance, and prevents all interference with the pupil's mind from without, from established forms of conduct, opinions, creeds. A character thus grows up without any one touching it, and without any other force upon it than the inevitable laws of nature. Under the shelter of such a system, its original tendencies, which are all good, have fair play, and necessarily come out; and human nature, with evil from the first excluded, and protection given from the impure and corrupting usages of society, arrives at its perfect proportions and designed growth. Upon this philosophical foundation arose the first French Revolution, with its extravagant expectations and wild talk; its ideas of the largeness of human benevolence, and the majesty of human reason; its dreams of a rapidly approaching era of social perfection. The weight of the doctrine of human corruption removed, the notions of the age rose indefinitely; everything appeared possible of human nature; divisions of race, class, interest, language, climate, association, all disappeared, and one scheme of universal love embraced all mankind as one people, under one law. A reign of the most horrible ferocity which the history of the world has recorded accompanied this sentimental outburst; and consistently enough, for the selfsame error which was the basis of all this sentimentalism was a fit basis for all the ferocity too. That which keeps men patient under the evils of this present state of things is the idea of their necessity,—the notion, indistinct, but still real in their minds, that injustice and disorder are fundamental in this visible system. That idea removed, all evil, civil and economical, becomes so much gratuitous and superfluous wrong, and the apparent authors of it so many monsters of cruelty; wanton tyrants, delighting in inflicting evil for its own sake. Retaliation to any extent upon such appeared simple justice; and the same theory which produced extravagant expectations produced horrible anger at facts.

The error still lives, and the Communist theory, which has made such ground in France during the last few years, and collected such an enthusiastic, intellectual, and eloquent circle of disciples and expositors around it, is another result of the sentimental philosophy. The Communist theory demands, as a necessary condition of its development in the world, a time when private interests shall cease, and every individual be wholly absorbed in the interests of the community. It requires absolute love and disinterestedness, on a universal scale, in order to its success. It does not deny that it does this: it boasts of its demand, and vindicates its expectation. It literally contemplates a period approaching when mankind will submit to an economical system, which allows of no profit whatever to the individual, from any superiority of talent or skill, bodily or mental, but gives it all to society. It orders the individual to live for the body and not for himself; and it favourably, and with no little theoretical triumph, contrasts its aim with that of St. Simonianism in this respect. St. Simonianism, it says, aims at a system of complete distributive justice, which rewards every man according to his capacity; but what is such justice but selfishness in disguise? There is a higher principle, and that is love. That principle, carried out consistently and logically, makes the individual not a claimant upon society, but a benefiter of it. He contributes whatever talent, natural or acquired he may have, cheerfully to the promotion of the common good, and looks upon all his powers, not as his own, but as the community's.

"The following was the development given by the disciples to the ideas of the master.

"Accepting his division of mankind into artists, *savants*, and men of business, the St. Simonians occupied themselves, in the first instance, with verifying by historical induction that law of progress which constituted the basis of their belief.

"With respect to the order of feelings, they remarked that, in history, the course of humanity was from hatred to love, from antagonism to association. The conqueror, they found, had in the first instance set out with exterminating the conquered; by and by he contented himself with reducing them to slavery—the serf succeeded to the slave, the freeman to the serf. Again, they found a single family enlarging itself until it has become a city; the city swelling itself into a kingdom, the kingdom becoming a federation of kingdoms, until by degrees, from one step to another, a great number of nations united under the law of Catholicism. The march of humanity, then, was towards the principle of universal association, founded upon universal love!

"Studied with reference to the facts which concern *science*, history afforded them instruction of no less valuable nature. The development of civilisation had continuously augmented the importance of the intellectual man to the detriment of the strong man. And what a magnificent lesson was given to the world, in the spectacle of the church, organised otherwise than the state! On the one hand, a spiritual power obtaining acceptation for itself on the basis of reason, and its intrinsic merit; on the other, a temporal power imposing its authority, by right of conquest, or by right of birth. In the middle ages, the hereditary principle was represented in the person of the emperor; the contrary principle by the pope. Now, down to the time of Leo X., who surrounded himself with a court, like a temporal prince, who sold indulgences to defray the cost of his sister's toilet, who transformed himself into Cæsar, which of these two powers, the church or the state, eclipsed and mastered the other? Was there no profound conclusion to be drawn from the example of a monk, who, the one day quitting the obscurity of the cloister to ascend the pontifical throne, on the next, saw the proudest among the monarchs of the earth, kneeling submissively before him, and reverentially kissing the dust from off his sandals? Humanity, it was clear, was marching on towards an organisation in which there should be given to each according to his capacity, and to each capacity according to its works.

"In what concerns industry or labour, the law of progress was manifest. Habits of industry had unceasingly been gaining the ground which habits of war had as continuously been losing. War, it was true, had not yet become banished from history, but its object was no longer the same. Where nations formerly armed themselves for purposes of devastation, they now armed themselves in order to establish marts of trade. The commercial conquests of England had become substituted for the triumph-conquests of old Rome. The military class was daily giving way before the mercantile class. Napoleon himself, the man of battles, Napoleon had held out to the ambition of his armies commerce and peace as the objects for which they were to contend. Humanity, then, was marching on towards the organisation of industry.

"As results of these historical investigations came the three following formulæ:—

"Universal association, based upon love; and, as a corollary, no more hostile competition.

"To each according to his capacity, to each capacity according to its works; and, as a corollary, no more hereditary possession.

"Organisation of industry; and, as a corollary, no more war.

"Such doctrines as these tended directly to shake down the entire fabric of existing social order. Their announcement caused great sensation, consternation. Yet they are deficient alike in logic, true grandeur, genuine courage.

"In preaching forth the universal association of mankind, based upon love; in demanding that industry should be regularly organised, and should establish its empire upon the ruins of a system of disorder and of war, the St. Simonians showed a thorough comprehension of the laws which, at a future period, will be the rule of mankind. But they overturned with one hand the edifice they were raising with the other, by this celebrated maxim: *to each according to his capacity; to each capacity according to its works;* a wise and equitable principle in appearance, but in reality unjust and subversive.

"Whether inequality, the mother of tyranny, takes her stand in the world in the name of mental superiority, or in the name of physical conquest, what matters this to us? In the one case, equally as in the other, charity disappears, selfishness triumphs, and the principle of human brotherhood is trampled under foot. Take a private family, and examine its proceedings: the father, in the distribution of that which he has to give his children, does he take into consideration the difference in the services which they render him, or does he not rather guide himself entirely by the wants which they feel? He himself, he who bears the whole burden of the domestic association, does he not readily abridge his own enjoyments, that he may be able to satisfy the requirements of a sick child, or promote the happiness of a child who is under incapacity from a diseased mind? Here you have charity in action. Let the state model its proceedings after those of the private family. If it does not, there can be nothing but violence and injustice. Give to each according to his capacity! What then is to become of the idiots? What of the infirm? What of the incurably helpless old man? Are these to be left to die of hunger? It must be so if you adhere to the principle that society owes nothing to its members beyond the value of what it receives from them. The St. Simonian logic then was a homicidal logic? No: it was merely inconsistent: for elsewhere it admitted of hospitals for the incapable, and of Bicêtre for the insane. To assert it to be fitting that a man should adjudge to himself, in virtue of his intellectual superiority, a larger portion of the worldly goods than to other members of society, is at once to interdict ourselves the right of execrating the strong man, who, in the barbaric ages, enslaved the feeble, in right of his physical superiority: it is a mere transference of tyranny. The St. Simonians, indeed, went upon the principle, that it is good to stimulate talent by the prospect of recompense; seeking in social utility a justification of this maxim of theirs. But is it necessary that recompenses should be material, should have a money value? Thank heaven! mankind have shown that they can be influenced, and more efficaciously, by other and far higher motives of action. Incited by the promise of a bit of ribbon, to be stuck in the button-holes of the bravest by their emperor, whole armies of Napoleon's soldiers rushed on to meet death. The word *glory*, well or ill understood, has directed the destinies of the world. By what fatality shall that which has sufficed to inspire great deeds, when the work in hand has been destruction, not equally suffice to inspire men when the work in hand is production? Have not the truly great ever sought and found their principal recompense in the exercise of their high faculties? Had society desired adequately to reward Newton, its whole means would have fallen short: the great and sufficing recompense of Newton was the glowing happiness which filled his soul when his genius had discovered the laws which govern the world of space. There are two classes of things in man: wants and faculties. By his wants, man is passive; by his faculties he is active. By his wants he is thrown upon his fellow-men for assistance; by his faculties he is enabled to assist his fellow-men. The wants are the indication given by God to society, to point out what it owes to individuals. The faculties are the indication given by God to individuals, to point out what they owe to society. Then there is the more due to him who has the greater wants, and we may fairly require more of him who has the greater faculties. Then, according to the divine law, written in the organisation of each human being, higher intelligence is called upon to contribute more extended and useful action, but is not entitled to greater remuneration; and the only legitimate rule, with reference to inequalities in aptitude, is that from those who are less apt for the duties of society, less duty shall be required. Adjust the social scale according to capacity: this is well, it is productive of all good; but the distribution of the public means, according to capacity, is worse than cruel; it is impious."—*Louis Blanc's History of Ten Years* 1830-1840, vol. i. pp. 553-556.

It is evident such a state of things as the communist here contemplates is neither more nor less than a state of social perfection founded on the universal abandonment of self-interested aims. He dwells with satisfaction upon the logical completeness of his system, the harmony of part with part, and admirable results of it supposed to be in operation; and sees nothing absurd and preposterous in the supposition he has to make, in order to secure its operation in the first instance; because he does not believe in the fundamental disorder of the nature and the world to which he belongs.

In opposition, then, to all such philosophy as this, the Book of Job witnesses to the fundamental hold which injustice and disorder have over this visible system of things; compelling us to look on them in their true light, not as accidents capable of being removed, and for the removal of which schemes are to be set on foot in the same spirit in which are instituted reforms in finance or commerce, or jurisprudence or police; but as part and parcel of this world. It substitutes for the sanguine view a sober and matter-of-fact one, and dissolves delusive futures: it tells men to measure their expectations by their experience; and, as they should be just before they are generous, to be wise before they are prophetic. It puts a stop to the fondling and caressing of human nature, and rebukes a luxurious and a carnal faith. It condemns sentimentalism. And as it witnesses to the fundamental hold which practical injustice and disorder have over the present system, it gives, we may add, a no insignificant hint at the same time, as to the force and prevalence of error in opinion to be expected under the same system. It were strange, indeed, to expect any large reign of pure unmixed truth under such circumstances. The gospel contains a specific promise that truth shall never be conquered and overpowered in the world; but it does not promise such a direct contradiction to the first principles of natural religion as that moral evil should not affect injuriously religious belief, and that the course of truth should run pure in a world of alloy. Why should truth be maintained to move thus by itself without sympathy with what is going on in our nature at large; and religious belief be the one single point on which mankind, on a very large scale, should go on from age to age correctly and without error? The reason of the case suggests that the mode in which religious truth is entertained, handled, used, and brought out in the world, must be affected by the state of the world practically, and that, if that state be bad, it will suffer with it. To expect, accordingly, that the received belief of that vast promiscuous mass of human minds which compose the existing Church over the world, the practical creed of the visible Catholic world, should be correct in the sense of being free from error, seems an approach, in the department with which it is concerned, to the sentimental philosophy. It is expecting too much of the human body, and imagining what does not harmonise with the world's state. It may be said that the Church is not the world. True: it is very distinct from it in one aspect, but it is largely identical with it in another. It has admitted the world on a vast scale into itself, and has become so far materially identical with it; the same masses of persons that compose the Church composing the world too. Numbers are the test; if the many are not the world, where is the world? And being so far identical with the world, the Church is so far subject to the same law of imperfection to which the world is, as regards the mode in which truth is held and handled in her.

Under this injustice and disorder, then, strongly laid down as part and parcel of this world, Scripture proceeds to enjoin a certain attitude and a certain temper of mind.

It is very evident from the history of human thought that the deeper part of mankind have always had an eye toward the construction of some temper of mind to meet this state of things. Of the various types of character which ancient philosophy struck out with this view, the Stoic and the Epicurean are the most conspicuous and complete: creations of very different schools, but both obviously evoked by the same want, and constructed with the same aim. Both of these formations of character show one great common ground; the means employed for the mind's protection and security amid the difficulties around it being in both a kind of absence of feeling. Ancient philosophy diverged remarkably from ancient poetry on this point; and while in Homer and the tragedians a standard of character appears which admits feeling prominently, in the ancient philosophies for the most part the only question seems to be how they can most effectively suppress or expel it. The Stoic took a high moral ground against feeling; he treated it as a kind of disease, which philosophy was to cure; just as medicine cures the humours and distempers of the body. Thus Cicero in the Tusculan Disputations, where he favours not an extreme, but a modified and gentle Stoicism, and professes rather to temper and combine different philosophies than to push out any one, has one judicial formula against the feelings which he brings in at every turn of the discussion. " *Omnis commotio insania*," he says; feelings are perturbations, and are therefore wrong. They are opposed to the proper constancy, gravity, and dignity of the human mind, and must be discarded by the wise man. The Aristotelian argued for the admissibility of " moderate perturbations " into the mind of the wise man; but he will not hear of it. " Do you uphold moderation in vice," he asks, " or do you not rather insist on its removal altogether? Do you stand up for moderate injustice, moderate indolence, moderate intemperance? no more can you defend moderate perturbations—*mediocritates perturbationum*."[1] The opponent pleaded that " men were not flints ;" that there was an element of softness and tenderness in the very material of which human nature was composed, which made certain affections and passions not inappropriate to it; and that apathy was not its designed state. But he rebukes the pleader with judicial severity, and bids him beware of assenting to weakness and effeminacy under the cover of considerateness and discrimination. " Not so," he goes on to say; " the philosopher must not allow half measures; he must not content himself with amputating the boughs, he must pull up the roots and fibres of human misery. Something indeed will be left after all, so deep is folly rooted in us; but it will be what is necessary and no more." In this spirit the philosophy of the Tusculan Disputations marches over the whole ground of human affections and emotions; all are sentenced under one common head, as being commotion in distinction to stillness and repose ; and the wise man, in accordance with his essential constancy, tranquillity, and fixedness, is pronounced free from the invasions of anger, fear, envy, grief, and pity. Grief, for example, it is decided has not its existence in nature but in opinion: a man grieves because he is under the obsti-

[1] " Omne enim malum etiam mediocre magnum est. Nos autem id agimus, ut in sapiente nullum sit omnino. Nam ut corpus, etiam si mediocriter ægrum est, sanum non est; sic in animo ista mediocritas caret sanitate."

nate prejudice that he ought to grieve; he could prevent himself if he chose to exert the will, and see that it was not necessary for him to be in such a state of mind. Anger is equally gratuitous, equally superfluous; man has reason, which tells him what ends to choose, and how to arrive at them; he wants no other stimulus or aid: reason is his substance, and all else is disease. "*Quid Achille Homerico fœdius!*" says the philosopher, as he dwells upon his own portrait of a perfect man, and contrasts it much to his satisfaction with the rude standard of ancient poetry.

In the very extreme of this direction, then, was the type of character which the Stoic chose, to fit himself for the world in which he lived. He assumed an artificial hardness and rigidity to meet the pressure upon him, and cased himself in a kind of buckram: he would not confess that he felt anything, and would not allow evil a single opening at which to get at him. Acknowledging the fact, he professed to ignore the power of evil, and treated it as something irrelevant, and in which he had no concern; just as persons in society affect a lofty ignorance about this or that individual who is displeasing to them. And this explains the extraordinary position given to the affection of pity in the Stoic moral code. It comes in promiscuously in the general list of the passions and diseases of the human mind; and the wise man is not chargeable with pity, just as he is not chargeable with envy, or anger, or fear. Such a bold contradiction to the instincts of our moral nature as that which turns pity into a fault is called for by the necessities of the system. The Stoic wanted a complete inaccessibility to evil in the mind of his perfect man, and that was his idea of moral strength and dignity; but pity was a medium of contact with evil, and subjected him to actual results in the shape of impressions received from it. It appeared to bring him under its power, and bend him before its presence. In this one point of view pity stood on exactly the same ground with envy, though the one was a benevolent affection, the other a selfish one; and the prohibition accordingly was as strong against it as against envy.. As the Stoic assumed an artificial hardness and rigidity, the Epicurean, again, assumed an artificial indifference, as a mode of meeting the state of things in which he found himself placed. He pretended to a secret of ease and pliability, which enabled him completely to fit in with the state of things here; to a power of mind, which acted not so much by hardening the man as by the much more complete method of softening the event. A secret indeed it was, which was not maintained without the cost of great self-command to the possessor. The Epicurean took the greatest care about his mind, and was always engaged in a preventive process, by which he kept himself just out of those relations and those influences which really fasten upon and penetrate the mind. He just stopped short of the impressive and absorbing point; and so just forestalled the stage of disappointment and depression. This was a real work of self-control, but, properly done, he pronounced it to be most effectual. He had no misunderstandings, because he had no friendships; he had no disappointments, because he had no zeal; he had no defeats, because he had no cause; he suffered no injustice, because he never conferred any obligations; he had no fears, because he had no lookings forward; and he had no regrets, because he had no lookings backward. He was thus quite safe, and felt quite composed. He was always in harbour, at some expense of care and watchfulness, indeed, in keeping himself there, but still, as being there, enjoying the immunities of the situation. This was his account of himself; though, like the Stoics, it must not be supposed to be all true. It is evidently a forced and assumed character, as the other's was; no one ever really brought himself to such a state of mind; and though approaches to both types are seen in human character occasionally, they are very imperfect and superficial ones. It was an effort, as the other was, made to meet a want; a character constructed upon a theory, and because the system of things here appeared to the originator to require it.

There is a form of character, again, not either of these two singly, but a tempered and modified combination of both, which is often actually met with in society, and is not a mere erection of theory; the character, in the more favourable sense of the phrase, of the man of the world. It is evident that experience has a tendency to form a particular habit of mind with respect to the world. No person of sense can see like fact after like fact taking place, and suppose every one of them in succession to be only a curious coincidence; he must, from the repetition, begin to suspect the existence of some sort of law or order of things. Thus, in place of that favourable theory of this world which presented to him at starting every cross incident as gratuitous, and therefore intolerable, a new basis of expectation is formed; and the idea abandoned that something good must always be happening to it, the perpetual vicinity to self-congratulation, which was always irritating because always disappointing it, human nature assumes a ground much more reasonable, and therefore much less trying to the temper. It might be thought beforehand, that the greater number of like facts, of the bad sort realised, would only cause the greater offence. But we know it is generally the reverse. Repetition has a peculiar power of unsubstantiating; a law converts individual facts into reflections of itself. All the world over, we see the human being taking refuge in the universal as a kind of counterbalance to the particular, and reposing in some impersonality or other as a relief from that definite and personal agency which immediately surrounds him. And this is one great reason, perhaps, why fatalism has been so popular, and gained such ground, wholly moulding the religion of vast portions of mankind. It extinguishes the personal agency in the world. Impatient of the injustice it sees around it, the mind falls back upon one summary antidote, and gets rid of the fact by converting it into fate; and fatalism has recommended itself by deadening the sense of wrong, and allaying the internal sore, like some stupefying medicine. And a modified and harmless form of this feeling is observable in all minds; for people all the world over console themselves with reflections on the universal, as soon as they have anything to complain of in their own particular case. Such is, more or less, the state of mind which experience produces; a cooler, and calmer, and we may add, a more benignant and forgiving one. Men of the world have acquired a regular habit of mind, which turns them away from the particular act to the class to which it belongs.

They go about with general exemplars of human conduct in their minds, to which they refer all individual acts they come across; which acts, therefore, affect them less strongly, as being no fresh realities, but only illustrations of an old familiar one. The philosophy which realises the weakness and frailty of the race, leads to a charitable estimate of the individual. It treats him as the reflection rather than the substance of evil, and tempers its feeling about him accordingly. It excuses, shields, and bears with him, and is a long-suffering and considerate judge. And thus it is that a favourable specimen of a man of the world is so popular. People take refuge in him from the caprice and violence of undisciplined minds with a sort of confidence; they repose in his sober kindness, his equable courtesy, his tolerant and disciplined good-nature, his sympathy, and acquaintance with mankind. There is moral form about his mind which engages them; he bears the Ulyssean stamp, and shows the effects of a species of discipline. Though, it must be added, all this need not be very deep morality. The whole character is an imitation of the true moral temper, rather than the temper itself. An Epicurean pliancy, a callousness, and a materialism often mingle with the discipline of life, and undermine the fabric of character so attractive to the eye.

The Christian type of character with reference to these points is one of stronger feeling and deeper nature than any of those mentioned. It does not produce an artificial hardness, like the Stoic; or an artificial indifference, like the Epicurean; nor is it one of accommodation to events, like that of the man of the world. It does not abandon the old poetical type altogether, as these philosophical creations do. At the same time, it is not to be classed, as in the popular sense of the term, a poetical character. A character is made more poetical, that is to say, more dramatically pleasing, by the very circumstance of a certain defect of internal control. Nature is more interesting than art or discipline; and passion is nature, and the control over it is art and discipline. So that to a certain extent, that is to say, within those limits which a high nature of itself imposes, natural passion is more pleasing not under rule than under rule. And youthful minds seem to have some such notion as this, and to go upon it, when the question of temper comes practically before them; they often give their feelings vent from a real latent idea that it is more noble and grand to do so; that is to say, upon a ground of reason, as it appears to them, and thinking self-control to be, however well intended, a mistake in morals. The Christian character has too much self-control in it for a poetical one. It is a practical character; a character which attends to work, and is full of the sense of duty. It is difficult to read the portrait of the charitable man, or true Christian, given by St. Paul, without feeling that it is a practical rather than what we call a poetical character, which is described; that of a person who is in a scene in which he finds all kinds of men and things which are difficult to bear, but to which he is always actively adapting himself, and doing the right and proper thing in each case : " suffering long, and being kind, not envying, not vaunting himself, not being puffed up, not behaving himself unseemly, thinking no evil, rejoicing not in iniquity, but rejoicing in the truth; bearing all things, believing all things, hoping all things, enduring all things." The Christian has this practical character, however, not because his strong feeling has vanished under artificial systems or a worldly experience; but because, existing and living in him, it is controlled by definite religious reasons. He knows the shortness of this life, and the eternity of the one which follows. In so short and passing a state to prepare him for so long a one, he feels that he must be doing and acting as much as he can, and must not spend too much time in contemplating, however deeply, the system in which he is for the time placed, and examining the features of the road which takes him to his journey's end. It is ignorance to mistake the anteroom for the room, and be absorbed in the task of unthreading the bustle and crowd in it. In all preparatory places, the mind is naturally pushed aside from its nicety; and simply thinks of acting for the best under the circumstances. "The time is short: it remaineth, that both they that have wives be as though they had none; and they that weep, as though they wept not; and they that rejoice, as though they rejoiced not; for the fashion of this world passeth away." And this practical spirit gives a cheerfulness to the Christian character; for action is necessarily cheerful. We see this effect in the case of all persons engaged in honest worldly callings, to which they industriously and conscientiously attend. The husbandman "holdeth the plough, and giveth his mind to make furrows. So every carpenter and workmaster laboureth night and day, and is diligent to make great variety. The smith also sitteth at the anvil and considereth the iron work; the noise of the hammer and the anvil is ever in his ears, and his eyes look still upon the pattern of the thing that he maketh; he setteth his mind to finish his work, and watcheth to polish it perfectly. So doth the potter sitting at his work, and turning the wheel about with his feet. He fashioneth the clay with his arm, and boweth down his strength before his feet; he applieth himself to lead it over, and is diligent to make clean the furnace." The honest labourer and artisan derives unfailing cheerfulness from his task, because it is his task; and because a whole part of his nature, which would otherwise lie gnawing him within, finds an external vent and is satisfied. It is the same in moral employment. Whether this takes the shape of definite works of charity without, or that of self-discipline simply within, makes no difference; so long as it goes on, the mind feels itself to be doing something, making some way. Whatever difficulties there may be in the world around it, its own situation here is fully accounted for and explained, and the system approves itself, as far as the individual is concerned, in its results.

His intensity of feeling, again, is checked by his faith, as well as by his practice. For what occasion is there for vehemence or excitement? There is no danger; all is safe; a good ultimate issue stands before his eyes, and has only to be waited for. Men are vehement and excited when they are under some impression, conscious or unconscious, that a cause is tottering and needs some speedy support to prevent a fall. Whenever there is insecurity felt as to the end, there is a motive for hurry as to the means; for it may depend on those means being taken immediately and on the spot, whether the end is accomplished. We see a great difference, indeed, in this respect in the temper which some men, and the temper which others, exhibit in the management of all questions. Some persons may have the best argument in the world to maintain, and they will not maintain it with effect, because they want the principle of confidence, and do not fairly realise even a true argument's weight, or grasp its necessary upshot; they are never wholly without some latent apprehension that it may fail; and therefore they are vehement and hurried in their mode of conducting it, throwing out their defences without giving themselves even fair time to state them, and snatching at, if not forestalling, every pause which admits of a remark, as if they were propping up a weak argument, instead of enforcing a strong one, and felt a constant call for their instantaneous succour to what was always on the point of giving way. There is something analogous to this in the attitude which the mere undisciplined generosity of nature assumes toward the evil which is in the world. Minds of this class are excited at the first news of any case of injustice and oppression which occurs in the world around them; and are, if their feeling were analysed, for final punishment upon the spot; as if they felt a latent insecurity that that punishment would come at all, if it did not come then, and wanted to have the testimony of their eyes to the justice of God's government. Put the government of the world into their hand, and they would convert the course of Divine justice into a series of hurried acts; and, because hurried, weak and ineffective, they would choose a justice which mistrusted its own powers, and was always forestalling the proper issue, because it did not fully believe in it. Such is not the temper of Christian faith with respect to this visible order of things, and its issue. It is self-possessed and calm, because it is confident of the issue: and sees beyond this or that apparent obstacle. And thus the admirable harmony and accordance of that whole new code of injunctions, " Resist not evil," " Let every soul be subject," the injunction involved in the parable of the tares and the wheat, and the like, by which the Evangelical Law lays down the relations of the Christian to present evil, and limits his moral, as a civil constitution does his natural, rights, with the new light of Evangelical promises and revelations. It was quite suitable, quite in keeping, that the same dispensation which enlightened, should tranquillise, the same promise which elevated, chasten; that feeling should be calmer where faith was stronger, excitement vanish with its excuse, and the toleration of present evil be enjoined where final good was assured, and life and immortality fully brought to light. True it is, that a deep hostility to a mysterious antagonist, who, unseen himself, has his visible representatives throughout the realms of this lower world, pervades all moral nature; for moral nature would not be itself, if it had not fundamentally adhering to it, and never parted with, the hatred of evil. But, in proportion as this nature rises, this hostility becomes disciplined. The generous sort of brute animals, over whom, as possessors of a rude, subordinate kind of moral nature, some shadows of this great enmity seem to fall, execute a dreadfully summary vengeance on those intruding species whom the apocryphal writer calls hateful and undesirable, unpraised and unblessed, annihilating their vile life with a frenzy of despatch, as if the mere sight of their existence were intolerable. But this is brute justice. Rational justice is a sober and tempered feeling, allowing time, preparation, and trial; introducing its operations with preliminaries, conducting them by rule, and consummating them with gravity. And Christian justice is—more than sober and tempered—passive and self-denying. Now, justice assumes its most majestic temper, and feels the strength and the repose which mathematical science and logic do in their respective spheres; a strength and a repose arising from clear-sightedness—the certainty that, as the problem must produce its demonstration, the argument its conclusion, so a moral constitution of things must issue in a Day of Judgment. Now, acting in the highest stage of character, and become a quality, not of a simply feeling, or of a simply rational but, of a spiritual nature, it imitates the temper of Him who, seated high above this world and all its movements, and strong in His own omnipotence, is supreme in His hatred, and supreme also in His toleration of evil: "Who maketh His sun to shine on the evil and on the good, and sendeth rain on the just and on the unjust;" "the Lord God merciful and gracious, long-suffering, and abundant in goodness and truth; keeping mercy for thousands, forgiving iniquity, transgression, and sin, and that will by no means clear the guilty."

PROFESSOR MAURICE'S
THEOLOGICAL ESSAYS.*

(JANUARY 1854.)

THE publication of these Essays has, as our readers are well aware, led to the removal of Mr. Maurice from King's College. His removal, whatever reasons have compelled it, is the loss to that institution of a man of great ability, energy, zeal, and disinterestedness, who has lived above worldly motives, and devoted himself to public interests, religious, moral, and social, and who, as a theological professor, has imparted life and interest to a subject too often abandoned to technicality, and made dry and distasteful to students by its mode of treatment. We cannot however, after reading these Essays, own to much surprise at such a result, however we may regret it; or consider Mr. Maurice a safe guide to theological students. He will himself readily allow that there are other qualifications which a divinity professor ought to have besides high personal character or animation as a lecturer and writer, though he will differ from us, and from the authorities of King's College, as to what those qualifications are.

---

* 1. *Theological Essays.* By FREDERICK DENISON MAURICE, M.A., Chaplain of Lincoln's Inn, and Professor of Divinity in King's College, London. Cambridge. 1853.

2. *Grounds for laying before the Council of King's College, London, certain Statements contained in a recent Publication, entitled 'Theological Essays, by the Rev. F. D. Maurice, M.A., Professor of Divinity in King's College.'* By R. W. JELF, D.D., Principal of King's College, and Canon of Christ Church. Oxford and London. 1853.

3. *The Word 'Eternal,' and the Punishment of the Wicked: A Letter to the Rev. Dr. Jelf, Canon of Christ Church, and Principal of King's College.* By FREDERICK DENISON MAURICE, Chaplain of Lincoln's Inn. Cambridge. 1853.

But we will defer these critical points for the present. We had rather meet Mr. Maurice, to begin with, on more general subject-matter, such as can be discussed and commented on without any charge affecting orthodoxy being involved. The Essays are highly discursive, and embrace much material belonging to ordinary philosophy and thought. And though a taste for philosophy does not necessarily make a philosopher, Mr. Maurice's taste for this department is such as to give an interest to his reflections and speculations in it, and to claim a respectful examination of them—a task which is attended, indeed, often with considerable difficulties in the case of a writer whose strength is that of vehemence rather than accuracy, and who thinks less like a reasoner than a rhetorician; who employs, to prove his conclusions, rather a determination of the will than the ordinary instrument of argument, and is too generally almost as obscure as he is emphatic; but a task at the same time which will not be without its reward, as bringing us into contact with a mind of considerable gifts and resources. It is fortunate for the world in the long-run that all the men who come forward to instruct and enlighten it are not cast in the same mould, and that some, according to their natural bent, reason, and others prophesy. There is a depth of mind which explains itself and unfolds its ideas in regular order, and there is also a depth which asserts itself, which throws out its contents, to produce their impression and make their way as such. The former is the more perfect method humanly, the latter is more divine. It is a kind of inspiration, and has an authoritativeness from the absence of art. Indeed, in proportion as minds are full of an idea or ideas, it is difficult for them to arrange or methodise them, or put them in the order of proof as addressed to other intelligences. Luther is little better than a chaos; Jansen the same. Even St. Augustine disguises much involved repetition of himself under the charms of an antithetical and highly-worked style. The reason is, these men were exceedingly full of the ideas to which they respectively devoted themselves. The consequence was that they could not afford to adopt that stationary attitude of mind toward them which was necessary to see them in their argumentative place. It may be pretty safely said that no one can see clearly except he stands still. But the act of standing still is exceedingly distasteful to minds under the impulse of particular ideas. To go forward is their natural bent; the instant they feel themselves stopping they are as uneasy as passengers in a quick train. Quiescence, however short or provisional, is to them stagnation, torpor, and death. They feel a total cessation of their inner life the instant the active office of putting forth and expressing stops; they are tormented by a sense of barrenness and shame, as if they were idle and vain portions of the universe. They consequently never get one fair look at the idea which is impelling them, so as to examine it and see on what it rests. To minds cast in a critical mould, on the other hand, the attitude of rest and examination is comparatively easy. Mr. Maurice will, we are sure, not take it amiss if we put him into the order of prophets, and assign strength of conviction rather than of argument as his forte.

We will begin with Mr. Maurice's philosophy respecting conscience, and his reflections on the defects and uncertainty of Bishop Butler's doctrine on that subject. "As Butler is commonly interpreted," he says, "he assumes all moral principles to depend entirely on probable evidence." He regards Butler as entertaining "strong *presumptions* in favour of a moral constitution of man," but apparently no more than presumptions. We wish Mr. Maurice had stated positively what he considered Bishop Butler's grounds to have been, and not put his assertion respecting those grounds into the ambiguous form of an assertion respecting them "as commonly interpreted." But as he considers this to be the common interpretation of Butler, and nowhere endeavours to prove that this interpretation is a wrong one, but proceeds to argue at length on the supposition of its truth, we shall suppose Mr. Maurice to state that Bishop Butler "assumes all moral principles to depend entirely on probable evidence," and to assert that his scheme only puts forth "strong presumptions in favour of a moral constitution of man." And when Mr. Maurice proceeds, as he does, to lament the scepticism of such a scheme, and to treat it as erecting the whole moral law upon a basis of uncertainty, we understand him to describe consequences which, in his opinion, flow from the natural interpretation of Bishop Butler's doctrine respecting conscience.

Now, of such a charge against Bishop Butler we can only say that we cannot easily understand how any one can make it who has read Butler's statements on the subject of conscience and human nature with ordinary attention. Probability has been defined by Butler himself—and his definition is one which nobody can object to—to consist principally in *likeness*. Where we have no actual *perception* of any thing or event we may still argue the truth of it from the fact of its likeness to other things or events which we have perceived. Probability, therefore, does not apply in the case of things of which we have actual perception; these are not probable, but certain. And though there may be cases in which we do not know for certain whether we perceive or not, and in which, therefore, probability comes in, still so far as we perceive, so far we are certain about a thing. Now, Butler places moral obligations upon certain plain and immediate perceptions inherent in our nature—perceptions which distinguish some actions from others, and attach to them the respective epithets of good and bad. It is almost frivolous to prove by extracts what runs through the whole of the Sermons on Human Nature, and either appears in or is supported by every statement which Bishop Butler makes respecting morals from one end of his works to the other. "There is a principle," he says, "of reflection in men by which they distinguish between, approve and disapprove, their own actions. We are plainly constituted such sort of creatures as to reflect upon our own nature. The mind can take a view of what passes within itself, its propensions, aversions, passions, affections, as respecting such objects and such degrees, and of the several actions consequent thereupon. In this survey it approves of one, disapproves of another, and towards a third is affected in neither of these ways, but is quite indifferent. This principle in man, by which he disapproves his heart, temper, and actions, is conscience." Here is a certain act of the mind described which is plainly that of perception, to approve or disapprove being evidently to *see* a certain character, good or bad, in the actions which come under our view. And just as the act of conscience is an act of perception, so the authority which attaches to this act is an object also of perception. And supposing a man to allow the fact of a conscience, but deny its authority, Butler tells him in reply that the *authority* of conscience is perceived. "The principle of reflection or conscience being compared with the various appetites, passions, and affections in men, the former is *manifestly* superior and chief, without regard to strength." It "manifestly" is superior and chief, *i.e.* it is *seen* quite plainly to be so. The appeal which Butler makes throughout is to certain immediate and clear perceptions in our nature, and it might as well be asserted that the evidence of our bodily senses rested upon presumption as that moral obligations did upon Butler's system.

But it may be said that though Butler places morality upon the basis of natural perception, he places religion upon a basis of presumption simply; and that for the grounds for believing in a Divine moral government of the Universe, and a final state of reward and punishment, he refers us to analogy;—to the circumstance, that is, that we see a moral government in this world, and therefore that we may expect it in another. Now it is quite true that Butler does not—and it would be absurd if he did—represent the evidence of religion as being that of immediate perception, but neither does he represent it as being merely presumption. There is a mode of proof which is neither immediate perception nor presumption, which is commonly called reasoning; that act of the mind by which we see a certain conclusion follow from certain premisses before us, without being actually in or part of those premisses. There are, it is true, different kinds of this sort of proof—different kinds of reasoning. There is demonstrative, or mathematical; and there is a less urgent kind, such as the argument from final causes: but both kinds are in strength far above the argument of mere presumption or analogy; and Butler moreover proved the truth of religion by both these modes of reasoning.

First, he held the existence of a God to be proved demonstratively, in the same way in which mathematical conclusions are deduced from their premisses. And there later philosophy does not appear to go along with him. But this mode of proof was part of the religious philosophy of the age in which he lived, and which he seems to have adopted out of respect to high names, and—we may almost say—contrary to his own better judgment. Locke and Clarke proved the existence of a God by demonstrative reasoning; they argued from the principle, that all things that begin to exist must have a cause; and by a keen and subtle use of this argument, professed to reduce the atheist to the position of a man who denied that two and two were four, or that things that were equal to the same were equal to one another. Locke begins his chapter on the proof of a Deity with these words,—" We are capable of knowing *certainly* that there is a God : " and by " certainty " he proceeds to say that he means " a certainty equal to mathematical certainty ;" adding indeed—" if I mistake not "—a rather ominous commencement of such a proof, but of which the spirit does not appear to last or to operate as a hindrance on him. His reflection upon his argument, after the explanation of it, is— " From what has been said, it is plain to me that we have a more certain knowledge of the existence of a God than of anything our senses have not immediately discovered to us. Nay, I presume I may say that we may more certainly know that there is a God, than there is anything else without us." " It is as certain," he says elsewhere, " that there is a God, as that the opposite angles, made by the intersection of two straight lines, are equal." Clarke expanded the fundamental axiom on which all this reasoning went, and said not only, " everything that *begins* to exist must have a cause," but " everything that *exists* has a cause,"—a startling proposition, but which he makes orthodox by means of a larger sense which he annexes to the word *cause*. " Whatever exists has a cause, a ground of its existence, a foundation on which its existence relies ; a ground or reason why it doth exist, rather than not exist; either in the necessity of its own nature, or in the will of some other being." The former of these two grounds or reasons he then applied to the case of the Supreme Being, and laid down a necessity for the existence of a God, as contained in the existence of Time and Space, which, as being not substances themselves, but modes and attributes of substance, implied a substance which supported them; and, inasmuch as they were infinite, an infinite and eternal substance. This necessity for the existence of a God he calls " a necessity absolutely such in its own nature," *i.e.* nothing else but " its being a plain impossibility, or implying a contradiction to suppose the contrary," —a necessity of which " the relation of equality between twice two and four is an instance ; it being an immediate contradiction in terms to suppose these two unequal." And upon this proof of the existence of a God he bases this reflection : " From hence it follows that there is no man whatsoever, who makes any use of his reason, but may easily become more certain of the being of a Supreme Independent Cause, than he can be of anything else besides his own existence. For how much thought soever it may require to demonstrate the other attributes of such a Being, as it may do to demonstrate the greatest mathematical certainties, yet, as to its existence, that there is somewhat eternal, infinite, and self-existing, which must be the cause and original of all other things,—this is one of the first and most natural conclusions that any man can frame in his mind : and no man can any more doubt of this, than he can doubt whether twice two be equal to four. 'Tis possible, indeed, that a man may in some sense be ignorant of this first and plain truth, by being utterly stupid, and not thinking at all. But this I say, there is no man who thinks or reasons at all, but may easily become more certain that there is something eternal, infinite, and self-existing than he can be certain of anything else."

It may appear indeed somewhat strange that it did not occur to a philosopher that he was getting out of his depth when he argued that the existence of the Deity was necessary as the substratum of time and space ; and the correspondence between Butler and Clarke, given in the common editions of Butler's Works, shows that that suspicion was entertained by Butler, though then a youthful thinker, and expressed as became a young man writing to the great metaphysician of the day, with the utmost modesty and caution. "I cannot say that I believe your argument not conclusive; for I must own my ignorance, that I am really at a loss about the nature of space and duration. But did it plainly appear that they were properties of a substance, we should have an easy way with the atheists; for it would at once demonstrably prove an eternal, necessary, and self-existent Being; that there is but one such; and that He is needful in order to the existence of all other things;—which makes me think that though it may be true, yet it is not obvious to every capacity; otherwise it would have been generally used as a fundamental argument to prove the being of a God."

Now this metaphysical ground for the existence and attributes of God has its weaknesses, but one weakness certainly cannot be laid to its charge, viz., that of being too diffident and too doubtful. It professed to be a demonstration, a mathematical proof of the existence of a God. And so far as Butler acknowledged this ground,—and he always does appeal to "abstract reasonings," as proof of religion,—so far, certainly, he cannot be said to have based the evidence of religion on mere probabilities and presumptions.

But such arguments as these could not prove the moral government of God. To prove this, philosophy has used the second sort of reasoning. It has argued from the moral nature of the creature to the moral character of the Creator; and from the moral character of God to His moral government. This common recognised argument of religious philosophy is always supposed and its validity taken for granted by Butler. He regards conscience as the "voice of God within us," and its approbation and disapprobation as anticipations of a future and final Divine judgment. This is not demonstration; but neither is it an appeal to mere chances and presumptions.

To Mr. Maurice's charge then—that Butler "assumes all moral principles to depend on probable evidence," our answer is plain. If by "moral principles" are meant moral obligations, moral principles are maintained by Butler to be the objects of clear mental intuition : if by "moral principles" are meant the Divine moral government, moral principles, we then allow, are made by Butler to depend on probable evidence; but only on probable evidence as distinguished from demonstration, not as being mere guess and presumption; on sound, valid, and irresistible probable *reasoning*.

But it will be said, that the arguments which Butler has *put forward* are at any rate arguments of analogy or presumption; and that he has written the book called the *Analogy*, which is entirely devoted to them. He has; and nothing can show more clearly that which we assert of Butler—that he did not rest the evidence of religion on analogy—than the ground which he assigns to analogy in this book. He tells us expressly that he adopts analogy as an appeal to men who will not acknowledge any other ground. He says in the advertisement, "It is come, I know not how, to be taken for granted by many persons, that Christianity is not so much as a subject of inquiry, but that it is now at length discovered to be fictitious. And accordingly they treat it as if, in the present age, this were an agreed point among all people of discernment, and nothing remained but to set it up as a principal subject of mirth and ridicule, as it were by way of reprisals, for its having so long interrupted the pleasures of the world. On the contrary, thus much at least will be here found, not taken for granted, but proved, that any reasonable man, who will thoroughly consider the matter, may be as much assured as he is of his own being, that it is not however so clear a case, that there is nothing in it. There is, I think, strong evidence of its truth; but it is certain no one can, upon principles of reason, be satisfied of the contrary." He is arguing then with men who do not acknowledge the ordinary evidences for Christianity. And it is the same with respect to natural religion. He is arguing with men who do not admit the ordinary evidence for natural religion, and the Divine moral government. Having excluded themselves then from the strong ground of evidence, he offers, or rather fastens upon them, another much weaker, but still better than none at all. "There is, I think, strong evidence of the truth" of religion; but that evidence he does not now bring forward, because it consists of an appeal to our moral nature, which can be strong evidence only to those who admit that moral nature.

He is obliged to confine himself to a kind of evidence which leads to a much weaker result, and does not prove that religion is true, but only that it cannot be set down as false—" that they cannot be satisfied of the contrary." But as that is the only kind of evidence they acknowledge, he uses it. It is evidently a gain if even such a result can be produced. Evidence which leads even to an inferior conclusion is valuable if it is of a species which is admitted and recognised by the persons addressed, while to address evidence to them which led to the most positive conclusion would be wholly useless, if the evidence itself was of a species which they did not recognise. The argument, then, on which Butler *himself* considered the truth of religion to rest, was a different one from the argument used in the *Analogy*. Does not Mr. Maurice himself admit this?

" He did, however, use words addressed to the loose thinkers of his day, the men of wit and fashion about town, which seem to confound ' probabilities ' with ' chances ;' to suggest the thought that we are to calculate the likelihood of religious principles being true, and that if there is even a slight balance in favour of them—nay, none at all—we are to throw in the danger of rejecting them as a makeweight, and so to force ourselves into the adoption of them. I groan over these words as I read them, feeling how much a great and good man was sacrificing of what was dearest to his heart, for the sake of an *argumentum ad hominem*, which, after all, was not an argument that ever reached the conscience of any man, or that could do so, if the conscience is what Butler affirms it to be."—Maurice's *Theological Essays*, p. 234.

Why does Mr. Maurice groan? We see no reason for it, even according to his own statement. He calls Butler's argument an *argumentum ad hominem*. But is not an *argumentum ad hominem*, by the very force of the expression, an argument which a man uses out of accommodation to another, and not the argument upon which he rests himself the truth of the conclusion in which he believes? Does a man give up his own stronger ground, because he uses another weaker one, out of accommodation to another man, who will not listen to the stronger? And if he does not, what is there to deplore? Truth is not injured, and a charity is done.

Not that the *Analogy*, though addressed primarily, is addressed solely to those who do not admit the stronger ground of evidence for religion. Undoubtedly, however we may admit that stronger ground, analogy is a confirmation of it; and that testimony of conscience to the moral and immoral character of actions, on which we substantially base our anticipation of a future judgment, is strengthened when we see that as a matter of fact these actions are, to a large extent, respectively rewarded and punished in this life. But this again does not make analogy the *ground* of our belief in religion. On the contrary, it makes it presuppose that ground. Nor can anything be more distinct and express than Butler's own statement on this subject. "*It is not the purpose*," he says, "*of this treatise properly to prove God's perfect moral government over the world;* but to observe what there is in the constitution and course of nature to confirm the proper proof of it, supposed to be known. Pleasure and pain are, indeed, to a certain degree, say to a very high degree, distributed amongst us without any apparent regard to the merit or demerit of characters. And were there nothing else concerning this matter discernible in the constitution and course of nature, there would be no ground from the constitution and course of nature to hope or to fear that men would be rewarded or punished hereafter according to their deserts. *And thus the proof of a future state of retribution would rest upon the usual known arguments for it, which are, I think, plainly unanswerable, and would be so, were there no additional confirmation of them from the things above insisted on.*"[1] Again, "That there is an intelligent Author of Nature and natural Governor of the world, is a principle gone upon in the foregoing treatise, as proved and generally known and confessed to be proved. And the very notion of an intelligent Author of Nature, proved by particular final causes, implies a will and a character. *Now, as our whole nature, the nature which He has given us, leads us to conclude his will and character to be moral, just, and good, so we can scarce in imagination conceive what it can be otherwise.*"[2] This is the proof then, according to Butler, of the truth of religion and

---

[1] Chapter on the Moral Government of God (near the end).
[2] Conclusion of First Part of Analogy.

the Divine moral government, viz. not analogy, but something which analogy supposes, "an argument which is plainly unanswerable, and would be so were there no additional confirmation of it from analogy,"—the argument that we have a moral nature, and that, therefore, the existence of a God, the maker of that nature, supposed, His nature and character must be moral too.

It would be a hard task to go into all the mistakes which Mr. Maurice makes, in consequence of supposing, against Butler's own distinct protest, that analogy is the *original* evidence of religion in his scheme, and not a mere secondary and confirmatory one. But his comparison between Butler's moral system and Mr. Combe's physical one should not be passed over. Mr. Combe proves that the observance of certain physical laws is necessary for the welfare of man, and, therefore, that these laws have, according to the design of the Author of nature, a claim on our attention and obedience, as guides to life. Butler proves the same of moral laws. Mr. Maurice, on a comparison of the evidence brought forward by the two for their respective sets of laws, asserts Mr. Combe's to be based on sure scientific observation, and Butler's on mere guess and presumption; and remarks, " Whenever guesses are balanced against laws, guesses must kick the beam; if divines and moralists have nothing but guesses to produce, and Mr. Combe has laws, it is not a matter of doubt, but of certainty, that he will be the teacher of the world, and that they must make their way out of it as fast as they can."

This comparison is evidently founded on the mistake we have noticed, viz., on Mr. Maurice's idea that analogy is Butler's primary argument for the truth of religion. Analogy being supposed to be his argument, Butler's argument, and Mr. Combe's argument, are both arguments of the same kind; the proofs are the same in both cases: Mr. Combe observes as a fact that certain *physical* antecedents produce certain consequences, painful or pleasant; Butler observes, that certain *moral* antecedents, or actions and ways of life, produce certain consequences, painful or pleasant. The arguments of the two are therefore, on Mr. Maurice's supposition, arguments of the same kind:

they are both of them inductions; and Mr. Combe's induction is a much more correct, accurate, and certain one than Butler's. But Butler's primary argument for the truth of religion is *not* analogy, and implies no induction at all; it is an appeal to our consciousness of a certain moral nature within us in the first place: it is an immediate inference from that moral nature in the next. His and Mr. Combe's therefore are different arguments, and cannot be compared.

Indeed, if Mr. Maurice will only reflect, he must see how perfectly inconsistent Butler's whole view of morals is with induction as its basis. Whatever uncertainty may attend Butler's view of morals, he is yet regarded by Mr. Maurice as maintaining morals, in the true sense of that word; *i.e.* as holding a fundamental distinction between good and evil in actions. But he could not, by possibility, get at such a distinction by induction. In induction we observe facts, and put them together, but we cannot get beyond this colligation or summary of the facts themselves, or get at an internal quality or characteristic of them, such as the moral one. To observe that intemperance, veracity, pride, lying, temperance, honesty, fraud, and many other habits and lines of behaviour, in the department of human life, are connected as antecedents with certain consequences,—such as intemperance with disease, lying with dishonour, veracity with credit, and so on,—is not to arrive at the quality of moral good or evil attaching to these respective ways of acting. That can only be discerned by an internal sense. The argument of the *Analogy*—we mean the argument put out there, as distinct from any ground presupposed—is indeed one of this simply inductive sort. Nothing being taken for granted with respect to the intrinsic moral good and evil of actions, and without saying that temperance is at all better morally than drunkenness, or veracity than lying, all the actions that take place in human life are in that argument simply looked upon as *facts;* and Butler asserts the present experienced connection of certain pleasures or pains with them, in the way of antecedent and consequent, exactly as a medical man would connect one physical state or habit with another, or as a chemist would observe that certain results were produced when certain materials were brought together. The argument of the *Analogy* is thus a purely inductive one; and we will admit further, that as an inductive argument it is much weaker and much less conclusive than Mr. Combe's—simply for this reason, that the facts in Mr. Combe's department are so much more fixed and clear than in Butler's. That some things produce health, and other things produce disease, is a much more uniform connection of antecedent and consequent than that virtues produce happiness, and vices misery, in this world. It is admitted that the facts in this latter department are not constant; that there is a large disturbance, that evil is often triumphant, and good depressed. And this causes the manifest weakness and poverty of the argumentative result of analogy pure. It cannot be helped. The result is, indeed, as far as it goes, decided. There is a clear balance on the whole in favour of virtue; and that being the case, a man is as really bound by the result as if it were a much larger one. Still, the facts are inconstant, and the induction must represent the facts. Admitting, however, that the argument of the *Analogy* is of itself an induction, and that a necessarily poor induction, we repeat that Butler did not rest the evidence of religion on the argument of analogy.

But now we must turn the tables upon Mr. Maurice, and having stood so long on the defensive, must become the accuser on this subject. We have explained what induction is, and its inherent weakness as an argument in morals. But, after charging Bishop Butler with resting morals on a weak and uncertain ground, what does Mr. Maurice do himself but rest the evidence of moral truth upon this very ground—that of induction? This is certainly implied in the following passage, which is given at large, marking what part we especially refer to :—

"'But though there may be this single point of agreement amongst Christian doctors on this subject, are there not the greatest disagreements among them; such disagreements as entirely bear out Mr. Combe's assertion that nothing is settled about the moral or spiritual constitution, while *he* is able to argue from the most certain data respecting the physical?' Before I answer this question, I wish to inquire what those data are, from which Mr.

Combe argues, and what is his method of coming at conclusions from them. These data, I conceive, are certain facts respecting the condition of men in different circumstances; respecting their states of health and of disease; respecting the treatment, mischievous and beneficial, which has been applied to them. Such facts have not been merely observed, loosely and carelessly: they have been submitted to a series of searching experiments. There have been experiments on the bodily frame which illustrated those on the influences to which it is exposed; the anatomist, physiologist, chemist, geologist, each contributing his quota of observation and thought to the confirmation or correction of the other. Thus, after many theories have been accepted, and thrown aside, some simple law has been brought to light, the great test of which has been, its power of explaining facts, new and old; so far as it can do that, it sustains its character; when it fails, it is not discarded, but it is supposed that some deeper, more comprehensive law is yet to reward the toil and humility of the inquirer. What can be better or truer than investigations of this kind? What duty can be greater, than to avail ourselves of the results to which they lead? *But the more we study them and admire them, the less shall we adopt those loose expressions which represent this evidence as something altogether different in kind from that which is open to moralists and divines, if they like to make use of it.* I do not believe that Butler intended to distinguish the probable evidence to which he appeals in his Analogy, from this kind of induction. On the contrary, he is applying the inductive method with the same hesitation and unwillingness to accept hasty generalisations, with the same readiness to look at facts and test them, which characterises the physical inquirer. And he wished his reader to feel how satisfactory that method was, what a guide it was to practical decisions, what a deliverance from mere vague hypotheses."—*Ibid.* pp. 232-234.

To say that we understand this passage as a whole would indeed be boastful. The author thinks that Butler distinguished, though without intending it, probable evidence from induction. What does he mean? Butler, in the *Analogy*, founds the probability of a Divine moral government *upon* an induction, *i.e.* observation of present facts. So much, however, is clear, that Mr. Maurice says the argument which moralists and divines ought to use for their conclusions is the argument of induction, which Mr. Combe uses. But what can Mr. Maurice be thinking of, with his dislike of uncertainty, to rest the evidence of religion upon induction? How can he think that a "satisfactory method" of proof? Will he say Butler has not made so much of it as he might have done? We shall be truly obliged to Mr. Maurice if he will make any more of it. Will he prove what Eliphaz the Temanite, Bildad the Shuhite, and Zophar the Naamathite, wanted to do,—that virtue and vice have uniform consequences respectively of pain and happiness in this world? But till he does that, the induction from the facts of this life in favour of the truth of religion, or the ultimate reward of virtue and punishment of vice, must remain a very imperfect one. And, even supposing him to succeed here, a still greater difficulty awaits him. With the most perfect induction as to the consequences of actions in this world, it would be still a mere presumption and no more that there would be the same consequences in another. Religion would rest on the most uncertain basis, if induction were its primary proof.

Again, after objecting so strongly to the uncertainty of Butler's proof in morals, what does Mr. Maurice do but actually charge Butler—and a most serious mistake he thinks it—with too great certainty in that proof? We allude to the remarks on the subject of conscience. Butler thinks that conscience, though liable to be occasionally disturbed by superstition, is, in the main, to be depended on as a guide, and puts it forth as a sound foundation of morals. Mr. Maurice disputes this, and sees in superstition, not that mere exception to, which Butler does, but a general and wholesale proof against, the trustworthiness of conscience.

"The student of Butler's doctrine on the Conscience is often forced even more painfully upon this conclusion. For he will say to himself, My conscience ought, you say, to be a king. But it is not a king. It is a captive. How shall it be raised to its throne? And when it has got a temporary ascendency, can I trust it? Does not Butler himself admit the possibility of superstition acting upon it, and deranging its decisions? Is that a slight exception to a general maxim? Does not all history show that the decrees of this great ruler may be made contradictory, monstrous, destructive, by this disturbing force, which Butler notices, but hardly deigns to take account of?"—*Ibid.* p. 221.

Who is it here who is throwing doubt and uncertainty

upon morals?—Butler, who maintains the trustworthiness of conscience, or Mr. Maurice, who seems to think conscience a mere guesser, and a very bad one? We have not time or space to enter at present further into this question, which is undoubtedly an important one, or explain how conscience may be an authoritative guide to us in action, though we may know it is not an absolutely infallible one. We shall content ourselves with saying that we think Mr. Maurice greatly exaggerates the errors of conscience, and, over-occupied with the effects of one disturbing force, forgets the many large fields of action on which it is quite clear-sighted and not liable to mistakes: and with reminding Mr. Maurice that if he unseats conscience as a guide, he is indeed throwing us on the wide world for any standard of action or rule of life. He may think he has a corrective for this defect which he has discovered in conscience, but it is much easier to pull down than to build up again, and to inflict a wound than to remedy it. His remedy appears, as far as we can understand him, to lie in a certain "regeneration" of the conscience. "Christ, the true bridegroom of man's spirit, is ever drawing it towards Himself —is holding out to it freedom from evil, and the knowledge of Himself as its high reward. Owning Him, the man rises out of dark superstitions, out of immoral practices; he recognises the fitness of all God's arrangements in the physical and moral world; he claims for the body as well as the soul a redemption from all which corrupts and degrades it." He enforces this discovery by a prayer of great earnestness:—

"But Thou, O strong Son of God! give Thy servants grace with all boldness to speak of Thee as that Lord of the inner man, in confessing whom each of us knows himself to be a person, knows himself to be a subject: knows that he is meant to rule the turbulent impulses and energies within him, because they are Thine, and have all been redeemed by Thee, and are all consecrated to Thee. Suffer us not to shrink through any shame, or through the desire of being reputed philosophical among philosophical men, or religious among religious men, from making this confession of Thee, seeing that Thou, who didst raise up men in other generations to speak that which was needful for them, hast mercifully awakened some of us to feel, that only in this way can we be saved from sinking into the deepest pit of unbelief, the most practical denial of that conscience, which, yet, not a few are ready to put in the place of Thee."—*Ibid.* p. 229.

We do not see, in spite of Mr. Maurice's earnestness, any correction here to the doubtfulness which he has thrown over the dictates and guidance of conscience. A "regenerated" conscience is undoubtedly a better guide than an "unregenerated" one; but how is a man to know that his conscience is "regenerated"?

We have thought it right to notice this very groundless attack upon one of our great class-books in morals and philosophy; and now we go to other and more critical portions of Mr. Maurice's Essays. And first, we shall make some remarks on the chapter on the Atonement.

Many statements and arguments in this chapter appear to us not only highly dangerous, but positively unsound, and opposed to the doctrine of the Atonement as revealed in Scripture, and always understood in the Church. At the same time we are anxious, in justice to Mr. Maurice, to make a distinction. He appears to us sometimes more unsound as a destroyer than he is as a constructor. He has a bias against all existing forms of opinion, all doctrines in the way in which they are actually held and received, and seems to consider it his special vocation to assail them. But allow him to construct the doctrine himself, and put it out in his own formula, and it will be not so very unlike the original one. In the following passage, he protests against the doctrine of the death of our Saviour as a satisfaction for the penalty of sin. The first portion of it is not his own protest in form, so much as that of certain parties whose scruples and objections to orthodox doctrine these Essays are written to meet, and whose sentiments he here expresses. But, so far as that point is concerned, he avows agreement with their protest; and we must add that we cannot, from the whole context, but regard him as agreeing in the main with the arguments on which it is founded.

"But I admitted that there were grave and earnest protests against much of what is called the Protestant doctrine of the

Atonement. 'You hold,' it is said, 'that God had condemned all His creatures to perish, because they had broken His law; that His justice could not be satisfied without an infinite punishment; that that infinite punishment would have visited all men, if Christ, in His mercy to men, had not interposed and offered Himself as the substitute for them; that by enduring an inconceivable amount of anguish, He reconciled the Father, and made it possible for Him to forgive those who would believe. This whole statement,' the objector continues, 'is based on a certain notion of justice. It professes to explain, on certain principles of justice, what God ought to have done, and what He actually has done. And this notion of justice outrages the conscience, to which you seem to offer your explanation. You often feel that it does. You admit that it is not the kind of justice which would be expected of men. And then you turn round and ask us what we can know of God's justice: how we can tell that it is of the same kind with ours? After arguing with us, to show the necessity of a certain course, you say that the argument is good for nothing; we are not capable of taking it in! Or else you say that the carnal mind cannot understand spiritual ideas. We can only answer, We prefer our carnal notion of justice to your spiritual one. We can forgive a fellow-creature a wrong done to us, without exacting an equivalent for it; we blame ourselves if we do not; we think we are offending against Christ's command, who said, Be ye merciful, as your Father in Heaven is merciful, if we do not. We do not feel that punishment is a satisfaction to our minds: we are ashamed of ourselves when we consider it is. We may suffer a criminal to be punished, but it is that we may do him good, or assert a principle. And if that is our object, we do not suffer an innocent person to prevent the guilty from enduring the consequences of his guilt, by taking them upon himself. Are these moral maxims in our case, or are the opposing maxims moral? If they are moral, should we, because God is much more righteous than we can imagine or understand, attribute to Him what we should consider a very low righteousness, or unrighteousness, in us?'

"These questions are asked on all sides of us. It is obvious that they are most deep and awful questions. They touch upon the very principles of morality and godliness. I know well how clergymen persuade themselves that it is right and safe to pass them by. They say, 'Such doubts bewilder the minds of our flocks upon a doctrine which is, of all others, the most vital. Let one of these objectors,' they say, 'go with us to the bedsides of some of the humblest, purest Christians. We will show them those who have grown up from their childhood in love and good works. We will show them penitent Magdalens. The testimony of both will be the same. "To lose this doctrine, of God having reconciled sinners to Himself, would be to lose everything. Without it we do not care for life here or hereafter. We do not know what life here or hereafter could mean!" Are we to rob such souls as these of their treasure, because some captious people find the casket which contains it disagreeable to their pride—because they cannot bend their reasons to the Cross?'

"I answer, No; you are to defend this treasure to the death. You are to let no man take it from those suffering spirits, or—if you have it—from yourselves. You are to desire that all, you among the rest, should be brought, with all your notions and theories, to the Cross. But what is the treasure which you see your humble, dying saints, grasping with such intense resolution? Is it not the belief which is expressed in our collect for Passion Week, that 'God of His tender love towards mankind sent His Son, our Saviour Jesus Christ, to take our flesh upon Him, that all mankind should follow the example of His great humility'? Is not this love of God, this perfect obedience of Christ to His Father's loving will, the ground of all their confidence, their hope, their humility? Has their confidence, their hope, their humility, anything whatever to do with the theory that has fastened itself to this doctrine of Atonement, and, in many minds, has taken the place of it? Do you hear any allusion to it amidst the pauses of that sepulchral cough? Does the feverish hand clasp yours with thankful joy, when you speak of a Divine justice delighting in infinite punishment? Does the loving, peaceful eye respond to the idea that the Son of God has delivered His creatures from their Father's determination to execute His wrath upon them?

"But go from the dying chamber to the house across the street, or, it may be, to the fashionable withdrawing-room below, and there you will find what hold this doctrine has upon your people. There you may hear some religious dowager, with the newspaper from which she derives her faith and her charity on the ottoman beside her, denouncing a youth just returned from Cambridge, and, as you enter, imploring your help in delivering him from the horrible scepticism into which he has fallen, respecting the faith which is her only consolation in time and eternity. That faith is *not* in the tender love of God, in the obedience of Christ, in His great humility; it is in the theory of the satisfaction He has offered to offended Sovereignty, or, as she calls it, justice."
—*Ibid.* pp. 137-141.

Here, then, Mr. Maurice plainly refuses to admit the

doctrine of our Lord's atonement, in the sense of a satisfaction for the penalty of sin. He asks, "Does the loving, peaceful eye respond to the idea that the Son of God has delivered His creatures from their Father's determination to execute His wrath upon them?" meaning, of course, that such a doctrine is essentially repugnant to true spiritual thought and feeling. He speaks of "satisfaction to offended Sovereignty," *i.e.* to the Divine wrath, as "a theory" which fashionable dowagers, devoid alike of faith and charity, may hold and repose in; but which the contrition of real penitents thrusts aside as revolting, foreign, and unedifying. But what, may we ask, *is* the doctrine of the Atonement, if it is not the doctrine that Christ's death and sufferings have been accepted as a sacrifice in our behalf; and, whereas our sins would, in the natural course, have brought eternal punishment upon us, this sacrifice has redeemed us from it? We do not say that deliverance from punishment is the only mode of expressing the benefit of the Atonement: that benefit is deliverance from sin as well. The two consequences, indeed, cannot be considered apart, so far as this, that the individual cannot have deliverance from punishment, if he does not exhibit a deliverance from sin too. But the one consequence cannot be regarded as absorbed in the other; nor can we afford to throw aside the deliverance from punishment, as if it had no separate and independent interest to us. All that deliverance from sin can amount to, even if by grace we have cast off our sins, is repentance and reformation. But reformation can only affect our future life; it cannot prevent the sins we have committed. And if those sins remain, how do we escape their natural consequence, unless the atonement of Christ is a special rescue from that consequence—a satisfaction for, and removal of a punishment, which would otherwise have been executed upon us? Accordingly, when Bishop Butler defends the doctrine of "a Mediator and Redeemer," this is the doctrine which he defends. "The Son of God loved us, and gave himself for us, with a love which he himself compares to that of human friendship; though, in this case, all comparisons must fall infinitely short of the thing intended to be illustrated by them. *He interposed in such a manner as was necessary and effectual to prevent that execution of justice upon sinners, which God had appointed should otherwise have been executed upon them;* or in such a manner, as to prevent that punishment from actually following, which, according to the general laws of Divine government, must have followed the sins of the world, had it not been for such interposition." If repentance cannot of itself do away with the natural effects of our past sin upon ourselves—a power it is plainly repugnant to revelation to assign to it—we are evidently left without a remedy for those effects, and are still under sentence of eternal punishment, unless the Atonement is what Mr. Maurice denies it to be.

We do not argue, however, with Mr. Maurice. All we are concerned with, is to show that the doctrine which he impugns is the doctrine of the Atonement as held by the Christian body throughout the world, and supposed and taken for granted by divines in their defences and explanations of it. Indeed, Mr. Maurice almost admits this himself, for he admits it to be the doctrine in defence of which Archbishop Magee wrote his book on the "Scriptural Doctrine of the Atonement;" and he allows that both parties in the Church accept the doctrine defended in that book.

"Men of the Evangelical school, who did not like Archbishop Magee's book, because they found nothing in it which responded to the witness of their hearts, yet accepted it on the poor calculation that it was a learned book, and might defend what they were pleased to call the outworks of the faith. Men of the Patristic school, who knew how little it accorded with the divinity they most admired, yet argued œconomically, that it might serve the purposes of such an age as ours is, and might confute objectors who did not deserve to be acquainted with any higher truth. I acknowledge the dishonesty and faithlessness of both decisions; I feel most deeply the mischiefs which have followed from both; but I see how much there was to make them plausible. I believe it is only a peculiar discipline, and some very painful experience, which has led me to abandon them, and to say boldly, I must give up Archbishop Magee, for I am determined to keep that which makes the Atonement precious to my heart and conscience; to keep the theology of the Creeds and the Bible."—*Ibid.* pp. 148, 149.

Whatever reasons, then, he may give for their respective

approvals, the fact is admitted that men of the Evangelical school, and men of the Patristic school,—that is to say, the whole of the Church,—accept that doctrine of the Atonement which Archbishop Magee defends; while he has "been led by painful experience to say boldly, I must give up Archbishop Magee."

The arguments in apparent deference to which the received doctrine of the Atonement is thus rejected, are the ordinary arguments of Sceptics and Deists, which we meet with in the controversial treatises of divines who have undertaken the defence of the doctrine of the Atonement. There is the argument drawn from the Divine benevolence, that it is unworthy of the Divine nature to suppose that God does not forgive sin simply upon repentance, without the condition of atonement and mediation. There is the argument drawn from the Divine justice, which, it is supposed, is contradicted by making an innocent man suffer for a guilty one. There is the argument against all punishment, as being a sort of vengeance. Our first remark on these arguments is, that it would have been more satisfactory if Mr. Maurice had distinctly stated how far he agreed with them, and how far he did not. As it is, he puts forth certain arguments with a great appearance of sympathy; he accepts the result to which those arguments lead, in the minds of the parties whom he represents; and he puts forward for this result no other arguments as his own in their stead. We do not say that these are, under such circumstances, to be regarded as Mr. Maurice's own arguments; but this we must say, that for a Professor of Theology in a Church of England College to treat with the greatest apparent sympathy and respect a class of arguments which are known as the common arguments of Sceptics and Deists, without ever stating dissent from them, or giving his readers any mark by which to separate the sentiments of the represented parties from those of their mouthpiece, is, if it is not an appropriation of those arguments, an inattention to what was due to his position as a Theological Professor in the Church of England.

Our next remark is, that as the Essay advances this ambiguity is somewhat lessened—to the satisfaction of the reader so far as he wants to know what Mr. Maurice's own arguments are—to his grief, inasmuch as he finds that Mr. Maurice's own arguments are but too like in character those of which he was the mouthpiece. He says,—

" What we have a right to insist on is, that no notion or theory shall be allowed to interfere with this fundamental maxim, that if any one, by any means, leads us to suppose that Christ did not simply submit to the will of His Father, and carry it out, but sought to move it or change it, he shall be held to have departed from the faith once delivered to the saints."—*Ibid.* p. 144.

Again :—

"The Scripture says, 'The Lamb of God taketh away the *Sin* of the world.' All orthodox teachers repeat the lesson. They say Christ came to deliver sinners from sin. This is what the sinner asks for. Have we a right to call ourselves scriptural or orthodox, if we change the words, and put 'penalty of sin' for 'sin ;' if we suppose that Christ destroyed the connection between sin and death —the one being the necessary wages of the other—for the sake of benefiting any individual man whatever ? If He had, would He have magnified the Law and made it honourable ? Would He not have destroyed that which He came to fulfil ? Those who say the law must execute itself,—it must have its penalty—should remember their own words. How does it execute itself if a person, against whom it is not directed, interposes to bear its punishment ?" —*Ibid.* p. 146.

These are arguments which Mr. Maurice himself brings against the Atonement as effecting a delivery from a sentence of punishment which would otherwise have been executed. He says first, that to suppose this is to suppose that "*Christ sought to move and change*" the Father's will; and secondly, to suppose that Christ destroyed the connection between sin and death, and so violated, instead of fulfilling, the law. Both these are rationalistic arguments. A change in the will of God, such as is supposed in the doctrine of the Atonement, is of course a mystery. We do not mean to say that God's will is changed in the sense in which a human will is ; that would be repugnant to our idea of the Divine Nature. We only use such language as a way of expressing some act of the Deity, which cannot really be expressed. Not to allow such modes of expression as these is rationalism ; because it is a clear limiting of the truths of religion to such truths as we can understand. The same answer may be made to the argument that Christ did not destroy the connection between sin and death. Let it be said—which is not true—that our natural idea of justice demands that real guilt should be punished, just as it demands that real virtue should be rewarded; while the doctrine of the Atonement represents real guilt as let off its just punishment. Still this is only a mode of speaking. It is the expression of a mystery to which our thoughts cannot reach, and which is only expressed in this language because there is no language by which it can be truly and adequately expressed.

We have been viewing Mr. Maurice as an assailant, and we find him not very tender about the arguments he uses. It seems to be *quocunque modo rem*. He appears to regard established forms of belief as things to be knocked down; as so many incrustations, harsh and artificial, which surround the essential truth, and exclude the mind from access to it. But after knocking down the established formula, when he comes to give his own, we find that it does not, substantially, so much differ from the established one. Mr. Maurice, we find then, is no rationalist, though he could use rationalist arguments before. It makes all the difference in this respect, whether he is the destroyer or the constructor. His own edifice is sacred, and no rationalist even wishes to touch it. He has found a formula which is open to none of the objections to which the established one was, while it does not gain this security by any concession; which satisfies reason much more, while it exercises faith quite as much. After laying down various principles, he concludes,—

"Supposing all these principles gathered together; supposing the Father's will to be a will to all good; the Son of God, being one with Him, and Lord of man, to obey and fulfil in our flesh that will by entering into the lowest condition into which men had fallen through their sin;—supposing this Man to be, for this reason, an object of continual complacency to His Father, and that complacency to be fully drawn out by the Death of the Cross; is not this, in the highest sense, Atonement? Is not the true, sinless root of Humanity revealed; is not God in Him reconciled to man? May not that reconciliation be proclaimed as a Gospel to all men?"
—*Ibid.* p. 147.

If this passage means, what it appears to do, that the life and death of our Lord, regarded as one sacrifice, are perfectly pleasing and acceptable to the Father, and that for the sake of that life and death He is reconciled to or forgives the sins of man, we must confess we do not see the great difference between Mr. Maurice's doctrine and that which he has been so strongly impugning; nor can we see exactly the reason why this Essay has been written. This Essay is written to show that the ordinary idea of the doctrine of the Atonement—the idea, viz., that our Lord "has delivered His creatures from their Father's determination to execute His wrath upon them;" the idea "of satisfaction to offended Sovereignty"—is erroneous, and contrary to our fundamental notions of the Divine Nature; he has declared his sympathy with the objections of Socinians to this doctrine, and made common cause with them against it. But if his own formula to express the Atonement is to bear its natural meaning, what does it amount to but to this very doctrine? It supposes God to be offended with man, and asserts His wrath to be appeased and removed by Christ's life and death. "God is reconciled" to man in consequence of His delight in the Life and Death of the Incarnate Son. Does Mr. Maurice imagine that he has satisfied the scruples of Socinians against the doctrine of the Atonement by the substitution of such a formula as this for the one he impugns? If he does, with all deference to his knowledge of Socinian grounds of scruple, we cannot but think him mistaken as to what the ground of scruple in the minds of Socinians to the doctrine of the Atonement really is. This ground of scruple is a general one against the *vicarious* principle in moral and divine things. They do not see in reason why one being's goodness should make any difference in the Divine regards towards another being; why God, being offended with man on account of his own acts, should be reconciled with him on account of Christ's. But Mr. Maurice's formula acknowledges the vicarious principle as much as the established one does. His language is that God, in consequence of His delight in the obedient, is reconciled to the disobedient. Nor does he avoid the vicarious principle implied in this language by speaking of our Lord as "the sinless root of humanity," as if man were pardoned in consequence of something within himself, and not external to him. For the Socinian will say, "What is this mysticism? I do not understand it; it is contrary to my common sense to regard one man as the root of another. Every man is his own root, and must rise upon the basis of his individuality." He will see that this language only expresses the vicarious principle under another form.

We shall go now to the subject which, though occupying but a small space in these Essays, has furnished the principal charge against Mr. Maurice, has filled the correspondence between him and Dr. Jelf, and has supplied the avowed ground for the Professor's dismissal from his office—we mean the subject of eternal punishments. We enter on such a question with great reluctance, but as one already agitated, brought into public discussion, and obtruded upon the attention of the whole world, we cannot avoid noticing it; though we see, as clearly as any one, the evil of bringing so deep and mysterious a doctrine into the common field, and subjecting it to ordinary criticism, and cannot therefore but express our deep regret that Mr. Maurice should have thought it necessary to bring it forward, and excite a controversy about it. We agree with Dr. Jelf in saying that there does not appear to be any general disposition in the present day to use this doctrine uncharitably. The Church preaches the doctrine which Holy Scripture has given to her, that the finally impenitent will be eternally punished; but who are the finally impenitent she does not profess to know, and she warns her children against any other use of the doctrine than such as is edifying to themselves, and sharpens the wholesome principle of fear as regards their own salvation.

Mr. Maurice's declarations of opinion on this subject are such as prevent, we confess, any surprise at the step which the Council of King's College has taken. The Church of England allows, it is true, considerable latitude to her members, and even to her teachers, in their mode of holding and expressing various important truths. Such a liberty nobody would wish to destroy; but there are, though not very clearly defined, certain recognised limits to this liberty. It is felt when a man has transgressed these, he has violated truths which the general body holds to be sacred, and has departed from the recognised ground and standard of the Church. The results connected with such a question as the present, too, come home with peculiar and alarming force to men's minds; the connection between error of doctrine and of practice is more immediate and more visible in the case of this doctrine than in that of some others as near to the foundation of the faith. Nor could the Council be expected to regard with any other feelings than those of the deepest alarm the teaching of a Professor who inculcated upon a rising generation of clergy, preachers, and expounders of Scripture, from whom future congregations were to receive Christian instruction, an interpretation of Scripture which wholly unsettled, if it did not overthrow, the powerful sanctions of religion contained in the doctrine of eternal punishment.

The objections ordinarily made to the doctrine of the eternity of future punishments are made upon what—to use the word in a somewhat large and mixed sense—we may call a moral ground; that is to say, upon the ground of the repugnancy of such a doctrine to the Divine Attributes. It is urged that eternal punishment is contrary to the Divine Love. Or if that objection is seen not to be valid, inasmuch as the Divine Love is not inconsistent with the punishment of an evil being, and eternal punishment supposes the being punished to be eternally evil, another is made on the ground of the Divine *Power*. It is urged that Almighty Power must be able to stop this moral evil in His creatures.

But this is not Mr. Maurice's ground of objection to the doctrine of eternal punishment. He betrays some tenderness on this latter point, and expressions which he uses every now and then show a considerable inclination toward the position that eternal punishment is positively inconsistent with the Divine Attributes. Indeed, we can give no other meaning to the concluding passage of the "Essays," to which great attention has been called.

"We do not want theories of Universalism; they are as cold,

hard, unsatisfactory, as all other theories. But we want that clear, broad assertion of the Divine Charity which the Bible makes, and which carries us immeasurably beyond all that we can ask or think. What dreams of ours can reach to the assertion of St. John, that Death and Hell themselves shall be cast into the lake of fire? I cannot fathom the meaning of such expressions. But they are written; I accept them, and give thanks for them. I feel there is an abyss of Death, into which I may sink and be lost. Christ's Gospel reveals an abyss of Love below that; I am content to be lost in that. I know no more, but I am sure that there is a woe on us if we do not preach this Gospel, if we do not proclaim the name of the Father, the Son, and the Spirit,—the Eternal Charity." *Ibid.* pp. 442, 443.

In this passage, though he first says that we do not want theories of Universalism, he proceeds immediately, if his language is to have its natural meaning, to give one. For he says that there is *below* that "abyss of death, in which he may sink and be lost," an abyss of love. An abyss of love must be a state of salvation; and therefore the ultimate state appears, according to this passage, to be a state of salvation exclusively. But his language elsewhere avoids decision on this point. The spiritual mind, he says—

"Feels that God is altogether Love, Light with no darkness at all. But then that which is without God, that which loves darkness, that which resists love, must not it be miserable? And can it not fix itself in misery? Has it not a power of defying that which seeks to subdue it? I know in myself that it has. I know that we may struggle with the Light, that we may choose death. But I know also that Love does overcome this rebellion. I know that I am bound to believe that its power is greater than every other. I am sure that Christ's death proves that death, hell, hatred, are not so strong as their opposites. How can I reconcile these contradictory discoveries? I cannot reconcile them. I know no theory which can. But I can trust in Him, who has reconciled the world to Himself. I can leave all in His hands. I dare not fix any limits to the power of His love. I cannot tell what are the limits to the power of a rebel will. I know that no man can be blessed except his will is in accordance with God's will. I know it must be by an action on the will that love triumphs. Though I have no faith in man's theory of Universal Restitution, I am taught to expect 'a restitution of all things, which God who cannot lie has promised since the world began.' I am obliged to believe that we are living in a restored order. I am sure that restored order will be carried out by the full triumph of God's loving will. How that should take place while any rebellious will remains in the universe I cannot tell, though it is not for me to say that it is impossible. I do not want to say it. I wish to trust God absolutely, and not to trust in any conclusion of my own understanding at all."—Dr. Jelf's *Pamphlet*, pp. 7, 8.

There are leanings here, we say, toward the position which we mentioned, that of an universal irresistible grace. But Mr. Maurice keeps these in check, and does not give way to them. He speaks more strongly against any dogma in such a direction in his final Letter :—

"What I dare not pronounce upon is the *fact* that every will in the universe must be brought into consent with the Divine will. Stating the proposition as you state it, I should indeed tremble to affirm the contrary, and I think any man would. Dare you make it a positive article of faith that God's will, being what the Scripture says it is, shall *not* finally triumph? Nevertheless there is such a darkness over the whole question of the possible resistance of the human will that I must be silent, and tremble and adore."—Maurice's *Letter*, p. 16.

Mr. Maurice, then, does not take the ground which has been ordinarily taken against the doctrine of eternal punishments, and refuses to decide upon any inconsistency of the Divine Attributes with the doctrine. We are glad to admit this, though at the same time we will just remind him of one argumentative result of such a scrupulousness. The texts of Scripture declaring the eternal punishment of the wicked are so decisive and plain, that they must be taken to mean what they appear to do, unless some positive ground of reason or morals can be shown against it. The arguer upon the Divine Attributes professes to have such a ground, and therefore can, if his ground is proved, treat these texts as explained away, or proved not to mean that which they apparently do. But if an arguer can only say that he is doubtful as to the consequences of the Divine Attributes on this subject, he has no ground derived from this quarter against the apparent meaning of these texts: and in the absence of any reason against the plain meaning of the texts, that meaning must be admitted.

Mr. Maurice's ground against eternal punishments, in the common understanding of that term, lies in the sense itself of the word *eternal*, which he conceives to have been mistaken by the world at large, and which he himself thinks to be a sense necessarily disconnected with any idea of time or duration. Accordingly he does not require any argument for the purpose of explaining away a meaning admitted to be the apparent meaning of these texts. The apparent meaning itself of these texts is to him a meaning wholly disconnected with any idea of time or duration. "I believe that we must take the words of Scripture literally," he says, and their literal meaning, he adds, is one thus wholly removed from the popular one. And he appeals to Scripture for his proof:—

"The word 'eternal,' if what I have said is true, is a key-word of the New Testament. To draw our minds from the temporal, to fix them on the eternal, is the very aim of the divine economy. How much ought we, then, to dread any confusion between thoughts which our Lord has taken such pains to keep distinct,— which our consciences tell us ought to be kept distinct! How dangerous to introduce the notion of duration into a word from which He has deliberately excluded it! And yet this is precisely what we are in the habit of doing, and it is this which causes such infinite perplexity to our minds. 'Try to conceive,' the teacher says, 'a thousand years. Multiply these by a thousand, by twenty thousand, by a hundred thousand, by a million. Still you are as far off from eternity as ever.' Certainly I am, quite as far. Why then did you give me that sum to work out? What could be the use of it, except to bewilder me, except to make me disbelieve in Eternity altogether? Do you not see that this course must be utterly wrong and mischievous? If eternity is the great reality of all, and not a portentous fiction, how dare you impress such a notion of fictitiousness on my mind as your process of illustration conveys? 'But is it not the only process?'—Quite the only one, so far as I see, if you will bring Time into the question; if you will have years, and centuries, to prevent you from taking in the sublime truth, 'This is life eternal, to know God.'

"For what, then, is Death Eternal, but to be without God? What is that infinite dread which rises upon my mind, which I cannot banish from me, when I think of my own godlessness and lovelessness,—that I may become wholly separated from Love; become wholly immersed in selfishness and hatred? What dread can I have—ought I to have—besides this? What other can equal this? Mix up with this the consideration of days, and years, and millenniums, you add nothing either to my comfort or my fears. All you do is to withdraw me from the real cause of my misery, which is my separation from the source of life and peace; from the hope which must come to me in one place or another, if I can again believe in God's love, and cast myself upon it."—Maurice's *Essays*, pp. 436, 437.

So completely does he dissociate the meaning of eternity from any idea of duration, that he actually supposes eternity may end. The reader must defer a logical comment, which will occur to him upon this mode of speaking. He says:—

"My duty then I feel is this, 1st, To assert that which I know, that which God has revealed, His absolute universal love in all possible ways, and without any limitation. 2d, To tell myself and all men, that to know this love and to be moulded by it is *the* blessing we are to seek. 3d, To say that this is eternal life. 4th, To say that the want of it is eternal death. 5th, To say that if they believe in the Son of God they have eternal life. 6th, To say that if they have not the Son of God they have not life. 7th, *Not* to say who has not the Son of God, because I do not know. 8th, *Not to say how long any one may remain in eternal death, because I do not know.* 9th, *Not to say that all will necessarily be raised out of eternal death, because I do not know.*"—Dr. Jelf's *Pamphlet*, p. 8.

Eternity having thus, in Mr. Maurice's opinion, nothing to do with our idea of time and duration, he wholly rejects the common and popular idea of eternal punishments as eternal in the sense of duration; he considers that sense as not only not intended by Scripture, but positively prohibited, and he is prepared to inculcate and propagate such a prohibition, as an essential part of the Gospel revelation.

Now upon such a mode of treating the word *eternal* as this, the first observation we must make is, that it appears to deprive that word altogether of any meaning which can be in the slightest degree perceived and apprehended by the human mind. The word *eternal* is obviously used in Scripture with reference to some meaning which the hearer can annex to it; and that, we will add, a meaning by no means far removed from ordinary comprehension. We say comprehension, not forgetting, of course, that the meaning is in its fulness incomprehensible; but only intending to say, that a meaning of some kind is supposed in Scripture to be immediately suggested by the word, and to rise up instinctively in a hearer's mind, even the most unlearned and uncultivated one. The texts in which mankind are warned of eternal punishments in a future state are evidently addressed to the whole of mankind, and meant to convey a particular meaning to the natural and average understanding of man. But if the meaning of "eternal" is to be entirely dissociated from the idea of duration, the word *eternal* ceases to have any meaning, which any man, learned or unlearned, can possibly in the remotest way apprehend. For what is the idea of eternity which is left, when all idea of it as duration is taken away? None. There is no idea in our minds, when we think of the word. There is absolute vacancy, and our mental interior is literally empty.

It may be said that we have the idea of simple existence; and that that idea of pure existence, abstracted from all idea of time, is the legitimate meaning of "eternal." And something like this we understand to be Mr. Maurice's meaning. But such an assertion will not bear examination. If I think of existence at all, I cannot think of it but as the existence of something or other; nor can I think of that something's existence, but as continuing or not continuing. You may tell me to think of existence absolutely, and to remove that foreign and irrelevant addition of duration, long or short, ending or not ending, that I have attached artificially to it; but if you do, you are simply imposing a task on me which the laws of human thought wholly disable me from fulfilling. I find in attempting to do so, that I simply make my mind empty, and my meaning nothing. If the idea of eternity then is reduced to the idea of pure existence, independent of duration, it is reduced to an idea which I have not got within my mind. And the notices of an eternal state in Scripture, so far from appealing to the plain average understanding of the human race, and being met by an instinctive meaning in our minds, find simply no response at all, and excite no idea whatever.

But our next observation must be that Mr. Maurice *does*

give a meaning to the word *eternal*, a meaning *contradictory* to the idea which we naturally assign to it. After protesting against any association of duration at all with eternity, Mr. Maurice uses language which, in its natural acceptation, plainly associates duration with it, only speaking of that duration as possibly a limited one, instead of being necessarily endless. "I feel it my duty," he says, "not to say *how long any one may remain in eternal death*," *i.e.* in a state of eternal punishment. Is not eternity here spoken of as time, and capable of a limit? What are the ideas which Mr. Maurice has before his mind, when he writes this sentence? First, he has evidently an idea of some space of time before eternal punishment begins; *secondly*, he has an idea of a space of time during which eternal punishment lasts; and *thirdly*, of a space of time which succeeds that. What is this but eternity positively imbedded in time, bounded by time before, and time to come? It is not only duration, but limited duration. The sentence following comes under the same observation, "I feel it my duty not to say that all will necessarily be raised out of eternal death." So then, Mr. Maurice has the idea, that in some cases, at any rate, men will be punished eternally, and after having been punished eternally, will enter another state and condition. That is to say, he first puts forward a transcendentally subtle idea of eternity, as pure existence without duration; and when he comes to apply it, he plunges into the very thick of time, and makes his eternity an intelligibly limited period. If this is the practical working, however, of a philosophy which professes to raise and refine the popular conceptions on this subject, we should, at any rate, recommend the adoption of another language; for, indeed, Mr. Maurice must allow us to tell him that it is eccentric to speak of eternity as ending.

The ground, it would appear, of this whole interpretation of the word *eternal* is the assumption, that our idea of time is not only not an adequate exponent—which none would assert it to be—but no exponent *at all* of eternity. But this is, indeed, a hasty assumption. Undoubtedly, if we have nothing in our idea of time to give us the least notion of what eternity is, it follows immediately that the latter is purely unintelligible, and that we take unauthorised and fictitious means for explaining it, when we put it before our minds in any way as time. But we wholly dissent from the ground, that our idea of time is to be regarded as no exponent at all of what eternity is. It is an inadequate and poor one, but it would be a great error to consider that it was designed to do nothing at all for us toward this object, that it was to be wholly separated from eternity in our thoughts, and that we ought to think of the latter as if there were no such idea as the former in our minds, *i.e.* to entertain no conception of it at all. We are expressly commanded to think of ourselves as existing beyond the grave; but we cannot think of ourselves as existing except in time. Then it is evidently intended that we should carry our ideas of time beyond the grave; only using such salvos and qualifications as reason suggests should be used in such a case. If this is forbidden us, God has imposed an impossible duty upon us.

If any one will be at the pains to examine his idea of time, he will find it to be by no means an inferior, sensual, or narrow idea. It is not like the idea of this or that particular external object. There is an evident distinction between it and the whole class of ideas which come in through senses, which proves a higher source. And that which gives it this distinction, and proves this higher and supersensual source, is the idea of infinity, which is involved in our idea of time.

The idea of infinity, with which we find ourselves endowed, is a very remarkable and peculiar idea, for this reason, that, while it is undoubtedly a true and in some sort apprehended one, it is at the same time only a preliminary and incipient idea, vanishing while we are upon its very threshold, and launching us upon the unknown and unconceived. We cannot rid ourselves of this idea of infinity; we cannot think of anything at all, but we may imagine that thing repeated once, twice, three times, three thousand times, till we exhaust ourselves with numbers; and then we feel ourselves as far from the goal as ever. Thus space widens on all sides of us into boundless space, and time stretches into an infinite time anterior and prospective. We cannot prevent the mind from exceeding the bounds of the objects and the sphere of its actual experience; because there is that in us which is ever growing and necessarily expanding, without capacity of check; and when we get to the very furthest horizon, we feel an action of excess or stretching over going on within our minds. But while we stretch over, we just stretch over, and no more. We cannot grasp that quantity and extent which lies beyond. It is unknown magnitude, unknown number. The idea of infinity is a true and an apprehended, but only an incipient idea, and Locke's distinction is a true one, in meaning, whatever defect there may be in his mode of expressing it, that we have an idea of infinity of space and time, but not an idea of space and time infinite. "The idea of infinite," he says, "has something of positive in all those things we apply it to. When we would think of infinite space or duration, we at first step usually make some very large idea, as perhaps of millions of ages, or miles, which possibly we double and multiply several times. All that we thus amass together in our thoughts is positive, and the assemblage of a great number of positive ideas of space or duration. But what still remains beyond this, we have no more a positive and distinct notion of, than a mariner has of the depth of the sea; where having let down a large portion of his sounding-line, he reaches no bottom: whereby he knows the depth to be so many fathoms and more; but how much the more is, he hath no distinct notion at all; and could he always supply a new line, and find the plummet always sink without ever stopping, he would be something in the posture of the mind reaching after a complete and positive idea of infinity. In which case, let this line be ten, or one thousand fathoms long, it equally discovers what is beyond it; and gives only this confused and comparative idea, that this is not all, but one may yet go farther. So much as the mind comprehends of any space, it has a positive idea of; but in endeavouring to make it infinite, it being always enlarging, always advancing, the idea is still imperfect and incomplete. . . . For to say a man has a positive clear idea of any quantity, without knowing how great it is, is as reasonable as to say, he has the positive clear idea of the number of the sands on the sea-shore, who knows

not how many there be; but only that they are more than twenty. For just such a perfect and positive idea has he of an infinite space and duration, who says it is larger than the extent or duration of ten, one hundred, one thousand, or any other number of miles or years, whereof he has or can have a positive idea; which is all the idea, I think, we have of infinite. So that what lies beyond our positive idea towards infinity, lies in obscurity; and has the indeterminate confusion of a negative idea, wherein I know I neither can nor do comprehend all I would, it being too large for a finite and narrow capacity: and that cannot but be very far from a positive and complete idea, wherein the greatest part of what I would comprehend is left out, under the indeterminate intimation of being still greater."
—Locke's *Essay*, book ii. ch. 17.

Such is the idea of infinity which we find in our minds, and from such an account we first infer that this idea is a true, solid, and constitutional part of our minds, and not a fantastic and fictitious conceit; and next, that it is what may be called a mysterious idea, or one of which we have only an incipient apprehension; which very dimness and imperfection is a result of its rank; because it is dim, and is imperfectly apprehended, only because it is out of proportion with the rest of our minds; because it is the threshold of a higher range of capacities, the border-line where our limited reason mingles for an instant with, and just tastes the greatness of another form and other laws of conception. Let no one suppose, that because this idea is concerned with simple magnitude and quantity, therefore it is not an idea of high rank; a man may think so for a moment, but the voice of nature will the next moment correct his fastidious criticism, and tell him that nature, reasonable and intellectual nature, admires magnitude. Whence it is, or how it is, we know not, but the very inner mind swells with the idea of extent and number, and feels in the contemplation of them a satisfaction to a certain innate ambition and high desire. The vastness of space, and the interminable lengths of time, fill us with awe, not only with reference to the objects and events there may be residing in them, but an awe excited by their own simple infinity. Every step in the world of magnitudes and extents is full of wonder, and the mind is subdued as in the presence of supernatural forms and powers.

We find, then, in our minds, an idea, such as Locke describes, a dim, indistinct, and mysterious idea of infinity ; and that, consequently, we necessarily think of time as infinite. The inference is that we have in our idea of time something which is exponent of eternity, and adapted to represent it to our minds. The infinity of time is representative of eternity, so far as eternity is simply endless and boundless. You say that eternity is a mystery, and that therefore time is no exponent at all of it. But time is a mystery too ; you do not think of that. We have not to go to another world for mysteries. Simple astronomical infinite time is a mystery ; its quantity is incomprehensible ; we have not, as Locke says, the idea of it. But a mysterious idea is, so far as we apprehend it, the fit exponent of a mystery —the mystery of eternity. We are let into the secret of infinity here, and something about eternity is already revealed to us in our natural reason.

But Mr. Maurice, as it appears to us, does not at the very outset do justice to this idea of time; and his mistaken conclusion seems to follow very naturally from this mistake at the outset. He acknowledges, indeed, that we have an idea of infinity and of infinite duration, but he speaks of it more as if it were a grotesque, fictitious, and fanciful conceit, than a solid, true, and noble part of our minds. He says,—

"I cannot apply the idea of time to the word 'eternal.' I feel that I cannot. Everybody feels it. What do the continual experiments to heap hundreds of thousands of years upon hundreds of thousands of years, and then the confession, 'after all we are no nearer to eternity,' mean, if not this ? Do they not show that we are not even on the way to the idea of eternity ? Might we not just as well have stopped at the hundredth year, or the first ? But this trifling becomes very serious and shocking, if there is a great and awful idea of eternity which our Lord would teach us, which belongs to our inmost selves, and which we are flying from by these efforts to get it into another region."—*Letter of Mr. Maurice in Dr. Jelf's Pamphlet*, p. 6.

"I am met with the complaint, that there is a simple, natural, admitted meaning of the word 'eternal' which every one understands, and which I am trying to get rid of. I ask for that simple, natural, admitted meaning, and I find it full of the strangest complexities and incoherences; one which cannot be set before simple people, without the most extraordinary devices to make it intelligible; devices which utterly fail, by the admission of those who resort to them."—*Ibid.* pp. 13, 14.

He throws aside our idea of infinity as in itself a low, absurd, and mean idea; it is "full of complexities and incoherences;" he sees in the representations of it that we make to our minds only "extraordinary devices;" as if the whole were a mere Chinese trick and puzzle. Undoubtedly the idea of infinity is a dim and indistinct idea, and we find in pursuing it apparent complexities and incoherences. But will any sane person deny on proper reflection that the idea of infinity is a true, a lawful, and a grand idea of our intellectual nature? Undoubtedly "we heap hundreds of thousands of years upon hundreds of thousands, and yet are no nearer to eternity;" but is infinite number a fictitious and mean idea? And because this idea of infinity falls short and owns its deficiency, is it not, as far as it goes, true knowledge, true perception? Do we apprehend no truth whatever, in any way whatever, in any degree whatever, when we have the idea of infinity in our minds? Are the ideas of infinity and nothing identical? Is it absurd to speak of an idea of infinity at all? Certainly this is not the case. All are conscious of the possession of a truth, a majestic truth, in this idea, though we feel ourselves but on the threshold of it, and cannot by possibility grasp that of which it tells us the existence. If Mr. Maurice, however, will not acknowledge any truth in our idea of infinity at all, it is no wonder that he should deny that our idea of time is any exponent of eternity; for our idea of time can only be such an exponent as involving the idea of infinity.

Upon this radical mistake rises the objection of Mr. Maurice to the term "endless," or "never-ending," as applied to a future life.

"Here we have your meaning of Eternal and Everlasting. You are not really pleading for either of the words which our translators have used. You are measuring both by a compound 'endless' or 'never-ending' which they have not used at all.

Now thus it seems to me you bring us under the conditions of Time in the most mischievous way. The 'measures of duration' which you try to escape, by speaking of an absolute duration, may be used—are used in Scripture—to raise us above notions of Time. 'I am Alpha and Omega, the beginning and the end, the first and the last;' 'the same yesterday, to-day, and for ever;' 'which is, and was, and is to come,' are forms of speech which do not chain us to a beginning or an end, to yesterday or to-day, to the past, to the present, or the future; but teach us of One who is living in these 'measures of duration,' and is not confined by them. But mere negative words, such as 'endless,' 'never-ending,' start from a ground of time; when I predicate them of God, I make him a mere negation of Time; I conceive of Him just as the Magians did, as 'Time without Bounds.'"—Maurice's *Letter*, pp. 7, 8.

The argument in this passage, as far as we can make it out, supposes that time is essentially limited in our idea of it; from which it follows that if we think of it as endless, we are entertaining "a negation of time." If this is *not* his supposition, we cannot conceive what he means by saying that "endless time," that "time without bounds" is a negation of time! Is an infinite quantity of brick or stone a negation of brick or stone? Is an infinite quantity of time a negation of time? If this *is* his supposition, we need not say how erroneous it is.

We have appealed to the idea of the infinite in our minds, as the true and intended guide in forming our notion of eternity, and referred Mr. Maurice's mistaken conclusion, on the subject before us, to his mistaken estimate of this idea. We do not mean to say, however, that this idea is of itself at all an adequate exponent of eternity. There is undoubtedly a great defect in an image of eternity which represents it as, however infinite, consisting of successive spaces of time. And this defect, though it cannot be remedied,—for we cannot think of time except under the mode of succession,—ought to be remembered in applying our idea of infinity to eternal duration. But this defect in the idea does not exclude it altogether as an exponent to us of eternity, but only qualify it. The *elements* of infinite duration have to be disposed in a different way from that in which we find the elements of present time to be: but the infinity *itself* of that duration is still truly represented to our minds by our idea of that time as infinite. And upon this basis the definition of eternity accepted in the middle ages was formed—*Interminabilis vitæ tota simul et perfecta possessio.* It is the definition given by Boetius, and adopted by Aquinas. Here first comes the idea of pure endlessnesss, infinity of duration. That is the leading and primary idea; eternity is *vita interminabilis.* But inasmuch as an infinite duration, going on, as present time goes, by a succession of moments, each in turn leaving the other behind,— inasmuch as the arrangement of past, present, and future is obviously unsuitable to eternity, this point is next looked to; it is added that the contents of the "interminable life" have the mode not of succession but of simultaneity, and that the whole of infinite duration is possessed at once—*tota simul.*

When Mr. Maurice, then, demands that eternity should be regarded, not as successive duration, but as a "fixed state," "a state subject to no change or succession," he is right; but why should he demand this characteristic, as he does, *in opposition to* the other. Why should the changelessness of the eternal state supersede its endlessness? He says, "The word αἰών, *ætas*, specially serves this purpose. Like our own word 'Period,' it does not convey so much the impression of a line as of a circle; it does not suggest perpetual progress, but fixedness and completeness. The word αἰώνιος, or *æternus*, derived from this, seems to have been divinely contrived to raise us out of our time notions—to suggest the thought of One who is the same yesterday, to-day, and for ever." All this may be so. But why should a particular mode in which infinite duration exists exclude that duration's infinity, and the duration, because it is *tota simul*, not be "*interminabilis*"? It is evident that we can form no conception of such a state of being; but in the natural order of our thoughts, the idea of eternity as infinite comes first; the fixedness is only a characteristic of such infinity, to distinguish it from an infinity of earthly duration. Earthly time is in idea infinite, but it is an infinity of passing moments; this is unsuitable to the heavenly state, and therefore we pronounce the latter to be a fixed and permanent infinity; but it still is infinity. Mr. Maurice appeals to St.

Augustine's description of eternity, as *semper stans*, and contrasted in that respect to the succession of past, present, and future in this life; but the *semper stans* of Augustine, like the *tota simul* of Boetius, supposes the endlessness of eternity, and does not exclude it. He might, had he thought it worth while, have claimed, with greater right, the authority of Cudworth, who appears to deny the possibility of infinity in material things, and so to condemn the common idea of infinity altogether as spurious; though he nowhere pushes his extravagant principles on this question to a definite conclusion.

We have endeavoured to point out and show the error of the ground on which Mr. Maurice appears to have founded his interpretation of the word *eternal*. If we are wrong, however, in our conjecture as to what that ground is, we can only —claiming some indulgence for a misapprehension not unpardonable in a criticism upon a writer whose depth is certainly out of proportion with his perspicuity—fall back upon our first objection, that, upon whatever ground this interpretation may be raised, it is one which deprives the word *eternal* of all meaning which the human mind can embrace or entertain. This is a fatal objection; but a simple negation of all meaning is—however bad a consequence in the case of a word evidently intended in Scripture to produce the most forcible impression upon us—far from being the worst consequence of such an interpretation. Such a negation of meaning would, practically speaking, issue in a meaning but too definite and positive; and this interpretation would no sooner pass from the minds of philosophers and theologians, to those of common men, than it would become a simple doctrine of the limitation of future punishment. It has hardly escaped this further stage in Mr. Maurice's own hands; and still less would it do so under the treatment which the mass would give it. Imagine a doctrine of eternal punishment pervading the world at large, which asserted that eternal did *not* mean "endless," or "everlasting;" what is the immediate meaning which *would* be given to the word? The difficulty would be solved, you may depend upon it, with sufficient ease, and the popular mind would suffer no long suspense. Men would of course say,—If eternity is not infinite, it is finite. Nor would such a result be in our opinion less valid as logic than it would be as plain common sense. Your very denial of endlessness is an appeal to our notions of time; but if you appeal to our notions of time, and reject time infinite, as applied to eternity, there can only remain time finite.

Let those then who at all doubt the effects of such a doctrine in society give Mr. Maurice the benefit of their doubt; but it would be doing great injustice to our own convictions if we owned to any doubt at all on this subject. We can hardly dwell upon the effects of any general spread of such a doctrine, even in simple thought, without alarm. The release from the notion of eternal punishment would be felt by the great mass as a relief from the sense of moral obligation; and, relying on the certainty that all would be sure to be right at last, men would run the risk of the intermediate punishment, whatever it might be, and plunge into self-indulgence without hesitation. It may be said that men do this now under the belief in eternal punishments: they do—and there is no limit to the powers of imagination by which men can suppress the reasonable certainty of the future and make the present everything. But the belief in eternal punishment is the true and rational concomitant of the sense of moral obligation. Destroy the punishment and you destroy the sin; limit it, and you make sin a light thing. Moreover, the belief in eternal punishment, however suppressed, leaves a blank and dark ultimate prospect before the sinner's mind; but this prospect is removed by the limitation of punishment, and in the place of a cloudy termination of the view, which the sinner at any rate had rather have removed, and which therefore must so far operate as a stimulus to that change of life which alone can remove it, he has a bright ultimate termination anyhow, whether he changes his way of life or whether he does not, and therefore he loses a stimulus to change which even the most careless must in some way feel. For even those to whom eternal punishment is thus a mere negation and suppressed idea had rather have a bright termination than this suppressed bad one before them. Conscious of his own religious convictions and aspirations after holiness for its own sake, Mr. Maurice may not see these consequences involved in his doctrine; but the practical working of it, were it to gain ground, would soon force them upon his observation. A general relaxation of moral ties, a proclamation of liberty and security, the audacity of sins which had before been abashed, carelessness where there had been hesitation, obstinacy where there had been faltering, and defiance where there had been fear, would show a world in which the sanctions of morality and religion had been loosened, and in which vice had lost a controlling power, and got rid of an antagonist and a memento. Whether or not the form and manner of its act could have been improved, the Council of King's College has done a substantial duty to the Church and the nation in suppressing at once a teaching that immediately interfered with the very foundation of religion and morals. This is not a question of this or that particular doctrine, however important; but it is a question whether we are to have religion at all amongst us, supported by its proper sanctions and endowed with its legitimate stimulants and motives. To have stood by and done nothing in such a case as this would have been a betrayal of their trust, an abandonment of a charge which the Church has committed to them, and for the execution of which they are responsible to that Church. The religious feeling of the country at large would not have allowed such indifference, and just clamour would have compelled them at last to do what their own consciences had neglected.

Meantime we are not judging Mr. Maurice himself, but only his teaching. We know this teaching has a very different character to his mind from that which it has to ours, and that he regards himself simply as in possession of a very deep truth of religious philosophy, viz., that eternity is pure existence, or some such truth as that. He disowns these consequences, and pictures to himself all the developments which we have given to his principle as so much irrelevant alarmist misapprehension. We are glad he does so; we should be sorry to think that he thought all these consequences true. So far as he is personally concerned, we are content to think of his truth exactly in the light in which he regards it, separating it from all the consequences which we have attached to it. But in this case he will allow us to say that it is not without real pain that we see a sincere, zealous, and able man losing his just influence and destroying his usefulness out of deference to a mere subtlety and a crotchet as impalpable as the air. We know he will immediately tell us it is not a subtlety but a vital truth—a truth intimately connected with practice; that he could not live for a day as a Christian without it; and that his whole moral and religious convictions would collapse if he had not this truth about pure existence, or whatever it may be, supporting him. We know he will maintain the urgent necessity of preaching this great practical truth to peasants and labourers, to ploughmen and artisans, to men, women, and children, in towns and villages, in fields and market-places; that he is convinced that these masses of uninformed and imperfect minds are crying out for this especial truth, are hungry and desperate for it, and that woe to him if he does not go forth to satisfy this forlorn, desolate, and consuming void within them. We know he will say all this with the most entire sincerity. But will he take it ill if we remind him that many men of sincerity equal to his own have thought particular truths of great importance at one part of their lives which they have not at another, and that what once rested on an all-absorbing necessity has come down to the rank of very secondary if not very ambiguous truth? In the excitement of philosophical thought we mistake the proportions of the great scheme of truth; we are led on by a favourite idea which becomes at every moment more necessary, more dominant, more fundamental, till it gains a complete throne and mastery. And such ideas often become stereotyped, and their dominion lasts for some time. But time, experience, fresh reading, new acquaintances, and other things, introduce us to new aspects of truth; the deep lines of a favourite idea wear insensibly away. We become aware that we can do without it, and the large and true foundations of religion take gradual hold of our minds, to the subordination of what was narrow, partial, and fictitious. It is possible that Mr. Maurice may some day not think the deep and subtle truth which he cherishes at present of such overwhelming consequence and weight. He may one day come to reflect that the great idea of time with which the Author of nature has endowed us is, after all, our intended and proper guide to a notion of eternity, and that, however reason may demand its qualification, we shall not gain by endeavouring to get entirely out of its reach in picturing to ourselves the life beyond the grave. He may come to consider that in this life we must be content with such helps as are provided for us in forming our conceptions of spiritual things, and that it is better to have a lower representation of truth than none at all. If such thoughts as these should ever at any future day approve themselves to him, we shall rejoice at the recovery of a person to utility and just influence who could only have lost them by the pardonable causes of a mistaken zeal and an unmanageable profundity.

We cannot, however, conclude this article without a slight notice of one particular claim put forward by Mr. Maurice in this controversy. For the *truth* of the interpretation of the word "eternal" which he has put forward Mr. Maurice appeals to certain grounds of metaphysics and to Scripture thus metaphysically interpreted; but his *liberty* as a Church of England teacher to inculcate this doctrine he rests upon the ground that the formularies of the English Church nowhere condemn that sense of the word "eternal" which he adopts, or impose that sense of the word which he opposes; that they use the word without marking the particular sense which is to be given to it, and therefore are to be understood as leaving it open to any person to attach this or the other meaning to it as he pleases, and to teach the doctrine of an "eternal" state of reward and punishment in his own sense of that word.

"I therefore pledged myself implicitly in my Essays, I pledge myself explicitly now, that I will not, God being my helper, give up my liberty as a member of the Church of England by accepting any *new* Formulary on this subject, or *new* explanation of the Formularies which I have accepted. To these I adhere in what I believe to be their literal natural sense."—*Letter of Mr. Maurice in Dr. Jelf's Pamphlet*, p. 21.

"The general notion which you encourage—that the King's College Council may demand of its professors an assent to a number of *et cæteras* not included in the Formularies to which, as churchmen and clergymen, they have set their hand—is one for which I own I was not prepared. It will alarm, I believe, many persons who differ very widely from me. I do not see how it can fail to alarm every man who attaches any sacredness to his oaths or his subscriptions.

"On this point I must insist very strongly. I said in a former letter that I accepted the words of our Formularies and of the Scriptures in what seemed to me their literal and simple sense, but that I would accept no new interpretation of them. In noticing this remark you have availed yourself, of course unintentionally, of the equivocal force of the adjective 'new.' You say, 'I wish for no new Articles nor any new interpretations of our Formularies,' meaning that your interpretation is the old one. But I submit that everything is *new* to the subscriber of a Formulary which is not contained in that Formulary at the time he subscribes it, however old or familiar it may be."—*Mr. Maurice's Answer to Dr. Jelf*, p. 3.

The ground advanced here is a general ground that whatever the formularies of the Church do not expressly and by word enjoin is to be considered as open, and that a man is bound by nothing but that which has been *nominatim* and specifically put before him for his assent.

But such a ground, we must say, appears to us obviously untenable, contrary to common sense and common equity, and fatal to any Church that should allow or connive at it. It is obvious that when a Church constructs formularies, and lays down articles of faith, it cannot possibly stop at every word to assign the exact meaning in which it is used. To do so, were it possible, would be to defeat the very object for which alone it could be done,—that, viz., of accuracy and clearness; to bury the whole formulary underneath an accumulation of definition and a load of words, which would simply perplex, harass, and overwhelm any reader. The articles, as they stand now, are not easy reading; but were they constructed on the explanatory principle just mentioned, the case would be desperate—no reader of human powers could extricate himself out of such a labyrinth of language as would surround him: once in, he could never emerge to light again, by any rational clew, but simply by cutting the knot in the Gordian way, and creating a meaning of his own. But in truth such explanation would be impossible. The compilers of formularies could not interpose to explain words which admitted of no explanation: words of which the meaning has been taken for granted in all ages, and to which all mankind have instinctively annexed one and one only idea, and that one which cannot be defined and analysed. How could one possibly expect that when, in the course of constructing the formularies of the English Church, the compilers came across the word "eternal," they should affix a parenthesis to explain what the word "eternal" meant? What had they to say about it? What could it mean but that which all mankind has always supposed it to mean? Nobody wanted an explanation; nobody could give one if it was wanted; and nobody could understand one if it was given.

But if it is impossible that the Church should stop to explain every word of her formularies as she constructed them, what is the immediate inference from such a state of the case? Clearly, that we are bound to something more than the express and specific terms as such,—the pure naked words of such formularies; viz., to the natural, commonly received, established meaning in which such terms were used; the meaning in which the Church has ever understood them, and in which therefore she imposes them. The impossibility of explanation demands as its correlative this attention and deference to those established and received meanings; allowance must be made for insuperable obstacles; and the necessities of the *imponens* turn to obligations in the subscriber. And though in smaller and secondary matters, where no strong intention of the Church can be supposed, and in doubtful matters where its intention cannot be certified to, every reasonable latitude must be allowed to subscribers, and the authoritativeness of received meanings not be made a minute, frivolous, and burdensome one; in important and vital articles of Christian teaching the established and received meanings of terms must be considered binding. The intention of the Church must be considered to be represented by the meaning which has been always given in the Church to the term; and the subscriber is bound by the intention of the Church.

To say then, as Mr. Maurice does, that because the meaning of the word "eternal" is not laid down in our formularies, its meaning is to be considered open, and that the most contradictory to the received one is to be allowed, and its inculcation by teachers in the Church not hindered, is to treat the Church in a way which is alike repugnant to common sense and common equity :—to common sense, because the explanation of such words is not to be expected; to common equity, because it is taking unfair advantage of such an absence of explanation. It is to approach the formularies of a Church in a spirit in which the merest lawyer would not approach a legal document, such as a contract or a will. In every document certain received meanings of terms must be taken for granted; nor are men allowed for an instant, in the interpretation of such documents, to assign some ingenious reason why the received sense of any of the terms employed is incorrect, and on that ground refuse to take the term in the received sense. Were such a system of interpretation allowed in secular matters, there would be an end at once to all good faith and stability in the dealings of man and man. And why should we treat the Church with less tenderness than we treat the world ? A fair claim has generally been made for some generosity to the Church, as no ordinary bargainer; but this is to deprive her even of rigid justice. It is to approach the formularies of the Church in a temper of ultra-legality; in the way in which a narrow lawyer applies himself to a hostile legal document, which he is determined to reduce to the very lowest and most necessary meaning in which it can be understood, and to get rid of that even if he can. We cannot but wonder that a man of Mr. Maurice's ordinary generosity should have adopted such a ground : that he should approach the formularies of the Church to which he belongs with the determination to defer to nothing but the absolute naked terms to which he cannot deny he has subscribed; and that, if the Church has not laid down expressly a certain meaning of a certain term, to suppose that he has a right to take advantage of the omission, though the whole world knows that the Church, in using the term, had a certain meaning and no other.

On such a system of interpretation as this, there is not the simplest and plainest article in the Creed that might not be explained away. Let us take the very first article in the Apostles' Creed—"I believe in God the Father Almighty, maker of heaven and earth." Here is expressed the elementary article of religion, that God is the Creator of the world. But a questioner may say, "What does that term 'Maker' or Creator mean? the Church does not express in what sense she uses this term. I shall therefore take the liberty of understanding this term to mean, not creating absolutely, but creating out of a certain primary unformed matter. For though I grant that the fair sense of the word *create* is to create out of nothing, its sense is still open, because it is not determined what *nothing* is. I shall therefore suppose, that by nothing is meant primary unformed matter or chaos; and that when the Church says that God created the world, or made it out of nothing, she leaves it open whether He made it out of nothing in the popular sense of the word, or out of nothing in the sense of unformed matter. I shall therefore maintain, as consistent with this article of the Apostles' Creed, the eternity of matter; which I do not believe was made by God, but has co-existed always with Him."

Are we trifling with Mr. Maurice and the reader in supposing such an argument? By no means. The specimen of interpretation of language here given is no invention of our own. Plato called all matter τὸ μὴ ὄν, or nothing; the later Platonists confined this term to the primary formless matter of which the world was made; still that which ordinary men would consider *something*, was called by this name. And this disguise of something, under the term "nothing," has been carried on by modern philosophers, who were thus enabled, under the outside of an article of the Christian creed, to hold a Platonic origin of the world, and to believe in "God as the maker of heaven and earth," and the eternity of matter at the same time. We quote from Mosheim :—

"Among modern philosophers, Robert Fludd, and many others, who have admired and endeavoured to propagate Plato's sentiments, have chosen to imitate the fashion of the Platonists, and to call matter nothing; which they seem to do for this reason, among others, that it may not be known how far their doctrine respecting the origin of nature differs from that universally received in the Christian Church. For though they make use of Christian expressions in speaking of the commencement of the universe, and like ourselves say that all things were produced out of nothing, yet they do not attach the same meaning as we do to the words, and by the word *nothing* they only intend a rude and shapeless kind of matter, which they will have to be a second principle of all things. These unfair interpretations have been well exposed among others by Peter Gassendi, whose words are worth quoting—'As respects creation,' says he, "it must not be understood as a production of something out of nothing, in the same sense as the Mosaic creation of the universe is commonly intended by divines. For though Fludd makes use of both the words and the narrative of Moses, yet he uses all these in a symbolical manner. By the word *creation*, therefore, he understands in the first place the production or generation of anything which is said to be made out of obscurity, or matter, which by him is called nothing.'"—*Mosheim's Dissertation, annexed to Cudworth*, c. 5.

One would have thought beforehand that the meaning of the word "nothing" was sufficiently clear, and afforded but little room for division of opinion. It is a word which has very decidedly its received and established meaning. Yet here we see another and more recondite sense assigned to the word, and upon the basis of that new signification, a doctrine of creation founded, which introduces, underneath the unchanged language of the Apostles' Creed, a pagan deity—a being who divides with primordial matter the empire of the universe. Dualism, Manicheanism, and the basest religions, that strike at the very root of the true doctrine of a God, insinuate themselves upon the strength of a certain meaning of the term *creation*, different from its popular and received meaning. But would such an idea of the Deity be allowed to be taught in our lecture-rooms and pulpits? Or would not the orthodox feeling of the Christian body at once reject it, and maintain the received meaning of the word "create," however unexpressed, as one which was supposed by the Church in framing the article, and only not expressed, because no other meaning was contemplated as capable of being held by Christians? And has not the word "eternal" its thoroughly received and popular sense, as much as the word "create" has?

Again, the Church has no expressed doctrine on the subject of inspiration. This is a most important and serious subject—the more so, because we cannot introduce it merely as an illustration of a principle, as we did the preceding instance, being quite aware that it is a question which is at this moment exciting deep thought, and which may before long come out in controversial shape. We are not going to discuss it thus incidentally at the end of an article; but we may at the same time be allowed to state what will not be disputed; and that is quite enough for our present purpose as regards the general question of subscription.

The Church implies, then, but makes no explicit assertion of the inspiration of Scripture. It is supposed that Scripture is inspired, because infallibility can only come from inspiration, and Scripture is infallible; any article of belief that can be proved from or shown to be contained in it being necessarily true. But because no doctrine of inspiration is formally laid down, is any Church teacher at liberty to maintain any doctrine of inspiration he pleases,—even the most ultra-German one, which virtually denies all inspiration? However unexpressed as a doctrine, the belief in the full inspiration of Scripture is one which lies underneath the whole Christian creed, and could not be removed without bringing the whole creed down with it. Thus Laud speaks:—

"Every rational science requires some principles quite without its own limits, which are not found in that science, but presupposed. Thus rhetoric presupposes grammar, and music arithmetic. Therefore it is most reasonable, that theology should be allowed to have some principles also, which she proves not, but presupposes. . . .

"The assurance we have of the penmen of the Scriptures, the holy prophets and apostles, is as great as can be had of any human authors of like antiquity. For it is as morally evident to any pagan, that St. Matthew and St. Paul wrote the Gospel and Epistles which bear their names, as that Cicero or Seneca wrote theirs. But that the apostles were divinely inspired while they wrote them, this hath ever been a matter of faith in the Church, and was so even while the apostles themselves lived, and was never a matter of evidence and knowledge, at least as knowledge is opposed to faith. Nor could it at any time then be more demonstratively proved than now. . . .

"The assent which we yield to this main principle of divinity, 'that the Scripture is the word of God,' is grounded upon no compelling or demonstrative ratiocination, but relies upon the strength of faith more than any other principle whatsoever. For all other necessary points of divinity may by undeniable discourse be inferred out of Scripture itself once admitted; but this concerning the authority of Scripture not possibly: but must rather be proved by revelation, which is not now to be expected; or presupposed and granted as manifest in itself, like the principle of natural knowledge; or by tradition of the Church both former and present, with all other rational helps, preceding or accompanying the internal light in Scripture itself.'—*Laud's Conference with Fisher* (*Anglo-Catholic Library*), p. 118 *et seq.*

It is evident, then, that there is *a* doctrine or idea of inspiration, which, however unexpressed, is a true and a most vital part of our creed, and to which subscription is implied when the formularies of the Church are subscribed to. And a test of there being such an idea is this, that contradiction to it could certainly not be formally and authoritatively allowed, without creating such scandal as would issue either in a withdrawal of the liberty, or a disruption of the Church—such a disruption as would show quite plainly that the Church at large has a belief on this subject, which it thinks essential.

On the whole, it is abundantly clear to us that no religious communion that had a definite creed at all, could hold together upon such a principle of subscription as that which Mr. Maurice, in his inference from the absence in our Articles of any particular interpretation of the word "eternal," has put forward. All human society requires for its maintenance and necessary order the bond of certain mutual understandings and implicit pledges; and if men begin to think themselves bound by nothing but by ink and paper, by seals and signatures, the cement of the whole fabric is loosened, and the materials part asunder. And religious communion requires the same substratum. No religious body can be kept together by statements and definitions solely: there must be something beyond these in which union is required: you may define and define, but something is left after all which is undefined; and that may be unimportant, and therefore open, or it may be most vital and fundamental, and therefore binding. The sound reason and common-sense of the Christian world must ultimately settle which the open and which the binding part of this unexpressed belief is, and the faith of the Church must discern what is necessary to it, and what is not. But some agreement beyond that which statements express, is essential to a Christian body, and must, when the occasion arises, be asserted and imposed on the teachers of that body.

Since writing the above article, a second edition of the Essays has appeared, with a new Preface, and a new concluding chapter on the subject of the word "eternal." The new portion contains no argument which had not appeared in the old, and leaves the controversy where it was. We will only notice two points.

Dr. Jelf has in his Letter accounted, in a way which we think quite satisfactory, for the omission in the Articles of 1562, of the 42d of the Articles of 1552, against those who deny the eternity of future punishments. It appears that this was one of a set of erroneous opinions held by the sect of Anabaptists, which in 1552 was of sufficient importance to make such special notice of its errors expedient, but in 1562 had sunk into insignificance; in consequence of which such notice was no longer expedient. Mr. Maurice, in the new concluding chapter, admits the reasonableness of this explanation, but draws from it the opposite inference to that which Dr. Jelf has drawn, and that which, we think, most people would draw. Dr. Jelf naturally gathers from the explanation, that the omission of the article is a proof only of the altered condition of the Anabaptists, and not of an altered belief on the question itself. Mr. Maurice gathers from it that the compilers of the Articles had changed their minds from thinking it necessary to impose a certain opinion on this subject, to thinking the subject an open one. "Here is an omission," he says, "a carefully considered omission in a document for future times, of that which had been too hastily admitted to meet an emergency of that time. The omission was made by persons who were probably strong in the belief that the punishment of wicked men is endless, but who did not dare to enforce that opinion upon others" (p. 461). The former appears to us the inference which common sense suggests. The latter inference is in the teeth of the facts of the case, which point to the decay of the sect exclusively, and to no change in the minds of the compilers of our Articles, as the reason of the omission. It would, if true, moreover, carry along with it the inference that the doctrine of the resurrection from the dead is considered by the Church an open one; the article on the resurrection and that on eternity having been inserted and omitted under exactly the same circumstances.

The second point we notice only for the sake of drawing a very obvious distinction. Mr. Maurice has, both in the old and the new portion of the Essays, but more pointedly in the new, condemned the philosophy of Locke as a materialist philosophy. We extracted in our article a description from Locke of the idea of infinity. We beg to say here, that we extracted it simply as appearing to us a true, forcible, and copious description of that idea, and not *because* it was Locke's description of it. So long as any philosopher restricts himself to describing faithfully any idea in, or any part of, our minds, we may make use of his assistance without committing ourselves to any general reliance on his system. Such an extract does not entail upon us, then, any share of the controversy respecting the philosophy of Locke, though we may be permitted to say that we think the judgment upon him as simply a "materialist" a harsh one.

INDIAN CONVERSION.*

(MARCH 1859.)

PREDICTION or prophecy—we are not, of course, speaking of inspired prophecy—may be founded upon one of two grounds. One basis of such moral anticipation or prediction may be the experience of actual present progress, when we see an opinion or a faith visibly advancing; when the new idea catches mind, and inoculates mind, and the current is obviously set in. This is an easy ground of prophecy, for, in fact, we do not so much predict as observe. Another is a more difficult one, when, in the absence of present progress, we predict upon a ground of reason, and see in deep, but as yet dormant, causes a certain basis of future conquest and success.

We do not wish to speak at all slightingly of the results of missionary labour in India when we say, that on the great question of Indian conversion the former ground of prediction is hardly at present open to us. A certain number of converts, however small when compared with the whole, may as a sample show, for those who want convincing, that the Hindoo mind opposes no organic hindrance to the reception of Christianity; but when we consider how very small this number is,

---

* 1. *Second Report of the Select Committee of the House of Lords on Indian Territories, together with Minutes of the Evidence. Session* 1852-53.

2. *Copy of a Letter from the Earl of Ellenborough, President of the Board of Control, to the Chairman and Deputy-Chairman of the East India Company, on the Subject of Education.* 29th *July* 1858.

3. *A Dialogue on the Knowledge of the Supreme Lord, in which are compared the claims of Christianity and Hinduism.* Cambridge. 1856.

4. *Articles on Caste in the "Times." April* 10 *and* 12, 1858.

5. *Government in its Relations with Education and Christianity in India.* By the Rev. GEORGE PERCY BADGER, Chaplain in the Diocese of Bombay. London. 1858.

what a mere fraction even of this is high-caste, and how many are not Hindoos at all, but rude aborigines, who had only the strength of a simple wild religion to oppose to the spiritual aggression of the missionary, we can hardly take the ground of present progress on this question. Providence has mercifully connected labour with hope: the smallest success of our own experience enkindles; and the missionary who adds a family or two to the Christian faith is immediately sanguine about the conversion of India. But an outside spectator, suddenly called upon to say whether, in his heart, he believes that the two hundred millions of India will one day be Christians, feels for a moment an alarmingly honest scepticism struggling with what is for the instant a conventional faith. There stands, in appearance, the impregnable fortress of Brahmanism as yet untouched. Hindoo immobility and the subtle tenacity of orientalism confront him, and India, like the Medusa's head, turns the believer into stone.

But though the anticipation of success founded upon present progress is hardly open to us in forecasting the future of India, the other ground we have mentioned is. We assume that the obstacle in the way of Christianity in India is that Brahmanism occupies the field; that if Brahmanism went, Christianity would by the force of those evidences, internal and external, for which the Gospel would be able then to procure a hearing, succeed to its place.

The question then is, Can Brahmanism stand? We believe, on the ground of Scripture prophecy, that it cannot; but independently of the scriptural ground, and subsidiary to it, do we not see a ground of reason, a great argument resting on the principles of human nature, biding its time, and only waiting for a fair and solid contact with that religion in order to demolish it—slowly and gradually, of course, but completely? We assume, that wherever existing under the sun, man is man, endowed with the plenitude of human reason in all that is essential to it, and with the whole moral and religious nature of the true human being. The question then is, Does Brahmanism answer to the religious type in human nature? Is it in harmony with the moral standard in human nature?

Is it in harmony with physical truth ? Is it in harmony with the ends of society ? If it is not, but is in disagreement with all these, then if human nature has only time, fair play, and moderate encouragement, human nature must gradually cast it off. We have, apart from present progress, an ultimate appeal to the original type of rational humanity.

Let us first of all take the department of religious truth, and in this department first the principle of Divine worship. On this subject the normal idea of the human race is the worship of one God. The human mind, in proportion as it becomes enlightened, is found, as a matter of fact, to demand this doctrine, which simply comes out with the growth of reason and civilisation in the human race.

We say the *worship* of one God. Intellectual pagans were not opposed to the unity of the Deity simply; their error lay in the article of worship rather than in the article of unity. They believed in one God, and they believed in a principle of worship, but they did not connect that Being with that principle, and make God the object of worship. They contemplated Him as the centre and the mainspring of the vast machine of the universe; but there they stopped short, and, having invested Him with the naked attributes of the Great First Cause, they gave their worship to a host of local deities or superior demons. We observe the coolness with which the ancient philosophers discussed the existence of a God. The Valeriuses, Balbas, and Cottas met and argued, some for and some against it : they talked with pleasant unconcern, they criticised with literary courtesy the strong and weak points in each other's arguments ; the snuff-box, as it were, went round, and all was philosophical ease and good-humour as the question, whether there was a God, or whether there was not a God, trembled in the balance. The truth is, that the question with them was entirely a philosophical as distinct from a religious question : it had nothing to do with practice ; no one duty depended upon it ; the idea of worshipping this First Cause never occurred for a moment to these men : it would have appeared a pure mistake, a simply absurd puzzle-headed confusion of two totally distinct departments. A theory of the origin of the universe was a branch of philosophy, not of religion, and had as little to do with practice as a Newtonian theory of gravitation. Will that sage who has just asserted with such force the existence of one Supreme Being, feel the smallest hostility to the popular worship of the day? Not the least. Not a particle of the spirit of St. Paul at Athens, or a spark of the honest fire of the iconoclast, rises in him, as he leaves the lecture-room to sacrifice to Neptune or make a libation to Ceres. But his distinction is plain: that was *philosophy*, this is *worship*. Worship is a principle by itself; it is not connected with the truths of reason: it does not apply to the First Cause of the universe: it applies to that order of beings to whom custom has appropriated it. That ancient primordial power of *impression*, which antedates not only reasoning but reason in our nature, and exists in us like the remains of a former creation, had established those mighty thrones in the air, and assigned them local and national relations. Reason then taught a Deity, irrational impression gave the object of worship.

Exactly the same distinction forms the basis of and gives the key to Brahmanism. Brahmanism asserts one Supreme Being, eternal, unchangeable, infinite, immaterial, omnipotent, omnipresent, God, Very God, Brahm. But the very next article prohibits the combination of *Deity* and *action*: those two great metaphysical poles and opposites must not meet; the union would be suicidal. Brahm is a motionless, characterless, quality-less, colourless essence, pure unity, pure simplicity,—a residuum of analysis, which it is difficult to distinguish from nonentity; without consciousness, without intellect: he neither does, nor understands, nor wills, but simply *is*, the substratum of everything, himself a nothing. All *soul* is indeed of this nature, according to one Hindoo school, and is distinguished from *intellect* on this point. The one *acts*, the other *knows*. Intellect is the busy principle: it designs, provides, develops, combines, harmonises, organises, constructs, and adapts means to ends; but it is simply a material birth from primary or plastic matter, the original element "indiscrete" and insoluble of the physical world—*Pracriti*. Soul is the sublime, quiescent looker-on, the complement of the action of the world, itself no agent; she is as the spectator who responds to the drama, which would be an imperfect performance without an outward eye: she gazes upon nature, "exhibiting herself like a dancer, going through many postures, and twisting herself into a thousand shapes" before her, and watches the play and sport of the multitudinous evolutions of elemental Pracriti. Were for knowledge, as the attribute of soul, substituted *love*, the distinction would border on a Christian truth, that pure intellect is not the immortal or spiritual principle in our nature, while love witnesses to its own spirituality and difference from a cerebral function. The whole creative and governing power of the universe, all that *does* anything, is thus laid down as *matter*, while soul only looks passively on: and the Deity, as the great collective soul, is the great universal motionless contemplator; the world with all its life, motion, and mechanism, being reflected upon the sublime mirror of the divine mind, as the hanging woods, the changing clouds, and clear sky of some scene of nature are pictured upon the unconscious bosom of the lake.

But how did such a Being as this create the world? This is the great difficulty with Hindoo sages. They *apologise* for the creation, and can only explain it as a great exception, if not mistake—the result of a convulsive moment in the organic life of Brahm, when he awoke from his solitary repose and said, "Let me become many." He returned to regular divinity immediately, but *nescit vox missa reverti*, the unconstitutional act could not be recalled. The issue of such an irregularity, however, is *Ajnana* ignorance, and *Maya* illusion, and it is the triumph of the contemplative life that it dissolves the fiction of created existence, and a divine *act*.

Such a Supreme Being as this is no object of worship or prayer, for we cannot worship an infinite negation; and the extraordinary phenomenon (which does not for a moment, however, agitate—as what does?—the sublime stolidity of writers of manuals) of a sect of Hindoo atheists, called Sankhyas, who, in a sphere of fanatical superstition are only regarded as mildly heterodox, receives an explanation in the fact that a

First Cause who is no object of worship may as well be the seminal matter of the heterodox Hindoo as the impersonal abstraction of the orthodox ; that it may as well be Pracriti as Brahm. Accordingly the Hindoo, like the ancient intellectual pagan, does not worship his Supreme Being. If scattered instances are found of it in the sacred writings of Brahmanism, the system does not recognise prayer, or prescribe one act of worship to Brahm, who has not a temple raised to him in all Hindustan. A host of demons or created deities—mere scintillations of the Supreme Deity, and delegated "guardians of the worlds," at the head of which are Brahma, Vishnu, and Siva, no true divinities, but emanations and creatures of Brahm —absorb the worship of the Hindoo. All these deities, says the Sankhya worshipper of them in Dr. Rowland Williams' dialogue, "are high forms, and probably very glorious and eminent forms of intellect . . . . but in the infinite roll of ages, they like ourselves must become subject to the eternal law of change; their wisdom and their power have bubbled up out of the froth of the abysmal ocean as it heaves into existence, and in turn they will subside and give place to others whether better or worse."

Intellectual Paganism and Brahmanism, indeed, both adopt unconsciously the great difficulty of philosophy as to the relations of man to an Infinite Being. How can you put yourself into relations with an Infinite Being, it is asked? Do you represent Him to yourself as infinite? That is impossible; you endow Him with personality, and you have no idea of personality but such as involves limitation. The Infinite Being may exist, then, but the being whom you worship is not an infinite being, but a finite. This is Hume's religious position. Hume expresses his entire belief in the existence of a God or intelligent Author of nature, but he refuses to worship Him, because worship degrades Him. "To *know* God," he says, quoting Seneca, "is to worship Him. All other worship is indeed absurd, superstitious, and even impious. It degrades Him to the low condition of mankind, who are delighted with entreaty, solicitation, presents, and flattery." Coleridge proved the impossibility of seeing a ghost by the simple argument that, if you saw him, he was not a ghost. Hume proves the impossibility of worshipping God by the argument, that what you worship is, *ipso facto*, not God. By putting yourself into relations with the Infinite Being, you make Him a finite one: a God worshipped is a demon, and his worshipper is an idolater.

As opposed, then, either to the worship of many gods, or the non-worship of one, and cutting through any philosophical difficulty in the way, the normal idea of worship in the human race is the worship of one Infinite God; and this idea can be used as a basis of prophecy, as an idea that must come more and more out, and cast out all others that are opposed to it. A rude polytheism or pantheistic polytheism is alike a forgery and an adulteration of the rational idea of worship, which genuine idea must always have the tendency to supplant the base one.

We come now to another great doctrine, that of a future state. The missionary counts on the matter-of-course belief of the Hindoo in a future state as a common ground between Christianity and Brahmanism. It is observed that the Hindoo has no difficulties on the subject, shows no trace of Western scepticism, takes a future state for granted, and requires no more argument to convince him why he should live hereafter than why he should live now. We prefer a faith which conquers doubt to that which has no element of doubt in it, and exhibits brute strength at the expense of the sensitiveness of life and reason. But what we are going to observe now is, that the Brahmanical idea of a future life is, however strong, not the normal or natural idea of man on that subject, but a corruption, a forgery, and an adulteration, such as we have shown the idea of worship to be.

The natural idea of a future state is an extremely simple one—that of continuing to exist beyond the term of this life in another world, just as we have continued to exist beyond yesterday in this. The preservation of our personal identity is thus the very essence of the idea; the state changes, but the person is for ever the same. Reason justifies to itself, on the ground that it is part of itself, that which would otherwise be the most extravagant of all dreams, and a speculation wilder than any of Gnostic or Valentinian, Norseman or Celt, this marvellous expectation, this universal second-sight in man, by which he is ever seeing a form beyond the boundary of time, and that form himself; this instinct which transplants personality and consciousness beyond the barrier of utter visible ruin, which levels all that interrupts, assimilates all that is heterogeneous, and extends the visible world in one plane into the invisible.

Now let us look at the Brahmanical doctrine of a future state. In the first place, the doctrine of metempsychosis utterly confounds, at the very outset, all our notions of personal identity. A man becomes, according to this doctrine, several men in succession; he is first the Great Mogul; he is then a Rajah; he is then a Brahman, and several other personages afterwards. All these are, according to all our plain natural conceptions, so many distinct individualities. A man is born, lives, and dies with the consciousness of being one particular person, the Emperor Aurungzebe; a man is then born, lives, and dies with the consciousness of being the Pandit Acharya, and nobody else; the same whole existence with the same exclusive consciousness is repeated in the persons of Shom, the Sudra tailor; of Damma Jee, the elephant-driver; of Musseeh, the ivory-carver; of Mullich, the Thug; of Dowlut Raow, the Rajpoot marauder. Nor is there any reason why the course of metempsychosis should confine itself to the Peninsula, or why, though the doctrine of it is Eastern, its action should be confined to Oriental blood, and prohibited from dipping into the heroic ages, the Olympiads, the *anni urbis conditæ,* the Anglo-Saxon, Norman, and Tudor periods, and adding to the above one, multitudinous, personality any successive names which we may choose to take, from Theseus to Sir Robert Peel. A ploughman and a cobbler are two as real distinct individuals as any two most distinguished historical personages in the world; and, therefore, if the former two can be one person, so can Plato and Pompey be, Attila and Peter the Hermit, Roger Bacon and Horace Walpole; and all six can be one person as easily as any two. Out of any chronological chart which gives every century in order, pick a succession of the most celebrated persons, with as much regard to variety in the kind of celebrity as you like,—all these may be one man; there is no limit to the number of apparent persons which, upon the doctrine of metempsychosis, may be only really one, except the condition of succession—that one man cannot be several apparent men alive at once, but must be those persons divided from each other by death; and, therefore, if the world lasts as long, one man may be fifty, five hundred, five thousand, five million apparent men. But who or what, in the name of reason, is he at the end of this career? what is the unit or single person which a Jewish high-priest, a Chinese emperor, a mediæval schoolman, an Elizabethan poet, a Nova Scotia baronet, Charlemagne and the late Mr. Joseph Hume, compose? Such a doctrine confounds all our notions of personality, and so violates, at the very outset, that which is the very point of the natural idea of a future state.

We have no doubt that were we arguing with a learned Brahman, he would bring forward many subtle and ingenious reasons to prove that we could not show any logical absurdity in the doctrine of metempsychosis—any metaphysical impossibility in one personality pervading any number of distinct lives. He would urge that we did not know what lay behind the phenomenon of infancy, or what impenetrable barrier of oblivion might separate a present from a former consciousness; he might admit that consciousness of past existence was the natural property of personality, and that, therefore, there was an apparent presumption against a man having once been somebody else in the circumstance that he was wholly unconscious of this entire past existence; but he might rejoin that, for anything we know, this exceptional and abnormal state might be corrected at the ultimate point or goal of the career of man, when all the chambers of past existence might be opened in the mind, and the individual at last see his whole real length of personality, and become conscious of himself and all his actions from the first. But what subtle philosophical arguments can possibly outweigh the intense natural conviction in the heart of every man that he—the self of which he is conscious—is one whole and one sole individual; and that, living and dying with no other consciousness than what he dates from infancy, such consciousness marks one person? We have, indeed, no other idea in our minds of a human person but this, which is therefore utterly violated by the supposition of personality embracing whole human lives entirely cut off from each other. The doctrine of metempsychosis has appeared to some a natural doctrine; but it can only be a natural doctrine to those who do not examine their own ideas, just as Eastern metamorphoses of men into horses and horses into men are natural to children; and though Pythagoras and Plato adopted it, the philosophy of those days, however deep in an imaginative and moral sense, did not excel in common sense or accuracy. If so many whole separate human lives disguise one living person, and so many separate individual consciousnesses are only the external crust of one true individual, this is a mystical incomprehensible personality, of which we have no conception.

But this confusion of personal identity is succeeded by another as great an adulteration of and contradiction to the natural idea of a future state. There is a great deal in a name. Warburton proves from their doctrine of a resolution into τὸ ἕν—the absorption of the departed soul into the Deity—that the heathen philosophers did not hold the doctrine of a future state; but that which Warburton calls the denial of a future life, figures in Brahmanism as a future life. The final state of the soul, that to which it aspires, and to which all these transmigrations tend, is absorption into the Deity; the individual soul is dissolved into the universal, and loses all personality and consciousness.

We might here comment upon so disappointing a termination of a career of disjointed personality, whole lives passed of which the individual does not remember one moment, and whole successive selves of which he has been altogether unconscious. We wait for the ultimate point when all these several links will reunite, and when, at any rate, the individual will be able to look back upon the complete past, assume the consciousness of the whole of his existence, and see the whole of himself.

But just at the point when he should be put in possession of his full self, he is absorbed into the universal soul, and he is annihilated as a conscious being altogether. But we go to another point. An absorption into the Deity has a grand sound about it, a pretence of ineffable elevation; but, upon examination, it exactly fails in meeting the true want of the soul, the natural instinct desiring the continuance of the very self, which the genuine doctrine of a future state satisfies. This is the craving which is implanted in us by God, to pretend to satisfy which by absorption into God, is simply to abandon all that is substantial and honest in us for a spurious shadow. We cannot possibly care for any state of things that does not carry our own true existence along with it: ourselves must first be provided for on this primary matter, and we can then begin to think of other beings besides ourselves; but, upon the strength of the Divine existence, to be indifferent to our own, is falsehood to that God who has made us the individuals we are, and made the continuance of that individuality our first interest, in comparison with which everything else is as dust in the balance. The empty, pompous idea of absorption, then, substituting grandeur for truth, does just not contain the kernel and true *desideratum*. This weak idea, which rises up when faith is not strong enough to admit the solid one, is not the real doctrine of a future state, but an *evasion* of the doctrine, covering a *denial* of it—offering a superficial medium between existence and non-existence, which is, in truth, the latter. When man dares not believe in a personal immortality, he substitutes the sham of an impersonal one, and talks about absorption. But ask any one resting or working, reading in his study, walking in his garden, or talking with his friends, speaking in the senate, or administering in the office, whether he had rather continue to be the person which he is or be absorbed into the Deity, and he will say undoubtedly the former. That is, then, the voice of nature; and those solemn forms that sauntered in eternal contemplation in the Elysian fields, or recreated themselves with eternal games of discus or bowl or javelin, mingling with them the memories of past deeds and friends—even the Scandinavian heroes in the hall of Odin, and the Red Indian hunter with his faithful dog, buried with him to be his companion in the new world—all these embody the natural idea of a future life more correctly than the simple liquefication and impersonal life of the Hindoo absorption.

The development of revealed religion and that of Brahmanism on this subject show a striking contrast. In revelation there has been a development on this point. The pious Jew rejoiced religiously in this life with its "butter of kine, and milk of sheep, with fat of lambs, and rams of the pure breed of Bashan, and goats, with the fat of kidneys of wheat, and the pure blood of the grape," as the gift of God and the mark of the Divine favour: he was satisfied with true present relations to an Almighty Being, and left the future as a distinct prospect to itself. But a time came when "immortality was brought to light," and when this life shrank into nothing. This was a change then, but it was a bright one: it prepared man for present chastening, but gave him a heaven above to look forward to.

So Brahmanism has had a development, but it has been a very different kind of development. The primitive Arya exhibits something of the spirit of the Jew—a genuine, simple appreciation of physical prosperity as a sign of the Divine goodwill: he rejoices in good fortune, victory, glory, plenty, exuberance, cows and fat pastures, butter and honey, corn and wine, overflowing larders and rich feasts; and he exults in it all as the mark of the favour of his gods, and the infallible token of his own matchless orthodoxy. It is a terrene, religious joy in a most successful compound of earth and heaven, the true faith mingling in delightful harmony with the teeming flock and fruitful field, not without a sense of satisfaction in the special circumstance that this mixture is enjoyed at the expense of the "infidel," *i.e.* the unfortunate aboriginal, whom at one stroke he has deprived of the two best possessions in the universe, his farming stock in the visible world and the Divine blessing in the invisible: the same victory which has gained the enemy's fat field having also proved his creed to be untenable and impious. The Arya's deities are personifications of the sunshine, rain, clouds, wind, the productive powers of nature, and the genial influences of earth and sky: one prime favourite is Soma, a personification of the rich milky juice of the Soma plant—a deity who, as an object of worship, would perhaps be analogous to a god of butter, or a god of curds and whey. The honest Arya prays, and thus does he pray :—

"A libation of milk, O Indra and Varuna! we pour it out for you, drink and be propitious. Guard the pious man from sin, protect his cows, and give him abundance. Preserve us, O Brahmanaspatis! that man does not perish whom Indra, Soma, and Brahmanaspatis preserve. I approach Sadasaspati, the wonderful, the beloved, the beneficent, for the grace of wisdom, also for the gift of opulence: he hears the thought of the devout; he endoweth the sacrificer with marvellous plenty. I have seen Narasansa, the most brave, most glorious, splendid as a star of heaven. O Agnis, amplifier of strength, whom we worship with an offering of butter, be favourable, O giver of meat, exhilarator, protector of households, lord of beatific nourishment! O Asvins, wonderful, veracious, let your horses bring you to my sacrifice: sit down, O men, on the carpet, bestowers of good things, and give us from air and sky all-delighting wealth."

The reception which the worshipper recommends for the "dasyus," or enemies, the "goat-nosed," or "noseless" aboriginal is very different :—

"Indra and Soma, burn the devils, destroy them, throw them down—ye two bulls—the people that grow in darkness! Hew down the madmen, suffocate them, kill them; hurl them away and slay the voracious. Indra and Soma, up together against the cursing demon! May he burn and hiss like an oblation on the fire! Put your everlasting hatred upon the villain, who hates the Brahman, who eats flesh, and whose look is abominable. Indra and Soma, hurl the evil-doer into the pit, even into unfathomable darkness. May your strength be full of wrath to hold out, that no one may come out again."[1]

Thus alternating between his creed and his dairy, the primitive Arya pours forth his rude and simple piety in the Vedic hymn; but a deeper spirit, in course of time, comes over Brahmanism; it too, like revelation, leaves the sacred sunshine of present life, and *looks forward*. But what is the

[1] Article on "Caste" in the *Times*, April 12, 1858.

prospect which it places before its eye when it does look forward? It is that prospect which is involved in the favourite *cultus* of Siva the Destroyer—a perpetual universal vanishing and passing away; generation after generation coming in only to disappear again for ever. The mind of man is indeed so marvellously accommodated in all respects to his mortal condition, that even this aspect of things is not without a subtle, latent pleasure constitutionally attaching to it: nobody can tell how much would be lost in the shape of pleasing melancholy were we all immortal here; everything around us has an interest derived from the simple circumstance of mortality which otherwise it would want: the dead are sacred because they are dead, the living little less than sacred because they are to die: the past is romance, the future is mystery, and the idea of succession is the basis of the poetry of life. So far we are all worshippers of Siva. We pause when some great man or some old man has gone, or when the last tip of the sun's orb has vanished from the western sky, and say—it is over. While life lasted, and while day lasted, the past was divided with the present: now we have an integral whole past, and we reflect that this is a sample of an endless succession of such wholes. But our doctrine of a personal immortality turns *us* away from this prospect to another; the Hindoo's empty shadow of an impersonal future allows *him* to be engulfed in it: his absorption is a shadow and an abstraction; *this* prospect is his real futurity: his immortality is endless mortality, an eternal succession of evanescent beings: he cannot escape from this idea; the knell of all nature tolls in his ear, and the universe is a vast funereal mystery to him, like the gloomy, interminable, inexplicable procession, which obeys the dreadful secret of a dream. Such is the practical result of a counterfeit and adulterated idea of a future life, which starts with confounding, and ends with destroying, personality. In the combination of metempsychosis and absorption, the true idea of immortality is lost, and the mind is thrown back upon that which inspires the whole later development of Brahmanism—the visible empire of Death.

From religion we turn to morals. If it is true that a change of religion is the only road to a change of morals in the Hindoo, it is also true that his morals are a strong lever for working a change in his religion; that, as evidence which must ultimately appeal to a natural conscience *against* Hindooism, it is, however temporally obstructive, fundamentally a weapon on our side in the contest with Hindooism. A religion which sanctions immorality must fall with the rise of the moral standard in the mind of its votary to a natural level.

The Hindoo moral system rises from two main foundations. One is an all-penetrating ceremonialism. The cravings of a shallow conscience are specially met and appeased by an unceasing course of easy, petty perfection, just as those of a deep one are disappointed and feel themselves trifled with; and the Hindoo ceremonial law combines, with subtle craft, the utmost completeness and finish with the utmost indulgence, by means of a scale of reward which allows no waste, crowning the perfect observer with the first prize, while the most negligent has his proportionate advantage, thus stimulating the zealous, not deterring the idle, and accommodating itself to everybody.

The other foundation is moral in a way, though a tremendous abuse of a moral power—*i.e.* a coarse, one-sided, and monstrous development of it. We mean what is called *power of will*. The inner criterion of a true religion, or the peculiar *nature* of its moral law, is quite as characteristic of it as its preference of the moral law to the ceremonial. Christianity demands the exertion of the will in subordination to another test of action. Is an act required or recommended as being in harmony with our relations to God or man? then you must exert your will sufficiently to do it; but the exertion of the will for its own sake, and as a mere feat, is no part of Christianity. But the will spiritual, in Hindooism, exerts itself for the sake of the feat, and exhibits its strength for the mere purpose of showing how strong it is. Hindooism *strains* the will, as if the pure quantity of it which an action or course of life showed were the moral test. Upon this principle arises the whole system of voluntary self-torture, one devotee surpassing another in the length and agony of self-inflicted pain. We need not go into details given in every book on India, the incredible violations of the animal frame and every part of it, the forced attitudes of body and mind sustained for years. These acts are truly astonishing as exhibitions of simple will, but that is all they are. Hindoo high morals are feats done for their own sake, like a conjuror's or athlete's. No wonder that such " boasting "—for boasting may proceed from the source of an inner moral law as well as from an outward and ceremonial —soon receives its punishment in the degradation of the saint into the mountebank, wandering about at fairs and showing off his self-inflicted tortures as an entertaining spectacle to crowds. A humiliating mirror for spiritual pride! But is there not a Western form of this moral disease, which sets up as the exclusive and idolised standard, not power of endurance indeed, but the analogous gift in Western life—*activity*? After all, the self-made trial is a poor disciplinarian weapon : there is a subtle, masterly, irritant, and provoking point in the genuine natural trial, and in the natural crossness of events, which the artificial thing cannot manage : we can no more *make* our trials than we can make our feelings, and the Manichean is overthrown, the Christian is perfected, by the venom of nature.

Raised upon such a foundation, Hindoo morality is a chaos —a mass of inconsistencies. The first virtues of man are those which suit his normal state; his normal state is one of health and peace, and therefore his first virtues are justice, honesty, veracity, charity : he must have, it is true—because he is not always in his normal state—other virtues, ability to endure pain, physical courage, and the like; but the former come first in order. But Hindoo law reverses this order, and turns morality topsy-turvy, makes it wholly absorbed, like the code of the savage, in the virtues of the abnormal state and the battle with pain, and bids it to neglect the plain virtues of common life, as if they were beneath notice. The result is, the monstrous anomaly of the same people, who gape with admiration at self-torture, recoiling with horror and loathing from those who are visited by chastenings of Providence. Pain is divine if a man inflicts it on himself, diabolical if God sends it—an extraordinary reverse, indeed, to the Gospel lesson of sympathy for pain. The victim who, by means of a hook in his back, is whirled round and round a pole, is applauded rapturously by the Hindoo crowd so long as the hook remains fixed; but if the miserable creature's flesh gives way, and he is dashed, with a concussion of the brain, to the ground, he is assailed with imprecations. If the test of true morality, as of true civilisation, is *consistency*, it is flattery to compare Hindoo morals to the civilised barbarism of the Incas, with its centralisation and *quipus*, marble, and thatch.

The common virtues, then, have no proportionate rank in the Hindoo system, and for this there is another reason. Another test of true morality, besides consistency, is *communicativeness;* this is part of its nature; it is a proselytising system; a good man wants to make others good. The much-criticised institution of preaching is an expedient by which the Christian body in the person of its representative exhorts itself: our literature and speeches are a preaching of society to itself. True morality is thus self-communicative, and by communicating it *sustains* itself, and keeps up the sacred flame. But Brahmanism locks up its really sublime moral truths, those high maxims and pure sentiments which our philosophers admire, in books, and the absurd and childish "Kutha" is the only trace of preaching in it.

The Hindoo has a facility for lying which astonishes and confounds a European. He has no regard for life: and first, not for his own life. Even this is a miserable trait; for where the moral nature is healthy, the implanted instinct of life must be strong, and nature can only become callous to it, as a limb becomes callous to pain, by disease and corruption. But this insensibility is a dreadful moral stain on character, when human life at large is the subject-matter of it, and murder is incorporated into a moral code. Hindooism, by not only conniving at but acquiescing in it as the established privilege of a class, has really sanctioned Thuggee, and made itself responsible for it; and Suttee and the Ghaut murders are absolute rites of Hindooism.

The question then—to come back to our old argument again—is, Is the Hindoo a *man*, endowed fundamentally with a human conscience? If he is, then there is ultimately an appeal to that conscience, at which this monstrous system must tremble. Can he, for example, remain for ever blind to the law of nature, "Thou shalt not kill"? If he cannot, he and the religion which says "Kill" must one day part. When man has been demoralised by a religion, his conscience is indeed, for that very reason, a perverted one, to which an appeal is not at once open; but its essential nature still survives, its foundation remains on which to work a recovery.

From morals we turn to science, and first to the metaphysics of Brahmanism.

We will not, in the face of Mr. Wilson's evidence, deny the existence of good strong logical heads in the Hindoo schools, who have written good school-books of logic; but what is called, *par excellence*, Hindoo speculation, does not seem to us to show strength of head. *Strength* is one thing, *depth* is another. Depth is a passive quality: it exists sometimes in children upon whom the shadows of great truths rest inertly, leading only to desultory wonder and subtle amusement; it comes out as a quality of note in a certain class of intellects, who throw interest rather than light upon philosophy. Deep ideas give a communion with truth, but not the grasp of it. There is such a thing as feeble depth, which is whirled helplessly by its own genuine and wonderful vortex. Coleridge's was a deep mind: Locke's was both a deep and a strong one. We cannot deny Hindoo speculation the attribute of depth. It broods upon all the deepest ideas connected with existence,—God, soul, the individual, the universal, the inward, the outward, infinity, eternity. Dr. Rowland Williams goes largely into this field, catches sympathetically the spirit of it, and, to use the popular term, *realises* Brahmanism. But Brahmanism is a philosophy of deep impressions, not of active grasp over ideas—a quietist not a hard-working philosophy. Locke examines an idea just as a chemist would a metal or fluid, and makes out what it is in this way. That is *our* notion of analysis, and of true metaphysics—accurate observation, the noting of the facts or phenomena of mind. But the Hindoo philosopher's is a barmecidal analysis, such as a man might perform in his sleep. We have a series of abstract *insides*: the outer body contains an inner, the inner personality, personality consciousness, consciousness intellect, intellect *Pracriti*. Or the abstract chain is linked thus—the intellect in each man (*prajna*) proceeds from the collective human intellect (*vaiswanara*), which proceeds from the divine creative intellect (*chaitanya*), "which again is intelligent," says Dr. Williams's Vedantist, "only in virtue of that which I despair of expressing in words. It is what we call the Fourth." The Deity sheathes himself in successive bodies, or forms of *Maya*, till from "the præcreative or præeternal spirit, before all thought, and itself the possibility of thinking," we come to the gross world of matter. "God is the implicit universe, the universe is developed God," and so on. There is no real analysis in all this, no observation. These are ready-made abstractions, put in a particular order. Working your way into the real facts of mind shows strength, and modern metaphysics have done this; but abstractions and subtleties are no signs in themselves of strength. There are some simple-minded people who think that all theology, and all speculation, and all metaphysics, are very difficult as such; but, setting piety aside, there are no two easier things to talk about than God and the universe. Hindoo philosophy betrays a real craving after an inner reality, of which this world is only the outside, but with a deep sentiment pervading it; as an investigator, the Hindoo sage only uses a formula, and rings the changes upon the great ideas of our nature.

Connected with this character of Hindoo metaphysics, one important characteristic of the religion must be noted—we mean its *actus salvans*, that state of the mind which unlocks the door of heaven, and admits the individual to the life eternal. This in Christianity is faith; with the Brahmanist it is *knowledge*. The Brahmanist's idea of meditation, like his idea of morals, is that of an extravagant conquest of nature. He goes into the woods with a long beard, and coarse gown and girdle, determined to see through a brick wall, to penetrate into the essence of things, and the mystery of the divine nature. He rejects all media, and directs his thought to Tad; he fixes himself in the meditative vice for the rest of the present, or, if need be, throughout a second or a third life, and awaits the issue. The issue comes at last in the shape of the great Brahman *gnosis*, the realisation of Brahm as the sole-existing essence; and the illuminate cries out, "I am Brahm." That is the consummation of the religious life which immediately unites the man to God, and gives him the final Hindoo salvation, absorption into the divine essence. Brahmanism has, then, for its *actus salvans* a position of mind which European metaphysics must expose as a complete sham. That science has formally shown the limits of human knowledge, and that the knowledge of God in Himself is beyond these limits. Christianity, then, however we may regret the approach in some Fathers to the adoption of a mystical gnosis, has, by its modesty in stopping short at faith, saved the encounter with metaphysics, while Hindooism, carried away by the bombast of a false religion, stands committed to a plain absurdity, which mental science and common sense alike expose.

But physical science is the great antagonist of Hindooism: its inspired books are inextricably committed to a collision with the truths of astronomy, chemistry, medicine, geography, and all the facts of modern science.

The Hindoo is what we may call a running inspiration. With the Vedas as its main seat and fountain-head, the popular stream goes on from age to age without coming to any line at which it abdicates, and hands over truth to fallible reason.[1] It thus accumulates a succession of books and treatises, and, in fact, grows into a library. Lost documents of revelation are

[1] The distinction between the Vedas and the subsequent sacred writings still leaves the ground of full inspiration for the latter. "The Veda alone," says the learned writer on Caste in the *Times*, "is called 'Sruti' or revelation; everything else, however sacred, can only claim the title of '.Smriti' or tradition. The most elaborate arguments have been framed by the Brahmans to establish the divine origin and the absolute authority of the Veda. They maintain that the Veda existed before all time; that it was revealed by Brahma and seen by divine sages, who themselves were free from all the taint of humanity. For what authority, the Brahmans say, could we claim for a revelation which had been revealed by Brahma to fallible mortals? It might have been perfect truth as seen by Brahma, but as seen by men it would have been affected by their faulty vision. Hence revelation, in order to be above all suspicion, *must be handed down by inspired rishis*, till at last it reaches, in its perfect form, the minds of common believers, and is accepted by them as absolute truth."

discovered in the dusty collections of temples. The late Babu Gunga Gobingha Singha, a Hindoo gentleman residing in a village near Murshedabad, spent a considerable fortune in making researches into the Shastras, and succeeded in bringing to light some valuable remains of inspiration.

Thus unchecked in its career, Hindoo inspiration, unlike the Christian, which confines itself to the great purposes of religion, undertakes all subjects; all is fish that comes into its net; every branch of knowledge and art, speculative or practical, from the nature of the Deity down to the art of dancing. The Shastras, or sacred writings, treat in succession upon astronomy, chronology, medicine, mechanics, metaphysics, the fine arts, geography, chemistry, botany, grammar, music, archery, etc. What such a theory of inspiration amounts to is, that age after age any treatise upon any subject that obtains reputation ranks as canonical, and makes part of a bible, which becomes simply another word for the accredited literature of the race. It is as if among ourselves, besides our standard books of divinity, and principal poets and philosophers, there had been admitted into our canon Bacon's *Essays*, Brown's *Religio Medici*, Evelyn's *Diary*, Walton's *Angler*, Selden's *Table-Talk*, White's *Natural History of Selborne*, Lindley Murray, Uvedale Price *On the Picturesque*, and a list of books that we could extend indefinitely. Such a theory has the effect of giving to inspiration a familiar, domestic, and, if we may use such a term, genial character. It brings everything within the holy precincts, and around the sacred hearth, and makes all the world a temple. Its disadvantage is, that inspiration under it incurs most formidable responsibilities, for, besides physical error, the questionable morality which has issued from venerable heads, looking as grave as sages and high priests, is known to all of us, and the same rule which would have included good old Walton and Sir Thomas Browne might also have brought Machiavelli into the canon.

It is the boast of the simple Hindoo that all science is revealed complete and perfect in his inspired books, and that nothing is left to the mere human intellect to discover. We need not go at length into these extraordinary puerilities. The chemical revelation lays down the doctrine of the five primary elements, ether, air, fire, water, and earth, each of which, in succession, produces the other. "Fire is born of air, because, being urged with force by breath, it increases; water is born of fire, because that which when disappearing enters fire must needs when it appears flow from the same thing." The medical revelation lays down the process of assimilation in the animal frame as threefold, turning corn into flesh, water into blood, oil into marrow; the finer part of corn supplying the mental organs, and the finer part of oil the faculty of speech : it elicits a hundred and one arteries from the heart, and places within the heart a corporeal being the size of a thumb—the whole man in miniature, which at death escapes through an artery. The Tantras, abandoning tangible medicine altogether, regard the human stomach as a region of speculative and theological truth. Six principal internal organs, called chakras or padmas, bearing a general resemblance to the lotus, extend from the pelvic cavity to the forehead; which are respectively the seats of the influence of different divinities, and the highest of which puts the individual into proper relations with the three sacred rivers of India, the Ganges, the Jumna, and the Saraswati. Following up the same plan, they construct a grand stomachic phrenological table or chessboard, with eighty-six divisions, which represents the human interior as divided into this number of moral, intellectual, metaphysical, theological, grammatical, vocal, alphabetical, corporeal, chemical, arithmetical, social, chronological, digestive, pathetic, and many other compartments. The compartments from nineteen to thirty-six run as follows :—"The place of the mind, fire, the state of profound sleep, passion, the vowel u, Vishnu, false ostentation of wisdom, attention, the place of intelligence, water, Orjya, ignorance or darkness ; the letter m, Shiva, false ostentation of bodily accomplishments, egotism, the place of life, the air." The astronomical revelation lays down a regular scale of ascending distances from the earth, through the sun, moon, and planets, to the pole-star, and gives a very extraordinary explanation of the moon's wane, and of solar and lunar eclipses ; though the later Siddhantse adopt the Ptolemaic system. The geographical revelation represents the earth as consisting of seven large circular belts of land, divided from each other respectively by circular seas. At the centre of this terrestrial target is placed a round continent of land, which may be called the bull's-eye of the earth; and at the centre of this round continent rises the mountain Meru, to the height of 240,000 miles, adorned with trees and pleasant streams, the haunts of gods and celestial singers, and with a splendid mineralogy of gold and precious stones; carrying on its top the heavens of Vishnu, Siva, Indra, and other divinities, and covering with its base the seven infernal regions of Brahmanism. This whole central target is engirdled by a circular belt of gold, the golden belt is protected by a circular chain of mountains, and the mountain circle is surrounded by outer darkness. An inspired local geography represents Hindustan as 72,000 miles long from north to south, and consisting of nine divisions, the first and last of which are the abodes of gods, with their retinues of heavenly musicians; and conducts the Ganges, after its journey through the habitations of men, through regions of celestial songsters, terrific giants and demons, gigantic snakes, and successive haunts of unknown and supernatural tribes and species, alternately beautiful and appalling.

It is difficult to separate one element from another in this mixed, heterogeneous mass of fairy tale, allegory, and physics: it contains however, mingled with other matter, the rude science of the early East, which science was gradually adopted as revelation, for which revelation Hindooism is accordingly now responsible. We naturally ask, indeed, how an ancient Brahman could profess to discover by thought the truths of geography: the earth's surface is a fact which can only be got at by observation; its mountains, rivers, seas, races of men, and species of animals are matters of ocular evidence, of which the most profound meditation in the deepest cavern of the earth cannot put you in possession. But to ask such questions as these is not to realise the dream which constitutes Oriental thought. In dreams the intellect is magnetised: we ask no questions; we are disturbed by no inconsistencies; we confound place and time, bring the living and the dead together, and see the dome of St. Paul's from the banks of the Nile. The popular Oriental reason succumbs to the fascination of solemn externals as the guarantees of truth : it reposes in the ceremonial of wisdom. A grave countenance, a venerable beard, a priestly costume, are the tests of a correct and capable informant, nor does it advance beyond the spectacle or rite of knowledge. Its ideas of matter of fact itself are vague. The region of fact is altogether an heraldic and mystical world to an imagination overpowered by the spell of a whole ritualistic scene, in which temples, incantations, sacrifices, sacred oxen, sacred rivers, sacred trees, sacred men, and sacred suns and moons, make up a waking dream, and convert life into a solemn show, which soothes into quietism and a quasi-holy lethargy and torpor. Geography is especially a dream amongst rude people, mingling with the supernatural as soon as it leaves the familiar confines of a district. The primitive imagination pictures the earth's surface extending onward and onward, till by the pure mystery of surpassing distance and remoteness, a change takes place, new laws of nature steal in, new forms of life appear, the mountains are the abodes of gods, the woods of satyrs, the valleys and ravines communicate with a subterranean world ; a dark river is crossed, and you are in the realms of the dead, the spectres glide peacefully along verdant avenues, or cower in murky hollows under instruments of torture. The same Homer who enlarged the bounds of literal geography yet abounds in the mystical, and lands Ulysses and his companions by a natural voyage over a natural sea upon the twilight of the Cimmerians and the region of departed spirits. The Fortunate Islands, the Homeric Ogygia, the garden of the Hesperides, were all oases of the supernatural or immortal life, boldly lodged within this world, not timidly relegated to another. So the sidereal world above us, which is but an extension of our own physical space, figures to this day as the region of the life supernatural, in the idea of a mistaken piety which cannot wholly separate the visible and the invisible. Thus, by an assimilating process peculiar to the primitive kind of intellect, the natural world glides into the supernatural and mingles with it. Under the jealous eye of philosophy, indeed, a certain resemblance of this process goes on: this actual time in which we live and this actual space in which we stand, with its numbered stellar orbs, run up into regions of insoluble enigma, where monsters of metaphysics reside, transcending all the centaurs, sphinxes, and dragons of fable; time which never began, universal space which is not a *whole*, and number which is neither even nor odd—the nondescript forms of infinity. But the monsters of philosophy are always inaccessible, those of mystical geography are seen and conversed with.

To sum up now what has been said. Here is a succession of truths which appeal directly to the rational nature in man, which Hindooism contradicts; there are truths of religion, the worship of one God, and the doctrine of a personal immortality; there are truths of morals; there are truths of metaphysics; there are, lastly, the undeniable truths of physical science, and the plain facts of nature. Here is a combination of forces, then, which as soon as ever the Hindoo mind has risen up to the natural human level, and has had the proper facts laid before it, is ready at once to close in upon the system, and crush it completely and finally. There cannot be the slightest doubt as to the effect which will follow from these truths being apprehended; and the question whether the Hindoo mind will ever be brought to apprehend them, *i.e.* whether the original type of rational humanity in the Hindoo is practically accessible, is a question of our own resources and of the natural course of events.

The question of our resources for this purpose involves as its principal element the question of education.

The prominent controversy which the field of Indian education presents up to the year 1835, is that between the advocates of the vernacular and the English learning. The Mahometan College at Calcutta, the Sanscrit College at Benares, and the mixed Mahometan and Sanscrit Colleges at Agra and Delhi, represented the former principle, and the support of it by the Government; while the erection of the Hindoo College, an institution of private foundation at Calcutta, showed a strong movement in Indian public opinion toward the latter. The celebrated resolution of Lord William Bentinck in 1835, in which Mr. Macaulay concurred, decided the balance in favour of the European learning. Another important question, viz., that of language, whether the English or the vernacular were to be used as the medium for communicating this new knowledge, was also decided by the same resolution. The vernacular was a rather unmanageable medium for reflecting European ideas and facts: the recourse to the Sanscrit hardly mended matters. It was not surprising "if a very bad translation of the *Life of Columbus*, full of barbarisms, and full of obsolete terms of Sanscrit, did not sell:"[1] in addition to which defects the translation was expensive, while the English book was cheap. English was on these grounds adopted as the medium of European learning in India, in the higher class of schools, and 15,000 Hindoos were receiving an English education in the valley of the Ganges in 1853. The necessity of the vernacular for the education of the mass was at the same time recognised; and it was felt that if European knowledge was ever to spread generally in India, it must be through the native language. European knowledge has been introduced into the lower class of schools by means of new vernacular school-books composed by pupils of the English schools. A vernacular *Robinson Crusoe* is said to be a great favourite with Hindoo peasants, and "a rage for translation," Mr. Wilson tells us, has introduced Mill's *Political Economy*, Bentham's *Principles of Legislation*, Paley's *Natural Theology*, Marshman's *Scenes of History*, with many other books, to the cultivated Hindoos, and has furnished them with the *Encyclopædia Bengalensis*.

When we come to the working of this system of education, remarkable results appear, with considerable drawbacks upon them. The Hindoo is a quick learner, and has a great facility for acquiring language; the perfection of his English pronunciation astonishes you; he writes English well; he catches up quickly European ideas, and pursues mathematics, metaphysics, and astronomy keenly. Lord Ellenborough is much amused at young Hindoos "spouting Shakespeare," and the school examina-

[1] We quote here and elsewhere from the evidence before the Committee of the Lords.

tions exhibit a good deal for an Englishman to laugh at. If the glibness, however, with which the pupils at these scholastic celebrations define "capital," estimate "paper money," and prove the "origin of wealth," "the beneficial effects of the division of labour," "the consequences of a free trade in corn," "the advantages of accumulation," and "the influence produced on wages by the relation of capital to the population;" if the facility with which they "analyse" Locke and Hume, "criticise" Brown's *Theory of Causation*, correct the Platonists and Peripatetics, and "expose" Descartes, Malebranche, and Leibnitz; if these philosophical triumphs have their ludicrous aspect, part of the effect, perhaps, is due to the overforward zeal of the missionary schoolmaster, who is bent on producing striking results, and aims at creating a perfect Bengalese Scotch philosopher in three years. The enthusiasm and practical powers of Dr. Duff merit the highest admiration, but he must expect Englishmen to stumble at such questions as these, proposed to copper-tinted youths of the age of fourteen or fifteen—"Define the true philosophic spirit," "In what two lights are we to regard the mental affections?" "State how the philosophy of mind agrees with that of matter," "Define what is meant by the relation of mental equivalence," with others which would make our list tedious. Part of the effect, perhaps, is due to the law by which an element of the ludicrous always somehow or other mixes with the practical part of great movements. Theory can evade, and history can forget or overlook; but take the actual present working of any great cause, as it goes on before our eyes, and it is sure to contain a good deal of the ridiculous. The practical, the actual, are severe tests. It matters not what the cause is, whether it is Parliamentary Reform, or Catholic Emancipation, or the Corn Laws, or the English Church, or the Universal Church, or the evangelisation of the world, or anything else, every cause incorporates an element of the ludicrous in its practical working and machinery of means to ends. This comedy of education in India does unquestionably—and that is a serious result—revolutionise the Hindoo, so far as he is brought under the process. He does not shrink from the logical result of new truths, and, from the instant that he comes into contact with them, abandons his old faith once and for all. This is the uniform result. Dr. Duff describes graphically the first effects of the new education upon a large body of Hindoo youth in Calcutta; their utter amazement and wild holiday sense of boundless mental liberty, " on being suddenly thrown adrift from their ancient and natural ideas, and completely tossed from the moorings and the anchorages of old Hindooism."

All this, in spite of extravagances, is satisfactory as showing a certain European foundation in the Hindoo mind, that it is not a mere local offspring of the obsolete East, but the true mind of man, capable of modern sympathies, and susceptible of all those sensations which attach to new ideas and the discovery of truth, and even of the excitement of the European revolutionary sentiment, which, however dangerous a one among ourselves, is not wholly unwelcome in a Hindoo, as a sign of his participation in true human nature. On the other hand, we hear complaints that the educated Hindoos do not keep up their education when they go into life. Out of 2000 educated natives in Calcutta, only 130, Mr. Marshman says, took in English newspapers, and only 12 English periodicals; though this statement should be qualified by the information that native reading clubs and circulating libraries have of late risen up in Calcutta. What keeps up education is society; and when the Hindoo leaves school he does not find an educated native society to receive him, and does not venture upon English. Even the Parsee holds back. "I tried to persuade," says Sir Erskine Perry, "Sir Jamsetjee Jeejeeboy to come and dine with me, and to bring his own cook, but it was too much for a man of his years to encounter. I have no doubt that as the elders go off, his son, a man of forty, and others of his generation, will do it."

The inertia of the Oriental mass thus necessarily retards the growth of the European element thrown back upon it. Nor should it be forgotten that the blind faith of the poor ignorant multitude, however intellectually despised, yet exerts an unconscious pressure upon the imagination of the Europeanised Hindoo : this huge body of ancestral belief everywhere confronts and encompasses him. He is not convinced back again by it; but such a state of things has a tendency, as we have seen in Roman Catholic Europe, to produce that neutral attitude which rejects one form of religion without adopting another. The ignorant mass thus exercises a real power even over the educated.

Enormous retarding influences, however, are no more than what the springs of the greatest movements, the most powerful and effective causes of grand revolutions, have been originally saddled with. The obstructive force is always strong and obstinate up to the point at which the assailant cause turns the corner; but in proportion as the assailing cause gains ground, it also absorbs the obstruction. Whatever drawbacks may accompany it, education, with an active European influence to back it up, is a most powerful engine for revolutionising the Hindoo mind. Christianity can wield the weapon of science for the demolition of her rival in India without any fear of a recoil upon herself. Her religious military position gives her this advantage. Some may be disposed to deny her right to such a position, but as a matter of fact it is one which she makes good. Whatever apparent opposition there may be between certain passages of the Bible and truths of physical science, Christians, as a matter of fact, do not cease to believe in their revelation on account of the difficulty: Hindoos do immediately and finally reject *theirs*. Christianity, then, bears the appeal to physical science, Hindooism does not; and thus strong against the recoil, Christianity can wield effectively the weapon. The only question is as to the moral rules which attach to the use of this weapon; what restrictions accompany it; what is the constitutional use of it. On this subject many scruples are felt by reflecting and religious men, and we find ourselves introduced to the agitated question of the secular system of education in India.

Before we suggest any materials, however, for the decision of this question, it may be as well to take the precaution to state what the question itself is, and to define it with proper accuracy. This question is often generally and vaguely described as that of religious education *versus* secular, a phrase which would lead us to imagine that one side maintained that education in India was better without religion, the other that it was better with it. But this is an incorrect statement of the case. Both sides, we apprehend, allow that all education in India would be better in itself with the religious element than without it: the difference is, that one side maintains the existence of insurmountable impediments to the introduction of the religious element in certain connections. This is a dispute which only relates to a certain class of schools in India, viz., the Government schools: the question is not raised with respect to missionary schools, or any educational institutions supported by private charity, but only with respect to those in connection with Government. It is maintained, in the first place, that Government is an improper agent for purposes of religion; that representing, as it does, a religiously-divided nation, its attitude on this subject is essentially neutral, and that it could not teach any one definite creed. It is maintained, in the next place, that Government could not assume the character of religious instructor in India without great danger to the safety of our empire; that proselytism would be incorporated by such a step in our civil system; and that, however mild a form of proselytism it might in actual working be, only offering certain instruction, and leaving it entirely at the option of the native to receive or refuse it as he liked, it would, as connected with the Government, suggest to the Hindoo the suspicion of overpowering influence and force, and thus perpetually stimulate native fear and agitation. On these grounds it is maintained that the religious element must be excluded from the Government schools, and that they must confine themselves to secular education.

With the recent exception of Sir John Lawrence, the unanimous consent of Indian statesmen of all parties decides upon these grounds against the introduction of religion into the Government schools. Assuming then, upon the strength of their concurrent testimony to a state of facts of which they are the proper judges, the existence of insurmountable obstacles to this step, the question is, Ought Government to shut up its schools altogether? or is it justified in carrying on, and, as may seem expedient, in extending, a system of simply secular education in India? The effect of this education is doubtless to demolish Hindooism. What is said, then, is, that you have no right to take away one religion without teaching another.

Now, were there no other teaching or influence at work in India, except that of Government schools, there would doubtless be something in this argument, and the policy of demolishing without any attempt to build up again would be highly objectionable. But this is not the case. The Gospel is preached in India. Christianity is offered to the Hindoo, if not in the Government schoolroom, at any rate in institutions founded side by side with the Government school, and by the same people who, in their national character, erect the Government school. The Hindoos know that a revelation professing to come from heaven claims their belief: some actually go to hear what the missionary says about this revelation, others know that they can go if they like. With this general invitation to the Hindoos to hear the Gospel, which has its own institutions to support it, it cannot fairly be said that we are demolishing Hindooism without offering a substitute, simply because this substitute is not expressly offered in *every* institution connected with education. Taking one institution with another, and looking upon our teaching in India as a whole, we teach both science and religion; and schools which give a sound secular education are not fairly chargeable with an irreligious character when they exist in juxtaposition with missionary and evangelising labours and institutions going on side by side with them.

In the next place, whatever responsibility the Government schools incur, as giving knowledge which may simply lead to infidelity, is incurred substantially by the missionary English school as well. It is true that Dr. Duff teaches the Bible and all the articles of the Christian faith in his school, and that young Hindoos who still nominally worship Vishnu and Siva give accurate answers at the public examinations to the questions, "How may it be said that faith saves a sinner?" "What is the difference between justification and sanctification?" But can he insure the Hindoo ever believing one tittle of that revelation which he is thus made to get off by heart? Out of a school which had been going on for twenty-two years, and which had gradually raised its average attendance to 1380, only 40, he tells us, had been baptized. But while the conversion of his pupils by this religious knowledge is a mere contingency, the demolition of their Hindoo faith by the secular knowledge which he gives them is, according to his own showing, certain. He teaches geography, astronomy, and all the branches of modern science; but he tells us that "you cannot teach true geography and astronomy without exploding the false Hindoo systems," which systems "are contained in books inspired by the gods, and which are, therefore, of divine infallible authority." He teaches, then, what is certain to make infidels of them, as regards their own religion, while he can only secure a very small fraction of them accepting the proper substitute for it. These young Hindoos "are mastering," he says, "the subject of Christianity, as far as the human intellect, apart from Divine grace, can master it, much in the same way as they come there to master geography or astronomy." It is plain that the responsibility, whatever it may be, of the certain destruction of their old belief is very little relieved by the mere accompaniment of such religious instruction as this, which is, in the nature of the case, received by the Hindoo pupil at the time as so much mere historical or psychological information. Dr. Duff, who speaks of the general body of pupils whom the Government schools turns out as simply infidels, regards the unconverted mass which issues out of his own in a more sanguine light. "Many others (*i.e.* those who are not converted) do become *intellectually* Christians, and are therefore brought into a condition very much the same as that of the great bulk of intelligent Christians in this country, who are Christians in head or intellect, but not in heart." But is this more than a favourable mode of representing the same real result as that which takes place under the Government school system, viz., the production of a certain quantity of loose belief? And is not this difference between the unconverted of Dr. Duff's and the unconverted of the Government school, owing a great deal to the spectacles through which the two are seen? "Before I left Calcutta," says Sir Charles Trevelyan, "I had a list made of all the converts to Christianity from the educated class, and I found that at that time the majority of that class of converts, whose character, cultivation, and strength of mind offer the best assistance to Christianity, were from the Hindoo [Government] College;" while in point of number of conversions the evidence establishes a nearly equal result under both plans. Dr. Duff admits an improvement "in the working of the non-Christian system," which he attributes to the circumstance "that the young men brought up in the Government Colleges are coming more or less into contact with the other class of young men" who have been brought up "under Christian influence," *i.e.* in Dr. Duff's schools. The admission is valuable, as showing, at any rate, what we just now said, that the secular system of education in India is not to be judged of as if it was our only mode of approaching the Hindoo mind, but must be considered in connection with the existence of missionary efforts going on side by side with it.

The truth is, this responsibility, whatever it may be, must be faced in India, if we are to make anything of the Hindoo or of India; because the Hindoo must be *taught*. The missionary is in a position to teach him both physical truth and religion. The Government, not being in a position to teach him religion, is still under the obligation to teach him physical truth, because this is plainly something which he ought to know. He ought to know something about where he is, and what he is; something about this earth on which he stands, and the sun, moon, and stars above him; something about his own body, and something about the race of man to which he belongs. If you cannot go one step in this world of simple fact without demolishing his Shastras, that is not your fault; you have a right, and it is your duty, to teach him what he ought to know. The mere knowledge is proper for him; it is the knowledge of the Divine creation, of its system and laws, of the earth and its inhabitants; he is a child without this; it is what man as man ought to have: the call to give it him is imperative. We do not say that every individual Hindoo, any more than any individual Briton, ought to know geography or history, still less astronomy or anatomy; but the *society* ought to have the knowledge. The knowledge is also positively necessary for the improvement of the physical condition of the people, and for the development of the resources of India.

This responsibility being unavoidable, then, it is consolatory to know that it is not so hazardous a one as it is sometimes represented to be; that is to say, that even simple infidelity, should that unhappily be the result of new knowledge, is by no means a certain and clear disadvantage as compared with Hindoo faith. Infidelity takes its colour from the religion from which it is a departure: it is a clear loss as a departure from the true religion, but as a departure from a false and gross superstition it must be estimated differently. We hear of Hindoos becoming infidels, and we immediately connect them with all the associations of European infidelity, and put them on the same level with apostates from Christianity; but we should remember that they are infidels without being apostates. They have left a miserable religion, which taught false gods and bad morals: is there anything to lament simply in that fact? Certainly not: it might indeed be allowed that if, in abandoning a false religion, the unconverted Hindoo fell back upon simple atheism and a total rejection of the religious principle in every shape, in that case the exchange would be for the worse; because any religious tie, any hold upon the conscience, of however low a kind, is better than absolutely none. But does it at all follow that a man who abandons a false religion, even though he does not accept the true one, throws himself upon this extreme and desperate alternative? By no means: so far as he has gone he has done nothing to show such a disposition; he has simply acted according to the laws of reason and conscience; he has submitted to the plain evidence of facts, and given up a creed which did not stand the test of that evidence. The state of mind, then, out of which the change has come, being a reasonable and proper one, why should we suppose that the result should be desperate? It will be said, perhaps, that those who leave a false religion, and do not join the true, must gradually, even though they are not prepared for it at the time, fall into this desperate condition, simply from want of a religion to keep them up: but is it true that there is this absolute vacuum in the meantime—this complete absence of religion of any kind? A man who leaves a false religion upon proper grounds of evidence, not having done anything to blind his reason or conscience, naturally falls back, in the failure of his old religious ground, upon the evidences of natural religion, internal and external, contained in the material world around him and in his own conscience. He becomes what we call a Deist—only a Deist, we must remember, from being a believer in a false revelation, not from being a believer in the true one. Is natural religion in the place of Hindooism a change for the worse? We should be sorry to say that it was, especially as this very Hindooism is a corruption of natural religion. It will be said that this modern natural religion is not like the patriarchal which preceded revelation—that it stands aloof from revelation given. Doubtless there is a difference; but it may be inferior to patriarchal religion, and yet much superior to Hindooism. It must be remembered that the act of rejecting a false religion upon proper grounds leaves not only reason and conscience, but the principle of *faith* fundamentally existing in the character, no improper process having gone on in the mind to destroy it; and though there is doubtless a great defect in the use, exertion, and improvement of this natural faith, where it does not lead, as it ought to do, to the acceptance of the Gospel, it may still imply a real belief in important truths: for example, the existence of a God, a future life, and the essential distinction between virtue and vice; as being which and no more, without superstitious alloy, it may be not only equal, but much superior, to Hindooism.

And facts bear out this aspect of the case: the evidence decidedly preponderates on the side of the Hindoo being morally improved by the abandonment of his religion, even though he does not accept Christianity. "Those young men who received an English education," says Sir C. Trevelyan, "are notoriously more truthful than the natives in general.

Everybody who knows them will say so. In my time they were fervent admirers of truth and virtue in the abstract. Their moral state seems very similar to that of the most enlightened of ancient days." "As to moral principles, as to truth-telling," says Sir Erskine Perry, "they are far superior to the former class of officials that we had to deal with. I should say they are Deists, and sincere Deists too, many of them." Mr. Norton says that education "has greatly improved and elevated their moral feelings," and in particular thinks that "it has given a higher appreciation of the obligation of truth." Mr. Bird says, "they conduct themselves extremely well as public officers." Mr. Wilson distrusts the *intellectual* results of the English schools. "I do not think that they (the pupils) make such good reasoners that they would understand an argument or discussion, or would investigate the merits of a judicial case so well, or at anyrate not better than a pupil of the Madressa or Sanscrit College." But he has no doubt as to *moral* results : "I think that those who have been employed in the judicial departments as Sudder Amins, or as deputy collectors, are a better class of men, morally speaking, than we get from the native Colleges." Mr. Keane, the association secretary of the Church Missionary Society, after generalising strongly against secular education, is brought to the point by Lord Stanley of Alderley, and to the question, "Is it your opinion that education, unaccompanied with instruction in the truths of Christianity, is an unmixed evil to the natives of India?" answers, "No; because our English education is mixed with Christianity. You cannot wholly take Christianity out of an English education, and therefore there is a great deal of Christianity, though the Government pretend to say they teach none. I believe they teach a good deal; and it is that which gives us great encouragement with regard to the results of this system of English education in India." "As to truthfulness," says Dr. Duff, "there is no question that some of those who have acquired merely a secular education have shown a higher sense of honour in that respect."

Secular education, then, in India, while its infallible effect is disbelief in Hindooism, cannot, as an engine in the hands of

Christians, be for an instant compared with that policy which has been ascribed to the Jesuits, which instilled infidelity in order that the victim might in sheer despair take refuge in Rome. The Jesuit, in the supposed case, insinuates gratuitous doubts for the mere purpose of producing infidelity : we give a necessary knowledge which we are obliged, in simple consideration of the intellectual, moral, and physical welfare of the Hindoo, to give, which happens, without our seeking it, to involve this advantageous peril to his old faith. The Jesuit, again, risks the pupil's fall into monstrous error—such error as he himself would acknowledge to be much worse than his present one—for the chance of his pupil's attaining a higher truth. We risk no such fall, because here there is no common faith, but only a false religion to leave.

In this state of the case, then, we are furnished with an engine, which we have a full right to use, for the complete, however gradual, demolition of Hindooism—an engine of which, so far as it is brought into use and action at all, this is the natural inevitable working; and upon the demolition of Hindooism it stands to reason that Christianity must more or less succeed in its place. Whatever may be the time required for this education to penetrate into the enormous inert Hindoo mass, and whatever struggles may, in the meantime, arise between the educated and uneducated elements in that mass— struggles in which ignorant brute number may for a long time, we know not how long, completely prevail over the enlightened few—still the rule must work, that as education spreads Hindooism goes, and that in some large ratio, as one religion goes out, another must come in. " My first position," says Sir C. Trevelyan, " is, that even supposing them [the educated Hindoos] to remain in that middle state, still they are far superior to what they were; but they cannot remain in that state. The human being requires the comforts and hopes of a religion : he cannot do without them; and Hindoos are even less able to do without them than some Western nations that are made of a sterner and more self-relying stuff. These natives must have some religion : they cannot go back to Hindooism; they will not turn aside to Mahometanism; they must therefore go on to Christianity." Dr. Duff and the missionaries proclaim in the same way the important part which physical science is to play in the cause of Indian conversion—that Hindooism must be demolished by it sooner or later, and that Christianity must succeed Hindooism.

"The old story over again," we are prepared to hear some readers say; "you will create by this education a school of infidels, and will not be able to touch the ignorance of the mass, which will go on as devoutly Hindoo as ever." The history of modern Europe to a certain extent favours this picture, exhibiting as it does infidel sections that have thrown off the popular belief on the one side, and a superstitious untouched popular mass on the other. But there is a wide difference between the two cases. Romanism is in no collision with the plain common truths of material nature, nor is there anything to prevent the most educated scientific man from being a Romanist. But Hindooism is in direct collision with this class of truths, and is therefore exposed by a test which is intelligible to everybody. Admitting, then, that so long as education in India is confined to a small section, such section may remain mainly a school of Deists; its further advance, its spread over any fair amount of ground, must alter this sectional result. A group, a knot, a school, a section of men may be Deists, but no nation, no mass of men can be. The experiment of a Deistical nation was tried at the end of the last century in France, and quite broke down. Imagine, then, any considerable portion of the Hindoo population gaining in the same way that society does here—from school-books, or by a general understanding with its scientific section—a knowledge of the broad truths of nature, and consequently of the falsity of Hindooism, what becomes of it? Can we imagine a large Deistical population in India? We hardly can, such a fact is so wholly without precedent; and if we cannot do this, the only other reasonable alternative is the spread of Christianity.

We are, then, committed by our position in India to a course of policy which, without aiming at all directly at it, does in fact tend to a most important religious result. For we must educate the Hindoos. That is our clear duty, which we cannot avoid, if it is only because the physical and social improvement of the people, and the whole development of the resources of India, depend upon it. It is quite impossible that the handful of English in India can undertake to do all that is wanted in the way of drainage, irrigation, surveying, engineering, building, for the whole of India. Good medicine and surgery are one of the first requisites for physical welfare; we cannot undertake to physic the whole population, or set all the broken arms or legs of India. If all this work is to be done it must be by the natives themselves, taught by us—by native engineers, architects, surveyors, surgeons, all over India, standing after the first start upon their own basis, and handing on their professions to natural successors. But this domiciliation of modern science and the useful arts in India can only be brought about by extensive education. There is then, independently of all the claims of knowledge on its own account, a natural call for education in India in the physical and social wants of the people—a call which must both expand the area of education and also tighten the grasp of education upon the Hindoo mind. The complaint is now that the Hindoo does not keep up his knowledge after he has left school; but the same able witnesses—including Mr. Marshman, who observes this also—attribute the effect in a great degree to the want of that natural stimulus which professional occupation gives to sustaining knowledge. Give this stimulus, and education will keep up itself, and the physical wants of India, all agree, cry aloud for those lines of native professional employment which will supply this stimulus. "Would there be any difficulty," asks Lord Monteagle and Brandon, "in natives obtaining employment in India if they had acquired a practical knowledge of engineering, and were able to take levels, and lay out drainages, and assist in irrigation?" Mr. Norton replies, "They would be coveted on all sides; swarms of them would be employed." "It is impossible," says Sir C. Trevelyan, "to develop the resources of India unless we call the natives to our assistance; there is a very great demand for native engineers." "The demand for skilled and educated natives is increasing," says Dr. Wise; "they would be absorbed in the labour market of the country." Native youths have, at the instance of the late Mr. Thomason in the north-western provinces, and Colonel Napier in the Punjab, received an engineering education under English officers, and have been employed on the roads, bridges, canals, and surveys of those districts. When the experiment was first tried of a medical education, it was thought that the goat would have to furnish the only access to an Hindoo's knowledge of anatomy; but Dr. Chuckerbutty's degrees at our Colleges of Physicians and Surgeons are unanswerable tests of a larger acquaintance with the subject; and though Europeans cannot be brought to accept their services, we are informed that "natives have become good anatomists, expert surgeons, and sagacious practitioners, and that many of them are employed with great advantage in the large cities."

It will be said, perhaps, that all this is only professional education; but mere professional education must, as involving science, demolish Hindooism; and, moreover, you cannot separate one part of education from another. Here is a quantity of knowledge all got from a European source, it must bring in with it European ideas.

From the main subject of secular education in India we turn to a collateral question of policy connected with it. After much consideration we are not disposed to find great fault with the policy announced in Lord Stanley's reply to the deputation of the Religious Societies—that, viz., of Government not connecting itself at all with the missionary schools. Highly as we should appreciate the advantage of the grant-in-aid in itself, we doubt whether it would not be more than counterbalanced in the long-run by the difficulty which it might throw in the way of clear and secure relations between the English Government and the native population. We do not question the abstract right of the Government to give grants in aid to missionary schools, nor do we see that the support of a system of voluntary conversion would be any *aggression* upon the native religion, which is all that our understanding or compact with the native population binds us to refrain from. This is simply a question of expediency, but on this ground we incline to Lord Stanley's alternative.

Christianity is playing a long game in India, and for playing out this game the permanence of the English Empire is practically necessary. By "practically necessary" we do not mean to say that the Gospel could not possibly win its way in India without the shelter of our Government, but only that with the fall of our Government in India would be lost the principal apparent engine which Christianity has for the demolition of Hindooism. There would go that whole revolutionising movement which has been just described, which depends on British shelter for its advance; there would go civilised Europe's main access to the Hindoo. For this reason, then, the permanence of our empire in India is—short of points of conscience, which are not involved in the present question, which is only one of Christian expediency—our first consideration.

On the subject of the permanence of our Indian Empire we have two schools of Indian statesmen; one of these directly contemplates its termination, and regards us as only holding India for a time, however indefinite, till the natives are able to govern themselves; the other does not contemplate any termination of it. These two schools differ on two great practical questions bearing upon this important point of our stay in India. One of these is education. The former advocates zealously, upon the philanthropic ground, native education, and is prepared to take the consequence of it when it has raised the Hindoos to the self-governing level; the latter is jealous of modern education for the Hindoo, on the professed double ground of its inutility on account of his unfitness for it, and of its revolutionary tendency, as inflating him with empty conceit and disposing him to kick at our rule. Lord Ellenborough's letter of last April, and Sir George Clerk's memorandum, which he indorses, represent the opinions of this school on this point.

On this question then we differ, as our whole line of argument has shown, from what is called the old Indian school. The unfitness of the Hindoo for *modern*, i.e. *good* education, that instruction in natural and historical truth which is the inalienable heritage of the human mind, appearing to us a mere assumption, we do not see how, as rulers of India, we can possibly evade the plain duty of improving, as far as we can, both the intellectual and also the physical and social conditions of the Hindoo, for all which ends education is absolutely necessary. If we cannot develop the resources of the country without this instrument, that is in itself an imperative call for the use of it. The gravity and temperate tone of Lord Ellenborough's letter disguise his fundamental jealousy skilfully; but we cannot mistake the operation of such a rule as this—that "it ought to be made quite clear to the people that our Government does not desire to assist in the education of a single child not brought to the school with the full voluntary *unsolicited* consent of its parents." To throw upon the Hindoo the whole initiative in a process of which the issue can alone show the true value, would, to say the least of it, be a gratuitous shackle upon education in India, and one which would come rather unsuitably from us as the natural movers and originators in Indian improvement. And though we acquiesce in the principle that "education and civilisation should descend from the higher to the inferior classes," *i.e.* though we prefer this order of things abstractedly, we cannot but remark that Lord Ellenborough has himself introduced his recommendation "to diffuse education by endeavouring to give it to the higher classes *first*, by founding Colleges to which the higher classes alone would be admitted," with the preliminary information that "there is throughout India, especially *among the higher classes*, a strong prejudice in favour of *domestic* education." It would hardly be difficult to conjecture how school-education, confined expressly to classes who have the "strongest prejudice in favour of domestic education," would advance under the patronage of the rule which forbids all "solicitation" of the trial of the new plan. Philanthropy is too strong in this country to allow of such restrictions as these, and the necessities of the case require a broader use of the instrument of education, one not so much based upon rule, but left more to itself to work itself out as it can. We cannot expect to be able to conduct the great work of education in India exactly upon the principle which we should select in our own rooms upon any best plan or theory whatever; it will be a rough hand-to-hand work, done as it can be. But we cannot leave it undone, we must do it as circumstances enable us, and done anyhow it cannot fail of important results.

On another point of policy, however, which is discussed in connection with the question of the permanence of our Indian Empire, we cannot think so entirely with the Indian philanthropical school. What this point is will appear from three or four brief extracts from some quiet passages-at-arms between Lord Ellenborough and Sir Charles Trevelyan in the Lords' Committee on India.

"*Lord Ellenborough.*—Do you contemplate ultimately the almost entire suppression of Europeans in the judicial and revenue departments?

"*Sir C. Trevelyan.*—I conceive that will be the final result.

"*Lord Ellenborough.*—Would there not be another end at the same time? viz., the end of our dominion, or at least of the utility of it?"—Second Report, p. 146.

Again—

"*Sir C. Trevelyan.*—If the connection ceases according to the new system, we shall leave a grateful country, and a highly improved country.

"*Lord Ellenborough.*—Why should we ever leave it at all?"—P. 171.

Again—

"*Sir C. Trevelyan.*—Supposing the connection to cease, our trade with India would probably be more advantageous to us than our direct political connection.

"*Lord Ellenborough.*—Do you estimate as of no value the maintenance from the revenues of India of 6000 English gentlemen in situations of trust and great importance, and the maintenance of some 1500 more in this country upon the fruits of their services in the East, besides the maintenance of about 40,000 of our troops employed in that service?"—P. 172.

Again—

"*Sir C. Trevelyan.*—I will read a passage from Gibbon : 'When Alexander became master of the Persian empire, he early perceived that with all the power of his hereditary dominions . . . he could not hope to retain in his subjection territories so extensive and populous; that to render his authority secure and permanent . . . all distinctions between the victors and vanquished must be abolished,'" etc.

"*Lord Ellenborough.*—Is there any power in our Government to marry at once every officer above the rank of captain, and every civilian of two years' standing, to native ladies of great character and high birth, which was the policy adopted by Alexander?"— P. 174.

Regarding, as we do, the permanence of our Indian Empire simply in connection with the interests of Christianity, and as most important for those interests, we cannot wholly acquiesce in an administrative generosity which would thus entirely remove Europeans from the great official area of India. This substitution is doubtless only intended to take place when an educated class of natives has risen up large enough to afford a basis of selection, and therefore is still looked upon, even by its advocates, as comparatively distant; still a system of education, working under such a stimulus as this, might easily create an educated native class large enough for this purpose, long before the country at large had been at all penetrated by European knowledge; and we might thus be virtually abdicating before we had made the least impression upon the main body of Hindoos. The presence of some more English than the Governor-General and a group of principal officials is necessary to maintain English power in India. Bengal and Bahar alone employ 45,000 natives, receiving an aggregate salary of £572,000; how far we can safely continue our present comparative monopoly of the *higher* posts and salaries, without danger from native jealousy, is a question for Indian witnesses to settle. We may observe, however, that this substitution is put, in fact, more upon philanthropic than upon politic grounds; that as rulers of India we have the right to fill these offices, if we are ready to submit to the condition of expatriation appended to them; that the time must be incalculably distant when a large English official body will cease to be wanted for India; and that the interests of Christianity, so far as the course of events points out, evidently chime in with this arrangement, which is identical with a practical maintenance of English power.

It is on this ground, then, that we are inclined, on the whole, not to quarrel with Lord Stanley's decision. Of the permanence of our Indian Empire, secure relations between our Government and the native population are the first condition. When Government, then, can take the clear ground of saying that it has nothing to do with proselytising, is it worth while to disturb that ground, and with it those relations, for the advantage of a pecuniary grant? It must be remembered that these schools, however large a part of the education they give may be secular, are substantially proselytising schools, and that secular education is avowedly given there only as a bribe and a bait to catch the Hindoo for the purpose of conversion. However suitable such a policy, therefore, may be to the missionary, the school is, as a matter of fact, a proselytising school, and a Government grant to it makes the Government a virtual partner in a scheme of proselytising. Is the advantage of the grant worth the difficulty which it entails? That is the question. However narrowly jealous a guardian of our political interests in India, common sense goes with Lord Ellenborough when he says that "the apprehension of religious designs on the part of the Government must have had something to do with the late rebellion;" that "no cause of inferior power could have produced so great a revolution in the native mind." We have had enough of risk then; let us run no more risks than we can help; that is to say, let us not run one single risk more than our position as rulers of India imposes on us. A civilised Government is bound, as such, to improve the social and physical condition of the Hindoos; but not, as such, to proselytise. It is true, a religious issue, and an important one, attaches even to a physical and social movement in India; but this ultimate issue is not a very manageable weapon for the mutineer; as distant, it is not tangible enough for his alarmist cry,—as near, it shows a movement which has gone too far for him, and already won the intelligent and powerful classes over to its side. Such a movement, indeed, is self-protective, the issue may be foreseen by both sides, but it goes on by a law of its own, strong in human reason, and even in human selfishness; and the Brahman who is clear-headed enough to predict the result can only stand by as an idle prophet, unable to help himself, or to hinder the natural operation of the rule that man accepts his own physical good when it is offered him.[1]

We cannot conclude a sketch of the prospects of Christianity in India without a slight notice of that iron institution which has upset the faith of so many in the possibility of Hindoo conversion—the formidable institution of caste. It is now (1859) just fifty years since Sydney Smith, in the *Edinburgh Review*, thus described the operation of caste—

"Another reason *for giving up the task of conversion* [in India] is want of success. . . . If a Hindoo is irreligious, or, in other words, if he loses his caste, he is deserted by father, mother, wife, child, and kindred, and becomes instantly a solitary wanderer upon the earth. . . . We do not say it is difficult to convert the Japanese or the Chinese, but the Hindoos. We are not saying it is difficult to convert human creatures, but difficult to convert human creatures with *such institutions.*"

Since this description of caste as an impregnable bulwark of Satan, against which the Divine purposes in vain rage and swell, the monster institution has receded just enough at least to swear to. A glacier-like movement is perceptible in it at the end of half a century. It is an ascertained fact that it gives way to pressure from events, that it cannot resist the strong claims of obvious matter-of-fact convenience as new improvements from time to time try its hold. Brahmans now wear leather shoes, and travel in company with outcasts by railway; anatomy is found necessary for the science of human health, and the Brahman dissects the human body to make himself a medical man. We doubt the success of the plan of putting down caste by a vernacular translation of the Rig-Veda, showing the Hindoos its total omission there, and so the want of the highest scriptural authority even of Brahmanism

[1] Mr. Badger, whose missionary zeal and experience none will deny, accepts Lord Stanley's ground. "I do not see that as Christians we ought to require that Government should depart from the line of policy marked out by his Lordship. If our missionary efforts are not hindered by any State enactments—if we are free to propose Christianity to the acceptance of the natives of India—it is all that we can in fairness demand."

itself for it; we doubt it, because the Brahman's gloss would, in all human likelihood, be ten times more powerful than the naked text, backed as it would be by the whole force of tradition, custom, and subsequent inspiration, which would overwhelm the Vedas not less than the same weight overwhelms the Bible now in Romanist countries; while the set-off of a Hindoo "Reformation" would be evidence of more life and spring than we can attribute to a false religion; but we do not the less value the explanation which the acute Orientalist in the *Times* gives of the institution of caste itself. The ground on which caste arises is a natural one.

"Men who have the same interests, the same occupations, the same principles, unite in self-defence, and, after acquiring power and influence, they not only defend their rights, but claim important privileges. They naturally impose upon their members certain rules, which are considered to be the interest of their caste or company."

Caste is thus in substance the organisation of society according to professional distinctions, and rises up on the principle of our own associations, circles, leagues, guilds, and clubs; but it adds to this principle that of hereditary membership, and that of a Divine sanction, making it a religious as well as a social institution. While, then, everybody who leaves an hereditary faith must expect social persecution in some shape or other, the result of caste is, that this persecution assumes an extraordinarily compact and penetrating form; that it is systematic, iron, and inexorable; and that the convert, only having belonged to the whole community by the medium of a caste, finds himself, on his exclusion from the section, an outcast from the community. But taking, as we do here, the ground of ultimate issues, we need only remark that, as far as we know, no intimidation has been ultimately able to exclude truth from any human society or nation. The force of truth then is, in its own nature, stronger than caste, which must again constantly tend to decrease under the rule of a civilising power, that both weakens the old institutions, and raises a counter one in the shape of new circles and connections for the converts.

It only remains now to revert to the original point of view from which we started, and which we have used throughout this article as subsidiary to the great fundamental ground of Scripture prophecy. Politicians and practical men, as such, only recognise that ground of prophecy which is contained in present visible growth, and the ascertained strength of causes in actual operation, and in that ground Indian conversion is weak. But there is another ground, a real ground of prophecy, contained in the fundamental type of human nature. Is the Hindoo a *man*, veritable and complete, as ourselves? If he is not, then scriptural prophecy has no responsibility about him; it is nowhere prophesied that the Gospel will spread either among the beasts of the field, the fowls of the air, or the fishes of the sea, or in any ambiguous and indescribable genus of beings, but only in the race of man. But if the Hindoo *is* a man, then there is an ultimate certain appeal to the fundamental type on which he is fashioned. The normal idea of worship, the normal idea of immortality, normal morality, physical truth, must, at some time or other, receive his recognition. Consider the aspect in which the world's future would present itself to the mind of one of the old prophets. One small people alone maintained the worship of one God, amidst universal polytheism. Great empires, strong hierarchies, deep philosophies, venerable creeds—all that was imposing and monumental in the world, the whole array of the sage-like, were on one side. Yet with these overwhelming facts before him the prophet announced the certain future, universal spread of the true idea of worship. On what ground did he justify to himself this prediction? Doubtless he had a witness in his own breast to an extraordinary gift of prophecy, but he had also a ground of reason backing up that gift. What was it? Was it not that he saw that the worship of one God answered to the type of religion in the human mind; that that was the normal idea of worship, and that the reasonable spirit in man ratified and enforced it? He appealed, then, to that type, to that idea, to that reason in man: he saw that the polytheism of the world could be no more than a temporary fashion, and must pass away like an excrescence before the great archetypal creed : he saw that solid strength in human nature which must one day vindicate itself, the root of the matter there which must ultimately show life. The whole page of prophecy witnesses to this ground in the prophet's mind, being, as it is, one strong appeal throughout to human reason, awakening it to consciousness, and shaming it to self-vindication by every argument which a holy scorn could apply to an unreasonable worship. The Jewish prophet nearly three thousand years ago committed himself to this prediction : the prophecy is before us, and the fulfilment of the prophecy : the whole civilised world now worships his One God ! We are only using, then, now, the very same ground of prophecy upon which he, in his simply reasonable character, went ; and with the advantage of seeing a vast and overwhelming fulfilment of that prophecy which he did not.

The strength of Brahmanism, we are told, lies in its philosophy : were it only a rude superstition, Christianity would obtain an easy victory over it ; but its deep and subtle refinements are more than a match for us. But if the religious history of the world teaches any one lesson clearly, it is this : that the great practical ideas and instincts of religion in human nature are too strong for the philosophical ones, and beat them fairly in the encounter. Philosophy is strong as a *check* upon religious ideas, and we thankfully acknowledge the benefit of that check in our own days, amidst religious leaders and partisans, who, with the best intentions, certainly want it. But it is not the function of philosophy to *originate* in religion : strong as a *critic,* and useful with its *veto,* it makes a *foundation* of sand. As a foundation it tried its strength against Christianity eighteen centuries ago. Christianity adopts and dignifies the natural ideas of God—those practical instincts by which we regard the Maker of the universe as an object of worship, a Being who interests Himself in our welfare, temporal and spiritual, and answers prayer ; and standing upon this basis it came into collision with the great classical philosophies. What was the result, then, of that encounter ? Where are now all those great philosophies which acknowledged a Supreme God, but assigned Him a nature too pure and sublime for worship, that raised Him above the poor regards of man?—the Alexandrian philosophy that set up a genuine Brahmanical and Buddhist deity, too pure to possess even intellect?—all those great contemplative systems, with their abstract deities—where are they? Swept away like cobwebs. An idea of God which any one of these philosophers would have treated as the rude conception of a savage—akin to the warring and hunting god of the Scandinavian—the idea of a *negotiosus Deus,* full of human sympathies, busying Himself in human affairs, and interposing for human relief and punishment—in a word, the idea of a personal God who is an object of worship has supplanted them all. So the idea of personal immortality has supplanted that of an absorption into the Deity, which was taught in these systems: the practical instinct has ousted the doctrine of philosophy, that notion of eternal life which men form by speculation. Looking, then, to the contest with Brahmanism, we find, in fact, that every step of the ground has been gone over before. We are told that this is a totally new kind of conquest for Christianity, but it is not; it is only the carrying out of an existing conquest.

It is a striking reflection that civilisation does not adopt these philosophical ideas of the Deity: some have attributed to it that tendency, but as a matter of fact the civilised European's idea of God is far more simple, primitive, and childlike than that of the barbarous Brahman. Civilisation is a happy compound: as the nurse of the human mind generally, and the fosterer of all its powers, it has encouraged metaphysical philosophy; on the other hand, it has been pre-eminently a practical movement, promoting natural science, discovery, trade, and the social arts. Indeed, Bacon decidedly discouraged theological speculation or metaphysics; and had the movement obeyed his sole direction, it might have become something like Confucianism; but it has had more than one master. Civilisation has thus invested with authority, and given a compactness and system to the ideas of practical men; and this standard of public opinion keeps not only dogmatism but philosophy also in check. The practical religious instincts of human nature are protected by it against the invading force of speculation. The Brahmans and the Schoolmen are both, in their respective ways, examples of the extravagant lengths to which human thought will go, when men get together and sit by themselves spinning their own webs, without any external check upon them. But the advance of civilisation erects an external control and an authoritative standard of common sense. Speculators of the sceptical school are apt to think that, though their ideas are not accepted now, as the world advances they will be; but they mistake the nature of civilisation in this respect.

On grounds of reason then, and apart from the argument of Scripture prophecy, a certain mode of speaking of the conversion of India, as if it were a simple impossibility, is a mistake. Where does this impossibility lie? Is it that the *race* is unfitted for Christianity? The Hindoo is a *man*: nay, the scientific linguist informs us that he is a member of the same branch of the human race with ourselves.[1] Is it in the philosophy of Brahmanism? The Gospel has conquered philosophy. Is it in philosophy and superstition combined? That was the very combination which encountered Christianity on its first start, and was surmounted. Is it in caste? Caste can do no more than intimidate, and that is no new thing.

It is true that we cannot picture to ourselves with anything like accuracy the slow operation of great causes upon so large a scale as this. We cannot pretend to describe how so vast and long a process as that of Indian conversion will take place, and any prophetical picture must be a daub: still we know that where great causes are at work an issue is managed somehow,

[1] Mr. Dasent says: "They (the Hindoos) have been still the same immovable and unprogressive philosophers, though akin to Europe all the while; and though the Highlander who drives his bayonet through the heart of a high-caste Sepoy mutineer, little knows that his pale face and sandy hair, and that dark face with his raven locks, both came from a common ancestor away in Central Asia, many, many centuries ago. . . . We all came, Greek, Latin, Celt, Teuton, Slavonian, from the East, as kith and kin, leaving kith and kin behind us; and after thousands of years, the language and traditions of those who went east and those who went west bear such an affinity to each other, as to have established beyond discussion or dispute the fact of their descent from a common stock."—Introduction to *Popular Tales from the Norse*, pp. 19-22.

and that by steps which look, one by one, no more than natural and common at the time. What a prophecy would the formation of language have been at the beginning of the world! What genius of detail could have approached to the faintest conception of the grand slowness and minuteness of the actual process, of which that was the miraculous issue? Who could have pictured the multitudinous labyrinthal growth of inflexions, genders, tenses, parts of speech, governments, constructions, the creation of words, the incorporation of metaphor? What a prophecy would the civilisation of the world have been? What a prophecy would the growth of any art have been? What a prophecy would civil government have been? From the extreme confines of the middle ages the prophet of science, two centuries and a half ago, saw the dim outline of a great approaching manifestation of nature. Nothing, we may say, as yet had been done; but Bacon had a basis of prophecy in nature and in man as they presented themselves to him.

Such a basis of calculation does not hurry us. Prophecy, like geology, requires time, and there is no reason why it should not have it. There are many who *live* in time who do not *believe* in time. They have no adequate conception of time in their minds, of the room and space in it for courses of events, or even for the ordinary evolution of any plan of action. Give them any matter of business to manage, and their idea is either to do it at one stroke, or to put it off altogether: in either case there is a most inadequate idea of time, as if it were a simple point which gave no alternative between an absolute cram of action and a total absence of it. An animal instinct sustains the idea of indefinite duration, passively and for purposes of pleasurable sensation; but those whom we have spoken of do not fairly embrace it for purposes of rational action. But there are those whose mode of conception does not do injustice to time; who have an image of it as true room for the evolution of action, with self-extending stages and successive lengths ever projecting themselves into the unknown, long suites of apartments for the procession of events and gradual development of schemes; their inner eye looks down the lengthening vista of folding-doors which disclose in metaphysical state one after another the telescopic chambers of time. This adequate conception of time is one characteristic of a statesman's mind, which gives him so great an advantage over ordinary men in the arena of public life; he possesses the first preliminary to effective and successful action, a true belief in that which *holds* and *contains* action, in a real field of *time*, in which plans can germinate and grow; while others, for want of this preliminary conviction, do not dare to form such plans, but act from moment to moment. These ideal extensions and prolongations of time in the mind of the man of action, answer to the original spaces and measures in the mind of the orator; those great primordial rhythms, those blank clauses and climaxes, which pre-exist in his brain, like vacant bars of music, before he fills them up with words; and represent the mute passion of rhetoric, before they support, as a framework, its expression. Would an orator unlock, he would tell us how these spiritual embryos and unembodied forms of speech rose up like majestic phantoms before him upon the occurrence of great exciting questions; and inspired him for the public effort. Let us form our calculation of the probable issue of the agencies now at work in the world, and especially upon the Indian field, with the full understanding that we have time before us. No reflecting person can avoid, whether he takes a religious ground or not, the conviction that the world's future is a striking and wonderful one; we feel morally certain that were it revealed to us now, it would be inconceivably astonishing; we know that mighty changes must be in store; that things have been on the move since the beginning, and that they will continue to move after we are gone; we know, therefore, in general, that there must be some ultimate stupendous climax of such accumulated motion; we know that the future of prophecy is not at all more surprising than some or other result which must take place, and we can repose without distrust in the strength of those deep causes which point to the ultimate overthrow of all false religions, and the substitution of Christianity in their place.

THE ARGUMENT OF DESIGN.*

(July 1869.)

It may seem extraordinary, after the Argument of Design in Nature has been discussed in the world for two thousand years, that we who accept and uphold it should have to explain what we mean by the Argument of Design; but such curious descriptions are given of it in some quarters, and we are saddled with such unintelligible and preposterous conclusions in maintaining it, that this preliminary step becomes necessary. A plain man lately, on turning over the pages of the "Fortnightly," would have been somewhat astonished to find that, as a believer in the evidences of design in Nature, he necessarily held one or other of some half-dozen singular theories, of not one of which he had ever even heard the name. He was asked, "Do you hold the Aristotelian theory of Potential Existence? Do you hold the theory of Preformation? Do you hold the theory of *emboîtement?*" And if he said that he had never heard of the existence of any of these theories, another heading was still reserved for him, "You are certainly an anthropomorphist." He had in his simplicity thought that facts were his strong point; but the tables are completely turned upon him on that head, and he is asked summarily to apologise for gratuitous speculation, for holding a capricious, arbitrary, and wanton hypothesis, a rationale wholly *in nubibus,* and concocted out of his own head in contempt of facts. A bold surprise at a belief is sometimes the best argument against it; the imagination is affected by it, and for a moment weak

* 1. *Mr. Darwin's Hypotheses.* By George Henry Lewes. The "Fortnightly Review," April, June, July 1868.
  2. *Le Matérialisme Contemporain.* Par Paul Janet, Membre de l'Institut.

Nature really thinks it must have made a great mistake. We shall, however, resist the impulse, and, considering the mistake to be on the other side, call attention to the real basis of the Argument of Design.

The Argument of Design is, that there is a certain construction which the facts of Nature of themselves call for and necessitate, not admitting of any other—the construction, viz., of design which attaches to visible arrangement, system, and adaptation. This construction, we say, *adheres to the facts*, is cemented to them, and cannot be separated from them. That is our position. Look into the inside of an animal body. Is it not, as a matter of fact, a machine? Yes, the apparatus of organs, pipes, vessels, is simple *fact;* design is the construction, which, we say, cleaves to that fact. We have not gone to the clouds, then, for design; we have not invented the notion; we have not coined it; it has not been spun out of our brain; it has come *to* us out of plain, solid, external, material, tangible facts. It is stamped upon those facts. We have not sought it by speculation, but outward Nature has forced it upon us. We have not first conceived the idea independently of Nature, and Nature got the impress from our fancy, but the idea has been got out of Nature in the first instance, and we are only the recipients of it. People would draw us aside from this position, and ask a number of irrelevant questions, which we shall deal with further on. "Who is the Designer?" they ask; "what is the nature of His mind? You must settle as to the designer before you assert design." But we say, No; the construction adheres to the phenomena. Were we obliged to discover all about our designer before we asserted design, there would be an end of the Argument of Design. But we say we are not obliged to find out that, because reason attaches the conclusion of design straight to the *facts*—the facts of concurrence, system, mechanism; to certain combinations and juxtapositions of matter. By the constitution of our minds, and by the laws of thought, we cannot but construe facts as we do construe them; interpret plain and palpable mechanism as indicating intention and purpose.

How do we argue in the case of—what is not indeed

exactly the same with, but has something in common with, the idea of design—Law, physical law? The idea of Law, while an indistinct idea of the mind, is at the same time a most simple one; it is the idea of something which *makes* something else to occur, as distinguished from that something happening by chance. What we mean by this making something else to happen, a *cause* of its happening, we do not know; the idea is lodged amid the obscure foundations of our intellectual system, from which it never will be extricated. The evidence or *criterion*, however, of "law" is very plain—simple recurrence; the same fact being repeated again! Upon what argument, then, does this criterion of law depend? Have we any demonstration that because an occurrence in Nature happens again and again, it happens by law? None. It might occur two or three times by chance. Why then, when it goes on occurring, does it occur by law? A man throws double-six once. It is a chance. He throws them again. It still might be a chance. He throws them a third time. Still we would not say for a positive certainty that it could not be by chance. But if he threw them fifty times running, we should then be certain that it could not be by chance. We should be sure that it was by *law*. He might at each throw say, "It is true I have thrown double-six so many times, but why should that prevent me throwing it again this time? Chance is still free; it is not bound by the past; there is no physical obstruction, there is no mathematical obstruction to the throw. It may therefore be thrown again, and thrown by chance this very next time." This argument might be repeated at every throw, but a practical principle in our nature would still decide, and decide beyond all manner of doubt, that, if double-six were thrown fifty times running, they were not thrown by chance, but by law; *i.e.* that there was something which *made* the throw thus to recur and be repeated. It would, however, be a practical principle within our minds which ruled this question, and not a mathematical or demonstrative one. The matter is thus decided in the case of Law, and the same decision applies to the case of *design* so far as this, that it is a practical principle within us that decides that too. The disposition, the arrangement of certain particles of matter, is no demonstration. But when there is manifold coincidence and adaptation to an end, we say it is morally impossible that such machinery should not be by design; just as we say that, where there is uniform recurrence, it is morally impossible that such repetition should not be by law.

In the Argument of Design, however, the *end* is the great consideration which appeals to the reason, and demands the verdict that such work is by design. There must be a distinct perception of an end—something which all this machinery is for, and without which, indeed, this machinery is not machinery at all, but an unmeaning labyrinth of parts, such as an intricate engine looks to a man who does not understand it. It is this end beyond the machinery, but at once the complement and interpretation of it, which makes design. Blind material law can produce form and figure, curves and angles, which superficially simulate design, and have the look to the eye of having been moulded artificially. Crystallisation makes squares and pyramids, and gravitation with propulsion, circles and ellipses. But crystallisation is not mechanism, because there is no *end* connected with it; its squares and pyramids end with themselves, and there is nothing beyond their squareness and conicalness. In design, on the other hand, there is an end which the mechanism accomplishes, out of and beyond the mechanism itself.

And here we come to a consideration of the utmost possible importance in the structure of the Argument of Design. There is wanted undoubtedly for the full and perfect establishment of the argument, for its completion and clear hold of our convictions, the admission of a spiritual principle; because nothing but this spiritual principle can give us that strong pointed and masterly *end* of the physical apparatus, which our reason wants in order to crown that apparatus with design. There are approaches to an end indeed before we come to a spiritual principle, but they do not satisfy the mind to the extent which is required for a full and penetrating proof of an intelligent designer. The machinery of a plant or tree has in a sense an end attaching to it, which is the growth of that plant or tree;

but how can a mere vegetable life satisfy the mind as an *end* ? It cannot; for there is no importance whatever in such an end. It cannot signify in the slightest degree to the vegetable whether it exists or not; the plant terminates with its own material structure, and possesses no self or soul, or sentient being which benefits by that structure, *i.e.* exists in consequence of it. The vegetable is only endowed with a transposed end, coming up across the great chasm and division of Nature, in the animal kingdom; where it presents itself to us in the shape of animal nutrition. The plant assumes the existence of another nature, viz., the animal, in order to be invested with an end. In moving a step upward, however, we find that the animal apparatus is connected with a direct concomitant end in the life of a sentient being who benefits and exists by it, who is capable of pleasure and satisfaction in some or other degree, and whose existence is therefore of consequence to itself. But in the brutes, though even these exhibit an ascending scale, the end is so much on a level with the machinery, the life is to so large an extent *one with* the material frame, simply consisting in the enjoyment or use of it; there is so little individuality in the existence of the brute, that the end is not satisfying. It is only when we come to man, that an end in immediate connection with an animal machinery shines forth with such overpowering intrinsic evidence, and stands out in so conspicuous and irresistible a light, that the completing stroke and finish is given to the evidence of design. In man the end is so distinctly superior to the machine, the end is so clearly beyond the machine, that the argument strikes home.

What indeed can be more utterly different from, more *not* akin to an apparatus of flesh and bones, than a self-conscious human existence, with conscience, will, sense of moral obligation? The heterogeneousness is startling. When I think of myself, the conviction that *I* am a different being from any part, or the whole, of my solid material frame, forces itself upon me with an overpowering weight which I cannot resist; I cannot think of any single organ, of any one sense, or of all of them together, as being myself. My consciousness, my understanding, my will, everything that comes under that great head of *I*, constitute a spiritual unity which does not touch, which is divided whole worlds from, my corporate structure. I know, I perceive, that *I* and *matter* are distinct ideas. Can we conceive any greater and more absolute diversity than that between a personal consciousness involving the highest moral, the subtlest intellectual, perceptions on the one hand, and a structure of organs, stomach, heart, liver, muscles, tendons, sinews, arteries, veins, on the other? There is something in the junction of two such dissimilarities which, if we could represent it in any visible mode, and imagine ourselves meeting it amid the curiosities of productive power, would strike us as an enormous and prodigious freak of Nature; they have so utterly nothing to do with one another. But in proportion to the strangeness of the juxtaposition,—the heterogeneousness of the end of the bodily apparatus, as compared with the apparatus itself,—is the absolute distinctness and pointedness of that end; the certainty that this corporate machinery has a positive scope and purpose fulfilled in that end. The greater the moral interval between the instrument and the result, the more pronounced is design in that instrument. Can anything exceed the conviction with which any man, when he really thinks of himself, and thinks of his body, must say, This body exists for the sake of *me:* I am its end, all this machinery is nothing without myself as an explanation? A man cannot rid himself of this sense of the object of his own body, that it is for the sake of *him*—that personal self of which he is conscious: the purpose clings to the machine and cannot be parted from it. And therefore, inasmuch as *he* is a different thing from the machine, he sees distinctly that this machine exists for an end *beyond* itself, which is the coping-stone of the Argument of Design.

And hence the necessity, as we said above, of the admission of a spiritual principle in Nature, in order to the just completion and finish of the Argument of Design. A speculator who has forced himself to think—if, indeed, it is possible that he can think—that the personal being is the same identical fact with, and not a different fact from, his bodily apparatus—that matter and I are *not* distinct ideas—such a philosopher discards that end of the machine beyond the machine itself, which completes the Argument of Design; because the personal being, whom *we* call the end of the machine, is with him the same with the machine itself. And therefore the recognition of a difference between the two ideas of "matter" and "I," or an admission of a spiritual principle, is a postulate in the Argument of Design which must precede the full stroke of that argument.

One observation, which we will make in passing, bears upon this subject. Two great representatives of science concur in the refusal to assert the existence of a soul.[1] The position which Professor Owen and Professor Huxley have taken is an equal and impartial certainty of matter and spirit as impressions, and an equal and impartial uncertainty of them as substances or real things. This formula of parallelism is not a just representation of the fact of consciousness. My own substance, *i.e.* I myself, stands in a relation to my consciousness, in which the substratum of an outward object does not stand. *Cogito ergo sum* is an argument which I can apply to

---

[1] Philosophy, according to Mr. Owen, does not recognise "an immaterial entity, mental principle, or soul." "Matter and spirit," says Mr. Huxley, "are both names for imaginary substrata of groups of natural phenomena." The latter thinks the asserter of a spiritual principle or soul in man is placed in a peculiar difficulty by the discovery of "protoplasm." We do not see the difficulty. We do not understand why a common "physical basis and matter of life" with the vegetable, contradicts the existence of a soul in man, any more than does a community of the same with brutes; or why protoplasm is more materialistic than flesh. Whatever be the common matter in the three orders of beings, there are characteristic differences which distinguish them; and what is common cannot account for what is different. Man is an animal on the old hypothesis; he is fundamentally a vegetable upon the new; but if his animal nature did not preclude the existence in him of a rational soul, why should this be precluded by his vegetable nature? The greater the identity of the physical basis in all three orders, the less its capacity of accounting for the differences between them. If man has what the brute has not, and the brute has what the vegetable has not, there is something which enters in as cause here which is not protoplasm, which *all* have. But Mr. Huxley asserts that thought is the effect of protoplasm; while at the same time protoplasm exists without thought:—a position which violates the very grammar of induction, and the first rule of that grammar, viz., that the cause of a fact must not only always precede it when it does take place, but always omit this precedence when it does not.

myself; but I cannot apply it to a cabbage, nor can the cabbage apply it to itself. Mr. Huxley objects to "systematic materialism," or the dogmatic position of the non-existence of soul, as not only unphilosophical, but practically injurious—what "may paralyse the energies and destroy the beauty of a life." But if the denial of the individual that he has a soul is injurious to him, the systematic doubt whether he has a soul or not cannot be advantageous. A man must first believe that he exists, before he thinks it a matter of vital importance that he should be good. If we take those glorious and immortal men whose words and acts have renovated and converted mankind, the fount whence their goodness proceeded was the conviction that they themselves had souls. They felt, to begin with, that they had a substantial being; this certainty invested all their actions with an infinite and eternal importance to themselves, and this vital interest in them brought out their whole power. But without that first conviction they would have been paralysed.

It follows, then, that Man is the great disclosure of design in Nature; that man lets out the great secret of the authorship of Nature; and that man is the revelation of a God in Nature. In him a corporate structure is *for* a distinct personality—man himself. A final cause is declared in Nature, and the interpretation is pronounced. Had we to stop with the plant, the interpretation of Nature would be defective, because there is no end which satisfies the mind in connection with the plant itself, and her constructive power might have been explained as an intricate working of mere material law—a mechanical art or *solertia*, such as the ancient Hylozoists and Kosmoplastic philosophers attributed to her. But man as an instance of design differs widely from a plant as an instance of the same; here is the immediate contiguity of a decisive end—viz., man himself. Does not the great argument of Paley derive its real pungency from the reader having always, consciously or unconsciously, *man* in his mind in connection with the machinery of Nature? In the description of the eye, he thinks of man, of himself, who sees. The complex operations are conducted to a satisfactory terminus, and he is penetrated with the proof of design, because he has, directly or indirectly, this pronounced end of design before him.

And here one thing may be noted. There appears to be an inexorable law, some deep necessity in Nature, which demands that a subtle and intricate animal machinery should always accompany the higher forms of animal life; so that that life cannot be produced without these complex mechanical means and conditions. We do not know the rationale of this law, or why such higher animal existence cannot be possessed without the adjunct of this elaboration and artifice; nor is it a law which keeps step with the ascent in the scale of life; it includes man, but does not coincide with man. Still, why is it so? Our own consciousness of life is not in the least connected with the idea of mechanism or contrivance; we *feel* life, we think, we move, we are what we are, without the slightest inward thought of a subtle apparatus which is necessary for this result. Nay, we had a great deal rather—but that these were imperative conditions of being alive—be without all these details; so far from wanting to feel the manifold organisation by which we live, the more unconscious we are of it the better; anything that reminds us of its existence annoys us; we wish it away; *not* to know by sensation any part of this intricate machinery would be a happy, a truly paradisal privilege; and there are, fortunately for some favoured sons of Nature, blissful states of health in the world, which almost attain this spiritual climax. Some men live till they are fifty without being the least aware by inward feeling that they have a heart, liver, or stomach, trachea, arteries, or nerves. Their physical perfection almost emulates an ethereal existence; so little experience have they of the struggle with matter, and the inward entanglements of a physical frame. A perfectly healthy child is thus almost in his feelings a spirit; he *sees* he has a body, but, beyond that fact, all is a volatile essential life, consisting of motion, joy, love, anger, exultation; effervescences of the vital spirits which might belong to aerial natures, and show no contact with a disquieting or depressing frame. As far as the conscious sensation of life is concerned, then, we might have bodies as simple as crystals in their formation, or almost, we might say, no bodies at all. But, as a matter of fact, the complexer mechanism is the means to, and condition of, the higher animal life; and this law of Nature is accompanied by this valuable result—that we are surrounded on every side by *proofs* of design, which otherwise we should be without. The intricacy of our bodily structure is at once our trial and our lesson, both of which objects fit into each other, and harmonise with the purpose and end of life.

Now, then, to revert to the position which we have laid down with respect to the evidence of design, viz., that it is a construction which adheres to the *facts* of arrangement, system, and machinery in nature, and comes out of those facts themselves. If we keep this fundamental point of view clearly in our minds, we have in it at once an answer to sundry objections to the Argument of Design.

Let us take first the objection of the unmeaning and incongruous insertions in Nature : its eccentricities, its superfluities, its abnormal appendages. This is in essence a Manichæan objection, but it has assumed lately a more scientific shape, and been equipped with fresh weapons and a more exact bill of accusation by recent anatomical discovery. This has brought to light a number of what are called "rudimental organs" in different animals : organs which never come out of a rudimental state, and are therefore without known purpose—alien interpolations in the structure, whether remaining in it or passing away from it.[1] We need hardly refer to a well-known list of "atrophied or aborted organs," which Mr. Darwin gives as a sample, asserting the fact to be "extremely common throughout Nature :" " the rudimentary mammæ, very general in the males of mammals ;" the " bastard wing" of birds, which " may be safely considered to be a rudimental digit ;" the rudimentary lobe of the lungs in snakes ; the rudimentary pelvis and hind limbs in snakes ; the teeth in fœtal whales, " which when

---

[1] "A very strong case has been made out by Mr. Paget, in his Hunterian Lectures at the College of Surgeons, in favour of the rudimental development of organs being necessary to withdraw from the blood some element of nutrition, which, if retained in it, would be positively injurious, like a retained excretion."—" MS. Notes of a Physiologist," in *Vestiges of Natural History of Creation.*

grown up have not a tooth in their heads;" the teeth in the upper jaws of unborn calves, which never cut through the gums; the rudimentary teeth which can, it is stated by some, be detected in the beaks of certain embryonic birds; the reduced wings of many insects, lying soldered together under cases; the rudimentary wings in some beetles; the rudimentary pistils in plants.

Recent investigation into the embryonic stage of animal life has enlarged the stock of anomalies in Nature. Mr. Lewes, after deciding that "rudimentary organs are perhaps the strongest case against Final Causes," carries the inquiry into this department:—

"What rational interpretation," he asks, "(on the hypothesis of a creative plan,) can be given to the succession of phases each embryo is forced to pass through? He will observe that *none* of these phases have any adaptation to the future state of the animal, but are in positive contradiction to it, or are simply purposeless; many of them have no adaptation even to its embryonic state. What does the fact imply? There is not a single known organism which is not developed out of simpler forms. Before it can attain the complex structure which distinguishes it, there must be an evolution of forms, which distinguish the structures of organisms lower in the series. On the hypothesis of a plan which pre-arranged the organic world, nothing could be more unworthy of a Supreme Intelligence than this inability to construct an organism at once, without previously making several tentative efforts, undoing to-day what was so carefully done yesterday, and repeating for centuries the same tentatives, and the same corrections in the same succession. Do not let us blink this consideration. There is a traditional phrase which is in vogue among anthropomorphists —a phrase which has become a sort of argument—'the Great Architect.' But if we are to admit the human point of view, a glance at the facts of embryology must produce very uncomfortable reflections. For what shall we say to an architect who was unable, or being able was obstinately unwilling, to erect a palace except by first using his materials in the shape of a hut, then pulling them down and re-building them as a cottage, then adding story to story and room to room, *not* with any reference to the ultimate purposes of a palace, but wholly with reference to the way in which houses were conducted in ancient times? Would there be a chorus of applause from the Institute of Architects, and 'favourable notices in the newspapers' of this profound wisdom? Yet this is the sort of succession on which organisms are constructed. The fact has long been familiar; how has it been reconciled with Infinite wisdom?"

Mr. Lewes then objects to the existence of Design in Nature, upon the ground of certain irregularities in Nature: but if design adheres to the facts of adjustment, arrangement, machinery, and these facts are seen, what avails it to bring forward instances of *want* of adjustment, want of arrangement, defect of machinery in Nature?—the affirmative facts decide here, not the negative. The question is, Can you tear from those facts of arrangement which do exist the construction that cleaves to them, and that is united to them by the laws of thought? If you cannot, design adheres to those facts, and no want of the same argument from *other* facts can cancel the conclusion from *those*. The discordances, the abortive insertions in Nature, in a word, those parts of Nature which are *not* evidences of design, may fairly come in in a further stage of the argument, when we have to deal with the attributes or with the conditions of the Designer; but upon the primary question of the existence of design in Nature, such objections are, in the very nature of the case, inoperative. The positive evidence of design determines the conclusion; no negative facts can undo the effect of the positive; they have no contradictory function. No exceptional outbreak of the apparent undesigned can disprove the result which is drawn from the apparently designed. Because, whatever may be the case with the other facts, these facts must be accounted for; and this is the only way of accounting for them.

Let, *e.g.*, Mr. Lewes describe as he will the subtle transitions of the embryonic stage of life—let him call them the corrections and retractations of Nature, alterations of her plan, successive adoptions at first of types which are afterwards cast aside—in what way can this enigmatical side of the introductory stage of life interfere with the plain evidence of contrivance in it, its adaptations and provisions for the support of the fœtus during its sheltered growth, while it is gradually acquiring the proper figure and conformation of its species, and before it comes to its birth? That obvious economy of the embryonic state remains, the conduciveness of its arrangements to a particular end remains, and the success of these arrangements in birth of the offspring and continuation of the race remains.

But these mutations in the introduction to life are, we are told, traces of old laws, and vestiges of successive past landmarks in the formation of the species; as Nature raised the species from one step in the scale to another, she ought to have, at each successive new stage, obliterated the traces of the former one; and the circumstance of her not having done so shows that she does not proceed by design.

Now whether we do or do not adopt this hypothesis of Nature, and of the traces of former species, let us suppose it to be true; —to say that it disproves Design is a forced artificial inference, and shows a critic straining for an objection. How can we say that, a descent supposed, traces of that descent simply left in a stage in which they do no kind of injury, are in any sense mistakes? Why are they mistakes? They are mistakes on the supposition that all history is a mistake, but upon no other supposition that we know of. They are records of the past. Why should there not be such records? They simply accompany and do not interrupt the life-germ which, as Professor Owen says, "takes *ab initio* its own course to the full manifestation of its specific characters; each step of development moving to that consummation as its end and aim." Though we allowed that there were real encumbering superfluities remaining from an old apparatus, how could they undo and negative the fact of the visible machinery of the new one? Suppose we had before us some engine which had been improved by long progress, but retained in corners of its structure awkward remains of the old make, would that stand in the way of our seeing what the engine was, that it was an engine, and that it was constructed and contrived for a special purpose? Mr. Lewes says "the embryo is not the adult in miniature," as if it could signify what it was so long as it grew, and grew into the form into which it does grow. But Mr. Lewes looks upon the variations of outer form as indications of a want of fixed intention in Nature to produce the specific being which is ultimately produced. He speaks of her "instability," her "blunderings," her "missings of the path," her "feeling her way," her "tentative acts and after corrections." His charge grows as he reflects upon the perversity and dogged obstinacy of Nature in going on repeating this inconsistent process without cessation. She "*repeats,*" is his charge, "the same tentatives and the same corrections *for centuries.*" It might occur to the objector that if Nature does commit an inconsistency in any part of her system, to withdraw it with a handsome apology after the first act, is not the conduct that we expect from Nature. With her to do a thing, and to do it uniformly, is one and the same act; and a mistake once is identical with a mistake always. But we wonder that Mr. Lewes should consider a record to be a mistake at all; still more, that he should consider it a proof of instability of mind in Nature. We know no better proof of a fixed intention than a uniform result; and even a mistake which is always made and always corrected is, however enigmatical a proceeding, as certain an indication of a fixed purpose as the straightest of roads could be; for the final law of correction shows to a certainty that Nature is in favour of what she retains, and against what she discards.

And even if the whole of the rudimentary stage of Nature was an enigma, how could that cancel the machinery of her mature work? Whatever the introductory period may be, Nature leaves it very soon behind her, and presents to us a magnificent and consistent structure. Regarded as knowledge, the more accurate an acquaintance with Nature is, and the more minute it is, the more admirable it is. And therefore if the embryo of the Neritina Fluviatilis has not a shell, while the mature Neritina Fluviatilis has, that is an observation of true value. We accept it, we record it, we give the apparent aberration a place; and yet the great vital fabric of the Universe stands before us, not wholly eclipsed. Yet Mr. Lewes is overpowered and transfixed with astonishment that we *can* talk of an Architect of Nature when the tadpole of a land salamander has aquatic gills, and the embryo Nudibranch has a shell, which is rejected by the Nudibranch mature.

We do not object to notice being challenged to the enigmatical parts of Nature; what we only demand is that they should be introduced upon the proper question, and in the right stage of the argument. To bring them into the arena upon the primary question of the *existence* of design in Nature, is somewhat the same mistake as if a democratic lawyer were to bring forward the irregularities, the qualifications, the curious modifications of the royal supremacy, in order to urge them as objections, when the question before him was simply whether there was a king, and whether he had a supremacy. It is the same mistake as if a scholar were doggedly to fasten his mind upon some of the most subordinate of the side clauses of a constructed sentence, and insist upon disposing of them, before he had dealt with, or settled, or thought of the grammatical backbone of the sentence. The enigmatical parts of Nature may legitimately be brought into discussion, a design in Nature being assumed, upon the question of the attributes of the Designer, His Omniscience, Omnipotence, Perfect Goodness; but they are brought in prematurely and out of place when they are brought in upon the primary question of there being design in Nature. Mr. Lewes buries himself so in the anomalies and curious irregular corners of Nature, that he fails to grasp the great interpretation of Nature—the interpretation of her as a whole. Nature has what may be called her backbone construction, analogous to the grammatical backbone of a sentence, which may still contain a clause of ambiguous government. We meet many such a sentence in our best old writers; Mr. Lewes upon the strength of the ambiguous clause, reads the whole sentence as a parish boy, half way up the school, reads his part. We see the parish schoolboy making his slow interrupted passage through his apportioned sentence; he is an instance of a person who does not grasp the backbone of that structure with which he has to deal; and the results are gloomy; he has hardly advanced a step when there is a wavering; a small side clause receives him, and, we need not add, detains him; he tarries there, stays in it long and tentatively, carrying on a minor contest with the tougher syllables. He issues out of the enclosure with the main clew somewhat entangled: a few more painful steps, and now the great beacon-light of the nominative case is evidently vanishing; about half way, the earth yawns and fairly engulfs him; he has dropped into an abyss; he emerges again, but plainly all is lost, nominative, verb, and everything; the low level monotone betrays the impartiality with which he treats all parts of speech, nouns, adjectives, verbs, and adverbs, conjunctions, prepositions, and interjections; he passes through a succession of syllabical cavities, and he only sees the one in which he at the time is; no whole exists, and the sentence comes to an end like an addition sum. This is one instance of the loss of a backbone construction. But that which is the helpless failure of the parish schoolboy is the systematic philosophy of Mr. Lewes, who construes Nature as the other construes a sentence. He immures himself in some of the petty clauses of Nature which are obscure, and will not see the great construction of Nature's sentence, which is plain. He incarcerates himself in the odd corners of Nature with rudimentary organs, with incipient lobes, with fœtal teeth, with elementary digits, with aborted hind-legs, with unfinished commencements of gills, and with shells that are bestowed without being promised, and that are promised without being bestowed; and he forgets that that which is enigmatical cannot cancel that which is perspicuous— the facts of organic structure and the visible machinery of life.

Let us not be misunderstood. We appreciate the mysteries of Nature; but we only say that we must not reject her light. Mr. Lewes is not only an explorer of physical secrets, he is a successful biographer, a man of the world, acquainted with life and society. Will he tell us in what possible way anything can be proved in history, in politics, or on any subject, unless we allow a discriminative faculty in the human understanding which can distinguish between objections which are difficulties and objections which are disproofs; which can not only see objections but estimate their proportion, and which can clear a substantial line of proof from amid minor opposition and protest. Was ever case carried into a court of justice in which, however strong the evidence was on one side, there was nothing to be said on the other? Is all the counter evidence which comes forth in our trials against even certain verdicts *mock* evidence?

Is it a nonentity? No; some of it is real: that is to say, it possesses an opposing force more or less. How, then, is it overcome, and so completely overcome that nobody doubts the result? Because its proportion is estimated. It is seen that there is a main structure of proof, rising out of and amid the facts of the case, which dominates. This discriminating faculty is the cement which builds the whole fabric of knowledge and of truth. With no condition of proportion to satisfy, any objection would prevent any proof: yet Mr. Lewes frees himself from this condition in his argument against the proof of design. His rule is not Sir Roger de Coverley's, that there is much to be said on both sides; but a rule much more diluent of all certainty, viz., that there is no proof in any case in which there is anything to be said on the other side. We may theorise on paper upon such a principle, but the application of it to practice would be the destruction of knowledge and the collapse of society.

The objection, then, of the superfluities, the incumbrances, and the irregularities of Nature is not relevant upon the question of the existence of design in Nature, but must be reserved for the question of the attributes of the Designer.[1] Observe, however, upon what a vantage-ground such questions relating to His attributes are treated as soon as we have decided on the existence of the Being; because the existence of an Infinite Being becomes at once a valid reason for not pressing objections which are met by the answer of our ignorance. If we admit an Infinite Being, it need be no matter of surprise if we find that He does not work altogether after the type of a human artificer; if a world which comes out of mystery contains modes of procedure which we cannot account for. Manichæanism has thus, as a theory, perished. A God assumed, common sense has refused to see in such facts as these reasons for denying His power and goodness. Their inadequacy was plain upon such a standing-ground, and the belief in the attributes has been carried practically by the belief in the Being. Mani-

[1] Hume does introduce the objection of the imperfections of the system of Nature in this place, upon the question of the attributes of the Author of the universe, not upon the question of the existence of an Author of the universe. See further on.

chæanism is obsolete, and Atheism or Pantheism is modern unbelief.

And this brings us to another head of objections to design, viz., those drawn from the Infinity of the Deity. Design is a human conception, it is said: the essential offspring of a mode of thinking which belongs to a limited intelligence: we cannot attribute it to an Infinite Being. Mr. Lewes asks how we obtain our "knowledge of the Divine mind—very enviable knowledge, but needing some guarantee for its genuineness." This objection, then, comes out of the general Pantheistic arsenal, and only applies to design in common with all the moral attributes of an Infinite Being. Descartes, however, who was not a Pantheist, but demonstrated the existence of a God out of our innate ideas, still objected to the Argument of Design on the ground that we must know God before we can attribute design to Him.

The force of this objection, then, lies in the overpowering vastness of the idea of infinity, which makes it inconceivable that this infinite world should go back to such a unity as a mental design. We cannot contemplate the life with which the universe teems, its countless types and structures, without at first sight a kind of despair that its *Cause* should be a personal Being. All seems to evaporate in immensity. Take even any of those great exhibitions which bring out and place before the eye of the spectator the inexhaustibleness of Nature, animal and vegetable,—that interminable labyrinth of variability which, like the Cretan, lets no one out again that has ever once got in. When he has seen hundreds of varieties of hundreds of species, which never, perhaps, challenged his eye before, what is his first sensation? It is, of course, that of wonder; but there is something which enters in with wonder, and is not so pleasant: it is perplexity. Is it more than perplexity? Yes; it is dejection. A disturber has crept into our home; there is an ominous stir as if upon an unwelcome arrival; some alien thought has come into collision with the mind's faith—the thought of an impersonal life of the universe. Can the Being that coincides with this boundless life be personal? Is there a congruity between the truth of fact and the truth of religion? The idea of personality is strong in the home of our own hearts; but let us be brought face to face with the infinity of Nature in one of these astonishing and vivid spectacles of her multiplicity, and for a moment it totters. The vastness, the boundlessness of Nature is not only an overwhelming thought, a prostrating thought: it is a benumbing thought. Infinity is a cold idea, thus forced upon us; and there is a refrigeration of the mind as the notion of a paternal Being gives place to pure immensity.

And this momentary effect from a great spectacle is only an anticipation of the great power of the idea when systematically cherished. The idea of infinity combines two great and startling opposites, viz., that of being the most religious, and that of being the most sceptical, idea of the human mind. On the one hand, it is the foundation of all that is transcendental and aspiring in human prospects; on the other hand, it is the destruction of it all. It has been the favourite idea of religious minds on the one side. One religious philosopher, especially, who lifts up the curtain and discloses the realms of metaphysics in all their solemnity and grandeur, has pursued the idea with an insatiable affection and longing. Pascal is supreme master of those domains of mystical logic in which the conclusions, not of a venturous faith, but of a pure reason, are more eccentric and abnormal than the most extravagant creations of romance and the oddest misconceptions of a dream —a universe which is not a whole, number which is neither odd nor even, and time which never began. The prodigious speculative births, the sphynxes and chimeras of reason that rise up in his world of thought, and haunt, like the awful shapes of classical legend, the boundless solitudes over which the mind of Pascal ranges, prove the overpowering sense of infinity which pervaded his mind. The strength of the idea in him made it fructify and multiply into this ghostly imagery, this brood of logical apparitions. The idea even of *material* infinity fascinated him—the idea of simple sidereal space, because it bordered on the supernatural, and converted even this world of fact into such an incomprehensible problem. The vivid conceptions of immensity which his metaphysical imagination raised, inspired him with an ever-fresh amazement, awe, and dread. In the region of the idea he felt himself on the threshold of a higher world; and the spiral coils of the great enigma, though they ascended endlessly, still pointed up to heaven.

But, identified with faith in one mind, the idea of infinity becomes the very antagonist of faith in another. It is now an infidel idea. It is the great undoer, the great reverser, of all the religious verdicts of reason; they are dissolved as soon as they enter this strong diluent. The attributes of the Deity melt in the crucible of this idea; it has the power of converting everything it touches into nothing; eternity and immortality into nothing, *i.e.* God himself into nothing. All these become human conceptions, which the touchstone of infinity has detected. The forward current in us which goes all toward a personal Deity, retires before this great reactionary tide, which carries the whole mind back again into vacuity. Infinity thus becomes Nature's great retractation, her great revocation, her great recantation; whereby she gives up all she once held, withdraws it, and owns herself mistaken and deceived. It is the great destructive idea, the loosener of all that was once fixed. There is a passion for destruction in the mind of man, as strong as that of constructing, which delights in clearness of all kinds, and wherever it goes empties space; even the imagination enlists itself on this side, and makes a poetry of demolition. Infinity which makes a clean sweep of all creeds is thus the creed of the Pantheistic poet, and often of the imaginative man of science.

But if we keep clear in our minds the position that design is a construction which *adheres to the facts*, we can deal sufficiently with this objection of Infinity. If by the constitution of our minds we are compelled to construe actual machinery which effects an end as designed for that end, that compulsion is our justification. No insoluble question outside of this act of construction can interfere with or invalidate this act itself. If Descartes then or any one else objects to us that we must know the Divine mind before we can affix design to Nature, we reply, It is falsely put; we need not know God in order to put a construction upon facts; we can put a construction upon facts, if we have the facts. We have nothing to do with the speculative point at the other end of this question; we argue from *this* end of it,—from the facts of contrivance : design is tied to those facts and cannot be divorced from them. If we cannot argue indeed *up* to a God till we can argue *down* from Him, if we cannot interpret any signs that point to Him till we know they come from Him, then certainly the evidences of a God from Nature are impossible until they are useless; and there is no such argument as the Argument of Design. But this is not the state of the case. You mistake our argument; we assume no knowledge of the Divine designing mind; we only argue from facts *towards* one. Whatever be the mystery which lies on the other side of the ocean of infinity, it is consistent with these facts, and with the constitution of our own minds, which obliges this construction of them.

If, indeed, infinity is logically inconsistent with design, we come to a contradiction in Nature; a contradiction between the constitution of our minds which affixes design to Nature, and infinity which withdraws it. But where is the logical contradiction between design and an infinite quantity of design? In affirming human predicates of God, says Mr. Mill, we affirm the same that we do of man, only infinitely "greater in degree."

The analogy of human contrivance certainly deserts us in its application to Divine at one stage. In the use of any human structure, a watch, *e.g.*, we know that the contrivance is traceable to a definite point in some artificer's head; all the constructive power converges to that local point, and we trace the whole course of design consecutively from its goal to its starting-point. But when we come to a contrivance of Nature we have a piece of mechanism as compact indeed as a watch, but where is the designer? We look around and see only universal space, and the site of design, instead of contracting to a point in the known mechanic's brain, expands into Immensity. The elaborate definiteness of an apparatus of Nature contrasts strangely with the infinity from which alone it can come. There is something indeed in this contrivance without a contriver in Nature, in the high artificiality of physical mechanism, joined with the utter absence of the visible mechanist, which recalls the effects of a certain department of mystery in works of fiction. All motion without an apparent agent has a singular power of startling; if a door trembles, if a curtain rustles, we turn quick round, and have a momentary sensation of that which appears to be innate in us, the fear of what is *not* seen. The supernatural story avails itself of these native impulses of the mind, and introduces unexplained motions, sounds, and sights. The effect of Nature, as a great structure and a great motion going on before us, corresponds to this; it is the mysterious house without a builder; a vast, a perpetual, and a most significant movement without a mover. But though the infinity of the designing mind makes an undoubted difference, it is not such a difference as destroys design. Why should I think that mind ceases to be itself because it is infinite? If I think so, I think so because imagination transports me; I judge like a man under agitation and terror, who supposes that whatever makes a difference reverses the whole. I am seized with a blind alarm as to the effects of infinity upon the Supreme Being; as if He could be wholly changed from a moral and intellectual being by it. I attribute to this idea an irrational power of transmutation, as I would to some spell of magic. This is not reason, but fancy; not philosophy, but alarmist speculation. Nature gives us a clew to her own Authorship, and the direction of that clew is plain and evident though its terminus is infinity.

It is remarkable that the Argument of Design was accepted by Hume, whose admission of it, taken in connection with his scepticism, deserves one or two remarks. Mr. Huxley has lately appealed to this great philosopher as the annihilator of all "isms." There was, however, one "ism" which Hume strongly supported by argument, viz., Theism :—

"The whole frame of Nature bespeaks an intelligent author, and no rational inquirer can, after serious reflection, suspend his belief a moment with regard to the primary principles of genuine Theism and Religion."—*Natural History of Religion.*

Hume's defence of Theism was a defence, indeed, with sinister limits and conditions, which remove it from the head of properly religious arguments. He was profoundly sceptical with respect to the attributes of the Deity as taught by natural religion; he professed himself unable to reconcile the facts of the world with Infinite Power and Goodness, and as therefore disposed on his own part to accept a more moderate conception of a God. He rejected with scorn the appeal to the solution which another world was to give of the difficulties of this, which he designated "as building in air, and establishing one hypothesis upon another."[1] He did not assign God any worship other than the knowledge of Him, quoting the saying of Seneca—to know God is to worship Him; but all these irreligious qualifications of the truth still leave Hume maintaining a residuum of Theism, and in Theism of immaterial intelligent Being.

Doubt in Hume did not supersede a strong though hard and narrow common sense, which enabled him when he liked to control the excesses of a speculative imagination, and subject it to practical reason, as he understood reason's verdict. He soars in the *Dialogues concerning Natural Religion* into the empyrean of scepticism, where infinity destroys all parallel between universal contrivance and finite, and where order even in the Divine ideas is no more an ultimate account of Nature than the order of matter itself is; but when he comes to decide, he recalls imagination from its flight to embrace a plain truth. "The whole chorus of Nature raises one hymn to the praise of its Creator. You alone, or almost alone, disturb this general harmony. You start abstruse doubts, cavils, and objections; you ask me what is the cause of this cause. I know not, I care not; that concerns not me. I have found a Deity, and here I stop my inquiry. Let them go farther who are wiser or more enterprising."[2]

We now come to the *vexata quæstio* of physical *versus* final causes. Bacon, as is well known, had to deal with a set of philosophers who, when a fact of Nature was placed before them, refused to recognise the physical cause of that fact as a subject of inquiry, upon the ground that the final cause was

---

[1] *Dialogues concerning Natural Religion*, Part x.
[2] *Ibid.*, Part iv.

enough; that the fact in question answered a useful purpose, and was inserted in Nature by God *for* this purpose. The final cause of the eyebrows, that they might protect the eye from the descending moisture of the forehead; the final cause of the bones, that they might carry the flesh; the final cause of the leaves of trees, that they might give shelter from the sun; the final cause of the earth's soil, that vegetables might grow in it; the final cause of stone, that houses might be built with it; the final cause of iron, copper, and the different metals, that different implements or different ornaments might be made out of them;—these respective purposes and uses of these respective natural materials were the sole account to be given of the existence of these materials in the idea of the scholastic naturalists; and chemical, physiological, geological, and all scientific discovery was thus stopped at the fountain-head; every production of Nature being regarded as an immediate creation of God to answer a particular purpose. The maxim, then, which Bacon applied to the separate items of Nature was applied by the French philosophers to the mechanism and system of Nature; and because he insisted on a physical cause for the physical facts singly and separately, they quoted him as their authority for attributing only a physical cause to the *collocation* of those facts, their concurrence and adjustment in the organic structures of Nature; and upon the strength of this application of his maxim discarded final causes altogether; whereas it is the very difference between the separate facts of Nature and those facts in agreement and concurrence which constitutes the evidence of final causes. A physical cause can be assigned to every single material of which a house is built —every stone, every beam, the iron, the lead, the glass, the tiles, the plaster; but the separate items are one thing, the agreement and coincidence of these in a fabric is another; and the distinction which is true of a human building Bacon fully acknowledged with respect to the edifice of Nature.[1] 'Those brilliant naturalists, indeed, who have penetrated with such

---

[1] Dr. Acland draws the distinction in his Harveian Oration—a paper equally distinguished by philosophical candour and discrimination:—" We may, therefore, discard the *use* of Final Causes in Science, and yet not necessarily infer, as Comte did, the absence of providential government."

acuteness and subtlety the labyrinths of Nature, while they dissect and methodise physical material with the intuition of genius, show at the same time, as soon as ever they get on the other side of the border of their own department, an absence of rigid training in the school of reasoning. Had they been as close logicians as they were keen investigators they must have seen that physical causes, as being only the physical antecedents of particular facts, can only explain the particular facts of which they are the antecedents; that they can perform no other function as reasons, and that it does not belong to them to account for facts as contemplated in their corporate arrangement, in their concurrence in one physical apparatus and system. Physical causes are, indeed, so far from accounting for arrangement in Nature that they are evidently in themselves common to arrangement and disorder. Were the world a tumultuous and tempestuous chaos, every single component motion of that multitudinous discordant agitation would still have its physical cause in some immediate antecedent. But this crowd of physical forces would want what they have in the existing system of Nature, disposition and arrangement. It is evident that what is common to order and disorder cannot account for order. The physical causes are the same in a steam-engine and a volcano, in waterworks and a deluge, in the ventilation of a room and in a tempest. An excrescence, a wart, a mole, a hump back, has as accurate a train of physical causes as a regular limb. But they work differently in the two cases, and the difference of the working cannot be accounted for by an order of causes which in both cases is the same.

So much for the appeal to Bacon as an authority for physical in opposition to final causes. Upon this great question, then, we have first to defend against the Encyclopædist even the *prima facie* verdict of facts for Design. We say the *prima facie* verdict of facts is at any rate for design: he does not admit it. We never saw any argumentative formulas of Encyclopædists against design in Nature, which did not substantially amount to this, viz., to saying, Shut your eyes to design, and you will not see it. The philosophy involved in this dictum is exactly the same as that which we have in theirs, and it has the advantage of being more plainly expressed. Take their cardinal formula—" Conditions of Existence "[1]— that the structure of the body is not intended *for* life, but that life follows *from* it, and would not exist *without* it, *i.e.* that the bodily structure is the condition of existence, and no more. The ingenuity and plausibility, then, of this formula is wholly obtained by an omission, and by the audacity with which that omission is made; by the circumstance that it fastens the mind upon *sequence*, and thrusts aside and ignores the natural, the unavoidable aspect of *provision*. In every system or compages of forces which issues in some particular result, any one of the forces of which the whole is composed is the *condition* of the production of that result. In chemical combination each separate item is the condition of the whole. One pipe or one artery within the body, one single ingredient in the air outside of it, is the condition of existence. But it is evident that an apparatus, as one harmonious whole, stands in a different relation toward the result which it produces, from that of one or other single item of it; and that the relation of *sine qua non*, though included in, is not the complete and adequate expression of, that aspect of the machinery as a whole. That whole is naturally regarded by the mind not only in this light, viz., that something follows from it, but also in another light, viz., that it is constructed *for* something. We see a concurrent action towards, as well as a sequence from; we see more than conditions of existence, we see a provision for existence. The end does not simply come after the means, but the means intend the end. But the formula—" Conditions of Existence "—will only recognise a consequence; only see the retrospective view, not the prospective. It only sees in sentient life the upshot of the bodily combinations, and discards the aspect of it as the end and scope of them. The formula, therefore, attains its purpose by omission. Look only at a sequence, and you will only see a sequence.

Geoffroy St. Hilaire, who carried the art of shutting the

---

[1] " Les causes finales ne sont, en dépit de leur nom, que les effets évidens, ou les *conditions mêmes de l'existence* de chaque objet."—*Revue Encyclopédique*, vol. v. p. 231. " Cuvier seems to have adopted the term in a sense *not* opposed to final causes."—Owen's *Comparative Anatomy*, vol. iii. p. 787.[1]

eyes to a high point of philosophical perfection, applied a scientific culture to this act of the mind. The point of view which he constructed for the purpose of exactly cutting off the approach of the proposition of common sense, reminds one of some skilful piece of military engineering, which projects the angle of a bastion in the direction which cuts off the assault from one threatening quarter in the country around; and is a curious specimen of the dogged perversity of a man of genius when he does not like one direction in which things are going, and opposes to obtrusive evidence the science of *not* seeing. " Voir les fonctions d'abord, puis après les instrumens qui les produisent, c'est renverser l'ordre des idées. Pour un naturaliste qui conclut d'après les faits, chaque être est sorti des mains du Créateur, avec de propres conditions matérielles : il peut, selon qu'il lui est attribué de pouvoir : il emploie ses organes selon leur capacité d'action."[1] It is a misstatement, then, to say that the advocates of design look at functions first, and at the instruments for the functions afterwards; what they do is to look at both together, and argue from their concurrence. But this, looking at them both, and looking at them in concurrence, is what St. Hilaire prohibits; it is not our seeing one before the other, but seeing the two in relation, which constitutes our offence. He will not allow the instrument to be looked at as agreeing with the work, but only at the work as necessarily coming out of the instrument. That is his point of view. Looking at the case, then, in this accurately limited point of view, design is undoubtedly excluded. Granted the construction of the instrument, the employment of it, or the function, does not flow from the construction by design

[1] *Principes de Philosophie Zoologique*, p. 66. His illustration against design is—" A raisonner de la sorte, vous diriez d'un homme qui fait usage de béquilles, qu'il était originairement destiné au malheur d'avoir l'une de ses jambes paralysée ou amputée." It is, however, a most gratuitous transposition of the final cause to fit the man to the crutch, instead of what is much more obvious, the crutch to the man. We cannot but add, with reference to the defect of logical training which these great scientific investigators sometimes show, that it is singular that Cuvier and St. Hilaire should dispute over two hundred pages upon the identity of organs, *e.g.*, whether the fore-hoof of an ox is exactly the "same organ" with the wing of a bat, without it occurring to either of them to ask, whether they were using "identity" in the same sense or using it in different senses and different respects.

but by necessity. The instrument works, and works according to its make, and according to its component parts. How can it work otherwise? The function is the only action of which the instrument is capable, and therefore is an unavoidable derivation for the instrument. But though, this point of view granted, design is excluded, what right has St. Hilaire to impose this point of view? On what ground does he assert that the instrument works according to its construction, and that *that is all?* We say there is something besides the instrument working according to its construction, viz., that the instrument is constructed for its work; we assert this on the ground of the plain agreement and coincidence of the two. St. Hilaire says you have no right to see coincidence and correspondence; you have only the right to see the work proceeding from the instrument, you have no right to see the adaptation of the instrument for the work; you are at liberty to perceive the motion derived from the oars and sails, you are forbidden to discern the aptitudes of the oars and sails to produce the motion of the boat. But if there are two relations to be seen, why should we only see one of them?

Some turn round a corner in order that they may not see the evidence of that which they do not care to admit; the Encyclopædist looks it full in the face, and gives it the cut direct. There is in the whole history of philosophy no rougher and more violent despatch of great questions to be found, than the Encyclopædist's method of dealing with design. There is a piece of the Chinese puzzle that will project beyond the figure; abscission is his remedy. There is something in Nature which is not included in his physical plan, and he cuts it off as a workman would cut off an angle of a mass of rough stone that he had to fit into a place. Of two aspects of Nature he simply expunges one. The prospective look of Nature, the aim in her, is set aside as a fictitious idea of the human mind, obtained by a false reflection of the result, and the transposition of effect and cause: according to the explanation of Lucretius :—

> " Illud in his rebus vitium vehementer, et istum
> Effugere errorem, vitareque præmeditator,
> Lumina ne facias Oculorum clara creata,

> Prospicere ut possimus; . . . . .
> Nil adeo quoniam natum'st in corpore, ut uti
> Possemus, sed quod natum'st, id procreat usum."

But now—and this is the next step in this *vexata quæstio*—if it is once admitted that design is the *prima facie* interpretation of Nature, that *facts* bear the impress of design; this verdict of facts can never be subsequently reversed by causes. Upon the great question of design in Nature facts are masters of the position; the actualities of machinery are what must rule the decision. Take any part of the human body where there is a group or system of matter-of-fact functions, *e.g.* about the eye, where there is the eye itself with its component humours, coats, membranes, muscles, fibres, lubricating fluid, socket, bed of the socket, retina, pigment, the eyelashes, eyelids, eyebrows:—suppose there is a physical cause for every one of these facts, or that each of these facts could be traced farther back to some fact anterior to it: the eyebrows, *e.g.*, to the texture of the flesh upon which they grew, the eyelashes in the same way to their membranous basis, the eyelids to the extension of the skin of the forehead; if even the humours of the eye itself, the muscles, the fibres, could be traced all to some further facts of tissue or fluid—we should still have the *collocation* of these further facts to account for. It is the collocation which is evidence of design in the original facts; but the same collocation meets us in the physical antecedents. And however much farther back we could trace definitely the physical causes, we should have the same collocation to account for. The primary patent facts are represented in the successive stages backward by a corresponding group or system of physical antecedents; and the last traceable physical antecedents can no more explain their own collocation than the original facts could. The resort to design, therefore, if it is necessary in the case of the first facts, is equally necessary at every step of the retrogression; the claim of reason is only pushed further back, and that which had to be explained in the facts has to be explained in the causes. There is co-existence, there is coincidence, there is concurrence to be accounted for at the very close and vanishing point of physical analysis, just as much as there was upon the threshold of the simple phenomenon.

But when we say that the search for physical causes can only push the collocation we see in Nature further back, the reply is that we do not take into account the simplification which physical analysis accomplishes; that the further back it penetrates the greater unity it discovers in Nature, and that in proportion as it discovers physical causes it also reduces or resolves them, till at length it brings us to a unit—to a cause in which there is no collocation because there is no plurality. It is of course true, then, that in pursuing the chain of physical causation we come at last to causes which lie entirely beyond the cognisance of our senses, and in which the powers and the forces by which the mature structure in which they issue is produced are wholly hidden from us. But then, it must be remembered, if we do not see the cause, if we do not see anything at all, we do not see a unit; this professed simplification of causes or reduction of them to a unit is not proved, and does not appear; and therefore the argument rests exactly on the basis on which it rested before this simplification was attempted or pretended; there is the original fact of collocation, and design cleaves to that fact. When we come to such causes as these, we can only argue as to what they contain from what they produce; and we must, as the only course left to us, conclude that, if the result which they produce is a fabric or a machine, there are, however subtle and latent, methodical forces in them which correspond to such a methodical effect. So far as we can trace Nature visibly there is arrangement; if we come to a point where we can trace her no farther, we then see the cause simply as represented in the result, and therefore as in turn reflecting the harmony and system of that result. The elementary leaf-organ, we are told, "expands into a leaf upon the stem, contracts to make the calyx, expands again to make the petal, to contract once more into sexual organs, and expand for the last time into fruit."[1] Be it so; but this elementary leaf-organ must be a cause adequate to produce this manifold system of the flower and fruit which actually comes out of it.

[1] Lewes's *Life of Goethe*, vol. ii. p. 145.

Is it then a sensible thing which can be depicted and its composition brought to light? In that case it must show some arrangement and method in its composition, whereby it is enabled to produce what it does. It must exhibit the system of the flower in tendency, in seed. Is it an invisible first element of vegetable life? We must then reason on what it is and contains, from what it produces; and, if a systematic production is the result, infer systematic forces in the cause. The phenomenal actualities of the plant, then, are masters of the position. We do not see the concurrent forces in any ordinary seed, but we collect them from the structure of the mature plant.

The Argument of Design is completed, indeed, within the sphere of tangible Nature; its validity is, therefore, not affected by any pursuit of Nature into the intangible; arrangement on the visible side indicates design on the invisible; and there we stop. You say this ultimate invisible cause is a unit, but within the sphere of intangible physics this unit has just as much right to be considered a coalition of a thousand causes as one. When we get to the ultimate forces of Nature we get to something which is so absolutely spiritual that we cannot impose material conditions on it. Can anything be conceived more absolutely immaterial than the primary forces in a grain of wheat? Are heaven or hell, angel or archangel, all the hierarchy of the Empyrean, all the Powers of light or of darkness, more invisible than the productive powers of an acorn? If ten thousand angels, then, according to the scholastic saying, could dance upon the point of a needle, a system of ten thousand invisible physical causes could act in an invisible physical unit.

If we pass from unity of root to unity of plan of Nature— to the theory of unity of composition, according to which the structures of the several species are not separate plans, but all developments, according to circumstances, of one—this distinction is of no relevance as regards the question of design. It can only in the nature of the case affect the number of plans, not the argument from plan. With reference to this argument, one universal plan, which embraces all special plans, is an exact equivalent to all the special plans it embraces; and it matters not whether all specific organs are homologous and radically correspond or not with each other, so long as each shows arrangement in its relation to its own proper frame. St. Hilaire did not reject design because he started the theory of unity of plan, but because he rejected *in limine* the argument for plan. Professor Owen maintains the same unity of plan, and infers from it design.

Upon the question of design, then, in Nature, facts are masters of the position; results, those arrangements which meet the eye, are the tests. Causes cannot reverse the argument from facts; they are either sensible causes, and correspond to the facts, or invisible ones, and reflect them. The argument is thus independent of all theories of elementary formation— Evolution,[1] Epigenesis, Nomogeny, Thaumatogeny—because facts hold the key, and they are the same, however rudimental theories may conflict. Design once seated in Nature by facts, can thus never be unseated; once in, it can never be out again. If the argument of design is a bad one, as drawn from phenomena, let it be dismissed; but if good from them it is good for ever.

We come now to some great hypotheses of the origin of the existing system of Nature, constructed by philosophical naturalists, and we find that these theories require, for simply being started and set going, some principle of design in Nature. Take Lamarck's theory that the animal organs are developed by circumstances—new circumstances creating new needs— new needs new instinctive efforts to satisfy them, and these new efforts new bodily adaptations; that some short-necked bird, by trying to catch fish without wetting itself, converted itself into a heron; that some land-bird, urged to the water by want of food, in its efforts to swim, extended, by repeated separation of the toes, the connecting skin at their roots, and changed itself into a duck. The physiological law, then, that use and exercise strengthen and expand an organ, while disease

[1] Upon the theory of Pangenesis, indeed, according to which the whole body reproduces itself, all the component parts of the reproduced body exist ticketed and numbered from the very commencement; and their destination is as marked at the fountain-head as it is at the result.

atrophies it, was the foundation of this theory; the instinct by moving the animal to the exertion of the organ, called this law into operation, and the physical need excited the instinct. The theory, then, at its foundation assumes the existence of organs —of something antecedent to this law of use and exercise to which this law is applied—something which, by the very hypothesis, has the innate capacity of being developed harmoniously and serviceably. A rudimental plan, therefore, pre-exists, which the Lamarckian law causes to develop in concurrence with the variety in the outward constitution in Nature. And the instinctive efforts of the animal are determined in every stage by a pre-existing structure, and only act at the openings and in the channels laid down for them in that structure.

But of the position which we have laid down, viz., that if the facts of nature are admitted *prima facie* to show design, no subsequent physical explanation can undo the original verdict of the facts, the theory of natural selection will furnish the most remarkable instance. It is not Mr. Darwin's storehouse of facts chiefly, enormous as that is; it is his searching and elaborate power of reasoning which he applies to these facts, which constitutes his greatness as a naturalist. Mr. Grove is a great physical mathematician; Mr. Darwin is a great probable reasoner—in details. His accumulative arguments might be studied indeed with advantage, simply as specimens. But while he applies this power so strikingly to details, his great conclusion fails remarkably upon this very head. One of his most recent antagonists[1] is "A Graduate of the University of Cambridge," whose criticism of the theory displays much acute reasoning, as well as command of language; though he must allow us to say that his argument would have gained much by compression. We have only to do, however, with Mr. Darwin's theory with reference to the special purpose before us. For

[1] Professor Phillips, in his inaugural address to the British Association in 1865, adopts an attitude of suspense. He asks "what range of variation is indicated" by some classes of facts which he mentions; and adds, "Specific questions of this kind must be answered before the general proposition that the forms of life are indefinitely variable with time and circumstance can be even examined by the light of adequate evidence."

this purpose we need not say that we do, or do not, adopt the theory of the Transmutation of Species. Let us assume it to be true; it cannot be worked without a principle of design. And first, what is the place which natural selection has in it? Does it do everything? If it does, then the theory is as a theory complete without the principle of design. But if natural selection, according as Mr. Darwin himself defines its functions, does not do everything, but leaves a void and chasm in the theory which must be filled up by some other principle, what is this other principle, when we come to examine it, but design?

We know Mr. Darwin's own account of natural selection; and from this very account it allows that natural selection is not an agent at all, but a result. It is the effect which proceeds from a favourable modification, or development of structure in one animal in the struggle for existence with another animal not thus additionally endowed; viz., his survivorship and continuance on the field while the other perishes. There is an unknown reservoir and spring of productiveness in nature; and some improvement or augmentation is supposed to have come out of it, and some animal to have been the recipient of it; this is the *productive* agency in the case. This productive agency having operated then, there is a result, in the particular condition of scarcity of food under which animal life labours, which proceeds from it, which result is the preservation of one animal and the death of another; or natural selection. Natural selection, then, is not an agent but a result; and it is moreover only a negative or privative result. The favoured party in this struggle, the party that lives, would have lived all the same had there been no struggle for existence, and no natural selection; and he does not owe his existence and continuance to natural selection, he only owes his *sole* existence to it, as distinguished from the fate of a rival who perishes. The difference, therefore, which natural selection makes is not that one of these animals is preserved, but that the other is destroyed, and that is the one sole result in natural selection. Had the supply of food in the world been infinite and inexhaustible, both of these animals would have lived; for both would have had enough to live upon; but the supply being limited, one of them dies. Natural selection, then, has nothing to do with the creation of any favourable addition to Nature; it is only the removal of those who do not possess the addition. They perish, and the scene of creation thus becomes a very different one from what it would have been had there been no natural selection. Could we suppose an innumerable and inexhaustible supply of nutriment in the world, and consequently no struggle for existence, the area of Nature would have been a crowded field of irregular as well as regular forms of animal life; all those wide interstices which now separate species from species would have been filled up, and the earth would have teemed with a chaotic rabble of animal structures, lower forms and higher, perfect species and imperfect; the ascents of Nature being almost merged and lost in the gradational multitude; all would have survived, because there was food for all. Natural selection clears this ground, interposes intervals, and arranges Nature into groups and masses. But it does this work not as an agent, but only as an effect—the destructive effect of the scarcity of food. Without the struggle for existence regular forms would not have monopolised the ground; Nature would not have been seen upon the unencumbered pedestal on which she is now, or presented her present structural appearance. But natural selection only weeds, and does not plant; it is the drain of Nature carrying off the irregularities, the monstrosities, the abortions; it comes in after and upon the active developments of Nature to prune and thin them; but it does not create a species; it does not possess one productive or generative function.[1]

[1] Professor Owen justly calls attention to the distinction between his own suggestion in the volumes of Transactions of the Zoological Society, 1850, of (to anticipate terms) Natural Selection as the "cause of *extinction* of species," and Mr. Darwin's theory of Natural Selection, "which he applies not only to the extinction, but also to the *origin* of species." Professor Owen's statement in 1850 was that one cause of extinction "was the contest which each species had to maintain against the surrounding agencies which might militate against its existence." This, though no adoption—as understood by some reviewers recently, who spoke in ignorance of the date of this statement—of the Darwinian theory of Natural Selection, is a curious anticipation of Natural Selection in that which appears to us its only true function. —*Comparative Anatomy*, vol. iii. p. 798.

Natural selection figures in language, indeed, as an active and creative power. It "effects improvement;" it "checks deviations;" it "develops structure;" it has "accumulative action;" it "works silently and insensibly wherever opportunity offers;" it has made, indeed, every organ and limb of every existing animal. The species are its workmanship; they come out of the hands of this great artificer, who is described as fashioning the clay of life. Natural selection is not only an agent, it is even a designing agent; it "acts for the good of each creature;" it is "always trying to economise;" it has always an object before it, and acts with an aim. But all this is only the phraseology of metaphor, summing up and condensing consequences under the figure and impersonation of a cause. We meet an effect under the form of a cause, as we meet our own figure in a shop mirror in the street, departing from the very place at which we are going to arrive. Upon this very account natural selection designs perfectly, because it is, in fact, itself the successful result; it always hits, because the aimer is, in truth, the mark; its intention is only metamorphosed fact. We have to carry on this interpretation of the action and design of natural selection as we read Mr. Darwin; and though we by no means grudge him the liberty of metaphor, we are sometimes conscious of an exegetical task in extracting the real fact out of the language of figure. Natural selection is superior to human selection. What does this mean? That one is a better exercise of choice than the other? No; it means that whereas human selection is choice, trial, and experiment, and may therefore fail, natural selection is secure because it is the favourable result to begin with. In human selection the choice aims at the event; in natural selection the event makes the choice. Natural selection endows the woodpecker with its instrument—"a striking instance of adaptation"—*i.e.* it does not give *one* woodpecker its instrument; it has nothing to do with that; it only kills off another woodpecker who has not got it. Natural selection forms the flying squirrel with its parachute; *i.e.* it makes away with another squirrel who has not got a parachute, and is at a disadvantage in the locality. Natural selection has "reduced the wings" of some species of beetles in Madeira. That means that those species which *had* reduced or shortened wings were naturally selected or survived, whereas others with full wings, by reason of this very completeness of them, perished, because they flew; and, flying, they flew over the sea, and, flying over the sea, got carried away by winds, and could not get back again to land. We have thus to commute the language of natural selection as fast as we receive it; to drive metaphorically forward and really backward at the same time, and at every moment to transpose, by an understanding and arrangement with ourselves, the cart before the horse, into the natural order of the horse first.

If natural selection, then, has nothing to do with the production of favourable variations, but only adopts them when they arise; in the absence of any principle or law to dictate or direct in any way the course of such variations, nothing of which kind is as yet supplied to us; whence does Mr. Darwin get that succession of favourable variations which is necessary for the ultimate formation of a regular and highly organised species? It is obvious that not one or two which chance might give him are enough for this purpose, but that a succession is wanted, and a long succession. The gradual development of an organ or limb implies in the very process a gradual succession of slight advances in its structure, each taking up the work at the point at which the other left off, each fitting in to the different respective stage of the developing organ or limb which preceded. This has to be accounted for; more than this, a continuous development in several organs, and several limbs, all expanding in harmony, and growing into a composite and perfect animal whole, has to be accounted for. Natural selection is no account of it, because this assumes the variations, and does not make them. What does account for it?

Now we will take Mr. Darwin as he is popularly understood, and according to this general interpretation of him, we understand him to account for this succession by two agencies—Chance Variation, and Time. A rudimentary animal gets, by simply waiting, all the successive additions from this great fund of Nature which it wants for a high organisation. No principle of order or guidance in the efflux from this latent reservoir is needed ; there comes out an infinite quantity of augmentations and modifications from it; and among the rest the fitting ones. Why should not they come as well as the rest ? They will come, though at the intervals of thousands, of hundreds of thousands, of millions of years. Only let us command an infinity of time, and the proper modification which meets a given stage of development will arrive; and upon the same terms the next will, and the next, till a high species is completed. There is only wanted in addition the preliminary condition that the animal should continue long enough upon the ground to reap the advantage of these successive favours from Nature, and incomings from the stock of variability. And this, natural selection provides for ; because each successive favourable variation gives him the advantage in the struggle for existence with his unfavoured rival. He therefore survives, and a complete physical development accumulates and descends by a law of tontine upon the surviving party.

We must observe, then, that such an explanation of species by chance variability is an explanation which violates moral possibility. We do not see how chance, however long a time it had to work in, could possibly account for this succession of steps in Nature, all fitting in with preceding steps; this train of developments of, and additions to, a rudimental organic stock, all respectively joining on to the last one, and at length collectively forming an harmonious whole. Undoubtedly chance variability will give you in an infinity of time certain given variations, but in what character do these variations come ? Do they come as fixed and permanent modifications of the structure upon which they light, as the stable and settled acquisitions of a lasting formation ? No, they come as passing stages in a perpetual fluctuation of organic form, as vanishing lines in an unceasing tide of change. They come, but they do not stay: they are off again, and others come in their place ;— for we must keep faithfully to the hypothesis of a real infinite chance variation as the law of nature. If amid this crowd of changing forms of life, in this ocean of fluctuation and metamorphosis, some structural points stand permanently out as insulations in the scene; if these have a correspondence with each other, and form an harmonious animal fabric; if those arrivals, we say, which are fixed also cohere and agree;—this is not included within the hypothesis, and must be accounted for in some other way. The chances then that you get by the mere infinity of variation do not construct a species. You only regard your infinite variability on one side, viz., as furnishing your required chance; you do not regard it on the other as taking it away, when it has given it; you do not see that what is gained by chance is also lost by chance. Out of an infinite storehouse of variations you may command a certain number of favourable ones; what you cannot command is, that amid universal transition and mutation, those favourable variations should be fixed as well as coinciding; so as to form harmoniously developed structures, *i.e.* species.

Take another point of view, which only contains the same reasoning in another shape. An infinite chance variability will give you by waiting for it, a certain given variation or development which would *in itself* be a fit; that is to say, would be such a development as would join on to the pre-existing growth or section of the unfinished organ, supposing the stage of imperfection in the organ itself continued exactly the same throughout this long waiting interval, and met the supplementary addition at the close of the period, just in the shape in which it desiderated it, at the commencement; but how is this interval to be kept wholly clear, and the organ wholly stationary? We have, by the hypothesis, an infinite chance variability, working in all modes and directions, pulling matter about in every way conceivable or inconceivable, agitating and twisting promiscuously the whole universe of body, and keeping the vast framework of the animal world in one perpetual change and fluctuation. How do you keep this chaotic power off for this whole period, which is of course long in proportion to the security of your own advantageous chance at the end of it? How do you keep an oasis of rest immediately around your own organ, while all the world is moving; and guarantee a vacant interval to it, which is counter to the general law of disturbance? It must be remembered that pure chance is the wildest thing possible; for one turn or motion of matter that chimes in with a given stage of an organ, there are millions that clash with it, and that are destructive of it.[1] How do you keep all *these* chances at arm's-length, and secure a monopoly of the ground preparatory to the arrival of the other chance, *i.e.* needed variation? But suppose one period of waiting thus kept clear, with the coinciding addition at the end of it, how, according to any laws of probability, could you repeat it? Or if you repeated it once, how would you go on repeating it an indefinite number of times, *i.e.* all the times that were wanted for the structure to be completed? A succession of given variations, *in themselves* making up an order and chain, would be nothing, unless you could also keep the intervals in the succession vacant and clear; but this upon your own hypothesis you cannot do. You cannot keep your organ quiet. It has the constant liabilities resulting from a wild basis of Nature. It is threatened at any time by eccentricity and distortion. Of what use, then, is the guarantee of time for a chance variation coming, if you cannot secure your organ from metamorphose or from actual destruction before the required variation arrives?

The way in which a man conceives and represents to himself the working of chance, when he gets the result now spoken of out of it, seems to be this: he first puts to himself one period of waiting only, and decides that there is nothing counter to moral possibility in supposing that a favourable accretion to an organ or structure may come by chance in that time. Having constituted, then, a first period of waiting, with a happy coincidence at the end of it, he proceeds to repeat the same period with the same coincidence, thus, as it were, forcing chance, converting it into an accommodating material, arranging it, and bringing it into harness. But such a negotiation and compact with this wild power is impossible. Is not the advocate of natural selection deceived by the enormous intervals of time which he interposes between the successive steps of the progress, so that he forgets every time the succeeding

---

[1] "Si donc vous supposez l'œil se formant par une addition infinie de phénomènes, il y a infiniment plus de chances pour qu'il soit altéré ou détruit que perfectionné.— *Matérialisme Contemporain*, par Paul Janet, Membre de l'Institut.

step comes that it is a coincidence with a preceding one? These successive coinciding developments equally require to be accounted for, whether the intervals between them are minutes or ages. Suppose I throw in regular series from one to fifty, the chances against those fifty throws in succession are the same, whether there is a second of time between each two or a million of years. But the advocate of natural selection seems to think that, because he throws with ages between instead of seconds, the coincidence in his successive throws has not to be accounted for.

It is impossible, then, that promiscuous variability could construct the existing species, because under it no fit, no adaptation could be other than a chance coincidence, and this can not be repeated to the extent of the formation of a species without an absurdity. The theory of natural selection, indeed, would fain make existence itself a ladder of ascent, and constitute a perpetual rise by the perpetual extinction of an inferior. But though natural selection guarantees a superiority in the structure of the surviving party in any given struggle, it can not guarantee a succession of struggles upon a succession of ascending points in the animal structure. Take an intricate organ, such as the lungs or heart, and the succession of acts of Nature in forming the elaborate existing structure of it out of the asserted original rudiment becomes an insuperable difficulty.

"I can hardly doubt," says Mr. Darwin, "that all vertebrate animals, having true lungs, have descended by ordinary generation from an ancient prototype of which we know nothing, furnished with a floating apparatus or swim-bladder."

But the transmutation of a mere air-bladder, which contracts and expands, into the full system of the lungs, with the bifurcation of the trachea on the one part, conveying the air first into the large and next into the minute bronchial tubes and cells, and the bifurcation of the pulmonary artery on the other, conveying the blood by a ramification of the finest channels into juxtaposition with those tubes and air-cells; this is a process, the successful completion of which by chance variation is an accumulated impossibility. The necessity of accounting for such a work of construction is exactly the same upon the theory of transition and the ordinary theory of creation, and some other principle than chance is as much called for upon one hypothesis as upon the other.

Or to take again the crucial test of the eye. Mr. Darwin himself says :—

"To suppose that the eye, with all its inimitable contrivances for adjusting the focus to different distances, for admitting different amounts of light, and for the correction of spherical and chromatic aberration, could have been formed by natural selection, seems, I freely confess, absurd in the highest possible degree."

But if he thinks the facts of Nature so strong for design—if he thinks there is such an enormous difficulty in accounting for them on any other understanding—if he says any account which dispenses with such an understanding "seems absurd in the highest possible degree"—why does he gratuitously expose himself to this difficulty? why does he volunteer to dispense with this understanding? The progress of Nature which he supposes, may be held just as well *with* an inner law of design as *without* it. Why, then, when Mr. Darwin can hold this progress as designed, does he hold it as undesigned, as he appears to do by this confession of the apparent absurdity and shock to reason which his position contains? He does not, of course, see any absurdity—any apparent shock to reason—in the mere theory of development, as such; that to which the apparent absurdity and shock to reason attach is development without design. The apparent absurdity he sees in the growth of the eye is its growth by a mere accumulation of chance variations. But why in that case does he hold it as a growth by a mere accumulation of chance variations? Why does Mr. Darwin voluntarily dispense with a rationale by which the execution of his theory is not hindered, and without which his theory does, as he himself admits, "seem absurd"?[1] He must

[1] "Or, je le demande," says M. Janet, "à M. Darwin lui-même, quel intérêt a-t-il à soutenir que l'élection naturelle n'est pas guidée, n'est pas dirigée? Quel intérêt a-t-il à remplacer toute cause finale par des causes accidentelles? On ne le voit pas. Qu'il admette que, dans l'élection naturelle aussi bien que dans l'élection artificielle, il peut y avoir un choix et une direction, et son principe devient aussitôt bien autrement fécond."

remember that he is, as Dr. Acland opportunely hints, under a greater difficulty on this head than M. Comte is. Mr. Darwin is an optimist with respect to Nature; he thinks the result perfectly admirable and unimpeachable. M. Comte does not think so; he criticises and censures Nature. Mr. Darwin's estimate of facts, then, adds to the difficulty of the omission of a Providence in the explanation of them; and M. Comte's blame of Nature, if a worse judgment of results, is better fitted to, and corresponds more with, his rationale of the cause.

A pure variability which issues in organisation is in truth nothing but the natural philosophy of Lucretius:—

> "Primordia rerum
> Ex infinito jam tempore percita plagis
> Ponderibusque suis consuerunt concita ferri,
> Omnimodisque coire, atque omnia pertentare,
> Quæcunque inter se possint congressa creare,
> Ut non sit mirum si in tales disposituras
> Deciderunt."

Lucretius had not indeed any physical theory to account for the disappearance of intermediate and anomalous forms; but his fount of development is the same as Mr. Darwin's: Time—*ex infinito jam tempore*, etc. In the Epicurean philosophy, time exhausted chance, and inserted a period of organisation in the universal chaos, on the ground that disorder could not upon the mere principle of chance go on always, but wore itself out; and allowed order to have its day. This school thus really thought that it made a complete Eureka when it promulgated as the explanation of the physical world—chance. It congratulated itself on being the first discoverer of this great power, and expressed the utmost surprise that it had never occurred before to anybody to see what a vast fund of causation lay hid in it. For, they argued, chance in *time* can do anything—only give it an infinity of time: things must have some form or other; they have in the infinite past gone through every phase of monstrosity [1] that was possible: of which state of the world,

---

[1] "Multaque tum Tellus etiam portenta creare
Conata est, mira facie, membrisque coorta;
Orba pedum partim, manuum viduata vicissim,
Muta sine ore etiam, sine voltu cæca reperta,
Vinctaque membrorum per totum corpus adhæsu;

in the very nature of the case, we know nothing; but now that things have gone through all conceivable eccentric forms, a stage of organisation comes about by the doctrine of chance, and such an insertion in the infinite duration of the world is a happy coincidence that must take place sooner or later. Such a position is of course absurd, because no time can really exhaust chance. Chance is as infinite as time. Chance, therefore, could never bring the Epicurean his oasis of universal order in any extent of time. Nor could a simple undirected variability, a variability without scope or aim, ever produce the existing world of species; it could never exhaust its stock of incongruities and imperfections.

There is an evident chasm, therefore, in the theory of Natural Selection which we must fill up before it can work; there is something to be accounted for which is not accounted for—the mode in which the variability of Nature, in fact, operates, the succession with which its gifts come out, the adaptation and agreement kept up in a long series of separate additions to and modifications of organs from their rudimental to their final form, the accumulation of the resources of Nature in particular directions,—so as to make up at last harmonious structures. The external check of natural selection which comes *after* variation, cannot possibly account for this succession in it; there must be a guiding principle within variability itself, by virtue of which its additions come out congruously, follow up a line begun, and form a connected string of operations. The contents of the great reservoir (here for the purpose of argument assumed), as a matter of fact, come out upon, or so as to make up, a plan; the pieces set together however gradually and at intervals. We ask why? It is slow work indeed, ages are consumed in the progress; one piece comes in ever so long a time after another; but as a matter of fact they have all composed into one plan, which we see. How has all this been going on? As natural selection does not by its very

> Nec facere ut possent quicquam, nec cedere quoquam,
> Nec vitare malum, nec sumere quod foret usus.
> Cætera de genere hoc monstra ac portenta creabat;
> Nequicquam; quoniam Natura absterruit auctum."

function construct, there must be some prior principle which does; the hypothesis requires another hypothesis to work it; it needs complementing by a scope in Nature, a working toward an end, or a principle of design. "Nous ne sommes ni pour ni contre la transmutation des espèces," says M. Janet, "ni pour ni contre le principe de l'élection naturelle. La seule conclusion positive de notre discussion est celle-ci : aucun principe jusqu'ici, ni l'action des milieux, ni l'habitude, ni l'élection naturelle, ne peut expliquer les appropriations organiques sans l'intervention du principe de finalité."[1]

Does not, indeed, the advocate of natural selection, while he thinks he gets everything out of *it*, unconsciously manipulate his material, and supply, by an insensible understanding with himself, a sort of gradation and method to the issues from variability? Does he not provide out of his own mind, without thinking of it, by reason of the familiarity which he has with order in Nature, a succession and order for these outgoings from the reservoir of Nature?

The parallel which Mr. Darwin institutes between the process of variation and development as an artificial system, and the process in Nature, is not one certainly which goes against this conclusion. In artificial breeding we see a process of variation tending to the improvement and perfection of the species; but it is a process which goes on distinctly by design.

"Le véritable écueil, à notre avis," says M. Janet, "de la théorie de M. Darwin, le point périlleux et glissant, c'est le passage de l'élection artificielle à l'élection naturelle : c'est d'établir qu'une Nature aveugle et sans dessein a pu atteindre, par la rencontre des circonstances, le même résultat qu'obtient l'homme par une industrie réfléchie et calculée."

Natural selection is indeed that result in the field of Nature,

[1] "Un botaniste distingué, M. Naudin (récemment appelé à l'Institut) qui, avant même M. Darwin, a comparé l'action plastique de la Nature dans la formation des espèces végétales à l'élection systématique de l'homme, reconnaît que l'élection naturelle est insuffisante sans le principe de finalité. 'Puissance mystérieuse,' dit-il, ' indéterminée, fatalité pour les uns, pour les autres volonté providentielle, dont l'action incessante sur les êtres vivants détermine à toutes les époques de l'existence du monde la forme, le volume et la durée de chacun d'eux en raison de sa destinée dans l'ordre de choses dont il fait partie !'"—*Matérialisme Contemporain*, p. 180.

which answers to the success of an article in trade. The field of trade exhibits a struggle between different goods and pieces of workmanship for existence: the old article goes on being sold till the improved article makes its appearance, when the better production beats the old one out of the market, which consequently disappears and is no more heard of. But it would be absurd to say that the new and improved article was made *by* the old one being beaten out of the market. The natural selection of trade assumes the previous construction of the successful production by contrivance. In the history of a steam-engine a hundred improved engines have successively driven a hundred unimproved ones off the field. Civilisation is made up from first to last of conquests of improved methods, arts, manufactures, over unimproved ones. Science is a constant progress from defective hypotheses to sounder and more correct ones; and as the correcter ones are discovered, the defective ones are sent to the wall and disappear. But it would be absurd to say that this disappearance of old contrivances *accounted* for human progress; because it is human progress which accounts for that. The perfect steam-engine owes to the natural selection of trade the destruction of the imperfect steam-engine; and the Copernican hypothesis owes to the natural selection of philosophy the withdrawal of the Ptolemaic one; but both improvements owe *themselves* to constructive power. In civilisation there has been an intelligence taking advantage of each successive stage in the progress to rise to a higher one; the succeeding mind has known the discovery of the preceding one, has fitted on his own to it, and has risen by starting upon its platform: and a unity of design, though the current has used generations as its channels, thus appears in the construction of the work. So on the field of Nature natural selection, supposing Mr. Darwin's theory of Progress to be true, cannot relieve us from the need of some prior principle, some intelligence, however mysterious, which has worked for an end in Nature, and under whose guidance this progress has proceeded.

We have hitherto taken variability in a simple way, without reference to *laws*. But variability, we are told, is governed by laws—laws at present almost wholly unknown to us, and belonging to a region of utter physical mystery, but which nevertheless exist and are laws which produce as their results the whole of the fifth and sixth days of the Mosaic creation; *i.e.* are the laws by the operation of which the whole existing animal creation has been formed.

Upon which basis then, do these occult laws, when they produce this result, work—Chance or Design? That is the question. To say that they are laws simply, does not decide that question. To say that they are *laws* simply, does not in the least imply that their issue may not be an utter medley. Laws may be irregular, blind, unmeaning, promiscuous laws, without concurrence or understanding with each other, without consistency or scope, and still be laws, as being each uniform sets of occurrences; they may be mere capricious laws, such as that cats with blue eyes are deaf, and still be laws; they may tend to no structural result whatever, and they may still be laws; they may be a chaos collectively, and laws separately. Law is indeed a midway position between chance and design, at which many minds find it convenient to stop. Chance is an absurdity; design is a mystery; law has, or appears to have, the great advantage of a neutral ground. Stop then at laws, says the Comtist, says the Secularist; acknowledge uniform facts, but do not ask a single question beyond this. It is in vain. Reason cannot be suppressed. Laws are simply facts— only uniform facts. The question then has to be asked about laws, just as it has to be asked about facts—have they issued in what they have issued in, by chance or by design?

To the question, then, whether the existing species can be referred to chance *laws* of variability, the same answer may be given that has been given to the question, put simply, whether they can be referred to chance variability. The insertion of *laws*, in the form of putting the question, does not in fact make the slightest difference; and all the reasons which have been given why chance variability could not have produced the existing animal creation, apply to chance-working laws of variability. If I see an harmonious structure as the result, and you suppose as the cause a quantity of blind unsystematic laws, do you think I can be satisfied with that cause simply because it is law—a number of laws? It cannot be. Then I must suppose something different. I must suppose a system of co-operating laws. If we know nothing about those laws in particular, we know that they must stand in some relation to that which they produce ; that they must correspond to that which they produce, and that they must coincide, to produce results that coincide. We know that there must be inter-correspondence, that there must be relationship to each other in such laws; but, if there is, then such laws show design ; for there can no more be a fortuitous concurrence of laws than a fortuitous concurrence of atoms. Let us throw aside for a moment the philosophical fiction and conventionality of laws, and think only of movements of matter ; going on, if you will, for ages and countless ages, but going on with a growing and expanding arrangement—a rudimental world disposing itself gradually into intricate system, and separating, by different directions, into multitudinous forms and shapes of mechanism; this is nothing but the actual fact which Mr. Darwin places before us. But if we could suppose ourselves witnessing this spectacle, and endowed with those extended faculties which would bring the work of ages within a spectator's view and grasp, annihilating the intervals of time between the successive steps of the formation, what would be the effect ? Could we possibly suppress the interpretation that there was a mind working behind and underneath such a process ?

When we look, indeed, at the two or three fragments of the code of variability which have emerged out of the dark abyss into Mr. Darwin's notice, we cannot but make the observation that, though mere outer laws not concerned with the inner structure of the animal, on the rule of *ex pede Herculem*, they certainly glance significantly in this direction. The law that specific characters are more variable than generic, and extraordinarily developed parts than ordinarily developed ones, and the law of reversion, directly minister to the stability of Nature ; they supply an invisible anchorage and mooring. The law of " compensation or balancement of growth," by which Nature, in order to spend on one side economises on the other, carries, on the face of it, something of the nature of a purpose, because it prevents the vital resources from consuming themselves in the attempt to supply too large a demand. The law of correlation of growth has so obviously the look of an arrangement that it figures in Paley's theology as one of the proofs of design. For correlation of growth in the animal body is a different fact from the correlation of the sides of a crystal; it is correlation in a structure formed for use, and whose use stops half-way and waits for correlation to complete it; it is correlation *concurring* and chiming in with another fact, viz., an organic body, and joining in attaining the purpose of that body, and not simple symmetrical correlation. The Duke of Argyll well observes:—

"Two growths might be correlated as regards each other, and might yet be wanting in any corresponding correlation of fitness and of function towards outward things. But the first of these two kinds of correlation would be useless without the last. And this last is obviously the higher and more complex correlation of the two. It is higher, not only in the sense of being more complex, but as involving an idea which lifts us at once from a lower to a higher region of thought, . . . from the work of Forces with inherent Polarity of action, to the operation of Forces working under adjustment with a view to purpose."

Are we then at liberty to interpret Mr. Darwin as maintaining the existence of these unknown laws of variability in this *sense*, viz., as constituting collectively a system of laws indicating design? Such an interpretation of himself by Mr. Darwin would be no more than a legitimate consequence of an admission which he makes upon the very threshold of his theory. He admits that the first life-germ was a creation; and if there is design in *his* first organism, that primary design must be credited with the whole of the final issue. It is impossible to suppose that the Creator of the rudimental germ which was to produce as its issue this existing world could after myriads of years awake out of sleep, and be astonished at the actual result of His own creation-seed:—that it was so much more than he had expected; to conceive this would be to suppose not even the Supreme Being of philosophy, but the idol of the pagan; it would be to imagine a Deity such as that which Elijah mocked at, a Deity like the Zeus of Homer, who could not hear the grievance of Achilles because he had gone to sup with the Ethiopians. But if we cannot suppose a God who is genuinely surprised at His own universe, and startled at the sound which He himself hath made, then, if Mr. Darwin supposes one true original creative act, the universal result must be included in that act. If design has once operated *in rerum natura*, how can it stop operating, and undesigned formation succeed it? It cannot; and intention in Nature having once existed, the test of the amount of that intention is not the commencement but the end; not the first low organism but the climax and consummation of the whole.

We are not at liberty, however, to interpret Mr. Darwin. *We* say that these laws of variability, if they issue in, if they collectively account for an elaborate system, as by the hypothesis they do, must contain system themselves, and therefore contain design; but we have not the right to say that Mr. Darwin thinks so, and are therefore unable to do more than fall back upon an alternative in treating with him. He must take the choice of two alternatives for his hypothesis to work with, —Chance or Design. The intermediate position of laws is no resting-place. Does he allow that these *de facto* concurring and co-operating laws of variability contain design? In that case his hypothesis is worked by means of a design in Nature. Does he *not* allow that they contain design? In that case his hypothesis is worked by chance. It is worked by the extraordinary coincidence of these laws or movements of matter *happening* to meet together, so as to have a plastic operation. The laws are laws in respect of the separate uniformity of each; but their concurrence in a constructive effect, not being due to any purpose, not being attributed to any cause, is chance; and the fashioning of animal nature which is conducted by laws which are altogether chance *with respect to* that fashioning process, is as much by chance as if there were no laws in the case. He must either make his theory rational, then, by the admission of design; or by the omission of design he must leave it a substantially Epicurean hypothesis, accounting for the formation of the animal world by chance.

And so we come round to Paley again. Paley had some

great wants; he wanted religious imagination; he wanted the sense of mystery; he almost wanted the sense of wonder; he treated the world too much like an instance of ordinary manufacture; but one thing he did do—he brought out with an incomparable perspicacity, and with a power which no one had done before, the verdict of facts for Design. We append to his great statement the observation that, if the verdict of facts is once given, physical causes can never reverse it—can never extort from those facts a retractation of their sentence. We do not in this article either adopt or reject the principal physical hypothesis with which we have dealt, viz., that of the Transmutation of Species; we have only required for our purpose the supposition of its truth in order to extort from it the confession that Design alone can supply an imperative need in its structure, and fill up a chasm at its very foundation which otherwise paralyses and incapacitates it at the very outset as a working hypothesis.

THE PRINCIPLE OF CAUSATION

CONSIDERED IN OPPOSITION TO ATHEISTIC THEORIES.*

(JULY 1872).

BEFORE I go to my subject I will make some general remarks on metaphysics, regarded as adapted for popular thought. When people in general regard metaphysics, as they appear to do, as a curious puzzle, in which arguers give reasons for things which have nothing to do with nature or common sense, but entirely belong to an artificial speciality created by an understanding among themselves, they should be reminded sometimes of the fact that everybody is a metaphysician, and cannot help being one. Metaphysics could not possibly have had any existence except there had been some great leading ideas in man's mind upon the foundation of which they had arisen. These elementary metaphysical ideas, then, belong to everybody; nay, and they are evidently so simple a part of our natural reason that we do not look upon them as metaphysical at all. We are aware of a certain profoundness and grandeur that belong to them, which distinguishes them from other ideas; but they are as perfect realities to us, at the same time, as truths of ordinary common sense. They do not belong to any fictitious world, though they raise us to another type of truths, other modes of existence in this. They are actualities of a most stupendous kind. Thus, take the first idea of this class that occurs to one—the idea of Infinity. This is a metaphysical idea; it arises out of our own minds, it is not a copy

* *The Principle of Causation considered in opposition to Atheistic Theories.* A Lecture delivered in connection with the Christian Evidence Society, July 19, 1872.

from nature, as many images in our minds are. I need not say that we never saw any object or extent that was infinite; it would be a contradiction to say that we had. But there is something in me by which I know antecedently that space is going on all the same as space, however differently it may be occupied, beyond my sight as within it. Having raised in my mind the largest portion of space I can, so that if I try to increase I simply repeat it, I have still a sense of limitation. There is at the furthest line of the horizon an excess which baffles me; which is not included in the imagined space, or it would not be an excess, and which yet belongs and is attached to it and cannot be removed; an incipient beyond, which must be endless for the very reason that it begins; because this indefinable excess, for the very reason that it exists itself, must be succeeded by the like. Infinity, then, is a metaphysical idea; but is it an idea without reality, without interest, without popular attractions? On the contrary, it is an idea which appeals vividly to our imagination, which is impelled to efforts at the pursuit of it, vain indeed, but which exalt the intelligent spirit in the very act of overpowering it. And so far from being fictitious and illusive, it is an actual attribute of this material world; it belongs to the actual space around us in such a way that we cannot by any mental effort remove it; we cannot prevent this outward material portion of space in which we are from going off into an incomprehensible mystery. Give me a fragment of space, and I can understand it; but carry this fragment itself onward, and by simply extending, simply going on, it becomes as absolute a mystery as has ever been contained in a creed. The idea of infinity has within it, as soon as men enter into it at all, a perfect romance, which all the flights of human fancy cannot overtake; the strange and insoluble enigmas of reason which come out of it act as a spell upon the imaginative curiosity of the human mind. It is thus that the ideas of metaphysicians, so far from being unreal, are bound up with this very field of vision in which we are; and, so far from being artificial, dry, and technical, belong to the very mystery and romance of nature. Infinity is a fact, and at the same time a mystery. We can no more deny that there is Infinity on all sides of us, wherever we point a finger, than we can deny our eyesight; and yet what *is* material Infinity, sidereal space? endless everywhere? It is as mysterious as a spectre.

Everybody, then, is a metaphysician, just as everybody is a poet. Just as everybody is endowed with those elementary sentiments and affections, and is influenced by those associations which, taken up by language, become poetry; so everybody has the primary ideas and maxims of metaphysics. Even the Bible can no more be understood without the aid of these great metaphysical ideas than it can be without grammar.

So, when we take up the idea of Cause, which is the foundation of so large a branch of metaphysical argument, we go at once to an idea which is one of the most obvious of all our principles of thought, and which appeals to us as most simple and rudimental truth. It is a self-evident maxim that every event must have a cause. After contemplating any event in life or nature, I find myself going in thought beyond it, to consider how it came to pass; by some instinctive law, some constitutional motion inherent in my mind, I go in the direction of a cause of that event; something not merely antecedent to it, but which stands in such a relation to it as that, in consequence of it, that event or thing exists. The intellect pushes on to this resting-place, as a satisfaction of its own indigenous want and desire. It is evidently upon this principle that we entirely depend for the slightest real connection between the present, the past, and the future; otherwise, and but for this principle, this whole connection is annihilated. Is it, can we imagine it to be indeed the case, that anything can in a moment begin to exist without there being any cause for it? Then no link whatever exists between one event in the universe and another; the whole concatenation of things falls to pieces, and the whole fabric of the world is dissolved, other than as a mere spectacle to the eye. Everything is perfectly independent, has nothing to do with anything else, begins of itself and ends of itself.

But when we look into the idea of Cause, we find immediately that it involves the most astonishing thoughts and conceptions. We cannot help ourselves having it, we cannot help ourselves being bound by the necessity of it, we cannot release ourselves from its grasp; but it is at the same time such an unfathomable idea that we pause under the impress of it, and feel ourselves under some great solemnising shadow as soon as we enter into this region of thought. As soon as the gates of the awful kingdom of Causation have unclosed, we are instantly upon, I will not say magic ground, for that is to convey a sense of illusion and unreality, but upon mysterious ground; and we are in company with majestic, inconceivable ideas, which we cannot grasp, and yet cannot do else than accept. For while the movement *towards* a cause is part of my rational nature, I find on reflection that I can form no distinct conception of what a cause is. What is that of which existence is the necessary fruit and result? We can form no idea of what goes on previous to, and with infallible cogency and force for producing existence. All this preliminary agency is entirely hid from us, and our faculties completely stop short of it. The order of nature puts before us an endless succession of antecedents, but in no one instance can we see any necessary connection between the antecedent and its consequent. But though we cannot raise the distinctive conception of what a cause is, we are not the less absolutely certain that there must be a cause, and that nothing can take place without one.

Again, the very first consequence of this idea of cause, and one which is implied necessarily in the very conception of a cause, is a result which appals us by its tremendous inconceivability; and yet it is a truth of the most absolute and obvious necessity; nay, it is an absolute and certain fact, which every single rational being, whether he be a believer in religion or not, must accept as simply and unreservedly as he does the evidence of his senses; and that is, that from all eternity something has existed. "This is so evident and undeniable a proposition," says Samuel Clarke, "that no atheist in any age has ever presumed to assert the contrary. For since something now is, it is manifest that something always was. For whatever now is has a cause, a reason, a ground of its existence—a foundation on which its existence relies, a ground or reason why it doth exist, rather than not exist; and this foundation [of a thing which has come into existence] must have existed before it. That something, therefore, has really existed from all eternity is one of the certainest and most evident truths in the world, acknowledged by all men and disputed by none. Yet as to the manner how it can be, there is nothing in nature more difficult for the mind of man to conceive than this very first plain and self-evident truth. For how anything can have existed eternally, that is, how an eternal duration can be now actually past, is a thing utterly as impossible for our narrow understandings to comprehend as anything that is not an express contradiction can be imagined to be. And yet to deny the truth of the proposition that an eternal duration is now actually past, would be to assert something far more unintelligible, even an express and real contradiction."

The idea of cause is thus the key to an eternal past, which has contained being of some kind or another. By means of that necessary *regress* which exists in the idea, this mental principle holds the entrance into that interminable and infinite retrospect, which in metaphysical terms is called the *ex parte* ante-eternity. There the vista is; and so long as it is true that every event must have a cause, it must exist—this unceasing past duration, going back endlessly and for ever. An atheist and a materialist has this endless past that he must look back upon, just as much as a believer in a God has. In his view the action of matter goes back in successive steps, each leaning upon one still further back than itself, and the retrospective chain of operations never stops, but goes back for ever. This is indeed an absolutely inconceivable idea—the actual pastness, if I may use the term, of an eternal duration of time: that an eternity is now over. And yet an atheist must believe this, simply because it is a fact. It is just as much a fact as yesterday. Yesterday existed yesterday: that is certain enough. The day before existed next. And so every portion of time goes back to a prior portion, and in the eye of the materialist each has its material contents just as solid and actual as those of yesterday: this visible world goes back for ever. This is not a mere idea. A past eternity of material operations is an actual fact to an atheist, though a past eternity is utterly incomprehensible ; but a God, because He is incomprehensible, is not even an object of faith. Such a mistake would it be for the materialist to assume that because he believed only matter, he had therefore escaped from the yoke of mystery. That ghostly power waits like a giant, ready to pull him back as soon as ever he thinks he is out of his reach, and throws him into the coils of the very enigma which he had run away from. Space and time introduce to consequences which are as inconceivable as articles of faith ; and yet these consequences are actual facts ; just as much so as the experience of our senses.

We have now got as far as the idea of cause, or the instinctive maxim of our nature that every event must have a cause. And here I pause to make two observations. One is, that it is most important to distinguish between the philosophical idea of the necessity of a cause and any perception of the necessary character of *physical* causes—those phenomenal causes which precede events in nature; which precede them uniformly and invariably, and therefore obtain the name of physical causes, but which do not in the slightest degree reveal their own nature as causes, and therefore do not reveal their own necessity. To say in general that a cause is necessary, is not to say that we see causes in such and such phenomena. The one is a maxim of our intellectual nature, the other would be a judgment upon a fact, which we are unable to pronounce. But though the operation of real causes nowhere comes under our cognisance, but only a chain of antecedents, we have not the less still inherent in our minds the idea of cause, and the certainty that every event must have a cause.

The other observation is, that so long as we put the maxim that every event must have a cause in such a way to ourselves as recognises the necessary character of it, it is not of much importance what special philosophical explanation we adopt of it ; whether we regard it as an ultimate and primary law of the reason, or as a derivation from some prior and more general law. Hume denied indeed the necessary character of the maxim that every event must have a cause. "The separation," he says, "of the idea of a cause from that of the beginning of existence is plainly possible for the imagination; and consequently the actual separation of these objects is so far possible that it implies no contradiction or absurdity; and is, therefore, incapable of being refuted by any reasoning from mere ideas, without which it is impossible to demonstrate the necessity of a cause."[1] Hume accounted for the idea of the necessity of a cause by custom—the impression which the constant sight of uniform antecedence made upon the mind, which was the same as if they were necessary, or real causes. To which Sir W. Hamilton replies, that this could not create in the mind that idea of necessity which we actually find there, and concludes:— "The alternative is plain: either the doctrine of sensualism (*i.e.* accounting for the idea of cause from mere sensible experience) is false, or our nature is a delusion. . . . It is manifest that the observation of certain phenomena succeeding certain other phenomena . . . could never have engendered not only the strong but irresistible conviction that every event must have its cause."[2] But though the denial of all reality in the necessity of a cause of events, or the assertion that events can take place without anything really to cause them, must be rejected as a paradox, there is no reason why room may not be allowed for different philosophical explanations of the origin of the causal judgment. The more ordinary course has been to refer this to a special idea inherent in the human mind, to maintain it as a "primary datum, a positive revelation of intelligence;" and Sir W. Hamilton reckons Leibnitz, Kant, and Cousin as holding this position. He himself, however, is opposed, as he expresses it, "to the assumption of a special principle," and maintains that the idea of causation comes under a larger law, and is only one of the operations of that law. "The law of parsimony, which he regards as nature's general rule," he observes, "prohibits the multiplication of entities, powers, principles and causes, above all the postulation of an unknown force, where a known impotence can account for the phenomenon. We are, therefore, entitled to apply 'Occam's razor' to

---

[1] *Of the Understanding*, sect. iii.   [2] *Discussions in Philosophy*, App. i.

this theory of causality, unless it be proved impossible to explain the causal judgment at a cheaper rate, by deriving it from a common, and that a negative, principle." His theory reduces the judgment of causality "into a form of the mental law of the Conditional. ... The mind is astricted to think in certain forms, ... we must think under the condition of existence—existence relative—and existence relative in time. But what does *existence relative in time* imply? It implies that we are unable to realise in thought either an absolute commencement or an absolute termination of time. ... We cannot know or think a thing to exist except as in time; and we cannot know or think a thing to exist in time, and think it absolutely to *commence.* Now this at once imposes on us the condition of causality."[1] Sir W. Hamilton's theory, then, seems to be, that as we cannot conceive any real commencement, while at the same time there is phenomenal commencement, the cause is only the shape in which a thing exists, before its present shape —a rationale of causation which is substantially the same as Mr. Baines's, but which the latter extracts not out of metaphysics, like Sir W. Hamilton, but from physical science. "A great advance," he says, "in the mode of viewing causation is made by the discovery of the law named conservation of force. The great generalisation of recent times, variously designated the conservation, correlation, convertibility, equivalence, indestructibility, of force, is the highest expression of cause and effect."[2] Dean Mansel, however, does not accept Sir W. Hamilton's explanation of causation. "His statement of the causal judgment, as an inability to think that the complement of existence has been either increased or diminished, is open to various objections. In the first place, I am not conscious of any such inability. ... I have no difficulty in conceiving that the amount of existence in the universe may at one time be represented by A, and at another by A and B. ... In the second place, whether we represent the new appearance as a *change* or as a *creation*, we are equally compelled to suppose a cause of its taking place. To say that B previously existed under the form of A, is not to explain the causal judgment;

[1] *Ibid.*, Appendix i.   [2] *Logic*, iii. iv. 8.

for we have still to ask why A became B. In the third place, the theory fails to account for the origin of the idea of *power*, which, whether rightly or wrongly, all men instinctively attribute to the supposed cause. To represent it as a delusion is not sufficient; unless it can be shown how, consistently with the limits of thought, such a delusion could have originated."[1]

But while new explanations have recently been given of the causal judgment, or the maxim that every event must have a cause, our older metaphysicians, Locke and Clarke, were satisfied with the evident necessity which upon common principles of reason attached to the truth, and they treated it virtually as an axiom, the contrary of which was a plain absurdity, and involved an absolute contradiction. They regarded the reasoning that necessarily flowed from this metaphysical axiom as demonstrative reasoning. Nor, indeed, is it easy to see, if we treat this maxim as a necessary one, and consider it possesses self-evident force, how we can avoid the demonstrative nature of the truth. It would be a lame and impotent decision, such as could satisfy no rational person, to say that it was probable that every event had a cause; but if we say this maxim is necessary, then we must admit that it is of the nature of metaphysical mathematics. Notwithstanding, then, the modern ingenious rationales of this maxim which have been offered to us, I must confess myself disposed to fall back upon the judgment of our older metaphysicians upon this point.

If we apply this maxim then to actions and determinations of the will, all that every event having a cause can mean is that every action has an agent. The agent is the cause of the action in the sense of doing it, and it depends upon our theory of the will whether he is a necessary or a free cause of it. If he is a necessary cause, this is the doctrine of necessity in human actions; if he is a free cause, this is the doctrine of free-will, or that the will determines its own acts, and is a self-moving substance. But this maxim, as used in the metaphysical argument for the existence of a God, has only an application to events which happen in the sphere of substance

[1] *Metaphysics*, p. 271.

which is not self-moving, but the characteristic of which is that it is moved from without. If we except the invisible wills of moral beings, the whole world we are in belongs to this mechanical nature; not only the whole order of physical nature, but the whole of history and the whole course of human action, so far as it is visible and comes under the cognisance of our senses. War, trade, government and administration, manufacture, art, language or speech, everything that we do, so far as it is visible and tangible, consists of a number of material and mechanical movements which are all caused by prior material and mechanical movements, and these again by others as far as we can trace. Spiritually we are conscious of what we call free-will, or of a nature which determines its own acts, *i.e.* moves itself; but outwardly and visibly all nature is moved from without, and does not move itself. In every action we perform, all that is seen is the motion of matter, the same in speaking, the same in our looks and expressions. Certain muscles are put in motion, which produce certain effects on the body itself, which in some cases stop there, and in other cases go beyond the body, to surrounding objects. Such is all visible nature : either it is what we call the order of nature, or it is action of man : under either head, it consists of the motions of matter, and of matter alone, which is not self-moving, but is moved from without.

But with this application it is difficult to say that the maxim that an event must have a cause is not mathematical in its nature. We apply it to motions of such things and substances as do not move themselves. But if these motions do not proceed from the substances themselves, whence can they proceed from but from without them? But in that case, whatever it is without them which makes them move is the *cause* of that motion.

The maxim, then, that every event must have a cause, or that what cannot move itself must be moved from without, differs from mathematical axioms in this, that whereas mathematical axioms stop with themselves, and we do not apply them to actual things, this maxim we apply to the actual material of this world. Did we apply, *e.g.*, the axiom that things which are equal to the same are equal to one another to actual things, we should first have to ascertain the fact that the two things were exactly equal, which we could not demonstratively do. But we do not give the axiom an application to actual facts, but leave it resting upon an assumption or definition of two things as equal; which being the case, it continues a pure mathematical truth. In the same way, if we simply said that what could not move itself must be moved from without, or, which would be the same thing, if we made it enter into our definition of matter, that it could not move itself, and upon this definition asserted that matter must be moved from without, this maxim, that every material movement must have a cause, would be a mathematical one. But we do not let this maxim stay in this mathematical stage; we apply this definition of matter to the whole actual material of this world, and we say that this actual material cannot move itself, but must have been moved from without. Here, then, we no longer rest upon a definition, but we assert a fact; and we cannot prove this fact mathematically, but only take it as a moral certainty, which is evident to common sense. If matter possesses an original power of motion, or has will, all we can say is that we have made a great mistake; but appearances are universally against such a supposition. The maxim, then, that every event must have a cause, is the axiom of mathematical metaphysics that what cannot move itself must be moved from without, operating upon a supposition of *fact;* viz., that all actual matter comes under the head of this category, of what cannot move itself.

We have now got the idea of cause, with the preliminary considerations attaching to it. But now that we have got the idea of cause, or the principle of causation, comes the great distinction in the interpretation of the idea, upon which depends the issue whether we can apply it to constituting the proof of a God or not; whether we can raise a religious conclusion upon it or not; whether we can use it as the foundation upon which an Eternal and Supreme Moral Being can be shown to exist, or whether it is reducible to a barren and fruitless succession which ends in nothing. It is upon this question that the whole of the great metaphysical argument for the existence of a God from causation depends. We assert that the whole of this argument is strictly extracted and evolved from the idea of a cause, as it is naturally conceived and entertained in our minds; that it is simply the contents of that idea brought out, when by an act of the attention we have entered into the idea, and seen how it is constituted and what there is in it. On the other hand, this constitution of the idea is denied by the atheist; and he claims to hold the idea in such a sense as leads to no such conclusion.

When we speak of a cause then, and of the idea of a cause which we have in our minds, the question to be decided is, does this idea demand finality, or is it satisfied by an infinite chain and series of causes? We assert, then, that this idea demands finality; and adopting the maxim, "*Causa causæ, causa causati*," we say that if a cause goes back to a further cause, then the first of these two causes is not a true and real cause, and does not satisfy the idea of a cause in our minds; and so on through ever so long a chain, until we come to a cause which has no further cause to which it goes back. That is our interpretation of the idea of cause; and we say that any other interpretation of the idea is a false one, and sets up a counterfeit cause instead of a real and true one. Let us examine what we do in our minds, in conceiving the idea of cause. First we go back for a cause; the natural want and ὄρεξις is a retrogressive *motion* of the mind. But just as the first part of the idea of cause is motion, so the last is a rest; and both of these are equally necessary to the idea of cause. And unless both of these are fulfilled in the ultimate position of our minds, we have not the proper idea of causation represented in our minds; but a law of thought is violated, that law which we obey in submitting to the relation of cause at all. In other words, a cause, exactly by the same necessity of thought by which on the one side it causes, on the other side must be uncaused; as it is the cause of its own effect, so it must itself be the effect of nothing. That is what I call the rest, which the idea of a cause demands. There is an end implied in the idea: as things move up to a cause, so at the cause there is an absolute stop; and itself does not move back at all. It is not a whit more necessary to a real cause that it should be the cause of something else, than that it should be uncaused itself: and without both of these elements alike represented in our idea we have not the true idea of a cause in our minds. And the alternative is either to decide upon rejecting the idea of *cause*, and ridding metaphysical nature and the world of mind altogether of it, or taking this idea of cause.

But thus understood, the idea of cause has only to be applied to this universe, and it becomes the proof immediately of the existence of an Eternal Original Self-existent Being. For what are we to call that Cause of the universe, beyond which there is no further cause—the uncaused cause of the world—but this? The attributes of this First Cause of the universe, indeed, must depend upon what the universe is; the Cause must take its character and rank from what it causes. But that there must be an Eternal Self-existent Unchangeable Being is certain.

But while this is the necessary result of the idea of cause understood as we have understood it, let us take the idea of cause as fulfilled and satisfied by another interpretation: and no such conclusion as this will follow. There is such a thing as a proximate or secondary cause, which goes back for its own causal efficiency to a prior cause; and we may make the supposition of this dependence of one cause upon another going on indefinitely. We are familiar indeed with this notion, and we speak of a chain of causes, a series, a succession of causes. But it must be remembered that when we apply the term cause to a chain or succession, *i.e.* to causes which are caused, we apply the term in a secondary sense, and a sense which does not correspond to the true idea of a cause, as our minds possess that idea. The atheist then falls back upon this notion of a cause: he hangs the world up upon an infinite chain and succession of causes; and thus he satisfies himself upon the subject of causation, and at the same time avoids the admission of an Eternal Supreme Being. But the answer to such an arrangement is, that it does not satisfy the idea of cause which we have in our minds. *Causa causæ, causa causati*: if from one cause we have to go back to another, that which we go back *from* is *not* the cause, but that which we go back *to* is. The very idea of cause, as I have said, implies a stop; and wherever we stop is the cause. If we stop provisionally at any stage of this backward journey, we have a cause provisionally: but as soon as we go on to another the provisional cause vanishes and surrenders its character as a true cause. And so on until we come to an Universal Cause, *i.e.* a First Cause. A true cause is a First Cause. When, then, the atheist throws the universe back upon an infinite series of mechanical causes he must be told that an infinite chain does not represent the idea of cause; that it is a false conception, and a departure from the genuine principle of reason. An end is included in the very idea—a final rest and repose beyond which there is no advance; an appetency for a cause precedes in the idea, but rest in a cause concludes it.

Wollaston's illustration, with which we are so familiar, of the chain with an infinite number of links, suspended from the sky, of which he asks the question, what holds it up? one link holds up the one below it, but what holds up the whole?—this metaphor of a suspended chain simply illustrates, by a contrast, the actual idea of causation as we have it in our minds. It illustrates the requirements of the rational mind which that idea creates, and its corresponding dissatisfaction and sense of void when those wants are not satisfied. It is in form an *argument* with steps in it, but at the bottom it only states what the idea of causation in man's mind *is*. The atheist says, "I hold to causation, I believe in cause, but why am I obliged to believe in a *First* Cause? What greater difficulties are there in an infinite succession of causes than in an original and self-existent one? I cannot in the least comprehend an infinite chain of causes; but neither can I comprehend an original unchangeable Being, which goes back to all eternity. Both are absolutely beyond my conception, and both raise difficulties which I cannot solve, both issue in dilemmas out of which I cannot find my way. But if both are incomprehensible, why should I be compelled to choose one of them, and adopt the hypothesis of a First Cause instead of an infinite series?" The answer is—because an infinite series of causes does not make a cause, and your reason demands a cause. It is a false criterion of truth and falsehood, to judge simply by difficulties in the way of conception; there are undeniable difficulties, and insuperable ones, which result from truths which are certain, such as Infinity and Eternity; but we hold those truths because they are ideas which are part of our reason, and which we cannot throw off. And so with respect to causation. The question is, what is the idea of a cause that you have in your rational mind? And to that the answer is, that it is the idea which has been stated, viz., a cause which stops. But this idea of cause is not fulfilled in an infinite series. There is by the supposition no finality; but a final standing-ground is demanded by the very idea, as my reason presents it to me. An infinite succession of causes rests by the very hypothesis upon no cause; each particular one rests upon the one which follows it, but the whole rests upon nothing.

The atheistic idea thus does not correspond to the idea of reason. The atheist appears to acknowledge the necessity of a cause, and appears to provide for it; but when we come to his scheme it fails exactly in that part of the idea which clenches it, and which is essential to its integrity; it fails in providing a stop. His scheme represents solely the appetency for a cause, but not the rest in one; it represents only half of reason; it breaks down midway. One might say to him, Why do you give yourself the trouble to supply causation at all? You do it because you consider yourself obliged in reason to do it; but if you supply causation at all, why not furnish *such* a cause as reason has impressed upon you, and which is inherent in your mind—a cause which stands still, an original cause? If you never intended to supply this it must have been because you thought a real cause was not wanted; but if you thought a cause not wanted, why not have said from the first that causes were not wanted, and said from the first that events could take place without causes?

It is this in substance which Clarke does in his celebrated

work, *The Demonstration of the Being of a God*. He brings out simply at bottom the meaning and signification of an idea in the human mind; that there is implied in the very idea itself of a cause, firstly, that it causes something else; and secondly, that it is uncaused itself. He thus extricates the true and genuine *cause* from all confusion and mixture with secondary causes; and he brings the atheistic infinite chain to the test of simple juxtaposition, putting it side by side with the true idea. He virtually says to the atheist, This is the true idea, yours is a false one; and the false one is detected by being put by the side of the true; human reason recognises its own idea. The fault of Clarke is that he clogs his argument with superfluous positions, which he puts forward as different arguments, while they only are one and the same argument differently stated. But it would be the greatest mistake to say, as some do, that Clarke's argument is a mere train of technical subtleties and dry abstractions. This is what those say who acknowledge no reality in metaphysical ideas; all reasonings in this sphere are to them jejune and arid inanities, because the sphere itself is a vacuum to them. How can the evidence of the existence of God, they say, be contained in such hard abstruse forms of abstract logic as these, which it is difficult to endow with any life or force whatever appealing to our nature? But Clarke's chain of reasoning, when we examine it, is the bringing out of a fact of our nature; for an idea of our nature is a fact of our nature; it is the bringing out of the idea of Cause. Is there no reality, nothing vital, nothing solid in that which belongs to our nature, which is part of us, which influences our whole view of things? These ideas of our minds are as much facts as history is, and as our emotions, affections, and feelings are. These dry sticks of formulæ, which they are set down as being, have sap in them, sap which is derived from the trunk of nature. There is a kind of injustice done to arguments of this class, although the term is proper as distinguishing a class, by calling them *antecedent* arguments; an injustice in a popular aspect; for it gives an impression as if they were prior to anything *actual*, belonging to a region of emptiness before fact existed. Whereas this particular argument for a First

Cause is as much founded on a fact as any other argument can be ; it is founded on a fact of our nature, the sense of, and appetency for, a cause of things.

The use of such arguments as Clarke's is not, however, all shown by the mere logical aspect of the case. We have, as I have been saying all along, the sense of causation, the want of a cause in our nature; but it is astonishing how idle, how sleepy, how stagnant, and how comparatively dormant this lies in us, until some great appeal is made to it, or until some great argument awakens it. It is astonishing what an indisposition the mind has for thinking of a cause and realising a cause, even when we know perfectly that there must be a cause. With what effort do we pursue anything that we have, any work of construction—the watch in our pocket, our clothes, our furniture, our books—to their causes. We know, of course, they all go back to their rudimental state and birth, and that they have all very definite retrospects, which end in special arts of workmanship. But it is a decided effort of imagination to us. So it is to go back with any reality to early ages, to remote conditions of the world, to say to ourselves, This really took place at such a time—the earth was once in such a geological stage—all this once happened—it only requires a miracle of anachronism and I should have seen it. All retrospects to be real require imagination. I have been struck often with the thought in Wordsworth's celebrated sonnet, one of those on the River Duddon :—

> "What aspect bore the Man who roved or fled,
> First of his tribe, to this dark dell—who first
> In this pellucid Current slaked his thirst?
> What hopes came with him? What designs were spread
> Along his path? His unprotected bed
> What dreams encompassed? Was the intruder nursed
> In hideous usages, and rites accursed,
> That thinned the living, and disturbed the dead?
> No voice replies ;—both earth and air are mute ;
> And Thou, blue Streamlet, murmuring, yield'st no more
> Than a soft record, that, whatever fruit
> Of ignorance thou might'st witness heretofore,
> Thy function was to heal and to restore,
> To soothe and cleanse, not madden and pollute!"

Here is a call to a remote past. There must have been

some man who saw the River Duddon *first*—before any other human eye rested on it. What kind of a man was he? What was he thinking of at the time? What was he hoping for? Of what nature was his faith? The first seer of the River Duddon had all this attaching to him—he was a real man, with his own past and future, thoughts and hopes. But to go back in this way is an exercise of the imagination. And so even in the logical process of going back to a cause—reasoning here cannot do much without some imagination; it must be stirred and enlivened by it. Metaphysics, and other sciences as well, summon one to entertain vast periods, remote regions, immeasurable vistas, and the dim contents of time's infancy, before it can be thought of almost as being time at all. Here is the region of cause. Can we enter into it, or is it all delusion to us? The average human mind tends to a deep torpid stagnation in present fact, not wanting more; remoteness is inanity to it; origin or cause fiction; the lethargy of the hour hides distance from it, and the distant realm of reason among the rest. It is all unreal, all false to it. Now, here such a book as Clarke's comes in as a person determined to wake a man out of sleep; it forces him to reason; it says to him— You must, you shall believe that something existed before you; that there were causes of what is now present fact; that these stretch into eternity, and that there was Being in that eternity. The hard formulæ are vices into which the torpid reason of man is put till it is constrained to exert itself; the logical apparatus acts really as a stimulus to the imagination, forcing the mind to acts of conception.

The idea of causation applied to this Universe, then, as has been said, takes us up to an Eternal, Original, Self-existing Being. For "how much thought soever," says Clarke, " it may require to demonstrate the other attributes of such a Being, . . . yet as to its existence, that there is somewhat eternal, infinite, and self-existing, which must be the cause and original of all other things; this is one of the first and most natural conclusions that any man who thinks at all can form in his mind. . . . All things cannot possibly have arisen out of nothing, nor can they have depended on one another in an endless succession. . . . We are certain, therefore, of the being of a Supreme Independent Cause ; . . . that there is something in the Universe, actually existing without, the supposition of whose not-existing plainly implies a contradiction."

Kant agrees with Clarke up to this point in the argument. He coincides with him in the necessity of an ultimate or a First Cause, as distinguished from an infinite chain of causes. "The reason," he says, "is forced to seek somewhere its resting point in the *regressus* of the conditional. . . . If something, whatever it may be, exists, it must then be admitted that something exists necessarily. For the contingent exists only under the condition of another thing as its cause, up to a cause which exists not contingently, and, precisely on this account, without condition necessarily. This is the argument whereon reason founds its progression to the original Being. . . . I can never complete the regression to the conditions of the existing without admitting a necessary being. . . . This argument, though certainly it is transcendental, since it rests upon the internal insufficiency of the contingent, is still so simple and natural that it is adapted to the commonest intelligence."[1] Kant differs from Clarke, indeed, in a point which concerns rather the abstract subtlety of metaphysics than the actual strength of the conviction which the reasoning produces ; he does not allow absolutely the necessity of a being as an "objective reality," *from any train of reasoning*, except that which is founded upon the *very conception of the being itself*. In this case "the non-being of a thing is absolutely inconceivable ;" but if the existence of a being is founded upon reasoning from a mere *fact*, then, however necessary the existence of the being would be if the fact from which we argued was necessary, if this foundation fact is not necessary, the being—which is the conclusion from the reasoning from it—is not absolutely necessary either. But in the present case, as he observes, "the proof begins properly from experience ;" it begins from the *fact* of this world, and thence by causes it ascends to a necessary being ; but this world, as an object of sensible experience, is not a necessarily existing thing. "The proof *a contingentia*

[1] Kant, *Critick of Pure Reason*, pp. 406, 407, 428.

mundi, the proof of a necessary being which begins from experience, and is not deduced wholly *a priori* or ontologically," is therefore not with him a demonstrative proof of a necessarily existing being. But with this distinction Kant and Clarke agree in the proof from causation of an original and self-existing being. The English school of metaphysics was satisfied with the certainty of the existence of this visible world as a ground of reasoning; and when a train of reasoning was conducted with rigid accuracy from this starting-point, it was regarded as necessary reasoning.

This is the first stage of the argument for the existence of a God derived from causation. But now we come to the main part of the argument, that, viz., which decides the *attributes* of this Self-existent Being. "This is the question," says Clarke, "between us and the atheists. For that something must be self-existent, and the original cause of all things, will not bear much dispute." But can this self-existent being be called God? That must depend upon His characteristics and qualities; and the characteristics and qualities of the First Cause can only be gathered from the character of that universe which He has caused—its arrangement and disposition, and the order and rank of the existence which has been produced in it. Here, then, we take leave of demonstrative argument, and we depend on the evidence of fact, and upon the natural conclusion which is to be formed from it.

We see, then, that what has ultimately come from the First Cause and Original Being is not only a material and corporeal world, but that world as connected with moral and spiritual being. Whatever criticism the ordinary and popular distinction between matter and spirit may be subjected to, that there is something which we call spirit, which is different from something that we call matter, is a simple fact of our consciousness, which can no more be got rid of than our very selves can; we are conscious that we are intelligent, moral beings. But if this is the case, this intelligent and moral existence must, like all other existences, be traced back to the original Self-existent Being; and if it is traced back to that Being, how can it possibly not affect the character and nature of that Being? The argument of Clarke, Cudworth, and all our religious metaphysicians was the argument of an *adequate* cause—that there must be a proportion between the Cause and the Effect; and this is no more than a necessary and consistent carrying out of the principle of a cause. For what can be the meaning of acknowledging a cause at all, if anything is able to cause anything—the meanest material existence the highest moral existence? It is evident that we must combine adequacy and sufficiency with our idea of causes, or the whole doctrine of causation will go to the winds. Can the motion of a stone cause a man, or friction produce mind, or the nebular theory account for the moral sense? There must then be a natural relation between the cause and the effect, and if causation is true at all it must be proportionate. It may be said, How are we judges of proportion and sufficiency in causes? but reason does not allow its voice to be stifled by mere difficulties which perplex us, but which do not prevent us from seeing the plain and downright wants of reason. If there is such a thing as mind, will, personality, which has had a beginning and come into existence in the world; and if this is thrown back, through secondary and vanishing being, upon the original Eternal Being, that Being cannot be matter. What we call matter is obviously insufficient to cause mind. Human personality cannot be accounted for by mechanical causes. The cause of intelligence must be intelligent.

The materialists of the last century then denied the position that the cause of intelligence must be intelligent, upon the general ground, which they asserted to be true in physics, that a cause need not be like its effect. And it need not be said that the materialists of this century have wielded the same arguments, with all the advantage of that growth of physical knowledge which has been the special boast of this age. They have multiplied physical rationales of mind, and they have diversified this species of reasoning with the utmost ingenuity and power, and carried it into all those subtler and finer forms, which a profounder acquaintance with material causes has enabled them to discover. Thus it has been announced by a scientific man of this day, that thought is a secretion of the brain. And we have been told that "many who hold the evolution hypothesis would probably assent to the position that at the present moment all our philosophy, all our poetry, all our science, all our art—Plato, Shakespeare, Newton, and Raphael—are potential in the fires of the sun."[1] Undoubtedly then we see as a matter of observation physical causes wholly changing phenomenally in the effect; and the composition and combination of particles producing a totally different substance from the eye, taste, and touch from any or all of the ingredients separately; nor only do we see the greatest and most entire metamorphoses in chemistry, but even the very doctrine of causation itself requires a difference between causes and effects. Causes do not produce causes—they do not simply repeat themselves; they produce effects, which effects are different from what produced them. But though a cause need not be similar to its effect, it must be sufficient for its effect. A *sufficient* cause, as has been said, must be combined with *cause*; otherwise if anything can produce anything, the whole doctrine of causation goes to pieces. It is the only mode of carrying out the doctrine. What difference is there in saying that there is no cause of a thing, and that it need not have any; and giving an *insufficient* cause? If you say human intelligence need have no cause at all—it came into existence of itself: that is, according to the doctrine of causation, absurd and ridiculous; but if you say it came out of a metal, it issued out of volcanic smoke, it flashed out of an aurora borealis—that is just *as* absurd. Our reason does not see the slightest distinction between saying that intelligence has no cause, and giving it an inadequate one. One is just as much no cause at all as the other. A sufficient cause, then, is only the consistent carrying out of cause; and if you admit the principle of cause at all, you cannot say that matter was the cause of intellect; or, therefore, that the Original Self-existent Being need not be intelligent.

It is true that matter has lately been set before us as claiming more vicinity to mind than it has been usual to assign it; and a scientific man, of the highest genius, has regretted

[1] Tyndall's Discourse on the Scientific Use of the Imagination.

that "mind and matter have ever been presented to us in the rudest contrast—the one as all noble, the other as all vile." I am not aware that people now, or for many centuries, whatever the Gnostics and Manichæans may have done, have spoken more slightingly and depreciatingly of matter, than to say that matter cannot move itself. That is all. It is charged with inertia. Therefore, if Professor Tyndall wants an alteration in the ordinary language of mankind respecting matter, I know of no other alteration that can be made in it, except that matter *can* move itself. This is the only new rationale which is open, because the contrary of this is all that has been said. Hobbes, in the seventeenth century, anticipated this claim, and laid down " that all matter as matter is endued not only with figure and a capacity of motion, but also with an actual sense and perception, and wants only the organs and memory of animals to express its sensations."[1]

But were such a theory of matter revived, and revived with new gifts and attributes with which to awaken the inert substance, I know not what the whole metamorphose would have to do with the position that matter cannot be the cause of mind. You elevate matter into a higher rank, and you raise its pretensions to be the cause of mind. But then, in proportion as you have done this, matter has ceased to be matter, and become mind. The chasm then is as wide as ever between mind and matter in the ordinary sense; and the obstruction as strong as ever to matter, in the ordinary sense, producing mind. What ordinary people mean by matter is substance which is without mind, or any element of it. I assume this description of it, this is my definition of it, when I argue about matter; if the definition is wrong, the argument as such is not affected; for the argument assumes the definition, and is right upon that assumption.

What such a view amounts to is that intelligence in the world is a *growth*; and that it began in a very small way as a blind unconscious action of matter, from which it gradually ascended to its present height and greatness. And taking this as the position asserted, we may drop the term matter, which

[1] Quoted in Clarke's Demonstration.

is wholly irrelevant to it, and represent it as being the assertion that the highest intelligent existence may have been caused by the lowest intelligent existence (if we may call blind instinct such) through the medium of a succession of steps. But the lowest intelligence could not cause the highest; it is as obviously insufficient a cause as brute matter. If we suppose an original plan, upon which mind ascends from that of an oyster to that of Plato, there is no intrinsic objection to such a supposition; but in that case it is not the oyster which causes Plato, but the Intelligence to whom the plan is due, upon which the ascent from the oyster to Plato is made.

The attribute of intelligence, then, and the moral nature of the Self-existing Being, are shown by the beings whom He has caused possessing those qualities. Another great evidence of the intelligence of the Self-existing Being lies in the works of nature; and at this point the argument of causation for the existence of a God joins on to the argument of design; and one argument cannot be separated from the other. The contrivances of nature require a cause, and a sufficient cause; the properties of matter are not a sufficient cause. Another lecturer, however, has handled this subject, and done it with great ability, and I will only make one or two observations in connection with it.

We have a right, I think, to complain of the attitude of scientific men—a considerable section of them—in one respect; and that is, that they will neither say that the world was formed by chance nor that it was formed by design; and yet one or the other it must be. What they say is, that it was formed by Law; but this is saying nothing; Law is quite consistent with either of these, either with chance or design. Laws are simply uniformly recurrent facts; if then these lines of facts are in disorder and confusion; if they are unmeaning, if they conspire toward no end, and make up no structure, then these laws are by chance. If they make up, on the other hand, an elaborate and useful apparatus; then we say, they are by design. But the scientific men I refer to will say neither the one nor the other; they stay at law, and rest in law as an intermediate verdict between chance and design, which saves them the absurdity of chance and the mystery of design. This is not a consistent position. Laws must be just as much either by chance or design as facts must be; and it is just as untenable that men should stop at laws as an ultimate rationale of the world, as that they should stop at facts.

And yet there is a great deal said now about Mind in Nature, and scientific men talk enthusiastically about Mind; the old notion of chance is obsolete, and, in spite of the strength of a materialist school, there is a tendency to a consensus of scientific men that there is mind in the universe. Would any one in any public meeting of scientific men dare to stand up and *deny* that there was Mind in Nature? It would be thought monstrous. It would be set down as the revival of an old stupidity. They find it is the only form in which they can speak of nature which at all ennobles it, or satisfies their own idea of the sublimity of nature.

But if a Mind is admitted in nature, how can that Mind be excluded from design in nature? The state of the case is this: Nature has all the *look* of design, and is full of contrivance and construction, which force the idea of an intention upon us; and with this aspect of nature, we also, and at the same time, say there is Mind in nature. Why then should not that Mind have something to do with that look of design? If both exist, to make one have nothing to do with the other is indeed an extraordinary arrangement. If there *is* Mind, why should the construction of the world be singled out as the special subject of prohibition to it, from which its exclusion is necessary, and with which no interference on its part can possibly be allowed? There is at first sight a singular appearance of adaptation in the power to the work; if such care is to be taken to shut it out, and resist its intrusion, the reason must be an unusually recondite one. But this is the course taken by the scrupulous physical philosopher. He seems to have a conscience upon the subject. This Mind in nature must do anything but design. You are permitted to contemplate its majesty; but if you hint about intention on its part, it is quite out of order. If you whisper about construction belonging at all to it,—it is, Hush! speak reverently about the Universal Mind.

Again, if there is a mind in nature, and that Mind has anything to do with nature, that Mind must be in harmony with our own personal mind. It provides a frame for it. What is that but a connection with it, as a scope and object? And it must be a Personal Being, who thus *provides for and understands* a personal being. Creation has evidently man in its view; it shows its comprehension of, its insight into, what man is. That insight must belong to a Personal Mind in nature. The intelligence which is at the bottom of an elaborate contrivance *for* a person, declares in that very act something respecting itself; and discloses a secret affecting its own nature. Whether the apparatus might *of itself* reveal the truth or not, its *application* does; the application of it to the support of a personal being, discloses a recognition and cognisance of—if we may say so—a sympathy with, a consultation for personal existence, which is inexplicable, unless there is something in that Mind which, for lack of adequate language, we must call Personality; unless the mystery of that individuality which is *provided for*, resides also, in some sense, in the Universal Mind which *provides for* it. The personality which is at one end is reflected upon the other. The Divine nature is not all cloud, with no light breaking through. Here is a gleam of light. The contrivance in behalf of, with a view to, the life of a personal being, involves in the very act an idea of that personal mode of existing; a knowledge of it, and entering into it. And what mind could enter into personal existence, but one which had in some sense personal existence itself."[1]

[1] "The Cosmos without us displays an intelligence far reaching as the farthest fixed star, but this infinite power the physicist hesitates to pronounce a personality. That microcosmos, our moral nature, displays undoubted personality; and unless the intelligence which forms and transforms the whole universe is somewhat infinitely less than man, we have found the true God. . . . Why unsatisfied by long chains of sequency, by a world pendent upon nothing, moving no-whence, no-whither, and for no reason, do we, incredulous as to these airy nothings, seek after a First Cause, an Author, a Creator, and refuse to relinquish our quest? It is because we find the facts of Causation within our minds. Will is the cause, and we are directly conscious of our own will . . . Thus where the physicist hesitates the psychologist steps in. Our moral nature utters what is voiceless in irrational nature, and pronounces that will sovereign over all it creates is the one known, the only conceivable First ground."—*Right and Wrong*, a Sermon by the Rev. William Jackson.

Professor Tyndall's conclusion then may well be embraced for our own:—" Be careful that your conception of the Builder of the Universe is not an unworthy conception. Invest that conception with your grandest and highest and holiest thoughts; but be careful of pretending to know more than is given you to know." We *are* careful for our conception of the Builder of the Universe, and for that reason we attribute to Him design and personality. In what possible way can we, human beings, think of the Builder of the Universe really as such, except in this way? Of course we do not know what design in the Deity is; we do not know what personality in the Deity is—not, *i.e.*, as they are in themselves; but that is granted and allowed for in all our thoughts and reflections and considerations as to the Deity. This ignorance has its own effect proper to it; but this effect cannot be to prevent us from representing the Deity with practical truth relatively to ourselves: this practical truth then must not be undone by harking back again to our ignorance. This has already been taken into the calculation; it must not be taken in again and afresh, after all the proper reduction has once been allowed for it. Therefore His personality stands, His design stands, because this is the only way in which we can conceive a Deity *being* or *causing*.

It is untenable, indeed, to tie us up completely with ignorance, when you give something to do which wants knowledge. Whatever be the speculative defence of this method, it is practically untrue; because it is unfair—first, to make our ignorance an insuperable impediment to conception, and then tell us to conceive. Do not impose this on us, and ignorance is fair; but if it is assumed that we must think, conceive something about God—" if we are to take care that our conception of Him must not be an unworthy one;" then, however we may keep the fact of our ignorance as a truth in the background, we must practically assume some knowledge. God must be to us as God. How can He be without personality and intelligence?

But in the argument from causation for the existence of a God, there is yet a gap, which must be bridged over, before we can arrive at the religious conclusion; viz., the interval between even a moral and intelligent Self-existent Being, and a God. The argument from causation is essentially an argument from fact; we begin from the *fact* that we exist, and that runs up through causes to a Self-existent Being: we see the *fact* of a moral as well as a material world, and that runs up to a *moral* Self-existent Being. But God is an Ideal, an Infinitely Perfect Being, and how do we get an ideal out of facts? We have only in the world a sphere of actual fact; in mind, in will, in character, all is limitation; and we see no perfection. If the attributes of the First Cause then are to be gathered from the qualities of creation, how can we upon simple experience erect the existence of a moral Ideal, an Infinitely Perfect Being, of boundless intelligence and goodness? And yet unless we have argumentatively reached this Ideal, we have not reached the truth of the existence of a God; for God essentially means all this.

The older metaphysicians, then, made this gap in the argument less of a difficulty than the later school. Clarke extracts the ideal character of the Self-existent Original Being out of the simple pre-eminence and excellence of a cause as compared with an effect. "Since in general," he says, "there are manifestly in things various kinds of powers, and very different excellencies and degrees of perfection, it must needs be that in the order of causes and effects, the cause must always be more excellent than the effect; and the Self-existent Being, whatever that be supposed to be, must of necessity, being the original of all things, contain in itself the sum and highest degree of all the perfections of all things." With the older metaphysicians the effort of the argument lay in the proof of a Moral Self-existent Being; and that gained, they considered the infinity and perfection to follow as a matter of course; and certainly if one thinks of the mysterious nature of a cause, it leads us unavoidably to such a transcendental estimate of the First Cause of all things, as cannot naturally stop short of an Ideal. But Kant, on the other hand, fixes the great difficulty of the argument after a Moral Self-existent Being has been proved, viz., between a Moral Self-existent Being, and a God: he announces his utter perplexity how

upon a simple ground of experience or the basis of causation—
he is to erect a proof of the ideal. " For can ever experience
be given," he says, "which should be conformable to an *idea ?*
That which is peculiar to this last consists precisely in this,
that an experience can never be congruous to it. The transcendental idea of a necessary, all-sufficient, original Being is
so immensely great, so raised above all that is empirical, which
is always conditional, that we can never collect matter enough
or experience in order to fill such a conception." But when we
examine Kant's attitude as a reasoner to the ideal, it does not
substantially differ from Clarke's; Clarke gives up "demonstration strictly and properly;" and Kant allows a natural strong
ground of conviction. He considers that the chasm which
presents itself to the passive and composed intellect between
the actual and the ideal is arched over by an intuitive impulse,
which springs from the whole view of the Creation, and carries
the mind by a quick movement of thought, which it cannot
resist, to the transcendental conclusion of an Infinite, Perfect
Being. "The present world," he says, "opens to us so immense
a theatre of diversity, order, fitness, and beauty, whether we
seek after these in the infinity of space, or in its unbounded
division; that even according to the knowledge which our
weak reason has been enabled to acquire of the same, all
language lacks its expression as to so many and undiscernibly
great wonders—so that our judgment of the whole must ter-
minate in a speechless, but so much the more eloquent,
astonishment. Everywhere we see a chain of effects and
causes, of ends and means, regularity in beginning and ending:
and since nothing has come of itself into the state in which it
is, it always thus indicates further back another thing, as its
cause, which renders exactly the same further inquiry necessary; so that the great Whole must sink into the abyss of
nothing, if we did not admit something existing of itself
originally and independently, external to this Infinite Contingent,
and as the cause of its origin. The highest cause, in respect
of all things in the world, how great are we to think it? The
world we are not acquainted with according to its whole
extent: still less do we know how to appreciate its magnitude

by comparison with all that is possible. But what prevents us, that, since we require in respect of causality an external and supreme Being, we should not at the same time, in respect of the degree of perfection, place it *above everything else possible?* ... It would consequently not only be comfortless, but also quite vain, to wish to take away something from the authority of this proof. Reason, which is unceasingly elevated by means of arguments so powerful, and always increasing under its hands, although only empirical ones, cannot, through any doubts of subtly-deduced speculation, be so pressed down that it must not be roused as it were out of a dream, from any meditative irresolution, by a glance which it casts on the wonders and majesty of the Universe; in order to raise itself from greatness to greatness up to the highest of all—from the conditional to the condition—up to the Supreme and unconditional Creator." [1]

I would only add to this argument that it must be considered that an ideal is contained in the moral nature of man; and that we have to account for its being there. It is evident that the peculiar character or construction, as we may call it, of the conscience and the moral sense, is such, that the very instrument it works by is a kind of restlessness and discontent with all fact in us, and a desire to be something which we are not. The condition of goodness is not that of attaining a defined sufficient end: it is not that of reaching a resting-place. That is counter to the law of our being. St. Paul has given an exposition of conscience, which plainly and vividly describes it as insatiable, swallowing, like some unfathomable abyss, all the duty, sacrifice, and effort that is thrown into it, and still demanding more. And though in the Christian dispensation the sense of a Divine justification is the remedial and appointed relief for the natural insatiableness of conscience, there remains a sense of short-coming which is ineffaceable, and is inherent and rooted in the man. What can this be the effect of but the existence of an ideal in man, the spontaneous erection of his own heart, which dwarfs every act of his, and reduces his whole life to failure and imperfection? Moral

[1] *Critick of Pure Reason*, Book II. c. 1. div. iii. s. 6.

beauty,—goodness, rises up before him in his conscience in a form and height which has no embodiment in fact; he sees there a whole, while all experience only shows what is fragmentary. How has he got in his nature a type of which he has no representative in actual existence? The only answer can be, if we acknowledge causation, that whence he has the moral nature which he has, thence he has this *peculiarity and manner* of that nature: viz., from the original Self-existing Being. This ideal is implanted in him; but if so, how can that Being, who has implanted an ideal, be other than Himself the fulfilment of it?

IN MEMORIAM

OF THE REV. SAMUEL RICKARDS, Rector of Stowlangloft, Suffolk.

[MENTION has been made of the author's power of drawing character. The following portrait is given, both as an example of the gift, and also for its own sake as the record of one whose friendship lives in the memory of those admitted to it, as one of the privileges of their lives. Between him and the author, many years his junior, there was the attraction of agreement and sympathy on the points that most occupied the thought of Churchmen during the eventful twenty years that preceded his death; which took place September 2, 1865.]

The death of Mr. Rickards of Stowlangtoft must be felt as a serious loss, not only in his own diocese, but in the Church at large, and especially in a wide intellectual circle, social, clerical, and academical, in which the thoughtful solidity of his mind, his strong judgment, his powers of criticism, his large information, and his conversational gifts were deeply appreciated. This high set of faculties were brought to bear mainly on religious subjects, but by no means to the exclusion of other subjects which naturally interest the scholar, and society generally. His was especially an independent mind. Intimately connected in early life with the leaders of an enthusiastic movement in the Church, he yet never allowed himself to be led by the impetus of other minds, or by his own sympathies with religious friends, a step further than his own judgment and perception approved. He did not bend to ány standard thrust upon him from without; he measured every religious party statement and aim by a criterion in his own mind, formed upon combined scriptural and ecclesiastical principles, as his own reading and thought and the authority of the great English divines had interpreted those principles. His standard was a comprehensive one, qualified by the rightful claims of doctrine; and he possessed particularly the power of making a stand upon a ground taken. His aptness and readiness of expression, his presence of mind in anything like argumentative discussion, his sustained recollection of his own position in an argument, and the clearness with which he kept his point before him, eminently suited him for this defensive work, and this calm but strong hold of sober truth, amid opposite extravagancies. He was, however, pre-eminently aided in the exertion of this power by the extraordinary simplicity and sincerity of his religious character. Entirely unpresuming, and singularly guarded and watchful, he used, however, and benefited by the right which great purity of character gives the upright man— that, namely, of being conscious of his own uprightness, and deriving strength and vigour from that consciousness. He knew he had no selfish or private motive for anything he did, or any ground he maintained, and therefore he was perfectly unimpeded in the operations of his mind. Having given his heart to religion, and strong in the *conviction* that he had, he had no temptation to show his earnestness and the vigour of his Church principles by narrow and fanciful symbols. None saw with more acuteness the pettiness of mind, the pride, the self-aggrandising spirit, the dictatorial temper which works under religious forms, and even enthusiastic impulses; his quiet discernment soon removed the veil from these religious manifestations, and disclosed the real man. As, on the other hand, none perceived more quickly a sterling character underneath the rough or even forbidding exterior. Fidelity to truth was combined with fidelity to friends, from whom difference of view did not in the least separate him. Man was not in his eyes simply the holder of opinions,—man was man. He loved through life and was loved by men of different theological views from his own; because the object of his affection was the sterling human character, which, if there was a common large Christian ground, was enough for him.

Mr. Rickards' conversation was rich in the recollection of distinguished men, and especially in academical and College reminiscences. He could recall with great accuracy the old Oriel days, when Whately, Coplestone, and Davison disputed in the Common Room, and converted the social meeting of the Fellows and Tutors after their day's work into a scene of the highest conversational brilliancy and power. It was when he was first elected Fellow, and resided in Oxford. These giants of argument used to hit each other uncommonly hard; so that even they, used as they were to blows, would sometimes show the effect of an evening's combat in a certain shyness of each other for a few days afterwards. He gave Whately the credit of having done a very useful and important work in the Church—namely, of having brought the truth of Christianity home to a large number of argumentative minds that would not have received the conclusion unless through the channel of a great argumentative writer, who made the management and conduct of reasoning his main point. With Davison, who was his College tutor, he maintained an intimate friendship up to that distinguished writer's death, appreciating strongly the calm depth of religious reflection which was so conspicuous in him, his meditative spirit, his vast resources of learning, and his solemn and rich style—which, however, he criticised as too elaborate. His knowledge of books, and his critical estimate of them, showing that he never read without a definite exertion of judgment upon the book before him, were remarkable—the more so that this erudition was in most harmonious combination with the life of the village pastor. The country poor were his admiration, whenever they were what the poor ought to be, and he attached himself to them by ties not only of authority, but friendship. The early recollections, relating to men and country life, of the village patriarch gave him unfeigned pleasure and fed his poetical feeling.

His great enjoyment of this world, while his life was ever tending toward a better, was a remarkable feature in him, and it was one from which everybody about him benefited; for his was a communicative enjoyment. He was full of happy thoughts and feelings, flowing from the spring of his own heart and his active perception of beauty in nature combined. All natural objects, scenery, birds, flowers, the gaiety of the fields and the hedges, were a source of real delight to him; the pleasure he derived hence even increased as he grew older, and continued strong throughout his last illness. The quick sense of happiness which these objects imparted is expressed in some of his own verses :—

> " Go, unlearn the ways of men,
> Be a little child again,
> Doff thy mannish pride and shame,
> That make those early pleasures tame,
> And taste, untouched by critic lore,
> The joys that spring around thy door;
> Let thy heart dance in nature's glee
> With very childhood's ecstasy;
> Drink her pure draughts of pleasure up,
> E'en from the homely buttercup;
> And let her common beauties be
> Fountains of comfort still to thee."

It was an addition to his happiness that he had the *knowledge* of it; that it was conscious reasonable delight in those objects which were set before him in this visible creation; a sustained enjoyment of things designed by their Author to be enjoyed. His extraordinary cheerfulness had the peculiar effect of making people feel cheerful about him: when he came into a room it imparted itself to the circle. But no one who did not know him very well would have guessed his brightness and playfulness in the society of his intimate friends.

Mr. Rickards had one especial characteristic, which, together with his transparent religious sincerity and consistency, gave a singular wholeness and completeness to his character—personal *weight*. It was the result of his religious life, and yet it deserves attention, specially and by itself, as a characteristic. Without powers of oratory, or exuberance of language to develop a subject and impress his view upon minds around him by the quantity of his statement, he yet never spoke on any subject without weight, and without producing a serious impression upon others. An importance was given to what he said. How commonly do we see the richest gifts and resources of language, and all the armoury of logic, wielded without this accompaniment of *weight!* The speaker is copious and brilliant, but you do not attach importance to what he says; you have no impulse to think what he says true. It was the particular feature of Mr. Rickards' place in society, that people reposed in the sterling truthfulness of his nature, and in that at once moral and sagacious instinct, by which, without elaboration, he saw his way into the folds of a subject, and extracted the true point of view out of the many rival ones. This characteristic of weight was intimately connected, however, with the general composition of his religious character, his habitual self-watchfulness and command over his thoughts when by himself, which prepared and trained him for conversation with others, and gave him that singular recollectedness and presence of mind which has been already noticed. He unconsciously describes *himself* in one of his volumes of Parochial Sermons, entitled *Godliness the Ground of Self-command*, and the following passage will recall the writer to many—"Even so sanctify the Lord God, after this manner, in your hearts; and in the only way in which it can be done you will attain for certain that godly temper and Christian presence of mind of which one effect only is described in the text, where it is said that you shall be ready always to give an answer to every man that asketh you a reason of the hope that is in you with meekness and fear. Godliness properly and of its own nature produces modesty and manliness, the only strength of character which at once never flinches and never presumes." The weight of his character, however, did not only tell in his presence; it was, perhaps, even more felt in his absence, in the influence which he had as an image in people's minds, reminding them of deep truths and hopes, and impressing upon them the reality of goodness, and its *value*—what it could do for those who had it. He was one to whom those who had ever known him could always in their thoughts turn as a pattern and proof of the substance there was in religion for the confirmation of their own faith. His life, so plainly above the world, and in the intercourse of society so revealing its own peculiar groundwork, motives, and aims; so marked yet so unostentatious—how many has it strengthened, without the knowledge of the benefit he had conferred ever reaching him! He did not know the greater part of the good he did.

Such was the character of this Christian witness—one whose whole life was a fulfilment of a duty which is laid in the Gospel upon every individual Christian—that, namely, of witnessing to the truth of Christianity. A witness to Christianity is one whose life evidently requires the hearty belief of the person in the truth of Christianity to *account* for it. Such a belief is a key, and the only key to it. There are many lives which do not require any such key to explain them; and therefore such persons are *not* witnesses to the truth of Christianity. We turn from such lives, whether in Church or State, to that of the village pastor whom we have briefly described, with relief. Mr. Rickards, though a country clergyman, was in a good sense a man of the world. He mixed largely with society; he was acquainted with many of the leading men of the day; he was interested in all the questions, political and social, of the day; he lived *in* the world; and yet it was impossible for any one who knew him not to see that his life was a religious one—religious in its whole motive and aim. It was written upon his countenance, upon his whole demeanour among men, that what he cared for was religion. The light of Christianity shone upon his whole path through life. A power attaches to such a life; it effects more than many a public religious life, because it is the life of a *witness*. It is by such lives that faith in Christianity is kept up in the world.[1]

---

[1] [In interesting confirmation of this estimate of a character, the following passage from a letter signed H. E. M., of the date 1840, written prior to the author's knowledge of Mr. Rickards, is given:—

"I am delighted to hear you talk of Mr. Rickards in a way to prove that he is still the same Mr. Rickards, the admiration and pride of my inexperienced taste in youth, I think one of the persons, one of the very few persons of whom I can say with truth—If everybody was like him, the world would be too delightful. I consider Mr. Rickards as the type and model of a country parish and domestic priest. *All* his powers and energies are expended on and exerted for teaching, preaching, and talking. Bodily presence is his vocation; unlike some, writers and others, he must be seen to be felt, and, unlike others again, writers and others, the more he *is* seen the more he *is* felt. I have all my life said, and I remember saying to you in July 1832, 'I am never afraid of exaggeration in speaking of Mr. Rickards.'"]

The following Articles and other Works by Dr. Mozley appeared in the order here given.

Truths and Fictions of the Middle Ages, (*British Critic*), Oct. 1838.
The Lollards, ... *do.* Jan. 1839.
De Clifford, ... *do.* Jan. 1842.
Bishop Andrewes' Sermons, . . *do.* Jan. 1842.
Palmer on Protestantism, . . *do.* April 1842.
Development of the Church of the Seventeenth Century, ... *do.* Oct. 1842.
Strafford, ... *do.* April 1843.
Bishopric of Jerusalem, . . *do.* July 1843.
Plea of the Six Doctors, . . . (*Pamphlet*), 1843.
Dr. Arnold, . . . (*Christian Remembrancer*), Oct. 1844.
Laud, ... *do.* Jan. 1845.
I promessi Sposi, . . . *do.* April 1845.
Recent Proceedings at Oxford, . *do.* April 1845.
English Churchwomen, 17th Century, *do.* July 1845.
Blanco White, ... *do.* July 1845.
History of the Church in Russia, . *do.* Oct. 1845.
The Recent Schism, . . . *do.* Jan. 1846.
Dr. Pusey's Sermon, . . *do.* April 1846.
Carlyle's Cromwell, . . . *do.* April 1846.
Newman on Development, . . *do.* Jan. 1847.
Luther, ... *do.* Jan. 1848.
The Book of Job, . . . *do.* Jan. 1849.
Recent Arguments on Baptismal Regeneration, ... *do.* Jan. 1850.
The Oxford Commission, . . (*Quarterly Review*), June 1853.
Maurice's Theological Essays, (*Christian Remembrancer*), Jan. 1854.

A Treatise on the Augustinian Doctrine of Pre-
 destination, ... (*Murray*), 1855.
The Primitive Doctrine of Baptismal Regeneration, do. 1856.
Indian Conversion, . . (*Bentley's Quarterly*), Jan. 1859.
A Review of the Baptismal Controversy, (*Rivingtons*), 1862.
Subscription to the Articles, a letter to Rev. Professor Stanley, 1863.
Bampton Lectures on Miracles, . . (*Rivingtons*), 1865.
Observations on the Colonial Church Question,
 (*Pamphlet, Rivingtons*), 1867.
Of Christ alone without Sin, (*Contemporary Review*), April 1868.
Argument of Design, . . (*Quarterly Review*), July 1869.
Education of the People, . . do. April 1870.
Newman's Grammar of Assent, . do. July 1870.
The Principle of Causation. A Lecture written
 for the Christian Evidence Society, . . . 1872.
University Sermons, ... (*Rivingtons*), 1876.
Ruling Ideas in Early Ages, . . do. 1877.

NEW BOOKS AND NEW EDITIONS

IN COURSE OF PUBLICATION BY

Messrs. RIVINGTON

WATERLOO PLACE, LONDON

And at Oxford and Cambridge

January 1879

The Annotated Bible, being a Household Commentary upon the Holy Scriptures, comprehending the Results of Modern Discovery and Criticism. By the Rev. John Henry Blunt, M.A., F.S.A., Editor of "The Annotated Book of Common Prayer," "The Dictionary of Theology," etc. etc.

Three Vols. Demy 4to, with Maps, etc.

VOL. I. (668 pages.)—Containing the GENERAL INTRODUCTION, with Text and Annotations on the Books from GENESIS to ESTHER. 31s. 6d.

VOL. II. (720 pages.)—Completing the OLD TESTAMENT and APOCRYPHA. 31s. 6d.

VOL. III.—Containing the NEW TESTAMENT and GENERAL INDEX. [*In the Press.*

The Theory of Development. A Criticism of Dr. Newman's Essay on the Development of Christian Doctrine, reprinted from "The Christian Remembrancer," January 1847. By J. B. Mozley, D.D., late Canon of Christ Church, and Regius Professor of Divinity in the University of Oxford.

Crown 8vo. 5s.

Essays, Historical and Theological.
By J. B. Mozley, D.D., late Canon of Christ Church, and Regius Professor of Divinity in the University of Oxford.

Two Vols. 8vo. 24s.

London, Oxford, and Cambridge

Studies on the Collects of the Communion

Office, Critical and Devotional. By Edward Meyrick Goulburn, D.D., Dean of Norwich.

Two Vols. Crown 8vo. [*In the Press.*

Selection, adapted to the Seasons of

the Ecclesiastical Year, from the "Parochial and Plain Sermons" of John Henry Newman, B.D., sometime Vicar of St. Mary's, Oxford. Edited by the Rev. W. J. Copeland, B.D., Rector of Farnham, Essex.

Crown 8vo. 5s.

An Introduction to the Devotional

Study of the Holy Scriptures: with a Prefatory Essay on their Inspiration, and specimens of Meditations on various passages of them. By Edward Meyrick Goulburn, D.D., Dean of Norwich.

Tenth Edition, revised and enlarged. Small 8vo. 6s. 6d.

An Eirenicon of the Eighteenth Cen-

tury. Proposal for Catholic Communion. By a Minister of the Church of England. New Edition. With Introduction, Appendices, and Notes. Edited by Henry Nutcombe Oxenham, M.A.

8vo. 10s. 6d.

Sermons Preached in the Temporary

Chapel of Keble College, Oxford, 1870—1876.

Second Edition. Crown 8vo. 6s.

Rudiments of Theology. A First Book for

Students. By John Pilkington Norris, B.D., Canon of Bristol, Vicar of St. Mary Redcliffe, Bristol, and Examining Chaplain to the Bishop of Manchester, Author of "Key to the Four Gospels," "Key to the Acts of the Apostles," &c.

Second Edition, revised. Crown 8vo. 7s. 6d.

Daily Gleanings of the Saintly Life.

Compiled by C. M. S., with an Introduction by the Rev. M. F. Sadler, M.A., Prebendary of Wells, and Rector of Honiton, Devon.

Small 8vo. [*In the Press.*

London, Oxford, and Cambridge

MESSRS. RIVINGTON'S NEW LIST

For Days and Years. A Book containing a Text, Short Reading, and Hymn for every Day in the Church's Year. Selected by H. L. Sidney Lear.
16mo. 2s. 6d.

The Microscope of the New Testament. By the late Rev. William Sewell, D.D., formerly Fellow of Exeter College, sometime Professor of Moral Philosophy in the University of Oxford, and Whitehall Preacher. Edited by the Rev. W. J. Crichton, M.A.
8vo. 14s.

Sunday Evenings in the Family. Being Expositions of the Gospels and Articles of the Church of England.
Crown 8vo. 3s.

Analytical Notes on Obadiah and Habakuk, for the use of Hebrew Students. By the Rev. William Randolph, M.A., of St. John's College, Cambridge.
8vo. 5s. 6d.

The Orthodox Doctrine of the Church of England explained in a Commentary on the Thirty-nine Articles. By the Rev. T. I. Ball. With an Introduction by the Rev. W. J. E. Bennett, M.A., Vicar of Frome-Selwood.
Crown 8vo. 7s. 6d.

A Manual of Private Devotions. Compiled principally from the works of Jeremy Taylor and Bishop Andrewes.
Small 8vo. 2s.

The Guide of Life: a Manual of Prayers for Women; with the Office of the Holy Communion, and Devotions. By C. E. Skinner. Edited by the Rev. John Hewett, M.A., Vicar of Babbacombe, Devon.
Crown 16mo. 2s. 6d.

Easy Lessons addressed to Candidates for Confirmation. By John P. Norris, B.D., Canon of Bristol, Examining Chaplain to the Bishop of Manchester, and Vicar of St. Mary Redcliffe, Bristol, Author of "Rudiments of Theology."
18mo. 1s. 6d.

London, Oxford, and Cambridge

The Christian Year: Thoughts in Verse
for the Sundays and Holy Days throughout the Year.
New Edition printed in large type. Crown 8vo. 3s. 6d.

The Devotional Birthday Book.
Forming a New Volume of "Rivingtons' Devotional Series."
18mo. 2s. 6d. [*In the Press*

Ruling Ideas in Early Ages and their
Relation to Old Testament Faith. Lectures delivered to Graduates of the University of Oxford. By J. B. Mozley, D.D., late Canon of Christ Church, and Regius Professor of Divinity in the University of Oxford.
Second Edition. 8vo. 10s. 6d.

Sermons Preached before the University
of Oxford, and on Various Occasions. By J. B. Mozley, D.D., late Canon of Christ Church, and Regius Professor of Divinity in the University of Oxford.
Third Edition. Crown 8vo. 7s. 6d.

Christian Biographies. By H. L. Sidney Lear.

- MADAME LOUISE DE FRANCE, Daughter of Louis XV., known also as the Mother Térèse de S. Augustin.
- A DOMINICAN ARTIST: a Sketch of the Life of the Rev. Père Besson, of the Order of S. Dominic.
- HENRI PERREYVE. By A. Gratry. Translated by special permission. With Portrait.
- S. FRANCIS DE SALES, Bishop and Prince of Geneva.
- THE REVIVAL OF PRIESTLY LIFE IN THE SEVENTEENTH CENTURY IN FRANCE. Charles de Condren—S. Philip Neri and Cardinal de Berulle—S. Vincent de Paul—Saint Sulpice and Jean Jacques Olier.
- A CHRISTIAN PAINTER OF THE NINETEENTH CENTURY: being the Life of Hippolyte Flandrin.
- BOSSUET AND HIS CONTEMPORARIES.
- FÉNELON, ARCHBISHOP OF CAMBRAI.

New and Uniform Editions. Eight Volumes. Crown 8vo. 3s. 6d. *each. Sold separately. Or the Eight Volumes may be had in a Box,* 31s. 6d.

London, Oxford, and Cambridge

A Selection from Pascal's Thoughts.
Translated by H. L. Sidney Lear.

Square 16mo. Printed on Dutch hand-made paper. 3s. 6d.

The Priest to the Altar; or, Aids
to the Devout Celebration of Holy Communion, chiefly after the Ancient English Use of Sarum.

Third Edition, revised and enlarged. Royal 8vo. 12s.

The Armoury of Prayer. A Book of
Devotion. Compiled by **Berdmore Compton**, Vicar of All Saints', Margaret Street.

18mo. 3s. 6d.

The Child Samuel. A Practical and Devotional Commentary on the Birth and Childhood of the Prophet Samuel, as recorded in 1 Sam. i., ii. 1—27, iii. Designed as a Help to Meditation on the Holy Scriptures for Children and Young Persons. By **Edward Meyrick Goulburn**, D.D., Dean of Norwich.

Small 8vo. 5s.

Thoughts on Personal Religion; being a
Treatise on the Christian Life in its Two Chief Elements, Devotion and Practice. By **Edward Meyrick Goulburn**, D.D., Dean of Norwich.

New Presentation Edition, elegantly printed on Toned Paper.
Two Vols. Small 8vo. 10s. 6d.
An Edition in one Vol., 6s. 6d.; also a Cheap Edition, 3s. 6d.

The Greek Testament. With a Critically
Revised Text; a Digest of Various Readings; Marginal References to Verbal and Idiomatic Usage; Prolegomena; and a Critical and Exegetical Commentary. For the use of Theological Students and Ministers. By **Henry Alford**, D.D., late Dean of Canterbury.

New Edition. Four Volumes. 8vo. 102s.

The Volumes are sold separately, as follows:—
- Vol. I.—THE FOUR GOSPELS. 28s.
- Vol. II.—ACTS TO II. CORINTHIANS. 24s.
- Vol. III.—GALATIANS TO PHILEMON. 18s.
- Vol. IV.—HEBREWS TO REVELATION. 32s.

London, Oxford, and Cambridge

Manchester Sermons. By the Rev. W. J.
Knox Little, M.A., Rector of St. Alban's, Manchester.
Crown 8vo. [*In the Press.*

Miscellanies, Literary and Religious.
By Chr. Wordsworth, D.D., Bishop of Lincoln.
Three Vols. 8vo. [*In the Press.*

The Doctrine of the Cross: specially
in its relation to the Troubles of Life. Sermons preached during Lent in the Parish Church of New Windsor by **Henry J. Ellison, M.A.** (sometime Vicar of Windsor), Honorary Chaplain to the Queen, Honorary Canon of Christ Church, and Rector of Haseley, Oxon.
Small 8vo. 2s. 6d.

A Catechism on Gospel History, inculcating Church Doctrine.
By the Rev. **Samuel Kettlewell, M.A.**, late Vicar of S. Mark's, Leeds.
Third Edition. Small 8vo. 3s. 6d.

The Authorship of the "De Imitatione Christi."
With many interesting particulars about the Book. By **Samuel Kettlewell, M.A.**, late Vicar of St. Mark's, Leeds. Containing Photographic Engravings of the "De Imitatione" written by Thomas à Kempis, 1441, and of two other MSS.
8vo. 14s.

A Manual of Devotion, chiefly for the use of Schoolboys.
By **William Baker, D.D.**, Head-Master of Merchant Taylors' School. With Preface by J. R. Woodford, D.D., Lord Bishop of Ely.
Crown 16mo. 1s. 6d.

Dictionary of Sects, Heresies, Ecclesiastical Parties, and Schools of Religious Thought.
By various Writers. Edited by the Rev. **John Henry Blunt, M.A., F.S.A.**, Editor of the "Dictionary of Doctrinal and Historical Theology" and the "Annotated Book of Common Prayer," &c. &c.
Imperial 8vo, 36s. In half-morocco, 48s.

London, Oxford, and Cambridge

Genesis. With Notes. By the Rev. G. V. Garland, M.A., late Vicar of Aslacton, Norfolk. [The Hebrew Text, with Literal Translation.]
8vo. 21s.

The Knight of Intercession, and other Poems. By the Rev. S. J. Stone, M.A., Pembroke College, Oxford; Vicar of S. Paul's, Haggerston.

Fourth Edition, revised and enlarged. Crown 8vo. 6s.

Morning Notes of Praise. A Series of Morning Meditations upon the Psalms. Dedicated to the Countess of Cottenham. By Lady Charlotte-Maria Pepys.

New Edition. Small 8vo. 2s. 6d.

Quiet Moments; a Four Weeks' Course of Thoughts and Meditations before Evening Prayer and at Sunset. By Lady Charlotte-Maria Pepys.

New Edition. Small 8vo. 2s. 6d.

Twenty-one Years in S. George's Mission. An Account of its Origin, Progress, and Work of Charity. With an Appendix. By the Rev. C. F. Lowder, M.A., Vicar of S. Peter's, London Docks.

Crown 8vo. 6s.

The Young Churchman's Companion to the Prayer Book. By the Rev. J. W. Gedge, M.A., Diocesan Inspector of Schools for the Archdeaconry of Surrey.

Part I.—MORNING AND EVENING PRAYER AND LITANY.
Part II.—BAPTISMAL AND CONFIRMATION SERVICES.
Part III.—THE OFFICE OF HOLY COMMUNION.

18mo, 1s. each; or in paper Cover, 6d.

The Life of Worship. A Course of Lectures. By the Rev. George Body, B.A., Rector of Kirkby Misperton, Author of "The Life of Temptation" and "The Life of Justification."

Crown 8vo. [*In the Press.*

London, Oxford, and Cambridge

The Words of the SON of GOD, taken

from the Four Gospels, and arranged for Daily Meditation throughout the Year. By Eleanor Plumptre.

Crown 8vo. 7s. 6d.

Our Work for CHRIST among His

Suffering People. A Book for Hospital Nurses. By M. A. Morrell.

Small 8vo. 2s. 6d.

A Dictionary of English Philosophical

Terms. By the Rev. Francis Garden, M.A., Professor of Theology and Rhetoric at Queen's College, London, and Sub-Dean of Her Majesty's Chapels-Royal.

Small 8vo. 4s. 6d.

The Religion of the Christ; its Historic

and Literary Development considered as an Evidence of its Origin. Being the Bampton Lectures for 1874. By the Rev. Stanley Leathes, M.A., Minister of St. Philip's, Regent Street, and Professor of Hebrew, King's College, London.

Second Edition. Crown 8vo. 7s. 6d.

The Reformation of the Church of

England; its History, Principles, and Results. A.D. 1514-1547. By the Rev. John Henry Blunt, M.A., F.S.A., Editor of "The Annotated Book of Common Prayer," and "The Dictionary of Doctrinal and Historical Theology," &c. &c.

Fourth Edition. 8vo. 16s.

The Mystery of Christ: Being an Examina-

tion of the Doctrines contained in the first three Chapters of the Epistle of Paul the Apostle to the Ephesians. By George Staunton Barrow, M.A., Vicar of Stowmarket.

Crown 8vo. 7s. 6d.

The Prayer Book Interleaved. With

Historical Illustrations and Explanatory Notes, arranged parallel to the Text. By the Rev. W. M. Campion, D.D., Fellow and Tutor of Queen's College, and Rector of St. Botolph's; and the Rev. W. J. Beamont, M.A., late Fellow of Trinity College, Cambridge. With a Preface by the Lord Bishop of Winchester.

Ninth Edition. Small 8vo. 7s. 6d.

London, Oxford, and Cambridge

Apostolical Succession in the Church
of England. By Arthur W. Haddan, B.D., Rector of Barton-on-the-Heath, late Fellow of Trinity College, Oxford.

New Edition. 8vo. 12s.

Sermons Preached in the Parish Church
of Barnes, 1871—1876. By **Peter Goldsmith Medd**, M.A., Rector of North Cerney, Hon. Canon of St. Albans, and Examining Chaplain to the Bishop; late Senior Fellow of University College, Oxford, and Rector of Barnes.

Crown 8vo. 7s. 6d.

The Mystery of the Temptation: a Course
of Lectures. By the Rev. **W. H. Hutchings**, M.A., Sub-Warden of the House of Mercy, Clewer.

Crown 8vo. 4s. 6d.

The Life of Justification: a Series of Lectures
delivered in Substance at All Saints', Margaret Street. By the Rev. **George Body**, B.A., Rector of Kirkby Misperton.

Fourth Edition. Crown 8vo. 4s. 6d.

The Life of Temptation: a Course of Lectures
delivered in Substance at S. Peter's, Eaton Square; also at All Saints', Margaret Street. By the Rev. **George Body**, B.A., Rector of Kirkby Misperton.

Fourth Edition. Crown 8vo. 4s. 6d.

Words to take with Us: a Manual of
Daily and Occasional Prayers, for Private and Common Use. With Plain Instructions and Counsels on Prayer. By **W. E. Scudamore**, M.A., Rector of Ditchingham, and formerly Fellow of St. John's College, Cambridge.

Fourth Edition. Small 8vo. 2s. 6d.

The Book of Church Law; Being an Exposition
of the Legal Rights and Duties of the Clergy and Laity of the Church of England. By the Rev. **John Henry Blunt**, M.A., F.S.A. Revised by **Walter G. F. Phillimore**, D.C.L., Barrister-at-Law, and Chancellor of the Diocese of Lincoln.

Second Edition, revised. Crown 8vo. 7s. 6d.

London, Oxford, and Cambridge

An Introduction to the Study of
Painted Glass. By A. A.
Crown 8vo. 2s. 6d.

Spiritual Letters to Men, by Archbishop
Fénelon. By the Author of "Life of S. Francis de Sales," "Life of Fénelon," &c.
Crown 8vo. 6s.

Spiritual Letters to Women, by Archbishop
Fénelon. By the Author of "Life of S. Francis de Sales," "Life of Fénelon," &c.
Crown 8vo. 6s.

Sacred Allegories. The Shadow of the
Cross—The Distant Hills—The Old Man's Home—The King's Messengers. By the Rev. W. Adams, M.A., late Fellow of Merton College, Oxford.
With numerous Illustrations.
New Edition. One Vol. Crown 8vo. 5s.
The four Allegories separately. 16mo. 1s. each.

The Origin and Development of Religious
Belief. By the Rev. S. Baring-Gould, M.A., Author of "Curious Myths of the Middle Ages," &c.
New Edition. Two Volumes. Crown 8vo. 6s. each. Sold separately.
Vol. I.—MONOTHEISM and POLYTHEISM.
Vol. II.—CHRISTIANITY.

Prayers and Meditations for the Holy
Communion. By Josephine Fletcher. With a Preface by C. J. Ellicott, D.D., Lord Bishop of Gloucester and Bristol.
With Rubrics in red. Royal 32mo. 2s. 6d.
Cheap Edition. 32mo, cloth limp, 1s.

Lectures delivered at St. Margaret's,
Lothbury. By the Rev. Henry Melvill, B.D., late Canon of St. Paul's, and Chaplain in Ordinary to the Queen.
New Edition. Crown 8vo. 5s.

London, Oxford, and Cambridge

Pleadings for Christ. Being Sermons,
Doctrinal and Practical, preached in S. Andrew's Church, Liverpool. By **William Lefroy, M.A.**, Incumbent.
Crown 8vo. 6s.

Sermons on the Epistles and Gospels
for the Sundays and Holy Days throughout the Year. By the Rev. **Isaac Williams**, B.D., Author of a "Devotional Commentary on the Gospel Narrative."
New Edition. Two Volumes. Crown 8vo. 5s. each. Sold separately.
 Vol. I.—ADVENT TO WHITSUNTIDE.
 Vol. II.—TRINITY TO ALL SAINTS' DAY.

Not Tradition, but Scripture. By the late **Philip Nicholas Shuttleworth**, D.D., Warden of New College, Oxford, and Rector of Foxley, Wilts, afterwards Lord Bishop of Chichester.
Fourth Edition. Crown 8vo. 4s. 6d.

Questions illustrating the Thirty-Nine
Articles of the Church of England, with Proofs from Holy Scripture, and the Primitive Church. By **Edward Bickersteth**, D.D., Dean of Lichfield.
Sixth Edition. Small 8vo. 3s. 6d.

The Bishopric of Souls. By **Robert Wilson Evans**, B.D., late Vicar of Heversham and Archdeacon of Westmoreland. With an Introductory Memoir by **Edward Bickersteth**, D.D., Dean of Lichfield.
With Portrait. Fifth Edition. Small 8vo. 5s. 6d.

The Good Shepherd; or, Meditations
for the Clergy upon the Example and Teaching of Christ. By the Rev. **W. E. Heygate**, M.A., Rector of Brighstone, Author of "Allegories and Tales."
Second Edition, revised. Small 8vo. 3s.

Voices of Comfort, Original and Selected,
edited by the Rev. **Thomas Vincent Fosbery**, M.A., sometime Vicar of St. Giles's, Reading, Editor of "Hymns and Poems for the Sick and Suffering."
Fourth Edition. Crown 8vo. 7s. 6d.

London, Oxford, and Cambridge

Short Sermons on the Psalms, in their

order, preached in a Village Church. By W. J. Stracey, M.A., Rector of Oxnead and Vicar of Buxton, Norfolk, formerly Fellow of Magdalene College, Cambridge.

Crown 8vo. 5s. each. Sold separately.
Vol. I.—Psalms I—XXV.
Vol. II.—Psalms XXVI—LI.

Yesterday, To-day, and For Ever:

A Poem in Twelve Books. By Edward Henry Bickersteth, M.A., Vicar of Christ Church, Hampstead.

Eleventh Edition. Small 8vo. 3s. 6d.
A Presentation Edition, with red borders. Small 4to. 10s. 6d.

The Treasury of Devotion: a Manual

of Prayers for General and Daily Use. Compiled by a Priest. Edited by the Rev. T. T. Carter, M.A., Rector of Clewer, Berks.

New Edition, in Large Type, Crown 8vo, 5s.; or in morocco limp, 10s. 6d.
The Smaller Edition, 18mo, 2s. 6d.; cloth limp, 2s., or bound with the Book of Common Prayer, 3s. 6d.

Comment upon the Collects appointed to

be used in the Church of England on Sundays and Holy Days throughout the Year. By John James, D.D., sometime Canon of Peterborough.

New Edition. Small 8vo. 3s. 6d.
Also a Fine Edition, on Toned Paper. Crown 8vo. 5s.

A Commentary, Expository and Devotional,

on the Order of the Administration of the Lord's Supper, according to the Use of the Church of England, to which is added an Appendix on Fasting Communion, Non-Communicating Attendance, Auricular Confession, the Doctrine of Sacrifice, the Eucharistic Sacrifice. By Edward Meyrick Goulburn, D.D., Dean of Norwich.

Sixth Edition. Small 8vo. 6s.
Also, a Cheap Edition, uniform with "Thoughts on Personal Religion," and "The Pursuit of Holiness." 3s. 6d.

The Annual Register: a Review of Public

Events at Home and Abroad, from the Year 1863 to 1877.
8vo. 18s. each.

London, Oxford, and Cambridge

Library of Spiritual Works for English Catholics.

It is hoped that the "Library of Spiritual Works for English Catholics," which will comprise translations, compilations, and other works, will meet a need which has long been felt. As the devotional life of the Church of England has increased, so the demand for spiritual treatises has become more and more urgent, and has arisen from all classes of society. This series of books, some well known, some already oftentimes translated, and others, it may be, yet to be presented for the first time in an English dress, is intended to meet this want.

The aim of the translators is twofold. First, to provide the reader with a fair rendering of the original as far as possible unmutilated. It has been a common complaint of late, that translations have been marred by the absence of parts of the original, the exclusion of which a more intelligent view of Catholic devotion in the present day has rendered unnecessary. In these editions these omissions have been to a great extent supplied; yet at the same time any term or expression which may come under the imputation of being "un-English" has been reduced, as far as may be without destroying the thought, to its equivalent in Anglican phraseology and belief. Secondly, to translate the original into ordinary English, and thus to avoid the antiquated and stilted style of writing, which often makes books of this kind distasteful, or even sometimes unintelligible.

Elegantly printed with red borders, on extra superfine toned paper.
Small 8vo. 5s. each.

OF THE IMITATION OF CHRIST. In 4 Books. By **Thomas à Kempis.** A New Translation.

THE CHRISTIAN YEAR: Thoughts in Verse for the Sundays and Holy Days throughout the Year.

THE SPIRITUAL COMBAT; together with the Supplement and the Path of Paradise. By **Laurence Scupoli.** A New Translation.

THE DEVOUT LIFE. By Saint **Francis of Sales**, Bishop and Prince of Geneva. A New Translation.

THE LOVE OF GOD. By Saint **Francis of Sales**, Bishop and Prince of Geneva. A New Translation.

THE CONFESSIONS OF S. AUGUSTINE. In 10 Books. A New Translation.

The Volumes can also be had in the following extra bindings:—

	s.	d.
Morocco, stiff or limp	9	0
Morocco, thick bevelled sides, Old Style	12	0
Morocco, limp, with flap edges	11	6
Morocco, best, stiff or limp	16	0
Morocco, best, thick bevelled sides, Old Style	19	6
Russia, limp	11	6
Russia, limp, with flap edges	13	6

Most of the above styles may be had illustrated with a beautiful selection of Photographs from Angelico, 4s. 6d. extra.

CHEAP EDITIONS.

32mo, cloth limp, 6d. each, or cloth extra, 1s. each.

Of the Imitation of Christ.
The Spiritual Combat.
The Hidden Life of the Soul.
Spiritual Letters of Saint Francis of Sales.
The Christian Year.

These Five Volumes, cloth extra, may be had in a Box, price 7s., and also bound in Roan, Calf, Morocco, &c.

London, Oxford, and Cambridge

New Pamphlets

A Charge delivered to the Clergy and Churchwardens of the Diocese of St. Albans at his Primary Visitation, October—November 1878. By **Thomas Legh**, Bishop of St. Albans.
8vo. 1s.

A Charge delivered to the Clergy of the Diocese of Llandaff, at his Tenth Visitation, August 1878. In Three Addresses. By **Alfred Ollivant**, D.D., Bishop of Llandaff.
8vo. 1s. 6d.

Greek and Latin Translation of the Letter of the Lambeth Conference. Epistola Centum Episcoporum in Anglia Congregatorum, in Palatio Lambethano, Mense Julio, Anno MDCCCLXXVIII. Graecè et Latinè Reddita Jussu Reverendissimi, Archiepiscopi Cantuariensis.
8vo. 1s.

The More Excellent Way of Unity in the Church of Christ. A Charge delivered to the Clergy of the Archdeaconry of Maidstone, at the Ordinary Visitation in May 1878. With Notes. By **Benjamin Harrison**, M.A., Archdeacon of Maidstone.
8vo. 1s.

The Reform of Convocation. A Speech delivered at the Lichfield Diocesan Conference, in St. James's Hall, Lichfield, on Friday, September 28, 1877. By **Edward Bickersteth**, D.D., Dean of Lichfield, and Prolocutor of the Convocation of Canterbury.
8vo. 1s.

The Burial-Place of Edmund de Langley, fifth son of King Edward III. A Sermon preached at King's Langley Church, Herts, on Tuesday, February 26, 1878. By the Bishop of St. Albans.
8vo. 6d.

St. Paul's Message to Archippus. A Sermon preached in Lichfield Cathedral, on St. Matthew's Day, September 21, 1878, on the occasion of the Bishop of Lichfield's Primary Ordination. By **Edward Bickersteth**, D.D., Dean of Lichfield, and Prolocutor of the Convocation of Canterbury.
8vo. 6d.

Are "Vows of Celibacy in Early Life" inconsistent with the Word of God? or, Some Remarks on the Lord Bishop of Lincoln's Letter to the Ven. Sir George Prevost, Bart., entitled "Sisterhoods and Vows." By the Rev. **T. T. Carter**, Rector of Clewer; Hon. Canon of Christ Church, Oxford.
8vo. 1s.

The Present Movement; A True Phase of Anglo-Catholic Church Principles. A Letter to His Grace the Lord Archbishop of Canterbury. By the Rev. **T. T. Carter**, M.A., Rector of Clewer, Hon. Canon of Christ Church, Oxford.
8vo. 1s. 6d.

The Freedom of Confession in the Church of England. A Letter to His Grace the Lord Archbishop of Canterbury. By the Rev. **T. T. Carter**, Rector of Clewer; Hon. Canon of Christ Church, Oxford.
Second Edition. 8vo. 1s.

New Pamphlets

How many Persons were present with our Blessed Lord at the Last Supper? Some observations on the above question. By a Layman.
8vo. 6d.

The Work of Christ in Central Africa. A Letter to the Rev. H. P. Liddon, D.D., D.C.L., Canon of St. Paul's, and Ireland Professor of Exegesis at the University of Oxford. By the Rev. J. P. Farler, B.A., St. John's College, Cambridge, Missionary in Central Africa, and Chaplain to Bishop Steere.
8vo. 1s.

Liberty of Confession in the Church of England. A Sermon preached in the Church of S. Stephen, Lewisham, on the Eighth Sunday after Trinity, 1877. By R. Rhodes Bristow, M.A., Vicar.
8vo. 1s.

The Diocesan Synods of the Earlier Church. By W. E. Scudamore, Rector of Ditchingham.
8vo. 1s.

Reform in Convocation, with some Notes on its Existing Constitution; being the substance of Letters addressed to the *Guardian*, and of a Paper read at a "Devotional Conference of the Clergy," held at Bodmin, September 1877. By the Rev. Henry Overy, M.A., Vicar of St. Veep, Cornwall.
8vo. 6d.

Cyprus: a Sermon preached on July 21st, 1878. By the Rev. J. B. Harboard, M.A., R.N.
8vo. 6d.

Hymns for the Natural Seasons. By Edward Henry Loring, M.A., Rector of Gillingham, Norfolk.
Imperial 16mo. With *Music*, 6d. *The Words only can also be had.*
18mo. 1d.

*Form of Prayer prepara-*tory to Confirmation. To which are added Devotions to be used in Private, before and after Confirmation.
Second Edition. 12mo. 3d.

Pupil - Teachers : Their Training and Instruction; or, A Plea for the more careful consideration of Pupil-Teachers, so far as regards their Powers of Teaching and Learning, and the Demands made upon them. By the Rev. A. E. Northey, M.A., Principal of the Hockerill Training College, Bishop's Stortford.
8vo. 6d.

A Form of Prayer to be used upon St. Andrew's Day, or upon any of the Seven Days next following. Being the Day or Days of Intercession for a Blessing upon the Missionary Work of the Church. Approved by the Two Houses of the Convocation of Canterbury.

[Form, No. 2.]
Royal 32mo. 1d.

The Form for St. Andrew's Day or the Sunday next following, may be had separately.

[Form, No. 1.]
Crown 8vo. 3s. 6d. *per* 100.

London, Oxford, and Cambridge

MESSRS. RIVINGTON *issue the under-mentioned Lists, which may be had gratis and post free:—*

CLASSIFIED CATALOGUE OF BOOKS SELECTED FROM THEIR PUBLICATIONS.

LIST OF NEW BOOKS IN COURSE OF PUBLICATION.

LIST OF EDUCATIONAL BOOKS.

MONTHLY CLASSIFIED LIST OF ALL NEW BOOKS PUBLISHED IN THE UNITED KINGDOM AND ON THE CONTINENT.

CATALOGUE OF A SELECTION FROM THEIR EDITIONS OF THE BIBLE, PRAYER BOOK, ETC., AND THEIR DEVOTIONAL WORKS, IN EXTRA BINDINGS.

RIVINGTONS: WATERLOO PLACE, LONDON
and at 𝔒xford and 𝔒ambridge.

www.ingramcontent.com/pod-product-compliance
Lightning Source LLC
Chambersburg PA
CBHW051900300426
44117CB00006B/469